This Fabulous Century

To Jerry + Carole
from
all of us at Seven

This *Fabulous* Century

Peter Luck

LANSDOWNE PRESS
Sydney · Auckland · London · New York

Dedicated to Penny and Elva

Published by Lansdowne Press Sydney
176 South Creek Road, Dee Why West, NSW, Australia 2099
First Published 1980
© Copyright Peter Luck 1980
Produced in Australia by the Publisher
Typeset in Australia by Savage and Co. Pty Ltd Brisbane
Printed in Australia by Griffin Press Ltd

National Library of Australia Cataloguing-in-Publication Data

Luck, Peter.
This fabulous century.
Index
ISBN 0 7018 1430 6
1. Australia — History — 20th century. I. Title.
994.04

Cover photograph Ray Joyce

Previous page. *Lord and Lady Fuller and their Government House party pose before the 1912 Melbourne Cup.*

CONTENTS

Acknowledgments   6
Introduction   7
1 As Time Goes By   11
2 Heroes   73
3 Humour   97
4 War   121
5 Sport   147
6 Leaders   193
7 Fads, Fashion and Feminism   221
8 Fear and Tragedy   253
9 Stage and Screen   285
10 The Sunburnt Country   331
11 Landmarks in Time   357
Index   394

Junction Street, Nowra, at the turn of the century.

ACKNOWLEDGEMENTS

This Fabulous Century is one of the largest and most ambitious documentary television series produced anywhere in the world. And yet this thirty-six episode history of Australia in the Twentieth Century was made by remarkably few people. My sincerest thanks go to David Salter, who produced, directed and lived with the series since we first thrashed out the overall concept while trout fishing in the Brindabella Ranges. To Peg McGrath, researcher and panacea to so many of the problems which beset such an enterprise. To Cathy Flannery who made the planes run on time and managed to co-ordinate two hundred Australians to be at the right place at the right time. To Michael Chirgwin who reduced two million feet to 20 000 with superb skill, and to Les Fiddess who laid all the sound tracks. To Tony Wilson who shot the colour film and to Brian Morris who recorded all the sound. To associate producer Neil Balnaves, and Doug Paterson and Bonnie Low of Hanna-Barbera who proved that documentary television could find a commercial audience. To George Spitzer who handled what is ultimately the most difficult and dangerous part of all giant commercial productions, the money. And to the man who made it all possible—the one who gave the initial support, financial help and above all the incentive, Kevin Weldon.

This book is a testimony to the endeavours of each of this merry band of artists and artisans, but in particular my thanks go again to David Salter and to Sydney journalist Carolyn Noad, for their help in compiling a magnificent record of This Fabulous Century.

INTRODUCTION

A child born in 1980, the year this book was first published, will be just twenty-one when this century ends.

It was not so long ago that even the Orwellian year of 1984 seemed too far in the remote future to contemplate as reality, and yet the 21st Century itself is now imminent.

Who could have predicted what an astonishing period of history this would be?

The people of the late 19th century approached the 20th with the same awe with which we see the 2000s. The last two decades of the last century were a period of fantastic change, almost a social and technological bridgehead to storm the coming era. From that flurry in the 1880s and 1890s the new epoch inherited, among other things, the phonograph, the typewriter, the electric light and the petrol engine. That generation also gave us the Suez Canal and the first skyscraper. It was an age which produced Darwin, Edison, Mendel and Pasteur, Marx and Nietsche.

This fabulous century, then, would be a time of extraordinary achievement, a time when man would transform his planet and even threaten to destroy it completely. And then, amazingly, he would journey into outer space.

Australia has more than its share of eighty-year-olds sheltered in this great cocoon in the southern oceans, people who might have been distant spectators to the remarkable procession of events which has included two world wars and a score of major conflicts. Some may even have watched the best part of eight decades go by from the windows of a terrace house which has remained relatively unchanged throughout.

This house, built in the days of our first Prime Minister, Edmund Barton, may have been given a coat of paint in the days of Billy Hughes, renovated during the Menzies era and completely restored in readiness for the heralded utopia of the Whitlam years.

What goes on in one's street is, after all, what history is to most people. For an average man history is as much about minutiae as major events. Chances are we don't remember a year such as 1948 because that was when the Australian Capital Territory was given Parliamentary representation, or that was when the High Court invalidated parts of bank nationalisation, but that was when the basic wage was about six quid a week, and three hundred pounds would buy a good block of land on Sydney's lower north shore, and the first Holdens came out, and remember those first long playing records? . . . and someone invented something called a transistor, and tickets to the annual ball at the Trocadero were 14/10d. Next year Bob Menzies would become Prime Minister and that new radio serial 'Blue Hills' was due to begin . . . but that was next year.

Of course, nostalgia is not history. Perhaps nostalgia is history through rose coloured glasses, history which has been kindly blurred a little so that we tend to remember even the bad times as the 'good old days'. The history of the thirties for many Australians means not so much the Depression but the days of Phar Lap and Don Bradman or maybe there are simply memories of the girl next door or the kids down the street.

If the archeologists of the future ever dig for evidence of this age they will notice something extraordinary about this century as opposed to all those which have gone before it. For the first time in the story of the world they will be able to see human beings moving — the way they were.

In all the thousands of years of recorded life so far the images have been static — fossils, records, artifacts, pictures — all totally still. But suddenly, around the beginning of the 20th Century a miracle occurred. The image moved. It is as though history has always been frozen, and then dramatically released. The people who uncover our civilisation will watch fascinated as we, the ancients, flicker into life and walk and talk before them.

They will be watching the first century recorded on film: This Fabulous Century.

The word fabulous means given to fable, incredible, absurd—and unhistorical. This is not a history book. It falls in two parts—a decade by decade account of a few of the highlights of the century, and then some stories of the people, places and events which have interested, shocked, amused and changed our lives. Many aspects of our history do not appear in this book but as Ned Kelly is supposed to have said just before they sent him off, 'Such is life.'

Landing of the Governor-General at Farm Cove in 1901

This Fabulous Century

1

AS TIME GOES BY ...

You must remember this,
A kiss is still a kiss,
A sigh is just a sigh,
The fundamental things apply,
As time goes by.
STERLING MUSIC

ON THIS SPOT *The ceremonial rotunda erected in Centennial Park, Sydney, as it appeared at the moment Australia was proclaimed as a federated nation on 1 January 1901—the first day of 'This Fabulous Century'. The ornate structure soon deteriorated—it was made of plaster of Paris.*

The growth of a nation

It seems fitting that the oldest surviving film in Australia, shot just before the turn of the century, is of the Melbourne Cup—maybe the only event in the world which, to this day, stops an entire continent in its tracks. As the *Bulletin* of the day observed, 'It is something beautifully appropriate that the first Australian picture should be a horse race. Of course it had to be that or a football match.' It was perhaps not so beautifully appropriate that the film was shot by a visiting Frenchman, but that's a long story.

Australia became a pioneer of the world's film industry in a most intriguing way. Just before the turn of the century a Sydney photographer by the name of Barnett was returning from a trip to England. In the Taj Mahal Hotel in Bombay he met a despondent French cameraman who had been told by his employers, the Lumière brothers (who invented the motion picture camera), that his shots of life in the East had been ruined by heat and humidity. Barnett suggested to the Frenchman, Maurice Sestier, that he could find work with Falk's photographic studios in Australia. The idea obviously appealed to him. Sestier caught the next boat for New South Wales.

Australians had seen some film before. At the Melbourne Opera House in August 1896, just a matter of months after the cinematograph had taken Europe by storm, Harry Rickards presented the 'Premier prestidigitateur and illusionist in the world—in his conflux of apparent miracles—the greatest wonder of the nineteenth century.' Rickards told the public that for the first time in the southern hemisphere a certain Carl Hertz would demonstrate the 'photoelectric sensation of the day'. Australians sat spellbound as scenes of London flickered in front of them: Westminster Bridge, a scene from *Trilby* and the Kempton Park races.

But Sestier, who arrived in Sydney in the following month, would present a spectacle to amaze Australians even more: themselves. The Frenchman, in partnership with Barnett, began filming scenes of Sydney on sixty-foot spools of film. The Lumière brothers in Paris were ap-

THE OLDEST FILM IN AUSTRALIA *When the first practical film camera—the Lumière Cinematograph . . . was brought to Australia by a certain Monsieur Sestier, he thought the best way of promoting the invention would be to film a well-known national event. Monsieur Sestier must have been a gifted salesman, because he chose to film the Melbourne Cup. This picture is a scene from that film—shot in 1896—and to this day the earliest surviving film in Australia.*

parently quite happy with the arrangement because they supplied the film stock. But Sestier quickly ran into trouble. Not being a technician, he knew nothing of processing and developing and his first results were a failure. However, an Australian photographer designed some special equipment, and soon Sestier's films were part of the vaudeville programme at the Princess Theatre in Melbourne.

Within a few short weeks, however, Australians were already beginning to tire of scenic views and street scenes. Then in November 1896 Sestier produced his sensation: *The Melbourne Cup*. It caused such excitement that journalists practically fell over their new-fangled typewriters to describe Australia's first sporting film. As the *Argus* noted, 'By the Lumière principle a series of views were taken which will carry to London, Paris and St Petersburg an actual presentment not only of the Cup meeting but the most wonderful Cup race ever run over this classic course.' No doubt the Melbourne

Cup would have gone over in St Petersburg like lead in the saddle, but the point was there. Film was a way of presenting Australia to the world—proof that we really were down here on the bottom of the world. According to the advertisements of the day, 'Exhibitions of the wonderful tableaux of the Melbourne Cup were received with thunders of applause and unbounded enthusiasm.'

Sestier, though, would share little but the kudos in the industry he helped to pioneer in this country. After some unsuccessful screenings this forlorn advertisement appeared in a Melbourne newspaper.

Cinematographe Lumière. For sale, the original one brought over by Mons. Sestier with all fittings—complete for immediate exhibition. Sixty-three magnificent pictures.

Whatever happened to the foreigner who shot our oldest film is something of a mystery but by the time his camera was sold, Australian films were well on their way. And the men

SALVATION CINEMA SOCKEROO *The 'title' glass slide from* **Soldiers of the Cross,** *the epic mixture of film, 'live' address and magic lantern show which is claimed to be the first full-length film presentation in the world. Produced by the Salvation Army Limelight Unit,* **Soldiers of the Cross** *was an enormous success—and all on a budget of £600.*

who made our movie history came from the most surprising places.

In the audience of Carl Hertz's first Australian picture show was someone who in his wildest dreams didn't realise that he would become the creator of the first major film, not only in Australia, but in the world. Joseph Perry was, after all, a member of the Salvation Army, not a movie mogul. But around the turn of the century the Sallies were a pretty dynamic bunch. Their leader was Herbert Booth, son of the founder of the Army. He sent Perry to a picture show to investigate the potential of the medium as an aid to evangelism. There was no doubt there were exciting possibilities.

It is difficult to realise now that film was not simply a quaint novelty

that amused the Edwardians like some gigantic home movie. Film then, like television today, meant money and a tremendous amount of technological experimentation and development. Even before the turn of the century, the Australian cinema audience was in the millions and the business was subject to the predatory maraudings of celluloid sharks. Studios, cinemas and production houses came and went in rapid succession. The competition was cut-throat.

Amongst this frenetic activity the Salvation Army seemed an unlikely contender. But the Army preached 'Blood and Fire', and ultimately it would hurl itself into the film business with such energy that it would produce the most ambitious

work of all—a film production that has often mistakenly been called the world's first feature.

On the very eve of the twentieth century, the Salvation Army's Limelight Department completed *Soldiers of the Cross,* a truly amazing presentation of film, slides, music, and oratory which must have been at least equal to the elaborate stage presentations of the future such as *Hair* or *Jesus Christ Superstar.*

Soldiers of the Cross was not strictly a feature film. Although it comprised thousands of feet of re-enactments of the trials of early Christian martyrs, it was interrupted by coloured glass slides during the reel changes, and some fiery evangelism by Commandant Booth himself.

LIONS 28, CHRISTIANS 0 *One of the soul-stirring scenes of Christian martyrdom from* Soldiers of the Cross. *None of the original film survives, but this photograph shows the elaborate sets, costumes and even animal actors employed in the production.*

When the illustrated address was first presented at the Melbourne Town Hall on 13 September 1900, it was billed in a rather low-key manner: 'Town Hall this evening, 7.45 o'clock, Wonderful Limelight Lecture entitled Soldiers of the Cross.'

Nevertheless, despite the soft sell and atrocious weather, 4000 people attended the premier. The title was taken from a line in a hymn called 'Am I a soldier of the Cross?' It was a ferocious epic which might have turned even Cecil B. De Mille white. Martyrs were crucified, beheaded, hacked to pieces, thrown into pits of burning lime, burned at the stake and fed to wild animals. During the filming, demure Salvation Army wives had been transformed into lightly clad maidens of Roman times, and to simulate their ordeal in the Coliseum they were photographed outside the lions' cage at Fitzgerald's Circus in Melbourne. The whole effect was apparently so life-like that women amongst the audience on the first night screamed and fainted.

The show was such an extraordinary success that within a short time the Salvation Army was encouraged to step up the publicity.

Of interest to All Creeds
Everyone Captivated from Start to Finish
A Colossal Success
Never Before Witnessed in This or Any Other Country

The Salvation Army's own magazine *War Cry* thought that *Soldiers of the Cross* was a 'knockout', a word that the paper's reporter heard used on the steps of the Collingwood Town Hall. 'Thanks for the word, whoever you were', he wrote. 'Possibly "knockout" is slang but it is rapidly becoming good English, and we like to be a bit ahead of the times. The lecture was a veritable "knockout".'

The Army's elaborate new programme included critiques from the *Age* and the *Argus* which were impressed by the 'savage but soul-stirring realism' of the production. They apparently did not notice that the Roman soldiers' cardboard spears bent a little as they prodded hapless Christians into settings which were actually draped across the tennis court netting at the rear of the Murrumbeena Girls' Home at 1219 Dandenong Road. Joseph Perry once told the film buff Eric Reade that in one 'take' the hindquarters of a fake lion fell over and the front portion tried to pull the offending legs upright.

Perry, who had talked the Army into buying a Lumière cinematograph for the filming had been running the Limelight Department for nearly five years when *Soldiers of the Cross* was completed. His first studies had been modest, to say the least: *Wood Chopping at the Metropole* and *Richard Earning His Breakfast.*

But he became more ambitious and was soon taking thousands of feet of film dealing with the social work of the Army. Members of his family also worked on his films and some can even recall playing parts, as children, in their father's epic. Tragically, none of his great work survives. Not long after *Soldiers of the Cross* was shown, Herbert Booth resigned from the Army in a disagreement over policy. There was some suggestion that the problems of the early martyrs had been tackled with perhaps a little too much relish and that this was not the sort of screen violence that the Army should be peddling to the masses. But, whatever the reasons, Booth purchased the film outright for £300, one half of the estimated cost of production. He later exhibited the film in America, but it has long since disappeared. Fortunately the superb glass slides somehow survived and are now a treasured possession of the Film Archive of the National Library in Canberra.

In 1901, the same year that Joseph Perry's great work was lost to history, he was appointed as one of the official photographers to cover Australia's Federation celebrations. The film industry in the colonies was now well under way, but Australia as a nation was not even born.

The 1900s

The first day of the twentieth century, 1 January 1901, was a day the whole world had been waiting for with a mixture of confidence and apprehension. And in Australia it was a day of tremendous excitement. For us it meant Federation, the time when Australia at last became 'fair dinkum' about being a nation. The first day of the century would see the swearing-in of the first Australian Government. The separate Australian colonies were about to weld themselves together as states of a Commonwealth. It was in fact a really significant achievement because, with so many rivalries and jealousies between the various cities and their politicians, there had been bitter arguments for many years. At times it had seemed that Federation might never occur at all.

Sir John Robertson, for example, was five times Premier of New South Wales and plainly disliked Victoria. 'We cannot stand that progressive colony,' he said. 'They are rather too insolent.' He commonly referred to his southern neighbour as 'the cabbage garden . . . those bloody fellows across the Murray who produce just the same as we do, and all they can send us is bloody cabbages.'

Freedom of trade of course had a lot to do with the urge to unify the nation, and defence was also a sobering consideration. Rudyard Kipling observed, 'If you want to hurry up Federation, you ought to make a syndicate to hire a few German cruisers to bombard Sydney, Melbourne and Brisbane for twenty minutes. There'd be a federated Australia within twenty-four hours.'

Whatever the reasons, on the eve of the twentieth century, most of the differences had been resolved. The Federal Parliament was in Melbourne, but the first Prime Minister, New South Welshman, Edmund Barton, would be sworn in at the Federation ceremony in Sydney.

It rained on the last night of the nineteenth century, and there were fierce storms. George Cockerill, a writer for the Melbourne *Age*, sent this report by telegraph:

The Australian Commonwealth was inaugurated in Sydney today.

MISGUIDED EARL *His Excellency Lord Hopetoun, first Governor-General of Australia, whose ineptitude almost bungled the formation of the first national government.*

The old century went out amidst rain and storm; the new one made its advent amidst overhanging clouds and portending thunder. Disunity and parochialism made a tearful exit. Federated Australia was nevertheless ushered into being on a day that was full of sunshine and inspiration of life and hope and the spirit of buoyant youth.

Sydney was decorated like a wedding cake for the proudest day in Australia's history. From the early hours of the morning, groups began to gather in the streets, and soon there were half a million people watching almost five kilometres of procession as it wound its way to the Federation site in Centennial Park.

Even the reporter from the *Age* was impressed by Sydney's extravagance. He wrote:

There was so much of interest and beauty along that triumphant pageant that human eyesight lamentably lost its range. Look down George Street! The Collins Street of Sydney is bedecked in its gayest apparel as it may never be bedecked again.

At the head of proceedings was Lord Hopetoun, Australia's first Governor-General, who had arrived in the colonies only a fortnight earlier. Hopetoun, who had made a colossal vice-regal blunder by trying to appoint the wrong man as our first Prime Minister, would never be a very popular figure, especially when the taxpayers found he had remarkably extravagant tastes. Hopetoun's choice for first Prime Minister had been Sir William Lyne, Premier of New South Wales and an arch opponent of the whole idea of Federation. Needless to say he couldn't find the necessary numbers to form a government and the job fell to Edmund Barton.

But on this day everyone was determined that nothing would spoil their moment of celebration. More than 150 000 people gathered at Centennial Park, and as the boom of the one o'clock gun died away, the Governor-General approached the magnificent white pavilion. There was so much feathered headdress around the official area that it was almost comic—a veritable gaggle of Gilbert and Sullivan officialdom.

But this was serious business. Queen Victoria's proclamation was read, Hopetoun took the Oath of Allegiance, a twenty-one gun salute was fired and 10 000 children sang the Federation Anthem. The Commonwealth of Australia was born.

According to reporters, the beautiful grounds of Centennial Park would always be remembered as the scene of the historic occasion. But how wrong they were. Few people today could say where the Australian nation was officially born. Indeed, the pavilion where the ceremony took place is no longer there. It was made mainly of plaster of Paris and was only a temporary structure anyway. The elaborate Victorian filigreed decorations were stripped away, and the wooden framework and a small brass plaque now stand tucked away in a corner of a quiet suburban park at Cabarita—over fourteen kilometres from the original site of 1901. But Australians have never been ones for great political monuments. Federation was, after all, more an idea, more a symbol than a tangible event. And the man in the street in 1901 had more practical concerns.

Simply staying alive was one. At the turn of the century bubonic plague was still a major problem in the Rocks area of Sydney (that area of the city around the southern pylon of the Harbour Bridge). Conditions in some of the inner city were as grim as those depicted in a drawing by Hogarth or a novel by Dickens.

What was life like for the average Australian in that first year of the century? For a start, our population was only a little over three and a half million whites. (In those days we didn't even bother counting the blacks.) And the whites were ninety-five per cent British, and proud of it. We were xenophobic, still trying to rid ourselves of the 'problem' of the Chinese who had flocked here during the gold rush, and the black Kanakas who had been brought here as virtual slaves to work the sugar plantations of Queensland.

To make sure that we would remain 'pure' for the rest of the new century, we introduced in our first year of nationhood an Immigration Restriction Bill, a polite way of saying a 'white Australia' policy. It was a racial filter that we would keep in force for more than half a century. During debate on the Bill, John Christian Watson, who was destined in 1904 to become the first Labor leader in the world to head a national government, delivered this classic utterance. 'The question is whether we would desire that our sisters and brothers should be married into any of these races to which we object.'

At the beginning of 1901 Queen Victoria was still on the throne, and words like world war, aeroplane and radio still had to be coined. Mr Bell's amazing device the telephone, however, was spreading like wildfire. There were 10 000 telephones in Sydney alone.

The maximum wage for a skilled worker was sixty shillings a week and females were lucky if they could earn five bob. The forty-eight hour week was standard. It all compared rather unfavourably with Lord Hopetoun's take-home pay of the best part of $200 000 in today's money.

It was a myth then, as now, that Australia was a 'classless society'. At the turn of the century the working class aspired to be middle class, and the middle to be upper. A white collar worker might have earned about £300 a year, and he was extremely mindful of his position in the community. He was the unchallenged head of the household. His wife knew her place. The people at the office called him 'sir' and his children might have called him 'pater'.

In 1901 our Mr Middle Class paid only £7/10/- annually in taxes. In New South Wales it was a flat rate of sixpence in the pound on incomes over £200. In Victoria, the rate was only fourpence in the pound on incomes up to £1 000. There was no federal income tax for another fifteen years.

The average Australian wore clothes and lived in a house totally unsuited to the environment. The Queen Anne style villa was all the rage, although within a few years one might be considering a change to 'Federation' style. Traditional terrace houses with their iron lace were considered 'old-fashioned'. Those that managed to survive would experience a spectacular revival more than half a century later. But now, at the dawn of a brand new twentieth century, it was all elaborate decoration in wood, with soaring

ONLY ONE OWNER *The first car to be used in a 'Commercial Presentation', on display in Flinder's Lane, Melbourne. The chauffeur of the Oldsmobile is Harry Hawker.*

16

CABINET ORIGINALS *The first Federal Ministry late in its term of office. Prime Minister Edmund Barton is seated second from left, with Australia's second Governor-General, Lord Tennyson, in the centre.*

towers, turrets and tiled minarets, completely at odds with the landscape and the climate. Seventy-five years on, nothing had changed. Australians were building Tyrolean houses with steep roofs to shed the snow—at Surfer's Paradise.

The unique Australian phenomenon—a panorama of red roofs sweeping from the hills to the sea—began before the turn of the century. The Wunderlich Tile Company was boasting before the First World War that it had 'painted the town red' with the seventy-five million terracotta tiles which it imported between 1892 and 1914.

What else can one say about the citizen of Australia in 1901? Certainly he wasn't the easy-going bushman which mythology had led us, and the world, to believe epitomised the average Australian. Between a third and a half of all Australians lived in the cities, and Australia was progressively becoming one of the most urban nations on earth. Nevertheless, some of the mythology did appear to hold true. We did 'like a drop'. At the turn of the century the genteel state of Victoria had fifty breweries, and Sydney alone boasted twenty-one.

Our passion for grog was eclipsed only by our love affair with sport. We took great pride in adhering to the lofty ideals of amateur contests

such as the Olympic Games. In 1900 the nation's collective bosom swelled with pride when Fred Lane won Australia's first gold medals for the 200 metres freestyle and 200 metres 'obstacle race' at the second Olympic Games in Paris. Fred had also entered for the 100 metres and probably would have won except that organisation of those games was somewhat lax; when Fred made it down to the banks of the Seine he found that the race was already over. In 1902 Lane became the first swimmer in the world to break the minute barrier for the hundred yards, using the favoured style of the day, the 'Trudgeon'.

Melbourne's love affair with that remarkable game called Australian Rules was in full flower at the turn of the century. Even before the first decade of the century was over, 50 000 of Melbourne's population of only half a million turned out for the Grand Final.

We also took a healthy delight in a good juicy scandal, or better still a murder. A few days after the twentieth century began, a half-caste Aborigine named Jimmy Governor was hanged at Darlinghurst gaol in Sydney. Behind him lay a horrifying saga of death and mayhem which appeared to have been triggered by the problems of a 'mixed marriage'.

Jimmy, who many years later

FAST FREDDIE *Australia's first Olympic swimming medallist, Freddie Lane, who 'trudgeon'-kicked his way to two gold medals at the 1900 Olympic Games which were held in Paris.*

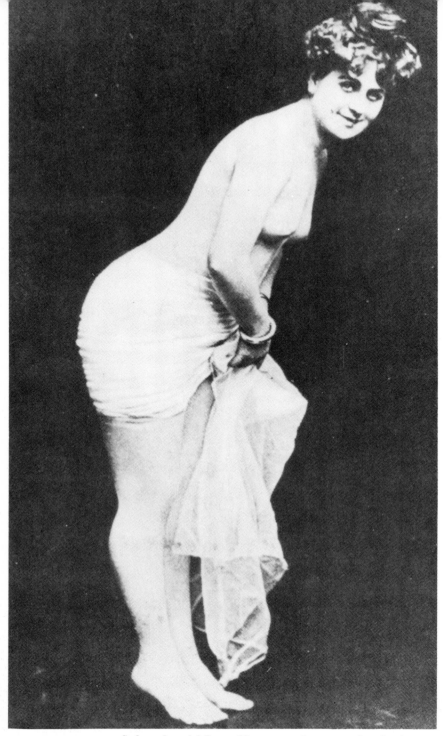

'THE BREAKER' *Poet Morant served in the Boer War but was executed by firing squad for murdering prisoners.*

EDWARDIAN PLAYMATE *Sydney showgirl Pansy Montague—who appeared under the stage name 'La Milo'—boasted statistics of 38-27-42 and an annual income of £10,000 per year. This saucy pre-dater of today's centrefolds was the nation's first pin-up girl.*

would be celebrated in book and film as Jimmy Blacksmith, married the white daughter of a local miner. He was hardly black himself. With his shock of red hair he was known in Gilgandra district as a good cricketer, fencing contractor and station hand. But one day Governor's pretty white wife overheard the wife of one of Jimmy's bosses discussing a coming cricket match and the words, 'If you pick those blacks for the team, I won't cook any cakes for the picnic.' This racial slur led to a rampage in which Jimmy Governor killed nine people, including old men, women and babies. Governor, his brother, and a friend were pursued over a good part of New South Wales. The killer's most relentless hunter was Herbert Byers, lover of a murdered schoolteacher, Helena

THE BARD OF THE BUSH *A. B. 'Banjo' Paterson styled himself as a bush balladeer although he was really a city slicker.*

Kertz. Governor was eventually riddled with bullets, but he survived to be hanged and to become the subject of hatred, awe and gossip for much of the first decade of the century.

In all, the turn of the century was an exciting if difficult time for the 'average' Australian. Some of the menfolk were overseas involving themselves in the oriental skulduggery which surrounded the Boxer Rebellion. 'Banjo' Paterson was with other Australians in South Africa chasing Boers and creating legends about such dubious heroes as 'Breaker' Morant. In Sydney, actress and generally naughty lady Pansy Montague, alias 'La Milo', was scandalising decent and not-so-decent folk with her picture postcard poses in the nude. And remember S. E. Gregory? Oh, well, they probably won't remember Dennis Lillee in seventy-five years either.

If 1901 was a momentous year for Australia, then perhaps it is worth noting what else was happening in the world during that first twelve months of the new century. For Britain no doubt the most significant single event had been the death of Queen Victoria. For the United States it was the assassination of President McKinley. He was succeeded by President Roosevelt, who concerned himself with such matters as America's brand new protectorate of Cuba, and the treaty for building a massive engineering project called the Panama Canal. It was in essence a quiet year internationally. Samuel Butler published *Erehwon Revisited*, Kipling presented the world with *Kim*. Toulouse Lautrec died, and Walt Disney was born. Rachmaninoff produced his Piano Concerto Number Two and rag-time jazz surfaced in the United States. The hormone adrenaline was isolated, Marconi transmitted radio messages from Cornwall to Newfoundland, J. P. Morgan organised his US Steel Corporation, oil drilling began in Persia, Britain launched its first submarine and recognised boxing as a legal sport.

Against this international background, Australia faced the first ten years of the new century. Before it

was over the inhabitants of the world's newest nation would see technological changes beyond belief.

Even by 1900 Australians were aware that the motor car had some potential in a country where the 'tyranny of distance' was to become a catch phrase.

The first all-Australian car, the Thompson Steam Phaeton, is in fact just as old as the twentieth century. In late 1900 the Phaeton's designer, Mr Herbert Thompson, of Armadale, Victoria, drove the vehicle from Bathurst to Melbourne at an average speed of 8.7 miles per hour (14 kilometres per hour). At that rate the journey did much the same for motoring as Burke and Wills had done for the concept of interstate travel. But, after centuries staring at the backsides of horses it was a novel change.

The year 1901 also saw the first Australian petrol-driven car built by Colonel H. Tarrant. The intrepid colonel went on to prove that the horseless carriage was quite a feasible instrument in which to travel from go to whoa. However, for the majority of citizens the solution to urban transport problems was the

tram and it would continue to be for most of the century. The good people of Melbourne have clung on to them until the present day and they may well have the last laugh. While other states have progressively ripped up the tracks in the name of progress, Melbourne's city fathers have nodded wisely and maybe suggested a new coat of paint. Today Melbourne still boasts one of the most efficient tramway systems in the world.

Initially trams were horse-drawn affairs. Sydney was first off the rank, introducing trams to the streets as early as 1861. Unfortunately in the haste to demonstrate the new wonder, the tracks were laid upside down, which made the streets so bumpy that the line was soon closed.

By 1885, Victoria had unveiled its version of the latest in urban transport, the legendary Melbourne cable tram. It was the beginning of eighty years of rivalry between the two capital cities over which had the better system. In many ways the Melbourne cable tramway symbolised Australia's new found faith in technology. The massive steam powerhouse which drove the endless

BONESHAKERS *This intrepid duo were waiting to be flagged away from the assembly point in George Street, Sydney, in the 1905 Dunlop Reliability Trial. The trial took 5 days to reach Melbourne, although one American daredevil did the trip in an amazing 23 hours.*

kilometres of underground cables was like some sacred monument to engineering. It was a splendid system even though only a few years after its introduction it was regarded as obsolete. Actually it would be 1924 before Melbourne reluctantly began tearing up the cableways that had been such a source of civic pride.

If the first decade of the century was marked by great technological change then it also saw considerable social advances.

In 1902 women (dammit, sir), were given the vote, and workers' compensation was introduced. Daylight bathing—a symbolic breaking down of the remnants of Victorianism—was pioneered at Manly. But in some areas perhaps we tried to change too much too soon. An Australian committee reported in 1902 that it was in favour of adopting decimal currency, but the Mother Country was unwilling to change, and it would be over half a century before our official D-day.

When the new Commonwealth came into being an entirely new force of public servants had to be recruited and almost immediately a search for a suitable site for a capital began. The site had to be well and truly in 'no-man's land', preferably on the border of New South Wales and Victoria, because interstate rivalries were still smouldering. At one stage the New South Wales Premier threatened to withdraw from the newly federated states altogether, and this led to Deakin's classic instruction to his secretary, 'Tell him to go to hell—three pages.'

In 1904 the world's first Labor government came to power, and the Commonwealth Arbitration Court was set up. One of its decisions not long afterwards gave some indication of the economic climate of the age. In an award for shop assistants in Sydney the court granted boys under fifteen a starting wage of five shillings a week which rose to seven and sixpence after fifteen.

The captains of commerce, however, were doing quite well, and some were well on the way to becoming institutions which would last

throughout the century. A company named Arnott was founded in that year. Soon afterwards they adopted a parrot motif which became almost as familiar to Australians as a boomerang. Arthur Arnott, one of five sons of the founder of the company, was a member of the Salvation Army. One day he christened a biscuit with the initials of Salvation Army Officer—SAO—and the rest is history. Seventy years later, this biscuit still outsold all of its rivals.

Two years after the Arnott company was established, another amazing success story began. The Kiwi boot polish company was a dynamic, thrusting concern which relied heavily on ingenious advertising. In fact one of the oldest film commercials in the world was made by Kiwi in London, and shows a good-humoured digger enlightening two street urchins as to the qualities of the product.

POLLY WANTS A CRACKER *The famous parrot trademark of the Australian biscuit manufacturers Arnotts—still the biggest bikkie makers in the land.*

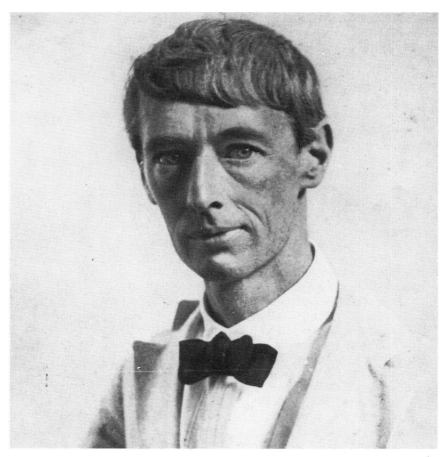

PORNOGRAPHER OR POET? *The classic study of Norman Lindsay by Cazneaux, which shows the wistful features of the most controversial Australian artist of this century.*

LOVELY RITA, NORMAN'S MAID *Today Rita Young is married and worlds away from the life of an artist's model ... but thirty years ago there must have been many painters who would've given anything to have her pose.*

RIGHT: OCTOGENARIAN PIXIE *For his whole adult life, artist Norman Lindsay waged an unceasing battle against the moralists and wowsers who found his paintings, drawings and sculpture lewd and obscene.*

As the new century unfolded and the Victorian influence dissipated, Australians had an extraordinary amount of difficulty in trying to work out their standards of decency and decorum. Norman Lindsay's *Pollice Verso* (Latin for 'thumbs down') caused a national outcry when it was purchased by the Melbourne Art Gallery for £150. The nudity in a religious setting aroused the ire of the wowsers to a pitch where they would feel obliged to hound Lindsay for half a century afterwards. Another of Lindsay's drawings, *The Crucified Venus*, caused even greater controversy when it was exhibited in Sydney. Julian Ashton refused to remove it from public gaze and eventually there was an absurd compromise. The picture was hung face to the wall. Lindsay, who was still working in his ninetieth year, outlived his most determined critics, but was somewhat bitter about them until the end.

RITA, NORMAN'S MAID *Artist Norman Lindsay had a well-publicised affection for the female form, and he liked his women to be substantial. Perhaps his favourite model in the second half of his long career was this woman ... Rita Young. He painted her again and again, delighting in the juxtaposition of her flashing good looks and splendid figure.*

SHOCK! HORROR! OUTRAGE! *The Norman Lindsay drawing* The Crucified Venus, *which so shocked the wowsers and clergy who flocked to view and condemn it at its showing in the Society of Artists Spring Exhibition of 1912. The drawing contributed greatly to Lindsay's reputation as an outrageous libertine and sensualist.*

It's a sobering thought that at the turn of the century, at the dawn of the modern era, bathing in daylight hours was prohibited in Australia. The strong, healthy bodies of a brash young pioneering country were apparently not suitable for public gaze. Wowserism still permeated our soul.

However, in 1902, in the Sydney suburb of Manly a newspaper editor named William Gocher decided to challenge public morality head-on. In December of that year, clad only in neck-to-knee bathers, Gocher plunged into the sea at high noon. He did it again on two more occasions, each time announcing his intentions in his newspaper.

On the first day a crowd gathered and oohed and aahed but police on the scene took no action. Eventually though, the constabulary decided it could no longer tolerate this flagrant challenge to the law and public decency. The police swooped and hauled Gocher off to court. Nearly eighty years on his daughter, Mrs Marie Mahony, recalls . . .

He asked to be taken to the High Court to see Inspector Fosby and the Inspector said, 'Mr Gocher, I've been reading with delight . . . you've won the day.' He said, 'All day surfing from now on as long

as the women are properly clothed. They must have neck-to-knee costume and the bosom must not be shown.' So of course Dad couldn't get home quick enough and we all went down with him and we were thrown into the water. We all had our costumes and had a lovely swim.

Gocher's victory was complete. Within a year daylight bathing was legalised and soon became as popular as it remains today. But not everyone approved. A Waverley alderman complained, 'I can no longer take my daughters for a walk by the sea because the recumbent nakedness is too indecent.'

The 1900s are probably the most forgotten decade of Australian history. With the whole of the first part of the century about to be eclipsed by the 'war to end all wars', those balmy days seem to have almost been lost to time. Yet in those first ten years there was a tremendous amount of development in all areas of antipodean life.

Australians had been besotted with sport ever since troopers kicked convicts around the decks of the first fleet. But now Australia was sending stout-hearted men back to the Old Country to wrest a variety of trophies from the British. In the first

year of the century Australian bowlers destroyed the Englishmen in Melbourne, M. A. Noble taking seven wickets for seventeen runs. In 1905 Australia and New Zealand sent a combined team to contest the Davis Cup, and two years later Norman Brookes, 'the Fox', became the first non-British player to win Winbledon. Then with his New Zealand partner he took the Davis Cup. The following year saw the remarkable Burns-Johnson world championship bout in Sydney, which was billed as 'the fight of the century'.

Nevertheless, Edwardian life was apparently not without its tensions. The magazine *The Lone Hand* was about half a century before its time when it reported in 1907 that 'what the drink habit is amongst men in Australia the headache powder is among women'. Despite the fact that it has been called 'the lucky country', it seems that Australia has always had a massive headache. By the twenties the Aspro company—with extraordinary advertising campaigns engineered by a remarkable character, George Davies—was using the slogan; 'Twenty Aspros a day keep a man's pain away.'

The amount of medical and dental quackery in the country lead to

FIRST FLIGHT *The first real flight in Australia was made by George Taylor in this glider. The date was 5 December 1909; the place Narrabeen Heads, NSW. In all 29 'heavier-than-air' flights were made on the day, and the best covered 110 yards.*

GO FLY A KITE *Australia's pioneer aeronautical inventor Lawrence Hargrave experimenting with giant box-kite flying machines at Stanwell Park, NSW in the 1890s. Hargrave was in fact lifted off the ground, but never achieved powered flight.*

THE HEADACHE BUSINESS *Hilton J. Nicholas, now head of the vast multinational company which began business selling Aspro—a simple aspirin headache cure invented by his father in 1915.*

a Royal Commission in 1908, and some of the bogus 'professors' were forced out of business.

As the first decade drew to a close, transport had made some astounding leaps, jerks and bounds. In December 1909, George Taylor made the first free flight in Australia in a glider.

Some Australians had been mucking around with heavier than air machines for many years and, indeed few people these days realise that Lawrence Hargrave, the man whose portrait appears on the $20 note, exerted a profound influence on the history of international aviation. Ten years before the Wright brothers flew their first powered aeroplane, Hargrave took to the air suspended beneath four box kites. The aerodynamic knowledge gained from this and other experiments contributed greatly to the development of aviation theory and the Wright brothers were among the many who corresponded with Hargrave about his work. A monument on a spectacular headland at Stanwell Park on the New South Wales coast commemorates Hargrave and his experiments, without which the Wright Flyer might never have got off the ground. Sadly, Hargrave himself never achieved powered flight, possibly because of the weakness of his propeller designs.

But soon after the turn of the century a number of other Australians were anxious to test their wings. In the same year that Taylor made his glider flight at Narrabeen Heads,

NSW, Mr L. A. Adamson, headmaster of Wesley College in Melbourne had been greatly excited by Bleriot's flight across the English channel. He sent a young man named Colin De Fries to Europe to purchase a Wright biplane and a Bleriot monoplane. On his return De Fries did manage to get airborne in that year. But the fact that he could not demonstrate his ability to control and steer his aircraft robbed him of the honour of being the first Australian to fly.

By a strange quirk of fate, the first man officially to make a controlled flight in a powered aircraft in Australia was the American escape artist and magician, Harry Houdini. On a tour here in 1910, he brought along his French biplane specifically to attempt the first real flight in this country. After waiting several days for the right conditions, Houdini duly made his ascent at Digger's Rest in Victoria on 18 March, but at the time no one realised that, just a day before, a young man in Adelaide named Fred Custance had flown an imported aircraft for three miles. Custance didn't seek any publicity, so the honour and glory went to the American magician.

STILL IN THE AIR *Australia's first home-grown aircraft, built with wire from wool bales by Victorian farmer John Duigan, is still proudly hung in the Victorian Museum. Duigan first flew in a paddock on his farm not much longer than this room.*

It wasn't long before Australians were keen to get airborne totally under their own steam, and just four months after Custance and Houdini, a young farmer named Duigan from the Mia Mia district became the first man to pilot an Australian-built aircraft. Duigan had designed and built the plane himself, although he'd never seen an aircraft. It was based on pictures of the Wright brothers' aircraft which Duigan had seen in a magazine, and it was lovingly assembled in a barn. On 16 July 1910 Duigan and his home-made plane flew into history books, with stays made from piano wire and fittings fashioned from the steel bands off wool bales.

The first Australian pilot's licence went to a Sydney dentist, William Hart, a dare-devil character who

MAGICIAN AT THE WHEEL *Celebrated American magician and escapologist Harry Houdini and his French-made Voisin biplane which he flew at Digger's Rest, Victoria, in 1910 to become the first man to officially make a powered flight in Australia.*

THE FLYING FARMER *John Duigan, a farmer from the Mia Mia district of Victoria, was the first Australian to build a successful aeroplane and fly it. The contraption was fashioned from locally collected materials including steel bands off wool bales.*

bought himself a Bristol Box Kite in 1911. Hart became the pioneer of inter-suburban flying and confounded the local sceptics when he made the epic flight from Sydney to Penrith, a journey of about forty miles. He took passengers for joy flights at ten guineas a time and thrilled Sydneysiders by once keeping up with a train travelling at a mile a minute. Hart was fined £10 for scaring some cows to death and he complained that at those prices the future of flying was bleak. Hart, like many other early Australian aviators, was almost killed in a crash.

At the beginning of the 1910s, Australia was already a considerably different country from what it had been in those heady days of January 1901. Science and technology were clearly going to change our society completely. Despite that huge continent, and despite the fact that we were told that we rode on the sheep's back, we huddled in cities on the coastline and prepared for the industrial onslaught.

There were now 360 000 trade unionists in the country. Towards the end of that first decade miners at Port Kembla struck over an issue which would foreshadow the anti-uranium protests of today. Miners considered that the use of electricity in the mines was dangerous. No protesters gathered with chants of 'Keep electricity out of the ground', but here was an early example of what the future was to bring.

BROKEN WINGS *William Hart never completely recovered from his last crash.*

THE "BIRDMAN" PHILOSOPHER

AUSTRALIA'S FIRST AVIATOR TELLS OF HIS SMASH-UP AND COMPLETE RECOVERY.

WILL FLY AGAIN NEXT MARCH.

For the "Sunday Times" by W. E. HART.

DAREDEVIL DENTIST *The cheerful face of Sydney dentist William Hart, the first Australian to hold a pilot's licence, in 1911.*

The 1910s

The next decade of Australian life was dominated by one great and hideous event: the First World War.

Not that Australia was bereft of development in the last few years before the conflict began. A man named Walter Burley Griffin won a prize for his concept of a magnificent new capital city. Australia now had its first 'skyscraper', a building nearly 52 metres high, Culwulla Chambers in Sydney.

The Australian Inland Mission was founded, the Murrumbidgee Irrigation Scheme began; we even had our first advertising agency.

By now we also had our first true film star, Lottie Lyell, who was described by the producer, Raymond Longford, as 'a little lady, an elocutionist, and strictly religious'. A far cry from Linda Lovelace perhaps, but the alliterative Miss Lyell made a great impact in *The Romance of Margaret Catchpole*, and appeared in dozens of films before her death in the prime of her career.

HERO'S WELCOME *Harry Hawker, who was forced to ditch his aircraft in the sea during an attempt to fly the Atlantic ten years before Lindbergh's flight, became a hero in London. He received £5,000 from the British and also the Air Force Cross.*

Another early darling of the screen was Louise Cabas, who, as Louise Lovely, went on to Hollywood to star in some truly forgettable 'silents'.

Ultimately Raymond Longford would be remembered for his classic film *The Sentimental Bloke*, but in the years just before the war he made *Australia Calls* which, in its story of a Japanese attack on Sydney Harbour, reflected the popular obsession with the 'yellow peril'. The visiting American fleet doubled as the Japanese naval force, and the rest of the action was done with models. However crude it may have been, Longford's film was also prophetic. The only problem was he predicted the wrong war. In the First World War the Japanese were not the enemy, but thirty years later, during the Second World War, Sydney Harbour did indeed come under attack from the Japanese.

In 1910, around the same time that Hart the dentist was earning Australia's first pilot's licence, a Melbourne man named Harry George Hawker was flying as test pilot for the legendary T. O. M. Sopwith in England. Hawker, whose legacy became the Hawker Siddeley and Hawker De Havilland companies, was Australia's first professional airman.

In 1914, Hawker was back in Australia to demonstrate a new aircraft. He had an appointment with the Governor-General who then resided at Government House in Melbourne. The story goes that Hawker was late for the appointment, but whatever the truth, when the time arrived the tranquil atmosphere of Government House was shattered by the noise of the new aeroplane's engine. A few seconds later the Vice-Regal couple

CHOCKS AWAY *Maurice Guillaux in his Bleriot monoplane makes a spectacular take off from the grounds of the Federal Government House in Melbourne in 1914. Guillaux was the first man to fly mail between Sydney and Melbourne.*

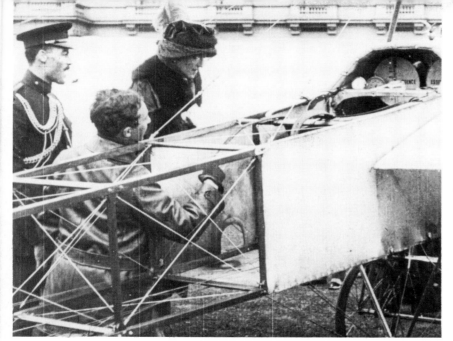

AND WHAT'S THAT? *Maurice Guillaux, the dashing French aviator, shows Lady Denman and a vice-regal aide the workings of his Bleriot monoplane in the grounds of Government House, Melbourne, then the seat of the Governor-General.*

the old Ascot race course in Sydney, was killed in Europe soon afterwards. Hawker, too, was destined to be involved in many remarkable aviation achievments, and was once awarded £5000 and a medal from the King after an unsuccessful attempt to fly the Atlantic. But, like most of our early aviators, he was fated to end his life in a crash.

The development of aviation during the conflict that was about to erupt in Europe would be remarkable. Once it was found that the aeroplane was useful for killing people other than pilots its future was assured.

The war did not burst on Australians overnight. The rumblings had been there for months. But the announcements came with surprising suddenness. On the eve of the outbreak, the issues which affected the Australian man in the street were the Irish crisis, the coming football finals and electioneering.

Andrew Fisher, the coal miner who became Prime Minister, suf-

who were engaging in a spot of tennis were greeted by the spectacle of a Sopwith biplane taxiing through the gardens.

Mr H. G. Hawker had arrived for lunch.

Flying into Government House became all the rage that year. Another who all but charmed the bloomers off the Melbourne ladies was the Frenchman Guillaux who flew the first air mail from Sydney to Melbourne. Guillaux, who pranged his aircraft spectacularly at

VICE-REGAL VARIETIES *The lawns of Government House Melbourne were treated to some amazing sights when it was still the seat of the Governor-General, not the least of which was a landing in the grounds by Maurice Guillaux the French aviator. In the same year, 1914, the Australian airman Harry Hawker also landed a Sopwith plane in the rose garden.*

DIE LIKE A SPORT *With staggering losses to replace, the Australian war effort invented bizarre themes on which to base their renewed recruiting effort. C'mon Aussie, c'mon.*

GOING FOR THE JUGULAR *Norman Lindsay's classic World War I recruiting poster appealed to a sure-fire soft spot—the innocence of children.*

fered similar vicissitudes to those of Gough Whitlam. Against a background of press and opposition cries of 'socialisation' Fisher struggled through three terms as Prime Minister between 1908 and 1915.

With such controversial items in its platform as a decision to form a Commonwealth bank and to introduce anti-monopoly legislation, Labor's position was always precarious. At the general elections of 1913 Labor very narrowly lost its majority in the House of Representatives, but increased its control in the Senate. The Conservative Government, in ironic contrast to the events of 1975, had its mandate frustrated by the Senate, and consequently the ministry fell.

During the election campaign in 1914 there was no mention of the imminence of war until the end of July. On the last day of that month both Fisher and opposition leader Cook broke the spell. On that night Fisher made his famous 'last man and last shilling' speech. This was not an original phrase, but one

which had tremendous effect on the electorate. The next night Joseph Cook made a similar promise, 'If there is to be a war, you and I shall be in it. We must be in it. If the Old Country is at war, so are we.'

Britain declared war on 4 August 1914, and the British Foreign Secretary made another memorable utterance, 'The lamps are going out all over Europe. We shall not see them lit again in our lifetime.' In the next four years Australia would send its sons overseas—often as not much more than cannon fodder. Almost 60 000 Australians were killed in action; nearly seventy per cent of our troops would be killed or wounded—the highest casualty rate of the Empire. British casualties were fifteen per cent less.

And yet for every man who went, a dozen Australians stayed home. Many of them were women and children but many of them were men too. Life did go on, sometimes with a zest. In 1914, two vaudeville performers, Nat Phillips and Roy Rene, formed a partnership which was to

become the most famous in the history of the Australian theatre: 'Stiffy and Mo'.

In that same year two brothers, George and Jim Coles, started a store with a motto 'nothing over a shilling'. It was the beginning of a business which would revolutionise retail trading in Australia. During the war George and Jim and their other brothers, Arthur and Dave, served with the AIF. Jim and Dave were both killed in France, but when the war was over George and Arthur opened another store with the slogan 'nothing over two and sixpence' and this would be their policy until the following world war. In 1979 the company declared a profit of $54 million.

There was no doubt that Australia enjoyed a blessed standard of living, even in those days. Our soldiers were called 'six-bob-a-day tourists' because they were the highest paid soldiers of the war. But the jibes seemed hollow when the 'tourists' were thrown almost as a sacrifice at the cliffs of Anzac Cove, Gallipoli.

In 1915 this little known Turkish peninsula became a byword for one of the most tragic and inept campaigns of the First World War. No other single event would do more to mould the national psyche. The campaign was not only tragic in its overall concept, but the folly was compounded by the fact that the first wave of Australians was mistakenly landed one mile from its true objective, in an area previously regarded as an impossible place for a night landing. As the Australians were slaughtered by the Turks their commanders suggested withdrawing, but the British General Hamilton on board the battleship *Queen Elizabeth* ordered them to hold on.

After eight months of hopeless fighting, trying to wrest the enemy from its topographical bastion, the Anzacs were finally withdrawn. They had lost 10 000 men. The Australians' heroism was such that nine of them were awarded the Victoria Cross. But the enduring hero of Gallipoli was a man who never won a medal—Simpson, the stretcher bearer who ran the gamut of Shrapnel Gully with his little donkey named Duffy.

Yet not all Australians were enamoured of the war and the press reports of deeds of derring-do. In 1916 a good many of the Irish community saw the conflict as a 'sordid trade war'. Their leader, Archbishop Daniel Mannix, fought vehemently against conscription. They made a martyr of Les Darcy, the young boxing champion who skipped the country and died in America while seeking fame and fortune. There were purges of the local German communities which admittedly had been rather nationalistic and insular since arriving in the colonies nearly a century before. The Germans were victims of a general hysteria about spies: some German-Australians were incarcerated, place names were changed, and South Australia banned the teaching of German and closed Lutheran churches.

Many of the passions and fears were understandable. On the western front alone 38 000 were killed. The general mood of the press, which had been strident and tub-

ORIGINAL ANZACS *An artist's impression of the historic landing at Gallipoli of Australian and New Zealand forces from the steamer* River Clyde *on 25 April 1915. The Gallipoli campaign did much to mould the Australian psyche.*

HORSEMEN AT THE APOCALYPSE *The determined young men of the legendary Australian Light Horse who fought so gallantly first at Gallipoli and then again in the desert campaigns.*

thumping at the beginning of the war, grew more sober. The heavy casualty lists appeared each day— surrounded by a black border.

The first Anzac Day was held in 1916 on the anniversary of the Gallipoli landing. By order of Billy Hughes, a dispatch by the British war correspondent Ellis Ashmead Bartlett was read out to schoolchildren all over the country. This was the stuff that made loyal Australian hearts skip a beat:

. . . not waiting for orders, or for the boats to reach the beach, the Australians sprang into the sea and, forming a sort of rough line, rushed at the enemy's trenches. Their magazines were not charged, so they just went in with cold steel.

By the end of the war 329 000 Australians had served overseas; 59 330 were killed and 152 710 wounded. Sixty-six Australians received the Victoria Cross.

The cost in cold hard cash had exceeded £370 million. Yet even then Australia could count herself fortunate. In Europe the daily war expenditure had been £164 million. Eight million people had been killed, twenty-one million wounded, and seven and a half million were missing.

When Billy Hughes returned from the Versailles Peace Treaty Conference in 1919 he said that he had no real idea of how much the Commonwealth might expect in compensation. Our claim for reparation was £464 million. Of this, Hughes thought we might get £50 million—if we were lucky. In fact only £5.5 million had been received by 1931, and after that no more payments were made by Germany.

During that conference Hughes was involved in some celebrated exchanges with the American President, Woodrow Wilson. Hughes insisted on what amounted to a 999-year lease over New Guinea. Wilson was shocked by the Australian Prime Minister's stubbornness in securing New Guinea and

DON'T SPEND IT ALL AT ONCE *Prime Minister W. M. Hughes officially welcomes Ross and Keith Smith to Australia after their epic flight from England to Australia and presents them with the Australian Government's cheque for the £10,000 prize.*

administering it under Australian law (a blatantly white Australian law at that). The following exchange was reported:

Woodrow Wilson: 'Mr Prime Minister of Australia, do I understand your attitude aright? If I do, it is this: that the opinion of the whole of the civilised world is set to nought.'

Hughes (adjusting his hearing aid): 'Very well put Mr President. You guessed it. That is just so.'

This sort of terrier-like activity endeared the 'Little Digger' to many Australians. Australia at the end of

EMPIRE GIRDLED! *The Vickers Vimy of Sir Ross and Keith Smith lands at Sydney in 1919—the conclusion of the first ever flight from England to Australia. The journey consumed 20,000 gallons of petrol and took 28 days to complete. The international call-sign of the plane was GEAOU—which the Smith brothers promptly turned into 'God 'Elp All Of Us'.*

BUNDABERG WELCOMES CAREFUL DRIVERS *'Hustling' Bert Hinkler, favourite son of the Queensland country town of Bundaberg, parades down the main street preceded by his plane—an Avro Avian—proudly towed by the local Shell dealer's tanker. The whole nation was proud of him, and celebrated his exploits.*

THAT'S MY BOY! *Conquering hero Bert Hinkler gets a tearful hug from his mother as he steps from the plane after completing the first solo flight from England to Australia.*

the war was much changed from what it had been just five years earlier. It had gone into the Big Stoush as the 'little boy' amongst the nations and had come out with a bit of a swagger. The returned soldiers formed an élite group in the community and reinforced their position each Anzac Day. They devoted a great deal of their energy to helping their comrades and families. No one questioned the fairness of the returned soldiers getting preferential treatment in areas such as housing, but whether it led to social harmony

and industrial efficiency was another argument.

The men who came home from the war found that the cost of living had risen by sixty per cent, and that you couldn't get a drink after six o'clock. Still, Australians were better off than the Americans, who were about to go through that extraordinary period known as Prohibition.

In 1919, with the hostilities over, the Australian Prime Minister, Billy Hughes, offered £10 000 for the first flight from England to Australia. Two Adelaide brothers, Ross and

Keith Smith took up the challenge. In horrific conditions—at times they nearly froze to death—they completed the journey in a Vickers-Vimy biplane. The trip took twenty-eight days, and that time stood as a record for the next ten years. It was finally broken by little Bert Hinkler, the young man from Bundaberg, Queensland, who had been crazy about flying since he was a child. He had built a glider as a teenager and by 1912 he was mechanic for the visiting American flyer Wizard Stone.

31

SYNCHRONISE WATCHES *Always punctual, Bert Hinkler checks his watch before taking off from Sydney. Suit, shirt and tie was normal dress for aviators in the 1920s.*

Hinkler, who was eventually killed in a crash in the Appenine Mountains in Italy in 1933, was a shy, introverted man who was devoted to his mother. His elaborate and maudlin funeral, stage-managed by none other than Benito Mussolini, would no doubt have caused the flier acute embarrassment.

When Hinkler took off from Croydon Aerodrome near London in February 1928 in his tiny Avro Avian biplane there was little fanfare. And yet he was about to make the longest solo flight in history ... England to Australia in little over a fortnight. When Bert flew into Bundaberg to see Mum the Hinkler backyard seemed to be almost the centre of the universe for this Queensland country town. The entire populace was ecstatic, as indeed was the whole of Australia. All around the nation they cheered him and wrote songs and poetry about him, a favourite being, 'Hinkle, Hinkle little star, sixteen days and here you are.'

'THE LONE EAGLE' *On a freezing dawn morning at Croydon aerodrome near London, little Bert Hinkler, wearing a suit coat with three buttons on the sleeves prepares to make the longest, epic solo flight in aviation history—from London to Australia in sixteen days.*

After being lionised by the Australian nation and the world, Hinkler tried to keep some of his flights, including a remarkable sortie across the southern Atlantic in a midget plane, secret. He shunned publicity and glory and became known as 'The Lone Eagle'. But there was no doubt that for most of Australia little Bert Hinkler, the boy from Bundaberg, was the public hero for the 1920s.

The 1920s

The popular image of the twenties is of the Charleston, flappers, crazes—'the roaring twenties'. It was a time of gay abandon and sheer joy, before we plunged into the gloom of the Depression at the end of the decade. To a large degree this mood did prevail in Australia. We did try most of the crazes, most of the fashions, most of the drinks, most of the dances. But the twenties was also a time of intense political and social change.

To most Australians the 'Bolshies' were little more than a 'bloody nuisance'. But there were real class struggles being fought. Police used bayonets to break up watersiders' demonstrations in Fremantle, and the Broken Hill mines had been closed for more than a year.

Politics was still a rough and ready business. Hugh Mahon, the member for Kalgoorlie, got stuck into the British for the policy on Ireland. That was acceptable, but when he referred to this 'bloody and accursed Empire' Billy Hughes organised a move to get him thrown out of the House. (Somehow people had now forgotten what Hughes himself had said about Britain in a fiery debate about the Boer War: 'This is the most iniquitous war ever waged by any race, and I hope that England may be defeated.')

Within a short time some fancy political footwork backfired on Hughes, and he would not taste the prime ministership again. In an attempt to placate big business, Hughes appointed the well-heeled Stanley Melbourne Bruce as his Treasurer. Soon Bruce was Prime Minister, and he led Australia through most of the 1920s. In many

HAVING A WONDERFUL TIME *Holiday weekend crowds on the St Kilda grassy swards in the early 1920s. Thirsty parents waited in orderly queues for their turn at the tea rooms, and a welcome 'cuppa'.*

ways Bruce's aristocratic and stylish image suited the times. We regarded ourselves as considerably more sophisticated than the eager colonial hicks who queued up for places on the troop ships ten years earlier. When the Prince of Wales visited Australia in 1920, the *Bulletin* urged that the Prince should be seeing 'the Australia that is friendly and hospitable but will lick no man's boots.'

Stanley Melbourne Bruce was our first businessman Prime Minister. And perhaps more by accident than design he ruled over Australia during an unprecedented boom period. By 1928 an increasingly materialistic Australia had 500 000 cars, 300 000 radios and 400 000 telephones. The population increased by twenty per cent and part of the increase was due to the influx of 300 000 migrants.

After the stagnation of the war,

the country was being pioneered once again. P. J. McGinness and Hudson Fysh, the two young men who had tracked by car the route for the 1919 flight from London to Sydney, formed Queensland and Northern Territory Aerial Services Ltd, or Qantas for short.

But enterprises were both large and small. The Golden Gate which opened in Sydney in 1921 became the best known soda fountain in Sydney, while on a slightly larger scale the boffins finally got serious and decided to call for tenders for a bridge across Sydney Harbour. In the same year the Old Melburnians were treated to a demonstration of the phenomenon of radio at one of their smoke socials. They were advised that it was 'quite unnecessary for any of the windows to be open' for the radio waves to get through.

33

HORSELESS CARRIAGE *The Cobb & Co. Royal Mail carriage leaving Longreach, Queensland in 1910, bound for parts unknown. It is not known whether the dog travelled as a non-paying passenger, or trotted along behind the truck.*

MOTORISED CHAOS *A splendidly disorganised traffic jam of cars, buses and trams at Anzac Parade, Sydney in the late 1920s. The two policemen on duty (in the white pith helmets) seem to be making little impact on the situation.*

Prime Minister Bruce allowed much of the frenzied commercial activity to develop unchecked. His motto could well have been 'Life was meant to be easy', but then, like Malcolm Fraser so much later, he could be extremely autocratic when the mood struck. His common ploy was to blame the Bolsheviks for all industrial ills. This was a successful tactic taken up by successive Liberal Prime Ministers.

By 1924 Australia was building 20 000 new factories a year. Woolworths went into business. Qantas declared its first profit in the same year that Cobb and Co. ran its last coach in Queensland. Horse-drawn trams were finally phased out, and work began on the Harbour Bridge and the new 'temporary' Parliament House in Canberra. Oil was struck at Lakes Entrance in Victoria, and although nearly 300 000 gallons of petroleum were produced there in the next thirty-five years, it was largely of a poor quality. This discovery was, nevertheless, of great significance in the development of Australia's oil reserves.

Australia was now fifth in the world for the number of motor vehicles according to the National Automobile Chamber of Commerce in New York. Of the world total of nearly sixteen million cars, America had thirteen and a half and Australia, bless her little heart, had more than 100 000.

By the mid-twenties Bruce was taking the 'big stick' to the unions, a tactic that would eventually bring about his undoing. He made an abortive attempt to have the ring leaders of the seamen's strike deported.

In 1925 Australia faced a far more insidious problem than some left-wing talk from the Bolsheviks. Over twenty million hectares of Queensland and New South Wales were covered with prickly pear, a vegetable plague, which had all descended from a single potted plant. The story of how the land was saved from the scourge is one of the great scientific sagas of the twentieth century.

Elsewhere in the world a man named Adolf Hitler unveiled a book called *Mein Kampf*. A chap named Clarence Birdseye succeeded in freezing cooked food and storing it, and Chiang Kai-shek became leader of the Chinese Nationalist Party. On a more parochial level, a Sydney real estate agent named Jack Lang became Premier of New South Wales. Lang was destined to become one of the stormiest and most fascinating political figures in our history, his career culminating in a dramatic dismissal which would not be parallelled until the Whitlam era.

In the same election that saw Jack Lang become Premier, a young man of thirty-one named Herbert Vere Evatt stood for and won the seat of Balmain. Evatt was quick to make his presence felt in Lang's government, playing a vital role in the framing of legislation introducing widows' pensions. Like Lang, Evatt was also fated to have a spectacular, dramatic and, at times, tragic political career. In Australia, he was eventually pilloried for his politics, but on an international level he rose to the highest position attainable: President of the United Nations.

After his early stint in state politics, Evatt became at thirty-six the youngest man appointed to the High Court. He left the legal profession to enter politics when the country was at war in 1940, and after the war he helped to set up the United Nations. At home his political career from 1949 onwards was thwarted by the smear that he was pro-communist. In those McCarthyist days the 'red' tag was enough to keep him out of office as Prime Minister. He remained Leader of the Opposition for a decade and his own party, the Australian Labor Party, split in two largely because of the strongly anti-communist and Catholic elements within its ranks.

By the late twenties, however, Australia was still under the benevolent dictatorship of S. M. Bruce. Although there was a general strike in Britain and the Hitler and fascist youth movements were on the rise, Australia was making the most of its ten years of peace since the First World War. We were happily separated from the gathering turmoil in Europe. The fact that Trotsky had

DAPPER AND DEBONAIR *Prime Minister S. M. Bruce during a day at the races. The top hat, pinstripes, gold chain and cigar did not exactly endear him to the nation's working class.*

A DAY THE UNIONS WILL NEVER FORGET *In 1927, at the height of a confrontation between the conservative government of Stanley Melbourne Bruce and an increasingly militant trade union movement, police and mine workers clashed in the Maitland–Cessnock region of NSW in what became known as the Battle of Rothbury. One man was killed, and forty injured. Police fired upon workers and the workers tried to fight back.*

been expelled from Moscow meant little, but the visit by famous Russian ballerina Pavlova excited press and public alike. A young Adelaide man named Helpman changed his name slightly, adding another 'n' for distinction, and joined her company. 1926 was a great year for the arts. Others who came were singers Dame Clara Butt, Chaliapin and Toti Dal Monte.

And if Pavlova inspired Robert Helpmann to greater heights, she did the same for a Perth hotel chef named Bert Sachse. Why the ballerina's lissome figure prompted Bert to create a highly calorific concoction of egg whites, sugar and cream is a mystery, but the 'pav' became one of Australia's favourite ethnic desserts; along with Peach Melba, created by the great Escoffier, and the lamington, a chocolate and coconut-covered cube of sponge cake named after Baron Lamington, Governor of Queensland from 1895 to 1901.

The disappointment of not being able to compete in the 1919 London to Sydney flight caused Kingsford Smith, in the late twenties, to make the most audacious flight of all—across the Pacific. We now had our own Lindbergh. In fact there were few international trends we could not match. We even had our own little crime 'czars' like Squizzy Taylor, who culminated his career by getting shot under mysterious circumstances in Melbourne.

Nellie Melba had ruled the international stage for decades, and in 1927 she sang at the opening of the brand new Parliament House in Canberra, while none other than the Duke of York turned a golden key in the door. The inimitable newspaper *Smith's Weekly* sent its boxing writer to cover the affair.

During a devotional interlude I noticed the Duke cast several nervous apprehensive glances towards the political gallery. Possibly he had just remembered his ancestor George the Third's illuminating outburst, 'Politics is the trade of scoundrels.' Orisons over, the Duke and Duchess vanished into the bowels of the building and the gallant Four Hundred charged the doorway.

As the twenties drew to a close, Australians could look back on a decade that hadn't been so frivolous after all. The CSIRO had been established, and the Australian Iron and Steel Company was formed to provide the vast sums for the projected Port Kembla steel works.

Australians had made international names for themselves even in the arts, although Frances Alda, prima donna at the Metropolitan Opera House for twenty years, was not too confident about the future. Asked whether she thought grand opera would show a profit in Australia she replied (to the delight of everyone, still with an Australian accent), 'Stick your money on a horse, son.'

In the late twenties it wasn't only grand opera which was having its financial difficulties. Unemployment, which was a problem of frightening magnitude, rose from seven per cent in 1926 to eleven per cent in 1928.

As the economic climate worsened we seemed to look more and more to our heroes for inspiration. Perhaps we took heart from the smiling faces of Smithy and Ulm when they conquered the Pacific, and little Bert Hinkler who flew solo from Britain to Australia. Hubert Opperman was voted the most popular sportsman in Europe. Don Bradman played his first Test Match. The name Phar Lap was on everyone's lips. The engineering wonder of the age, the Sydney Harbour Bridge, was under way.

But the reality was that most of us were now battling for a living. The Wall Street crash in America signified the start of the Depression and, although not hit as hard as some countries, Australia nevertheless suffered severely. Her economy relied heavily on overseas loans and the sale of primary products. Share prices plummeted and, as the value of our money dwindled, businesses closed, farms were abandoned and

DEATH AT THE PIT HEAD *Today this coal pit is called Ayrefield No. 3, but fifty years ago it was named Rothbury . . . and the name symbolised an infamous incident in Australian union history. In 1927, striking miners and police clashed in a bloody battle.*

THE UNLUCKY LEADER *James Scullin brought Labor to power in 1929 with an incredible landslide—just in time to inherit the financial catastrophes that would be known as The Great Depression.*

THE PREMIER GOES TO VOTE *Jack Lang, the N.S.W. Premier who was dismissed by the State Governor Sir Philip Game in 1932, walks into a polling booth on election day in his Sydney electorate of Auburn.*

people who could not pay the rent were forced out of their homes.

Prime Minister Bruce, more and more incongruous in his Saville Row suits and spats, not only lost an election, but suffered the humiliation of being the only Australian Prime Minister to ever lose his seat in Parliament as well.

Scullin, who became Prime Minister after Billy Hughes had led the revolt which toppled Bruce, lost important support soon after winning the election. He refused to intervene in the New South Wales coal strike in 1929. When the New South Wales government sent troops into the Rothbury mine and killed and injured strikers, many unionists never forgave him for ignoring the call for federal intervention.

It was a dramatic time in Australia. In Sydney thousands of people took to the streets to protest about the killing of the young Rothbury miner, Norman Brown:

Norman Brown's body lies a mould'ring in the grave,

But we'll go marching on.

Labor also failed to gain control of the Senate during the elections, and in March and May of 1930 the Senators threw out money Bills which Scullin considered vital. Scullin also became embroiled in combat with his Labor colleague in Sydney, Jack Lang. Lang tried to protect the people of his state from the effects of the Depression at the expense and in defiance of Canberra, and, more dangerously, Britain. It made him a hero of the people but it killed him politically.

And so the thirties began with unemployment worse than Germany's, and 125 000 out of work in Sydney alone. The decade would end with another world war.

The 1930s

The 1930s was not a happy decade for many Australians, although perhaps because of this, it is a period rich in folklore. Even the crimes of the thirties have an unsurpassed mystique: the 'pyjama girl' and 'shark arm' murder cases still arouse more curiosity than any of the thousands of murders which have taken place in the half century since. Bradman, Lindrum, Phar Lap and Jack Crawford were just some of the sporting giants of the thirties. The decade also saw the rise of perhaps the greatest of our political giants, Curtin, Chifley and Menzies.

This whole period was marked by bitter internal dissension in the Labor Party over the handling of the Depression by Scullin. Ben Chifley was one of Scullin's supporters and, because of this he lost the backing of many people in the Labor movement. Perhaps, more importantly, he made a life-long enemy of Jack Lang. In the elections of 1931, during the massive swing away from Labor, Chifley lost his seat. At the same time Lang and his supporters launched a plan to oust Chifley from his own union. The move was successful and Chifley faced 1932 without a seat in parliament, without membership, and without a job. He spent the next ten years out of parliament, but not out of politics, and, after a long battle, he did in turn have Lang expelled from the party in 1936.

After the outbreak of the Second World War, Menzies offered Chifley the job as Director of Labour Supply. Chifley lasted in the job for less than a year. He resigned to contest the seat of Macquarie and within a year his close friend John

Curtin appointed him to the post of Federal Treasurer, a portfolio he retained even after he eventually became Prime Minister.

But back in the 1930s, Chifley, Curtin and Menzies were still in the political wilderness. The Prime Minister for most of the decade was in fact a most unlikely character, Joe Lyons. Apart from the fact that he was one of those peculiar political animals who changed horses in midstream, Lyons seems an uninteresting character. Or was he? When he put himself outside the government and the Parliamentary Labor Party in March 1931 he was protesting against their handling of the economic crisis.

He fully expected that his political career was finished. Yet, within a year he was the country's leader, and he remained so until 1939. The secret of Lyons' success has puzzled many analysts.

Certainly, with the rest of federal politics in disarray in the early thirties, 'Honest Joe' came through the middle in a fashion not dissimilar to the rise of Jimmy Carter. The Nationalist Party Leader, John Latham, who had gunned down such figures as Billy Hughes, stood aside to let Lyons lead. There had been a hasty move to bury the Nationalist Party and create the United Australia Party and once again, a Labor 'defector' filled the opposition party leadership and gave it renewed stability. Latham, in turn, had the satisfaction, along with Menzies and Casey, of manipulating the less urbane and seemingly malleable Lyons. But just how much Joe Lyons was a pawn of the party is open to speculation. History has painted Joe and his famous wife Enid as a couple of simple, homespun, fundamentally decent Christian folks—a little at a loss in the hurly-burly of federal politics. But the idea that a couple could acciden-

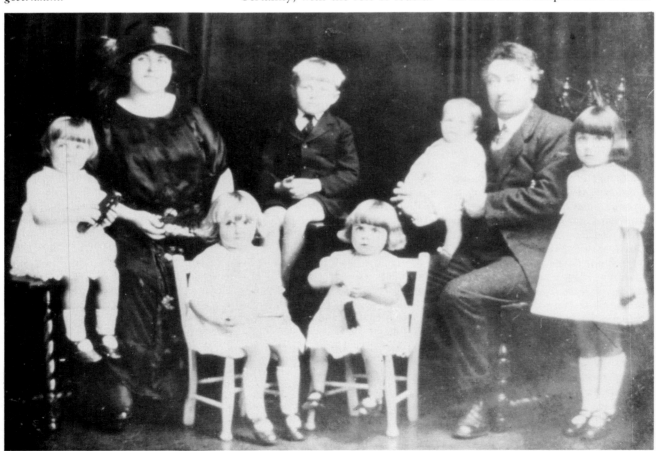

AND THEN THERE WERE SIX *The Lyons family when Father Joe was Minister for Education and later Premier of the Tasmanian State Government. By the time Joe was Prime Minister, his wife Enid had eleven children to look after.*

tally stumble into the top positions in the country seems absurd.

If the leadership of the 1930s was somewhat grey, then life was not altogether dull. We took up most of the Depression crazes: barnstorming, marathon ballroom dancing and mini-golf. There were other rages: art deco, airships, skiing, 'Odeon' style cinemas, cocktails, modern bungalows.

There was another important change to the way Australians saw themselves. The newsreels began— Cinesound and Movietone—and they really were the television of their era. They were surprisingly large-scale, dynamic and topical for such a small country, and we flocked to see them. There was a surge of activity in the film business. It was the beginning of the so-called 'golden age' of Australian film, and a not-so-golden start for a strapping young bloke named Errol Flynn, whose first role was in a documentary feature called *In the Wake of the Bounty*. Flynn got £10 a week for his part and had no idea then that he would go on to become one of the biggest stars in Hollywood. In that same year in 'tinsel town' Shirley Temple was making her first film, and Johnny Weismuller made his first appearance in a Tarzan movie.

But while Errol Flynn made a tenner a week, many were getting next to nothing. By 1933 a quarter of the workforce was still unemployed. It was the era of 'bagmen' and 'jumping the rattler', when men caught Murray cod, possums and rabbits to earn a meagre living. They transported themselves in boats called 'Murrumbidgee whalers', and jumped the trains, sometimes slowing them down to a comfortable jumping-on speed by greasing the tracks.

There was no building boom throughout the decade, and immigration virtually ceased. In fact, more people left Australia between 1930 and 1932 than entered it. Rural areas were hit just as hard as the cities. In the early thirties a country bank manager wrote:

Merriwagga is a dust storm fenced in, surrounded by mirages, dying

NON-STOP JITTERBUGGERS *In those crazy, madcap days just after the war when the nation was gripped by a common desire to enjoy themselves, these desperate young things jittered and bugged their way for miles along city streets.*

THOU ART THE LIGHT *During the 1930s Sydneysiders enjoyed playing mini-golf in the remains of the Theosophist Temple overlooking Middle Harbour.*

sheep and our clients. The principle industries are dust storms and uninhabited farms.

However, in the depths of the Depression, Australia built its proudest monument—that grand old pile of nuts and bolts called the Sydney Harbour Bridge. There was a tremendous amount of fuss at the opening when the political extremist De Groot cut the ribbon with a sabre and stole Jack Lang's thunder. For Lang it was a desperate time all round. At his right elbow on that sunny afternoon in March 1932 was Sir Philip Game who, two months later, called the Premier to his study at Government House and dismissed him.

For many, the dismissal was an outrage against democracy, but even Lang's sacking hardly aroused the kind of passions which surfaced during the infamous 'bodyline' cricket tour. Cricket became warfare and the sporting crisis reached diplomatic level. As England kept the Ashes, our only comfort was that Jack Crawford won the Wimbledon singles tennis. But we soon had other preoccupations which would help take from our minds the wounds left by 'bodyline'. The bizarre 'pyjama girl', whose body was kept in formalin for ten years until she was

identified, was the subject of ghoulish speculation and rumour until the mid-forties, as were the shady principals of the 'shark arm' case. The case began with an incredible coincidence. A shark in Coogee aquarium disgorged the remains of another shark, which in turn contained a human arm. On the arm was a tattoo which started police on one of the most frustrating and still unresolved murder cases in our history.

Such newspaper stories as the pyjama girl and shark arm cases, the mysterious loss of Kingsford Smith's airliner *Southern Cloud*, and the race riots in Kalgoorlie, momentarily distracted Australians from the problems of the day. Halfway through the decade there were still 400 000 unemployed. Australia's recovery from the Depression was slow, and full employment did not return until the outbreak of the Second World War in 1939.

However, the extreme severity of the Depression was thankfully not compounded by a collapse of the banks as had occurred in America (and indeed in Australia in the 1890s). As a response to the bank smash just before the turn of the century, Australian banks had strengthened themselves with a series of amalgamations, which reduced

their total number to nine. Nevertheless, there were many penny-pinching schemes which caused hostility and heartbreak. The New South Wales Married Women (Teachers and Lecturers) Act provided for the dismissal of married women teachers unless they could prove hardship. The official justification was that 'the married woman's sphere is the management of the home rather than breadwinning. It is the woman's lot to marry and share the home with the breadwinner.'

Now looking after our interests overseas was Stanley Melbourne Bruce, who after a brief comeback in federal politics, had accepted the job as resident minister in London, a job which he handled with distinction and *savoir faire*. He proved to be a hard bargainer at the Empire conference in Ottawa. At one stage, when Neville Chamberlain (then Britain's Chancellor of the Exchequer) was being unco-operative about meat quotas, Bruce retorted, 'I saved the bloody Empire on Monday. It's your turn to save it now.'

This conference did in fact go some way to 'saving the Empire', and established a trade pattern which was to last for thirty years. Chamberlain and Bruce were actu-

LET'S TRY AGAIN, SHALL WE? *NSW Premier Jack Lang finally completes the ribbon-cutting ceremony to mark the opening of the Sydney Harbour Bridge in 1932. Moments earlier, a political extremist had slashed the ribbon with a ceremonial sword.*

GENERAL AGREEMENT *General Douglas MacArthur (left), Commander of Allied Forces in the Pacific during WW 2 with Australia's military supremo General Sir Thomas Blamey, inspecting an air base.*

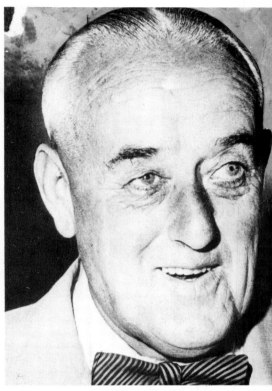

ENERGY DREAMER *William Walkley, the Australian who founded the Australian Motorists Petrol Company.*

ally friendly foes. When war seemed inevitable, Chamberlain offered Bruce the chairmanship of the BBC, but Bruce declined.

The situation in Europe was ominous. Hitler amassed ninety-nine per cent of the vote in the 1936 elections. The Spanish Civil War had begun. Edward abdicated to marry Mrs Simpson. The world seemed to be falling apart.

And, while the war clouds gathered, some of those who were destined to play major roles for Australia were going through the most traumatic periods of their lives. One was Thomas Blamey, who went on to become Australia's best known soldier and our first Field Marshal. After a highly successful career in the First World War, Blamey was, in the late thirties, the Victorian Police Commissioner, but he was involved in some scandals which nearly ruined his career. Soon after he took the post, Blamey's police badge, number 80, somehow came to light following a raid on an 'upper crust' Melbourne brothel. Blamey claimed

he had lost the badge some time before the raid, but a public scandal ensued. Nevertheless, Blamey survived the crisis and went on to re-organise the police force. In 1936, however, the chief of the CIB was shot in a gunfight when two men tried to hold him up as he waited in a car with two women friends to meet an informer. Blamey told the press that the superintendent had been shot accidentally while loading his revolver. But the true story came out, and in the storm that followed Blamey was censured and forced to resign. His official career seemed finished, and for a while he was a broadcaster on radio 3UZ.

In his talks on the radio Blamey warned of the growing dangers from Germany and Japan, and in 1939 he was made Controller-General of the recruiting secretariat. A year later he was appointed General Officer commanding the Sixth Division. Blamey was a man with many enemies, and many friends. When he died in 1951, 20 000 people passed through the Shrine of Remembrance.

With the war yet to begin, people still made their plans for the future. Who knew what lay in the days ahead?

Laurence Hartnett, a little Englishman who had come to Australia to solve some of the problems of the merger between General Motors and the Adelaide-born Holden Motor Body Works, dreamed of an 'all Australian' car. A man named Bill Walkley was fighting to establish the Australian Motorists Petrol Company, which eventually became Ampol. Even without the war, the odds seemed against them from the start. The Sydney Stock Exchange advised its members not to buy shares, and the major oil companies did their best to squash the new company. By 1937 the company welcomed the tanker *Garonne*, carrying its first supplies from the American Richfield Corporation. But the 'big boys' cut their prices to try to force Ampol out of business. Ampol lost more than £18 000 in its first six months, and employees had to hawk shares door-

One of the constant problems of inner city life in Australia has been low cost housing. The first half of the century has been marred by a struggle to overcome slum conditions.

THE STAYER *A young Robert Gordon Menzies, pictured on the occasion of his first elevation to the Prime Ministership on 7 May 1939.*

to-door to raise another £100 000 in capital.

The year 1938 was also the one-hundred-and-fiftieth anniversary of the founding of New South Wales. Charles Chauvel, watching the procession to celebrate the event, was instantly inspired to make his epic film *Forty Thousand Horsemen*. It was based on the exploits of his uncle, an eminent soldier, during the Palestinian campaign in the First World War, and it put 'Chips' Rafferty and Peter Finch on the road to international fame.

The Lyons Government, which had lasted for almost the whole decade, had been sound but unspectacular. When the Labor Party, led by John Curtin, began to look formidably strong in the late thirties the conservatives started to carve each other up politically. The one who came out on top was Robert Gordon Menzies.

Menzies had already earned his famous nick-name of 'Pig Iron Bob' after he had introduced severe punitiv measures to break a union ban on the loading of scrap iron for Japan. Menzies was growing impatient with the apparently feeble leadership of Lyons, and in 1938 launched a thinly veiled attack on

his leader by saying that 'Democracies could not maintain their place in the world unless they provided leadership as inspiring as that of the dictator countries.' It was a prophetic statement.

The speech by Menzies caused a Cabinet re-shuffle which did not suit the ambitious Victorian. For a start, Richard Casey was promoted to Treasurer, and it transpired that Lyons had chosen him as his successor. Within a matter of months Menzies resigned. His excuse was that the government had failed to carry out its 1937 election promise to create a national comprehensive insurance scheme. Menzies said this was a betrayal of the electors. But, whatever his reasons, neither Menzies nor any other non-Labor leader revived the idea of the scheme.

As fate would have it, Lyons died while the internecine struggles continued, and there was immediately a brutal battle for the leadership. There were desperate plans to revive Stanley Melbourne Bruce as Prime Minister, but he set down a series of impossible conditions for his leadership. The Country Party leader, Earle Page, tried to thwart Menzies and publicly denounced him, but

Menzies shrugged off the attacks and formed a new government.

As Robert Menzies posed for his first ministry photograph in 1939, with Casey on his right and Billy Hughes on his left, and with his United Australia Party colleagues and a few renegade Country Party men to back him up, the future looked shaky. Yet even now, it seemed war was not inevitable. The coalition government under Lyons believed, like the British coalition government under Chamberlain, that the aggressors could be appeased. In fact just a few months earlier Lyons had rebuked visiting English writer H. G. Wells for describing Hitler as a 'certifiable lunatic' and Mussolini as a 'criminal Caesar'.

On 1 September 1939 Menzies was booked to hold a meeting in the Victoria Hall at Colac, the venue where Andrew Fisher, on the eve of the First World War, had pledged that Australia would defend the Mother Country to 'her last man and her last shilling'. Menzies was dining before the meeting when he was told on the telephone that Hitler had invaded Poland. He went to the meeting, told the audience of the invasion, and returned to Melbourne to confer with his ministers. At 9.15 p.m. on 3 September, Menzies said in a broadcast to the Australian people:

It is my melancholy duty to inform you officially that in consequence of the persistence by Germany in her invasion of Poland, Great Britain has declared war on her and that, as a result, Australia is now also at war. No harder task can fall to the lot of a democratic leader than to make such an announcement.

The 1940s

More than twice as many Australians enlisted for the Second World War as did for the First, and yet only half as many were killed.

LATER TO BE PRIME MINISTER *In December 1919 John Curtin, lost his first attempt to be elected to the federal seat of Perth.*

While there had been sixty-six Victoria Crosses won in the First World War, only twenty were won in the Second World War. It was a different war. No longer was there a sense of derring-do or adventure. It was more business-like, more mechanised and more scientific. There were no bloody years of trench fighting, and medicine had improved. Nobody thought that the conflict would end in a futuristic nightmare—the atomic holocaust of Hiroshima and Nagasaki.

At the outbreak, the mood was calm and purposeful, not as excited and enthusiastic as it had been in 1914. Service throughout the war was primarily voluntary—not complicated by the divisive conscription battles of the First World War.

Yet, as in the First World War, Australia turned to a Labor Government for leadership. The Menzies Government's tenuous hold on power led to a revival of calls for a 'national government'. Although many, including Evatt, agreed with the idea, Curtin refused. While Menzies was beset with the problem of dealing with the unions, the Labor movement was strengthened by the return to the fold of the Lang Labor Party.

In 1941 Menzies went overseas and returned to find that his leadership had been completely undermined. Fadden took over, but two

HEAD TO HEAD *Australia's wartime Prime Minister John Curtin meets with the Commander in Chief of the Armed Forces, General Blamey. By independently declaring war on the Japanese, Curtin issued a new era of Australian foreign policy.*

independent members, one of whom described Menzies' fall as a 'lynching', took revenge on his behalf. They combined to defeat the Fadden Government and their action placed Labor in office for the remainder of the war.

In 1941 the new Prime Minister, John Curtin, made a direct declaration of war against Japan without consulting the British Cabinet. It was the first time in Australia's history that she had declared war on her own. Curtin also introduced a new era of Australian foreign policy in December of that year when he said:

> Without any inhibitions of any kind I make it quite clear that Australia looks to America—free of any pangs as to our traditional links of kinship with the United Kingdom.

For Australia this was perhaps the major difference between the Second World War and the conflicts that had gone before. For the first time in our history there was a possibility of a direct threat to *our* shores.

Within months war would actually come home to Australia, and it shocked the nation.

In the meantime Australian soldiers underwent a splendid baptism of fire at Bardia, capturing 40 000 Italians for the loss of only 130 of their own men. But we were not so fortunate in Crete. Trapped on the Greek peninsula by the German occupation armies, Australian losses were high. Yet, as with all warfare, the fortunes vacillated. Glorious pages of Australian history were written at Tobruk. At one stage the Australians found they had taken another 27 000 prisoners for the loss of just forty-nine men. But the untried Ninth Division was routed by Rommel in Tripoli in a retreat which was cynically called the 'Benghazi Handicap'.

In the early days of the war the Australian battleship *Sydney* sank the Italian *Bartolomeo Colleoni* in the first cruiser battle of the war. But in 1941 she met the German raider *Kormoran*, a heavily armed ship disguised as a Dutch freighter. *Kormoran* was on her

ARTFUL ARTIE *Queensland cunning politician Arthur Fadden who snatched the Prime Ministership from Menzies in 1941 when even the UAP refused to tolerate Menzies.*

UNWELCOME VISITORS *The most celebrated exhibit outside the War Memorial in Canberra—sections of two Japanese midget submarines recovered after their suicidal attack on Sydney Harbour in May 1942.*

way to lay mines in the Shark Bay area outside Fremantle, and surprised the *Sydney* as she was returning to port. The ships had closed to about 900 metres before *Sydney* asked for a secret sign of identity. The captain's reply was immediate. German flags went up, Dutch flags went down and she opened fire. A full salvo hit *Sydney* amidships. Both ships were crippled in the fire which followed, and as the Germans abandoned ship they caught sight of the *Sydney* about 16 kilometres away with her hull ablaze. The only trace of her ever found was a life float and lifebelts. Her amazing demise remains one of the great naval mysteries.

In 1942 the war came right to Australia's shores. Japanese midget submarines raided Sydney Harbour and Japanese planes bombed Darwin. They were bleak times. To our near north Singapore fell, a loss described by Churchill as 'the worst disaster and the largest capitulation in British history.' On 16 February Major General H. Gordon Bennett, leader of Australia's Eighth Division, escaped from Singapore believing he should return to his country to help in her defence. His reasons, however, were not accepted in Australia and he did not receive an overseas command for the rest of the war. In 1945 he was finally cleared by a commission which decided that he had considered himself a prisoner of war, and that it was his duty to escape.

The American role in the war was paramount. When General Douglas MacArthur arrived in Australia after his mauling in the Philippines, the American President sent a telegram to Curtin saying it would be 'very acceptable' if the Australian government would nominate MacArthur as the Supreme Commander of all allied forces in the South West Pacific. The Australian government agreed. MacArthur found what he later described as 'a sense of dangerous defeatism' amongst a large segment of the Australian people. Many disagreed with his assessment, and there were some who took the General's florid and studied oratory with a grain of salt.

Australians were already well

A HELL OF A PLACE *Members of the 16th Australian Infantry Brigade moving up along a track across the Owen Stanley ranges, photographed near Nauro, New Guinea.*

MAKING OF A LEGEND *Exhausted Australian infantry retreating along the mud-clogged Kokoda Trail during the fighting against the Japanese in New Guinea.*

aware of the American alliance. By the end of the war nearly a million American troops had passed through Australia, and the influx caused inevitable tensions. The American GI, with roughly twice the spending power of the Australian soldier and a somewhat more dashing uniform, cut a swathe through some of the flower of Australian womanhood. Eventually 12 000 girls went to the United States with American servicemen. There's a classic story about a GI who boasted that the Americans had pinched all the girls from the Australians, to which a Digger laconically replied, 'You didn't pinch 'em mate, you just helped us sort them out.'

Many Australians really resented the American 'invasion'. They described the Americans as 'over paid, over fed, over sexed and over here'. The liaisons between American ser-

vicemen and Australian girls eventually led to the 'Battle of Brisbane'. A group of Australian servicemen picked a quarrel with American military police. In the fight that followed nine Australians were shot, one of them fatally.

Late in 1942, the Japanese launched a two-pronged attack on Port Moresby along the Kokoda Trail and at Milne Bay. For a while it seemed that the Australians would lose Milne Bay, but the invaders were driven back into the sea. On the Kokoda Trail the defeat of the Japanese took much longer. The nightmare of Kokoda—the sheer hellishness of the terrain and the fighting—is known to most Australians. The casualties on both sides were high. In Papua the Japanese eventually lost 13 000 of their 20 000 men.

It is sometimes assumed that when

45

THE LIKENESS *At the time of the notorious 'Joshua Smith' case, the press posed this photographic portrait of Smith to help the public decide whether the painting was a true portrait or not.*

DISPUTED PORTRAIT *William Dobell's portrait of Joshua Smith won the Archibald Prize in 1943. Unsuccessful exhibitors at the exhibition took the Trustees of the Prize to court charging that the painting was in fact a caricature, and not a true portrait.*

a country is at war all other activity stops in respectful silence. On the contrary, many non-aggressive pursuits flourished during the war years, although not always without problems. The 1943 Archibald Prize for portraiture was marred by a ludicrous scandal which almost destroyed the life of artist William Dobell. An argument in the Supreme Court about whether Dobell's portrait of fellow artist Joshua Smith was a caricature was resolved in the artist's favour, although he suffered deeply after his public trial.

During the war years the courts also humiliated Max Harris, Sidney Nolan and others involved with an avant-garde literary magazine *Angry Penguins* after they had excitedly published the works of the hoax poet 'Ern Malley'. Malley and his free-form poetry had been concocted by two poets of the traditional school and, to add insult to injury, Max Harris was prosecuted for publishing what were considered indecent extracts from the phoney poet's works.

Lawson Glassop's famous book *We Were the Rats* was also prosecuted for obscenity in 1944. Diggers, it seemed, didn't use four letter words. Around the same time Dr Floyd began his record breaking run of concert programmes on the ABC, and the Commission also began broadcasting the legendary 'Kindergarten of the Air'.

In 1944, the year the Liberal Party was formed; Chief Havoc, a Sydney greyhound, broke five track records in one night; fifty-one people were killed in Victorian bushfires; and the D-day landings were made in Normandy. The Japanese were driven out of New Guinea, 232 Japanese died in a suicidal breakout from a prison camp near Cowra, and the

POINT DUTY *With the war just ended, business was booming. These Sydney shoppers had to dodge the trams and the baleful eye of the policeman to get across the street in one piece.*

PULLING UP STAKES *Forgotten victims of the massive Snowy Mountains Hydro-Electric Scheme were the hundreds of families whose farms and houses disappeared under the waters.*

first Aboriginal army officer was commissioned in Australia.

The year 1945 was one of the most momentous in the history of the century. It was a kaleidoscope of horror, and hope: the Americans entered Manila; British troops reached the Rhine; there was heavy United States bombing of Tokyo; Iwo Jima; Roosevelt died and Truman took over; Mussolini was killed; Hitler suicided; Germany capitulated; the Japanese held out in New Guinea until the end; atom bombs were dropped on Hiroshima and Nagasaki; thirty-five million had been killed in the war and ten million in concentration camps.

John Curtin, still a hero to many Australians, died just a month before the war ended. Ben Chifley easily won the position as Australia's Prime Minister. The London *Times* said in an editorial, 'Chifley is a true product of the Australian Labor movement. He is solid, hardworking and sincere, and his record suggests that since Curtin's mantle has fallen on him he will wear it worthily.'

On 12 July 1945 Chifley entered the Federal Parliament for the first time as Prime Minister and was greeted by a chorus of cheers from members of all parties. His first job was to announce the surrender of the Japanese, and for this occasion he arranged the first national broadcast from the House of Representatives in Canberra.

Chifley's primary objective as Prime Minister was post-war economic and industrial development. His government set up shipping, aluminium, whaling and atomic energy

SWITCHED ON *The scene at the main control room of Sydney's electricity supply in the late 1940s. During the coal strike in 1949 these switching points became the focus of national attention.*

industries. It started the Snowy Mountains Scheme and took over telecommunications. But it was Chifley's confirmed belief in nationalisation which led to his downfall; first with the airlines and then, more disastrously with the banks. Menzies, who was then Leader of the Opposition, later recalled:

In my opinion he was the most authentic labour leader in Australian political history. For him the socialist objective was more than a slogan, it was a principle of action.

Chifley's first attempt to nationalise

industry met with mixed success. He did not achieve a true monopoly, but TAA is still a testament to his success, and his initial sortie into the airline business did no harm to his standing at the next elections. Labor was returned with Chifley firmly in control.

During his second term as Prime Minister, however, Chifley made a decision which militant labour leaders still regard with distaste. Strikes in the New South Wales coalfields were causing a critical shortage of supply and Chifley, believing a communist plan was at work, sent the army to work in the mines.

'CHIF' *Joseph Chifley, a railway worker from Bathurst, NSW, led the nation from 1945 to Menzies' victory in 1949.*

MOVING MOUNTAINS *The massive scale of engineering works in the Snowy Mountains Scheme. One of the greatest public works projects ever undertaken, the system provides vast resources of hydro-electric energy for eastern and parts of South Australia.*

Chifley's most serious tactical error was his attempt to nationalise the banks. Chifley dissented from the findings of a Royal Commission into the banking system and introduced legislation which was passed through parliament in 1945. It gave greater control to the Commonwealth Bank, but the Melbourne City Council mounted a challenge in the High Court, claiming that the legislation was discriminatory. The abortive bank nationalisation plans were a nail in the coffin of the old Labor Party, which was about to be cast out of office. Labor would not see power again for another twenty-three years. Ahead lay the agonies of the crippling party 'split' and the years in the wilderness.

The legacies of Labor in the forties are very much with us today. The visionary Snowy Mountains Scheme is one example. Another of Chifley's more symbolic acts in the last months of his Prime Ministership was to welcome the first Holden motor car off the assembly line. Chifley, a constant supporter of

Laurence Hartnett, played a considerable part in the birth of the car which became an Australian institution.

The Menzies Government came to power in 1949 with promises of a softer life. Menzies' slogan for the election was 'Tip out the socialists and fill up the bowsers', and he won comfortably.

Whatever the achievements, for most Australians the forties was a good decade to leave behind. The first five years had been bloody and sad, the second rather drab and grey.

There's a story, now very much part of our mythology, which comes from the forties and which says a fair bit about that decade. An American visitor is sitting down to dinner at an Australian pub and he's given a plate of cold meat and potatoes:

'Do you think,' he asks adventurously, 'that I could have a little salad to go with this?'

'Did you hear that?' the waitress yells back to the kitchen; 'This bastard thinks it's Christmas.'

The 1950s
At the beginning of the fifties no one could have realised that one man would rule us almost until the 1970s. The 1950s and 1960s were the Menzies Years. He was in power longer than the combined terms of all the Labor governments in our history. Little wonder that they called his reign 'the Ming Dynasty' (from the traditional Scottish pronunciation of his name 'Mingus').

Many Australians look back on the 1950s and 1960s as balmy, troublefree days—a time when a silver-haired father figure in a double-breasted suit gave everyone a Holden, created the Snowy Mountains Scheme and then went off to watch the cricket at Lords. Menzies in fact had little to do with any except the last.

The early Menzies years were as politically turbulent as any in our history. When Menzies came to power in 1949 he had already been savagely 'rolled' by his own colleagues years earlier. He knew what political scrapping was about and his reign began with a tremendous series of battles over the issue of communism. It led to a divided nation and a 'split' which virtually destroyed the Labor Party as an effective opposition. On top of the problems at home, Australia was already fighting in Malaya and was soon to be embroiled in the war in Korea.

The early days of the fifties were hardly halcyon. Menzies has often been accused of engineering the turmoil to achieve his own political ends. But no politician is quite that clever, and it seems that when Menzies did emerge from the fray as victor, he set about seeking a quieter political road. Some said the secret of his success was that he did nothing at all, and although his achievements do not stand out like beacons, Australia did settle into a long period of stable government. It is also said that Menzies chose his time to be leader nicely, although other countries in the 1950s and 1960s saw the usual turnover of political leaders.

There is not much doubt, however, that the period between our involvement in the Korean and Vietnam wars was a time of contentment and prosperity for millions of Australians. The bogeys of today—over-population, the energy crisis and nuclear power—were still beyond the horizon.

Australian awareness of a nuclear future had only just begun in 1950. Just a year earlier a lone prospector named John Michael White stumbled across uranium deposits at Rum Jungle. The deposits were proved in 1951 and a jubilant White was paid a reward of £25 000 by the Commonwealth Government.

In those days nuclear fallout held little fear for Australians. We blithely let the British explode atomic devices all over the country. Yet, by the 1970s, there would be a collective national frenzy when the French were testing similar bombs on a Pacific atoll 4800 kilometres from our shores.

Looking back, the 1950s seem a somewhat smug period of Australian history. Proud of our lifestyle in the 'greatest little country on earth' we

worried constantly that the yellow hordes might still be casting greedy slant eyes on our vast land. The threat from the north became almost a national obsession as our standard of living increased. Those who preached about the peril of the communist tide drew maps with large descending arrows which showed that communist Chinese and others were going to descend upon us almost by force of gravity. (Some wags said the problem could be solved simply by inverting the map.) To the delight of those who had been predicting an Asian invasion, the situation actually began to get some real tension in the early 1960s during Indonesia's 'Confrontation' period under Sukarno. As the Indonesians adopted a menacing stance towards Malaysia and other Anglo-Saxon outposts like Australia, the fear of the 'yellow peril' waxed and then slowly waned again.

Although life in the early fifties was fairly insular we soon began to expand our horizons again. Australia sent a Davis Cup team to try to wrest the trophy from the Americans who had held it since before the war. Drysdale and Nolan, the Australian artists, held their first London exhibition. At the same

THE FICKLE FINGER *Robert Gordon Menzies (left) and W. M. Hughes, two Australian politicians who had both been toppled from the Prime Ministership.*

time, there was an aggressive new school here called The Antipodeans who attacked local abstractionists as 'second rate imitators of the Europeans'. It was rampant artistic jingoism, and while the big guns of the art world lined up on each side, some painters like Godfrey Miller, Passmore and Fairweather, said it was folly for artists to call themselves anything at all.

IT WORKED! *English defence scientist William Penney gives the all-clear as the atomic device his team had developed detonates in the Australian desert at Maralinga. This particular test took place in 1953.*

49

In 1950 a young woman named Joan Sutherland won a Mobil Quest and within a few years she would be strutting the international stage commanding a fortune as 'La Stupenda'. Other Australian women, however, were still struggling to make a quid. In 1950 the female basic wage was increased from fifty-four per cent to seventy-five per cent of the male rate. Today's feminists would no doubt respond 'big deal', but in that year women accepted the adjustment as 'progress'. A large body of Australian women were still a pretty mousey lot who even years later would sullenly oppose the idea of liberation espoused by their self-appointed champion, Germaine Greer. Ironically, too, Australian women were slow to adopt the fashion which eventually we came to believe we had created. In July 1946 the United States began its atomic bomb tests at Bikini atoll in the Pacific and in that month Louis Reard, a Parisian designer, made world news by introducing the first bikini swimsuit. However, in Australia the summer season of 1949-50 only saw the introduction of the strapless swimsuit, which was quite bold enough, thank you very much.

In 1952, the year Elizabeth became Queen and Australia sent its second battalion to Korea, Australians at home began once again to flex their sporting muscles. The fifties were a watershed for Australian sport culminating in the pride of staging our first Olympic Games in Melbourne in 1956. The war had interrupted the careers of some Australian sportsmen, and terminated many more, and in the late forties, save for the inexorable progress of cricket and football, sport had been in the doldrums.

Then, with a rush, we found ourselves gathering laurels around the world. Hoad and Rosewall, two seventeen-year-olds from Sydney, won the Wimbledon doubles. Marjorie Jackson won two gold medals at the Olympics in Helsinki, and the whole nation gave a collective 'tch, tch', when Marj, 'the Lithgow Flash', dropped the baton in the 100 metres relay, then went on to cross the line first just to show that we would have won. Jimmy Carruthers slaughtered Vic Toweel in 139 seconds to win our first official world boxing championship this century.

That was just 1952. In 1953 Ken Rosewall, at eighteen, became the youngest Australian singles champion. Russell Mockridge, the great cyclist who was to die in a tragic accident, won the Grand Prix in Paris. In the following year Peter Thomson won the first of his five British Opens and John Landy, our first four-minute-miler, racing against the world's first, Roger Bannister, turned his head in the last few yards to see where his opponent was, Bannister snuck past, and it was all over. It was the beginning of the professional era. Sport started to become big business. Sedgman turned pro with Kramer. There was a strong rear-guard action fought by amateur sporting bodies, but soon ambitious young people in all fields made a bee-line for the big money.

1954 was probably Australia's most momentous political year. Vladimir Petrov and his wife Evdokia defected to Australia in an atmosphere of hysteria. Russia and Australia withdrew their ambassadors, a Royal Commission into espionage was set up, and the scene was set for the Labor Party's exile from government for nearly twenty years.

The cold war got a little chillier, but life generally was loosening up—less austere than the grey days of the late 1940s. Encouraged by tours by Laurence Olivier and his wife Vivien Leigh, and then the Queen herself, a group of Australians led by Dr H. C. Coombs set up the Elizabethan Theatre Trust. Australian theatre was injected with new life with celebrated plays like Ray Lawler's *Summer of the Seventeenth Doll*. Australians generally had a sudden new passion for what Barry Humphries many years later would call 'the Yarts'. Sydney even decided to fulfil a grandiose dream and chose a site for an Opera House. Three years later the first Opera House Lottery—£5 a ticket—was introduced and fifteen years and $100 000 000 later the Queen would open the building itself.

One 'cultural' development that Australians eagerly awaited in the early fifties was television. In 1950 the Television Advisory Committee sent a group of advisers abroad to study the latest developments. There was considerable argument over

COBBERS *The fabulous tennis twins—Lew Hoad and Ken Rosewall—when they were still in their early teens. Evenly matched opponents in singles, they formed a doubles partnership which excited crowds at every major tennis tournament in the world.*

many years. Ben Chifley, for example, had wanted no commercial television whatsoever, and these days there are still a lot of people who wish he had had his way. Others wanted to aim straight away for a colour service, similar to those in other countries. But, by being unadventurous and settling for a black and white, at least we benefitted from the technological improvements which had been made at the expense of others. Television was postponed in 1951 because of the economic problems of the time, and the next significant move was the setting up of a Royal Commission in 1953.

The Australian way of life was changing both rapidly and slowly. When Malcolm Muggeridge, the English pundit, came here in the 1950s he noted that Geelong Grammar was 'even more snobbish' than Eton. The 1950s saw a burgeoning of the *nouveau riche*. One of them was a nuggety character with a nose for good dirt named Lang Hancock. In 1952 Hancock, a grazier and part-owner of an asbestos mine, became lost under thick cloud in his light plane while flying with his wife from their West Australian property, and flew into a gorge with rust-coloured walls. He returned later, and took iron ore chip samples. He found that they were of better quality than deposits being processed by the United States and was elated. He claimed that 'the greatest industrial might in the world was built around the Lake Superior deposits, and here is a deposit bigger and better.' Hancock's genius was that he not only discovered the deposits, just as John White had stumbled across uranium at Rum Jungle, but that he was able to hang on to 'a piece of the action'. It has made him as rich and powerful as a small government, and from his constant electioneering it is sometimes difficult to tell that this is not what he is.

Hancock is one of the new breed of Australian millionaires whose fortunes were founded in the 1950s. Australia still had its old rich, who in the 1950s were getting £1 a pound for wool during a boom due largely to shortages caused by the Korean

STOMACH IN, CHEST OUT *A young Paula Stafford, (seated) giving her mannequins the once over before sending them out to model her latest 'bikini' creations. In her determination to establish the bikini style, Stafford even talked to meetings of Catholic Mothers to assure them their daughters would be safe in a two-piece.*

war. But the new social giants were people who found new ways to tap the land of its riches.

After flying over promising looking oil country in the late 1940s, William Walkley took six years to raise the money and equipment to prove his theories. In November 1953 the first oil rose out of a drill site at Rough Range near the southern tip of Exmouth Gulf. It was the two-hundred-and-fiftieth well to be dug in Australia, and while several strikes had been made dating back to the 1920s, they ultimately proved to be of limited value. By the time of the first strike Walkley's company, Ampol, was working with Caltex in a joint venture. As they poured millions into the search for oil, these two companies found just what a difficult and frustrating business it is. WAPET spent $35 million before its big strike at Barrow Island.

While some Australians talked in millions, however, most talked in tens. The year 1953 saw tremendous conflict over the basic wage. In that year the Commonwealth Arbitration Court decided to abolish the system

of quarterly cost-of-living adjustments. The automatic adjustments had been part of the Australian way of life since 1921, and the decision sent a shock wave throughout the trade union movement. The circumstances which led up to the change were not dissimilar to the factors

IRON MAN *Lang Hancock, the grazier and mining entrepreneur who was instrumental in developing the vast iron ore deposits of Western Australia.*

GIVE ME YOUR MEEK *Immigration Minister Arthur Calwell welcomes another boatload of migrants to Australia. The gifts of footballs, kangaroos and koalas were presumably intended to transform these bewildered children into instant Australians. By the 1970s 2 500 000 migrants had started a new life in Australia.*

GIDDAY, HOW YA GOIN'? *Australia's millionth post-war migrant, Englishwoman Barbara Porritt, meets her new neighbours for the first time over the front fence of their house at Yallourn, Victoria. She and her husband arrived in 1955.*

which renewed the arguments in the mid-1970s. 1947 to 1953 was a period of high inflation and, after a series of extremely rapid price increases, the basic wage had risen in leaps and bounds from £4/18/- to 11 guineas. As it happened, because of a complex series of economic developments, the decision coincided with a drop in inflation. The unions pressed for restoration of the old system, and would continue to do so until nearly a decade later when the Board partially reversed its policy. In the 1970s the adjustments came back again and all the old arguments were revived.

In 1955 the labour movement split and Australia saw a new political force, the Democratic Labour Party, or more commonly the DLP. A group of vehemently anti-communist Labor men, who according to their enemies were controlled by a clandestine Catholic group called 'the Movement', the DLP never took a large share of the vote. But it was always enough, when preferences were distributed to the Liberal Party, to keep Menzies in power.

Just how the electoral system works in Australia is a fascinating numbers game. For example, when the DLP was at the peak of its influence in the late 1950s and early

IT'S ONLY A GAME *Flags of all the participating nations are dipped towards Australia's standard bearer John Landy as he reads the Olympic Oath during the opening ceremony staged at the Melbourne Cricket Ground for the 1956 Olympic Games.*

1960s it did not gain even ten per cent of the vote. But here's how important those votes were. Below is a breakdown of figures for the 1961 election which the Menzies coalition government won narrowly: ALP 47.99%, Liberals 33.53%, DLP 8.65%, Country Party 8.45%, Communist 0.48%.

The DLP was a staunch advocate of increasing Australia's expenditure on defence. In 1955 Australian forces were committed to the South-East Asia strategic reserve.

Since soon after the war our answer to survival in a hostile world had been 'populate or perish'. If we didn't fill this country up someone would. So in 1955 our one millionth migrant, Mrs Barbara Porritt, arrived in Australia with her husband Dennis, and was greeted with great ceremony. In the long run many British migrants—about 20 per cent—go home again, but the Porritts stayed and now live in Canberra where Dennis works with the CSIRO.

Fifteen years later the number of migrants had more than doubled. By the 1970s 2 500 000 migrants had travelled half way round the world to start a new life. More than fifty-five per cent of them are of 'British stock'. Despite the feeling of homogeneity, Australia has the highest proportion of overseas-born people in the population in the English speaking world. One million of its people are either bi-lingual or normally speak a language other than English. Melbourne is the third largest Greek speaking city in the world and there are more Greeks in Australia than there are descendants of the original inhabitants, the Aborigines.

In 1956 Australia saw its one millionth road casualty, Sydney got its first parking meter, its first computer and its first glimpse of Utzon's amazing concept for an Opera House. But we really only remember that year for two reasons: the Olympic Games in Melbourne and the coming of television.

The 1956 Olympics were the first held in the southern hemisphere, always the favourite sphere of reference for Australian claims to fame. Australian athletes responded by winning thirty-five medals, to come third behind the giants USA and USSR. Ron Clarke, a promising junior, ran in with the ceremonial torch. Betty Cuthbert, Dawn Fraser, Murray Rose, Marlene Matthews and Lorraine Crapp all made unforgettable names for themselves at those games. Australians dominated some of the traditional areas, particularly swimming, and performed admirably in other events. We only narrowly missed a gold medal in the high jump and the men's hundred metres. John Landy, who had injured his foot before the Games, still ran third in the 1500 metres. Rolly Tasker won the points for the gold medal in sailing but had to accept silver after a disqualification. Jock Sturrock won a bronze, and sculler Stuart McKenzie earned a silver. There were also medals in a series of events in which Australia has been completely overwhelmed in more recent Games.

The Games were memorable in many ways. In that same year Russians invaded Hungary and while a 5000 and 10 000 metres double by Russia's Vladimir Kuts electrified the crowd, a water polo match between Hungary and the USSR literally turned into a blood bath. The Hungarians survived the battle to go on and retain their title.

The opening of television was not so dramatic. TCN 9's first broadcasts were made from a church hall in Sydney. The programmes included 'Accent on Strings', 'What's My Line' and 'The Johnny O'Connor Show'. Bruce Gyngell, who eventually was to have the last word on television as head of the Broadcasting Tribunal, had the first words on 16 September, 'Good evening, ladies and gentlemen. Welcome to television.' For the first few months it didn't matter much what was on. Australians would have watched film of the grass growing. But, as time wore on, the programmers were already well aware of the importance of ratings. As Gyngell recalls:

Oh, we had highly educational programmes. We started with Jet Jackson, Rin Tin Tin, Jungle Jim. We had Disneyland. It started on the 28th January 1957 on a Monday night. I Love Lucy, and Father Knows Best were an enormous success. Frank Packer said to me when we did the first programme line up, 'Who was it that decided to put Jungle Jim in at 7.30 on Tuesday night?' I said, 'I did.' And he said, 'It doesn't augur well for your future in this business.' But when the ratings came out it turned out that they were highly successful.

Towards the end of the 1950s Australian society had changed noticeably. The Olympic Games and television alone had heightened our awareness of the rest of the world, and the population itself was tangibly more cosmopolitan. Change was seen on the most mundane level. Australians who would not have dreamed of anything more exotic than a pork sausage began their first hesitant experiments with 'wog tucker' such as salami. Pizza Huts

COP THIS, POSSUMS! *Australian Housewife Superstar Dame Edna Everage (actor Barry Humphries), flashes a thigh while swigging neat Barossa Pearl at the opening of Melbourne's artistic rendezvous, the Jam Factory.*

and Kentucky Fried were still in the future but the more adventurous Australian housewife now called a buffet supper a smorgasbord.

The most astonishing best seller of recent times was in fact a story about the life of an Italian migrant in Australia and the peculiar way this country has of embracing foreigners. *They're a Weird Mob* was written in 1956 by John O'Grady and published in 1957 under the pseudonym of Nino Culotta. The manuscript was rejected by Angus and Robertson and eventually published by Ure Smith. By 1964 500 000 copies had been sold, 350 000 in hard cover. It had little success outside Australia although it was made into a film.

Another stunningly successful cre-

ation which dates back to this period is Edna Everage, the vaguely malevolent mother-in-law of all Australians. Devised by comedian Barry Humphries, she has since become Dame Edna Everage and according to her creator she has all but disowned him since her international success.

But the smell of success is not always sweet. Throughout the 1950s the chances were that anything with a frame around it was 'a Namatjira'. Albert Namatjira, an Aborigine from the Alice Springs area, was possibly Australia's most famous artist but his story had an almost classical tragic progression. After picking up a few bob on a mission station carving mulga wood plaques,

MY COUNTRY *A typical watercolour by Albert Namatjira, the Aranda tribe Aboriginal artist who was first lionised, then destroyed by white society.*

VIDEO WUNDERKIND *Bruce Gyngell, the first presenter on Australian television.*

Namatjira was 'discovered' and fostered by the white watercolourist Rex Battarbee. Namatjira was soon grossing more than £1000 for an exhibition. But the black artist was inevitably caught in the land between two cultures. According to his tribal law as many as 500 'relatives' moved in for a share of the takings.

And white society made its own demands. Although Namatjira was not a full citizen and was not allowed to vote (or drink) he was expected to pay income tax. In 1951 when he tried to buy a house in Alice Springs permission was refused on the grounds that Aborigines were not allowed into town after dark. In a marvellous display of hypocrisy Namatjira was dressed up in a white suit and flown south in 1954 to meet the new Queen of England. In October 1958 the old painter was sentenced to six months gaol for supplying liquor to his relatives. After a national outcry the sentence was reduced. He was released after two months and shortly afterwards he died, a broken and bitter man.

THEY SHALL HAVE MUSIC *The Myer Music Bowl in Melbourne. This unique outdoor venue for concerts is one of the city's proudest possessions, and the intricate roof design won an international prize for the best architectural use of aluminium.*

TRAGIC MASK *The haunting face of one of Australia's most famous artists, the Aboriginal watercolourist Albert Namatjira.*

On the eve of the 1960s Australia's first nuclear reactor was opened at Lucas Heights. The last trams ran in Adelaide and Perth. Equal pay was now a reality for men and women performing the same tasks. Our population had reached the ten million mark. Construction of the Opera House began in Sydney and the Myer Music Bowl opened in Melbourne. But if Melbourne led Sydney as a cultural venue, film star Ava Gardner did not seem impressed. While in the southern capital to make the film *On the Beach* with Gregory Peck and Anthony Perkins she said, 'I came here to make a film about the end of the world and I certainly came to the right place.'

At the end of the fifties a phenomenon swept the world. It came to be represented in Australia by a young man, who was not overly talented, not overly attractive but an ebullient little character who embodied much of the new spirit of the sixties. The phenomenon was rock and roll and our local star was Johnny O'Keefe. Johnny was the idol of the generation of Australians now in middle age and with teenage children of their own, 'the sixties generation'. Johnny O'Keefe gave his life to rock 'n' roll, and a good many Australians at least gave it the best years of their lives.

The 1960s

The sixties began with a 'credit squeeze' which almost cost Menzies his position as Prime Minister. He survived the election which followed by just one seat—the only really nasty moment in his long ride at the top. It was also the closest Arthur Augustus Calwell would ever go to being Prime Minister. From then on the battered old campaigner—'Cocky' to friend and foe—would cling on to leadership of his party, warding off challenges from abler, younger men who just might have had a chance of toppling Menzies.

On the other side of the world there had been many changes. The Russians had sent a spacecraft to the moon, Kennedy was President of the United States, and Castro was President of Cuba; Kruschev, Macmillan, Eisenhower, and de Gaulle who held summit talks in 1960 were soon gone. But in Australia the political status quo was preserved and life in 'the lucky country' went on.

Our universal obsession with sport continued unabated. In these pre-swimming pool days the tennis court was still the badge of someone having made it to the upper middle class. 'Muscles' and 'Rocket', two names which only Australians could give their human sporting heroes, dominated professional tennis for the decade. Rosewall's professional career quickly surpassed that of his 'twin' Lew Hoad. But, blazing along the amateur circuit was a 24-year-old red-haired, freckled-faced Queenslander. In 1962 Rod Laver became the second player in tennis history (the first was Don Budge in 1938) to win the four major world tennis titles: the Australian, Wimbledon, United States and French. When Laver turned pro he was given a hiding by both Hoad and Rosewall and he won only two of his first twenty-three matches in world professional tennis. But he settled down and by the middle of the decade he and Rosewall would be sharing victories with monotonous regularity. Rosewall ranked number one player in the world in 1961, 1962, 1963 and 1964, but from 1965 Laver got the top berth by a wide margin. Rosewall came back again and again and was still winning tournaments against players half his age in the 1970s.

One who failed in his comeback was the boxer Jimmy Carruthers. At

GOOD LUCK TO YOU ALL *With those words, Prime Minister Sir Robert Menzies farewelled the Press (and perhaps Australia) at the end of his farewell press conference which was held in Canberra in 1963.*

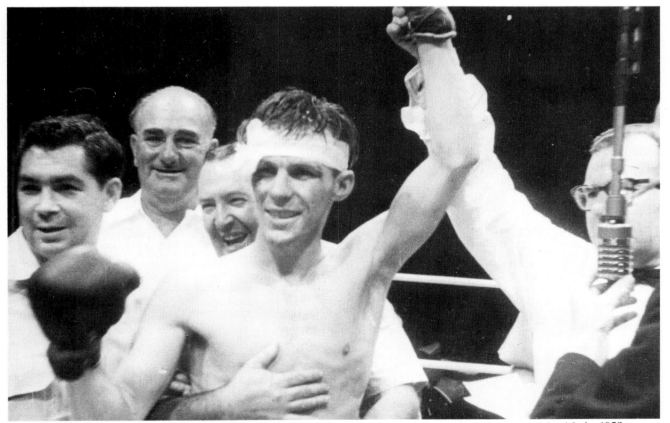

THE WINNER! *Jimmy Carruthers, after his win over American Pappy Gault to retain the world bantamweight title in 1953.*

the start of the 1960s Heather McKay was squash champion of Australia for the first of fourteen times. Wicket-keeper Wally Grout made a record twenty-three dismissals in one Test Match against the West Indies. And 1960 will be remembered by all cricket fans for a long time for possibly the most exciting match in the history of the game—the first ever tied Test, played between the West Indies and Australia in Brisbane.

In 1961 Yuri Gagarin was the first man in space. And there were even more significant scientific developments back on earth. Contraceptive pills began to be widely used and soon controversy was raging throughout the world. Australians, somewhat conservative about sexual matters, would not join in the debate in earnest until later in the decade.

Frank discussion of sex was not really seen in the media until the arrival of more liberated women's magazines at the end of the 1960s. Until then the most intimate secrets exchanged had been knitting patterns and lamington recipes. Sexual problems were considered 'dirty'. Within a few years the pendulum swung so far the other way a woman's magazine in Australia would be considered unsaleable without a generous helping of advice on virginity, menopause, VD, hysterectomy and every other conceivable 'female problem'.

But if sex was somehow 'unclean' politics got smutty indeed. At the start of the 1960s Gough Whitlam and Arthur Calwell set out on an unprecedented and much criticised campaign to win support from the press, considered traditionally hostile to the labour movement. They periodically dined with newspaper proprietors in Sydney and Melbourne. To some degree they succeeded in getting the papers to report ALP and trade union activities more sympathetically and even persuaded the conservative *Sydney Morning Herald* to come out in strong support for Labor in the 1961 elec-

tion. But Sir Frank Packer's right wing *Daily Telegraph* was dismayed by the development and it ran an extraordinary report of what it described as a wedding on Broadway (the address of the *Herald*). The story, illustrated by a photograph of Mr Calwell visiting the *Herald*, parodied a political 'marriage'. The *Sydney Morning Herald*, and Menzies himself, followed up with a famous 'thirty-six faceless men' campaign which made much of the fact that Labor's Federal Executive, not necessarily the elected members of the parliament, controlled Labor's policy. The politically clever adjective 'faceless' implied such sinister doings that Labor's stocks fell again and Menzies won the 1963 elections with a majority of ten seats.

Sir Frank Packer was almost as much a colossus on the Australian horizon as Menzies, his friend. The only difference between the two was that with Packer politics was really only a hobby. Another of the pastimes of the newspaper buccaneer

AND ALL WHO SAIL IN HER *Big men have big ambitions, and newspaper magnate Sir Frank Packer's dream was to win the America's Cup. For his first challenge in 1962 he built the* Gretel, *and although she didn't win she gave the Americans a fright.*

THE LAST TYCOON? *Media and business baron Sir Frank Packer at the height of his power and influence in the 1960s.*

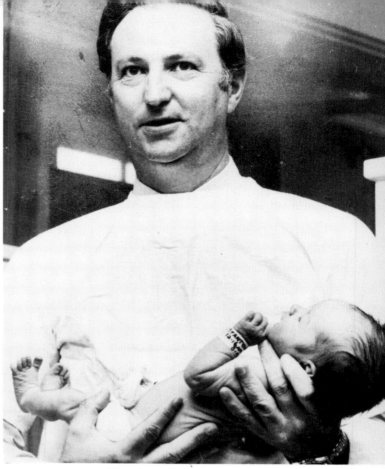

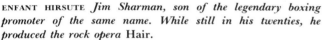
ENFANT HIRSUTE *Jim Sharman, son of the legendary boxing promoter of the same name. While still in his twenties, he produced the rock opera* Hair.

WILLIAM MCBRIDE *The Australian doctor whose persistent research led to the isolation of thalidomide drugs as a cause of horrific birth malformations.*

was sailing, and in 1962 he made the first of his quixotic tilts at the most elusive prize in sport—the America's Cup. It was one of the few times that he ever lost anything.

Australians were still faster through the water without a boat. In that year Dawn Fraser became the first woman to break 60 seconds for 110 yards freestyle. By now the Americans had also put men like Alan Shepard and John Glenn in space. Here at home our long distance achievements extended to an STD telephone service between Sydney and Canberra. On the other side of the world television was transmitted by satellite between the United States and Britain. But if our achievements were not always spectacular they were sometimes just as important. In 1962 the world became aware of the horrors of thalidomide and it was an Australian, Dr William McBride, who tracked down and exposed the reasons for the malformations caused by the drug. Another scientific find which has helped establish Australia as a leader in radio astronomy was the

discovery of 'quasars' by the radio telescope at Parkes in New South Wales in 1962.

In 1962 the seeds were sown for a tragic end to a decade of peace. Australian military involvement in the quagmire of Vietnam began—as it had for the United States—in an almost miniscule way. A team of thirty army officers joined American advisory forces training the Vietnamese military in South Vietnam. Later this was increased to a hundred, as well as six Caribou aircraft and RAAF crews. Inevitably the advisors were drawn into counter-terrorism. But even by 1965 only one Australian had been killed. On 29 April 1965, however, Sir Robert Menzies announced to a half-empty House of Representatives that Australia was to send a full battalion of troops. Within a few weeks of arriving three men were killed and ten wounded in a grenade attack on the American base at Bien Hoa. Australia was at war again. Nevertheless, the general attitude of the Australian public to events in South-East Asia would not turn until late

in the decade. 1963 was a disastrous election for Labor and Gough Whitlam began his long run for the leadership.

Compared with the momentous international stories which dominated the newspapers—the Profumo scandal, the great train robbery, the assassination of John Kennedy, the loss of the United States nuclear submarine *Thresher* even our major events such as the beginning of the Ord River Project seemed like small beer.

Yet at home one story dominated the front pages of our newspapers for not weeks but months on end. It was a weird murder mystery called the Bogle-Chandler case. On the morning of New Year's Day 1963, the semi-nude bodies of Dr Gilbert Bogle, a brilliant CSIRO scientist, and Mrs Margaret Chandler, a 29-year-old mother of two, were found on a bush track in Lane Cove National Park. They were last seen alive at a New Year's Eve party. Nearly twenty years later the cause of their death is still unknown. Police, scientists and criminologists

PRIME MINISTER AT PLAY *The informal style of new leader Harold Holt made a refreshing contrast to the double-breasted conservatism of his predecessor, Sir Robert Menzies. Holt's brief period as Prime Minister included a landslide election victory fought on the issue of Australia's continued involvement in the Vietnam war.*

all over the world have studied the case. Scores of theories, some sound, some bizarre, have been put forward but in the words of former Police Commissioner Norman Allan the case is 'the mystery of the century'.

Perhaps the biggest political issue of the mid-sixties was defence. Spurred on by the clamourings of the right wing DLP who pointed to the worsening situation in South-East Asia, in 1964 Menzies introduced Australia's most important peacetime programme for the armed forces. Selective national service was brought in in such a swift and definite manner that there was no chance for a repeat of the great political conscription battle of 1916 and 1917. Besides, as yet there was no war, only a vague feeling of menace to the north.

Although there soon would be a growing groundswell of anti-conscription feeling, Australians in 1964 were more concerned with another war between Dawn Fraser and swimming officials. At the Olympic Games in Tokyo that year Dawn won the gold medal for the hundred metres freestyle for her third successive Olympics. But her 'antics' in Tokyo led to her suspension for ten years.

SHE LOVES ME! *Yeah, Yeah, Yeah. The fabulous Beatles on-stage in Adelaide during their triumphal tour of Australia in June, 1964. They drew some of the biggest crowds they had encountered in the world on this trip.*

Donald Campbell was trying to be the fastest man on earth. He eventually set world land and water speed records in Australia. This caused considerable excitement. But some other English visitors that year turned the country upside down. The English pop group the Beatles were confronted by the biggest crowds they had seen anywhere in the world—300 000 in Adelaide alone. As if the British had not foisted enough on us that year, they sent scientists here to launch rockets including the Blue Streak. A good many of the tests ended in disaster. Some critics mocked the experiments but when China exploded an atomic bomb that year some at least acknowledged that perhaps we should know what a nuclear warhead was.

In 1964 Donald Horne, one of a long line of distinguished editors of the *Bulletin*, wrote a book and gave the nation a new phrase. Almost every Australian has at some time used the words 'the lucky country', even if they haven't read the book. 1964 also saw another significant contribution to Australian journalism with the birth of a national newspaper the *Australian*. Sceptics predicted that a newspaper covering one of the world's largest and most sparsely populated countries had Buckley's chance of survival, but fifteen years later the newspaper was still around.

By far the most significant development for Australia in 1965 was that decision to send the first full combat unit to Vietnam. And yet the announcement took many Australians by surprise. Even men in Menzies' own party and certainly the opposition were unaware of the impending announcement. Calwell and Whitlam had left Canberra a few hours earlier to help campaign for the forthcoming New South Wales elections. During the day Calwell had asked Menzies whether there were any major statements 'in the wind', and Menzies had replied that it was possible but that he could not say for sure. On the very afternoon of the announcement Senator John Gorton was asked a question without notice as to whether the government was planning to send a

SPEED FREAK *Son of an English world speed record holder who'd died attempting to set new record, Campbell speaks to the press shortly before he too died.*

ONLY ONE OWNER *Donald Campbell's 'Bluebird' streaks across Lake Eyre, during a 200-mph warm-up run in the 1964 attempt to set a new world land speed record.*

battalion to Vietnam and his reply was, 'I know nothing about the matter which the honourable gentleman has raised.'

When the announcement was made Labor was in some disarray as to its approach to the problem of Vietnam. Labor policy was ambiguous to say the least although the opposition did attack Treasurer, Harold Holt, on his return from America two days later for trading Australian lives for United States' capital. Holt announced that he had successfully dissuaded the American government from placing severe restrictions on American investment in Australia.

The slogan 'Diggers for Dollars' quickly gained currency but the government rode the storm easily. By the time Labor had resolved its line on Vietnam, Australia was already up to its neck in the mire. Ahead lay a bitter struggle at home and abroad—a struggle which contributed some catchwords to our vocabulary: 'Make Love Not War', 'All The Way With LBJ', 'Save Our Sons' and 'Hearts and Minds'.

The 1960s were frustrating for Gough Whitlam. When Herbert Vere 'Doc' Evatt retired as leader of the Labor Party, Whitlam only narrowly beat the popular Eddie Ward for the position as deputy to Arthur Calwell. He stayed there but he would have to watch Arthur Calwell lose three elections before having a chance to lose one himself.

In 1966 it seemed that Labor may have had a chance for victory. The indefatigable Menzies had left the stage, the first Prime Minister to retire in office, and given the nod to his chosen one, Harold Holt. Holt was less forceful, had less charisma and there was a strong issue on which to fight an election. But there were problems for the ALP too. The 1966 election was definitely the 'Vietnam election' but Labor was forced to adopt a difficult stance. With Australians already committed to a war that many supported, any criticism of involvement or the conduct of the war was easily dismissed as the arguments of 'ratbags and commies'. Arthur Calwell said the war was 'unwinnable', and although he would be proved right, his statement wasn't really that helpful as far as the public was concerned. Besides, Australians having been fortunate enough to be on the winning side in most of its wars, did not expect defeat—especially when aligned with the United States against a small underdeveloped Asian country.

Whatever the arguments, the Liberals won the 'Vietnam election' comfortably. But the war and particularly the conscription arguments increased in intensity. Australians suddenly found themselves grappling with unfamiliar emotional and intellectual arguments which had not intruded into daily life and the press for fifty years.

The year 1967 saw the death of Harold Holt. Before his untimely end in surf at Portsea, Victoria, Holt was beset with problems which had arisen over the issues of VIP aircraft for politicians and the complex aftermath of the collision between the navy ships *Voyager* and *Melbourne* which killed eighty-two men.

It was an unusual time in Australian politics because some of the main critics of the government came from among the Liberal ranks. John Gorton, a man destined to be Prime Minister himself, at one stage tabled papers embarrassing to the government. A group of Liberals and Independents attacked their leaders on the handling of the *Voyager* affair.

No doubt because of the serious-

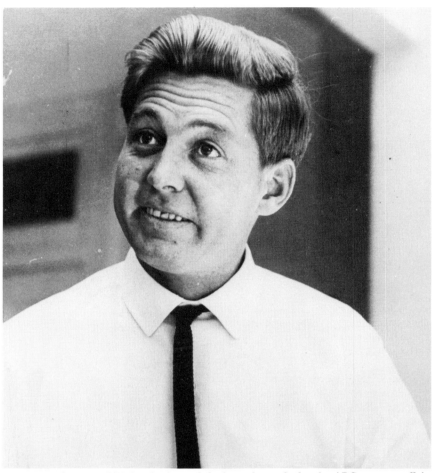

FRONTMAN *Compere Bill Peach pictured during rehearsals for the ABC current affairs show* **This Day Tonight** *which quickly changed the style of Australian television after its premiere in April 1967.*

ness of the issues involved, and their intensely human consequences, political debate took on a fervour which had not been seen for many years. Humanitarian issues were paramount. Conscription was one, and there was also a revival of the capital punishment issue fired by the hanging of Ronald Ryan at Pentridge Prison in Melbourne. There was also a great moral argument over the dismissal by the RSL of two of its members for opposing Australian involvement in Vietnam.

In the middle of this fervent period of social change, and perhaps even because of it, the birth occurred of the television programme 'This Day Tonight', which in turn would significantly affect the development of the medium during the next decade. Out of it evolved the television programmes 'A Current

Affair', 'Twenty-four Hours', 'Willesee at Seven' and 'Sixty Minutes'. The current affairs programmes arrived at a time of some turmoil, at least by Australian standards. Holt's death had almost a domino effect on the Liberals. There was a succession of leaders during the next few years.

The electorate, already highly charged because of the war and the instability of the political situation, was given an extra shot of adrenaline by a modern version of the gold rush. Already in the grip of oil fever Australia saw, in the late 1960s, a series of dramatic mining discoveries. Conzinc Rio Tinto announced its first nickel discovery in 1967. By 1968 the Broken Hill Proprietary Company Limited sent the Stock Exchanges wild with the news that Esso BHP would be able to supply two-thirds of Australia's total oil needs. Then the Western Mining Corporation announced fresh nickel finds at Kambalda.

But the most amazing share market flurry of the late 1960s centred around a company with the romantic sounding name of Poseidon. Late in 1969 the directors of the small and almost unknown mineral company excitedly announced a nickel and copper find. During the previous week, rumours alone had almost doubled the price of its shares. When asked by the directors of the Adelaide Stock Exchange for an explanation of the rise, the Poseidon directors replied that the find had yet to be assayed. Nevertheless, the Exchange went wild. A couple of hours after lunch on the same day shares leapt from $1.90 to $6.70. A week later they were $30. One reason for this reaction was that this find, unlike the great nickel discoveries a few years earlier, had been made by a small adventurous company. Nickel was much in demand, and the time was ripe for a rags to riches story in the grand Hollywood manner.

At the company's annual general meeting on the eve of the 1970s it was confirmed that the nickel strike at Mount Windarra could be as large as the Western Mining holding at Kambalda. In February 1970 the price of Poseidon shares in London was nearly $300. There were now runs on similar companies such as Tasminex, which merely looked promising. When it was finally announced that Tasminex had no substantial nickel at its Mount Venn site, the shares plummeted drastically until the Stock Exchanges suspended all dealings pending an inquiry.

Towards the end of the financial year, when money began to tighten up, the trading companies began to sell out, partly to realise their paper profits before the end of the financial year and partly because of a nagging sense that something was amiss. Once the signs of the first crack appeared the general trader began to follow the professionals, and the rush to get out started. Although there was another encouraging report

END OF AN ERA *While Australians admired William McMahon's work as the Federal Treasurer, they baulked at the chance to confirm his position as Prime Minister at the 1972 elections. His defeat ended 23 unbroken years of Liberal Party rule.*

from Poseidon the market failed to respond. Small companies such as Minsec, which had quickly found that they were theoretically among the biggest mineral producers in the world, saw millions wiped off the value of their shares. Many small investors lost their life savings and in June 1970 a Senate Select Committee was set up to investigate the crash. It was soon realised that some of the principals in the drama had a classic conflict of interests. Short selling, a device whereby the client sells shares he does not have in hope of covering his sale by buying at the lower price, was banned.

The end of the 1960s also saw some frenzied activity in Canberra. The most obvious successor to Harold Holt was William McMahon, Deputy Leader of the Liberal Party and experienced in the

POLITICAL SWINGER *Sir William McMahon picking up squash tips from world champion Heather McKay.*

63

UNLIKELY SUCCESSOR *In the bitter faction fighting which erupted during the Liberal Party's attempts to produce a leader to follow Harold Holt, the winner was Senator John Gorton, pictured here with tourist children immediately following his election.*

PRESSING THE FLESH *During a visit to Australian military forces engaged in the Vietnam War, Prime Minister John Gorton shakes hands with members of the RAAF's No. 9 Helicopter Squadron based at Vung Tau.*

ways of Treasury. But, as had happened with Billy Hughes fifty years earlier, the Country Party, in particular its leader John 'Black Jack' McEwen, would have nothing to do with McMahon. If 'Little Billy' got up, said 'Black Jack' the Libs could kiss the coalition goodbye.

The remaining candidates were a pretty unexciting lot including Leslie Bury, who had been twice sacked by Menzies, Paul Hasluck and Billy Mackie Snedden. However, a group of behind-the-scenes power brokers, including Malcolm Fraser, lobbied for another candidate from the almost unheard of background of the Senate. He was a Victorian orchardist and ex-fighter pilot whose face had a craggy and yet endearing quality caused to some degree by plastic surgery after a fighter crash during the war.

Gorton—'Jolly John' to the press gallery—had been around since the 1940s, had frequently clashed with Menzies and had remained on the backbench for nine years before his promotion to the junior portfolio of Navy. His rough and ready 'decent sort of a cove' image impressed the electorate, but his rough and ready government soon caused him problems. For a start, he was an iconoclast and an activist, opposed to the 'committee-style' of government. Not surprisingly the committees did not like it. He made enemies in the public service but if anything this only endeared him to the public. As with all Prime Ministers, Gorton caused some animosity amongst his colleagues—particularly those he kicked upstairs or downstairs—and there was constant reference to Gorton's 'kitchen Cabinet' and the 'Mushroom Club' in Melbourne. But by far the greatest controversy surrounded Gorton's private behaviour.

A visit by Gorton to the American Embassy on the night of the American announcement to halt the bombing in Vietnam became the most controversial story of the year. According to the ascetic politician and QC Edward St John, the evening had turned into a party during which Gorton had preferred to spend his time talking to a young woman journalist. Gorton survived the controversy and St John didn't (he lost his Liberal Party endorsement). But the Prime Minister's days were numbered.

The Liberals suffered a set-back in the ensuing election and discontent with the leadership was evident as soon as the voting was over. When Gorton put some more noses out of joint in a Cabinet reshuffle, some of the victims complained that the Prime Minister was unduly influenced by the opinions of his attractive young secretary. One of Gorton's deposed Ministers, Dudley Erwin, asked whether he had been the victim of subtle political manoeuvres, replied, 'Yes—it's shapely, it wiggles and its name is Ainslie Gotto.' Gorton remained Prime Minister for more than a year, but his ultimate undoing was brought about by one of the men who had helped put him into office in the first place. Newspaper journalist Alan Ramsay had written a story stating that the army Chief of Staff, in a meeting with Gorton, accused Malcolm Fraser, the Minister of Defence, of disloyalty to the army and to the Army Minister, Andrew Peacock.

Gorton released a statement indicating that the details of the conversation were untrue. Ramsay replied with a statement that Gorton had been given an opportunity to repudiate the story before its publication, but had not done so. Fraser then resigned from the ministry (accusing the Prime Minister of releasing news of his resignation before an agreed time and also accusing him of significant disloyalty). Then Gorton attacked Fraser in parliament and vigorously denied the contents of the story, whereupon Ramsay, in an unprecedented incident called out from the press gallery, 'You liar.' Soon after this incident Gorton's leadership was again put to the vote, and this time it was a tie between Gorton and McMahon. Gorton, in a puzzling move, cast his own vote against himself and stepped down.

So within a few short years after the abdication of Menzies, the Liberals were in disarray. The kindest observation one could make about McMahon was that he did not have

THE FIRST OF MANY *The funeral of Private E. Noack, the first Australian conscripted soldier to be killed on the battlefields of Vietnam. His death sparked a new determination in the anti-conscription movement in Australia.*

RUSH TO SAFETY *Australian soldiers dash to a waiting helicopter after contact with Viet Cong during the Vietnam War.*

the image of a leader and against Whitlam on the ascendancy he looked progressively shaky. He led the Liberals to their first defeat in twenty-three years.

And so the 1960s drew to a close. During the decade the government, backed by strong mandates from the people, had felt confident in steadily escalating its involvement in Vietnam. By 1968 more than 8000 combat soldiers, forty per cent of them conscripts, had been committed to the war.

BODY PROTEST *In 1966 when anti-Vietnam War protesters lay down in the streets of Sydney to stop the motorcade carrying American President Lyndon Johnson, Premier Robin Askin suggested to the police that they 'run the bastards over'.*

For some young men unfortunate enough to have their marble drawn in a lottery it was death in the jungles of Vietnam. For others it was days of wine and roses. In 1967 John Newcombe won Wimbledon. The following year—the first 'open' Wimbledon—it was an all Australian final with Laver beating Roche. The year 1968 saw the Test match between England and Australia. Australia had won eighty of these games and England sixty-five.

There were triumphs and tragedies, sometimes—as with our first heart transplant—a touch of both. The patient died soon after the operation. There were more Blue Streak failures, and a Viscount airliner crashed near Port Headland killing twenty-six people. HMAS *Melbourne* was involved in an incredible 'history repeats' collision in which another destroyer was cut in two. A Sydney to Melbourne express train, the *Southern Aurora,* collided with a goods train at Violet Town.

Morally we seemed just as confused as ever. Norman Lindsay died in his ninetieth year, while authorities in Victoria were still banning posters by the 'Victorian' artist Aubrey Beardsley. The record *Hair* was banned in Melbourne and in all Australian cities there was tremendous controversy over the nude scenes in the musical.

With the 1970s just around the corner, two men named Armstrong and Aldrin walked on the moon. Back on the ground Bob Hawke became president of the ACTU.

The 1970s

It is hard to look back on the 1970s with a sense of nostalgia, although even now the remarkable political events of November 1975 are beginning to gather the mystical aura of history. There will probably not be a bigger political story this century. Only the sacking of New South Wales Premier Jack Lang in the 1930s really equals the Whitlam dismissal in dramatic intensity and long-term import for the Westminster system of government. The other event of great magnitude in the 1970s was the destruction of Darwin by cyclone on Christmas eve 1974.

There have been numerous peaks and troughs in our inexorable development as a nation in the past ten years. We breathed a collective sigh of relief at the start of the decade when the Australian withdrawal from Vietnam was announced in 1971. The war had cost

NOT LONG FOR THIS WORLD *A proud moment for the Navy, but a short-lived one—the launching of HMAS* Voyager. *Less than ten years later she was sliced in half.*

the lives of 415 Australians and 2344 were wounded. It had been the most controversial war in our history fought for three major reasons—anti-communism, our geographical position, and traditional reliance on powerful allies. Our geographical position hasn't changed and neither has much else. The pessimistic view is that if we were prepared to fight a war for pragmatic reasons as recently as the 1970s then we probably will again.

Many years after the war ended Australia is still coping with its aftermath. Refugees, or the 'boat people', have arrived in Australia in their thousands. This pathetic flotsam from the war causes some resentment amongst comfortable and secure white Australians, but many accept that having waged bloody war in someone else's land we must take our share of the consequences.

AT LONG LAST—THE LAST *Some of the very last Australian military personnel to leave Vietnam arrive at Richmond air base near Sydney in December 1972.*

THE MORNING AFTER *A still-dazed Darwin resident searches through rubble in the devastated streets of the city after it had been flattened by Cyclone Tracy on Christmas Eve, 1974.*

Attitudes have altered. After centuries of fear of the 'yellow peril', Australians now calmly accept the sight of their Prime Minister happily snapping away with his Japanese camera as a tourist on the Great Wall of China.

But perhaps the most significant social change in Australia has been amongst this country's original inhabitants, the Aborigines. When Australia proudly welcomed the Queen of England here in 1970 to celebrate our two-hundredth birthday, Sydney's Aboriginal community threw wreaths into the water at Captain Cook's landing place at Kurnell. The arrival of the twentieth century—a fabulous century for white progress and achievement throughout the world—meant little

for Australia's black community. Shortly before the turn of the century Aborigines in one state, Tasmania, had been wiped out altogether. And even in this century Aborigines have been shot, enslaved and humiliated.

Official policy towards the Aboriginal race in Australia has ranged from Christian ministry to savages around the turn of the century; to a policy of separate development or apartheid in the 1920s and 1930s; to a half-hearted attempt to assimilation in the 1940s and 1950s; to a situation in the 1970s where Aborigines were finally given some rights to determine their own future. Some of them, like Neville Bonner of Queensland, chose the white way. In 1971 he became the first Aboriginal

parliamentarian when he was elected to the Senate. Ironically, he had achieved the feat in the state which is generally considered to be the most retarded in its attitude to the race problem. Because he had chosen the white way to power and influence—even to the point of standing for the Liberal Party, on the conservative side of the Australian political spectrum—Bonner had to suffer the inevitable criticism that he was an 'Uncle Tom'. But it would be a mistake to think that Aborigines are any keener about their own politicians than whites are about theirs, and Bonner seems to have been at least as successful in parliament as some of his Queensland colleagues.

But no story is more symbolic of

BIG MANDY *The BHP supertanker* Amanda Miller *before her launch in February 1971. Built at the Whyalla Shipyards the 62 000-tonne tanker is the largest built in Australia.*

THE SPOKESMAN *Just a few years after Australia's Aborigines had been granted the right to vote in national elections, Neville Bonner became the first black Australian to sit in the Senate.*

the Aboriginal struggle in Australia than that of the Gurindjis and their battle for land rights at Wattie Creek, about eight hundred kilometres south of Darwin. It began in 1966 when a group of Aboriginal stockmen walked off Wave Hill station owned by the British beef barons, the Vesteys. The Aborigines were being paid less than a quarter of the minimum wage of the whites and sometimes they got only salt-beef, bread, tobacco, flour, sugar and tea. The Gurindjis said they were sick of it, they wanted their own place. One day they simply took a bale of wire and fenced off some of the Vestey land. The Gurindjis' leader, Vincent Lingiari, was soon confronted by Mr Morris, the station manager. In Lingiari's words:

> We all got the wire for the fence and carry them on the shoulder—everybody bring it up here, and we start that morning, cutting up poles, and so we put it up. Straighten her up, right around, finish it. And Mr Morris came along and he said, 'Hey, you steal another man's country.' Oh yeah, that's alright. And I said, 'No, well, what was before the Vestey born and I born? It was black feller country.'

This statement crystallised the whole story of the Gurindjis' struggle for land rights. A pathetic band of Aborigines was prepared to fight one of the most powerful business concerns in the world. The Vesteys, a collection of English barons and earls, had acquired their original 36 000 square miles of the Northern Territory during the First World War. In 1970 they leased Wave Hill from the government for only fifty-five cents a square mile (2.66 square kilometres), and at that price the Gurindjis could probably have afforded their few acres. But for them the land was beyond value. They maintained that Seal George above Wattie Creek was sacred. They said it was the burial place for some of the thousands of natives they say were shot by early land-holders in the district.

According to whites in the district, Wattie Creek is no more sacred than a mission Sunday school. 'Next

LAND RIGHTS PIONEER *Vincent Lingiari, the Gurindji tribal elder who led his people's fight for land rights in the Northern Territory. It was the struggle he inspired at Wave Hill which helped make Aboriginal land rights one of the most volatile political issues of the 1970s.*

THIS BIN BLACKFELLA COUNTRY *Gurindji stockmen with their friend and publicist Frank Hardy (centre) at the Wave Hill cattle station, centre of their successful land rights strike in the Northern Territory.*

UNITED WE STAND *Deposed Prime Minister Gough Whitlam and ACTU President Bob Hawke share the podium at a 'Shame Fraser Shame' rally in December 1975.*

ONE DAY TO THE LODGE? *Bob Hawke—the man the polls say is the most popular leader in Australia—and the man likely to become the next Labor Prime Minister.*

thing,' they said, 'the Abos will claim Pitt Street in Sydney.' But there was no doubt that there was a principle involved that was very hard to argue with. So the buck passing began, and the Gurindjis found that Vesteys were not necessarily their main opponents. The company maintained a low profile throughout the affair and, in fact, their approach eventually embarrassed the government. When asked about the land they would say it wasn't theirs, it belonged to the government. The government on the other hand said land rights claims were out of the question because Vesteys had the lease until the year 2004. But in 1971 Bob Hawke was claiming that the government had known for three years that Vesteys had been willing to surrender the land.

Whatever the truth, the then Minister for Aboriginal Affairs, Mr Wentworth, promised to try to get about 21 square kilometres of land at Wattie Creek. Cabinet replied by offering about 4 square kilometres at Drover's Common near the Wave Hill welfare settlement. The Gurindjis rejected the offer and considering the welfare people planted trees there with a jackhammer, this may not have been surprising. Nevertheless, the government decided that this would be the new home for the Gurindjis and they spent $500 000 building a township there. The town came to be known as 'Dangled Carrot'. Ironically, the Gurindjis helped to build the town as paid labourers, but when applications came in from families to live there, there was only one from a Gurindji. Lord Vestey went over to Vincent Lingiari to ask why.

He said, 'Why don't you come in a decent house?' 'Where?' 'Down at the settlement and the new town.' 'Oh, no. I don't like going in there,' I said. 'I stay right here where I pick the place. Right-o. So he move off.'

Later in the 1970s anyone who doubted the determination of the Gurindjis to hold out for their land must have been starting to think twice. Admittedly a benevolent welfare service made life easier and the Gurindjis had support from people 'down south', including some communists and the waterside workers who at one stage raised $10 000 for their cause.

The turning point for the tribe was the 1972 federal election. On the previous Australia Day, William McMahon had rejected the idea of land rights, and it was clear that if the ALP wasn't going to do something about the situation no one else would. Sure enough, after the election the new minister, Gordon Bryant, and a big mob from down south came into the Gurindjis' camp. Captain Major was one who spoke with him:

He claim he shall be the minister. He come here, tell everybody he was the boss now. 'You OK out here?' Vincent said to him, 'Yes.'

He said, 'Alright, you can have this country, and you can put cattle on it and build a new village.'

So, after seven years, the Gurindjis finally had the official blessing of the government of Australia. But there was to be a succession of ministers, and indeed the whole Labor tribe would soon vanish. Yet the Gurindjis have held out. They've hardly turned Wattie Creek into a thriving cattle concern, but it was only meant to be a subsistence operation, and the tribe has been there ten years. It has been a remarkable stand summed up in the words of a remarkable song by Ted Egan.

Poor Bugger Blackfella, Gurindji,
Long time work, no wages we,

Work for Good Old Lord Vestey,
Little bit, flour, sugar and tea.
From Lord Vestey to the Gurindji.

Poor Bugger Blackfeller, this country,
Government law, him talk along we,
Can't givit land long blackfella, see,
Only spoilim Gurindji,
Poor Bugger Me, Gurindji.

Poor Bugger Blackfella, Gurindji,
Suppose we buy im back country,
What you reckon proper fee?
Might be flour, sugar and tea,
From the Gurindji to the Lord Vestey,
Oh Poor Bugger Me.

More importantly Wattie Creek has become a symbol of hope for all Aborigines. A hope that one day the land—theirs since the Dreamtime—will be rightfully returned.

SOCIALIST SAVIOUR *an ecstatic supporter kisses Whitlam's hand after the opening Policy Speech of his successful 1972 campaign. Despite the adoration his reign was short-lived.*

2

HEROES

SMITHY AND FRIEND *Sir Charles Kingsford Smith at the controls of the* Southern Cross, *the plane he affectionately called 'the old bus'.*

Our great folk heroes

Traditionally heroism is about war ... slouch hats and fixed bayonets ... acts of conspicuous bravery ... The Spirit of Anzac.

And yet who really remembers our military heroes? Of the scores of Victoria Cross winners in the First World War only the name of Albert Jacka is still well known, and, strangely, more recent VCs are even harder to recall. Some Australians remember the late Frank Partridge who became famous as a contestant on Bob Dyer's 'Pick-a-Box' show on television. Very few Australians remember the names of the four VC winners in Vietnam ... 'Dasher' Wheatley perhaps, but Badcoe, Payne, Simpson? Such is the price of military heroism.

In fact our truly unforgettable heroes come from a variety of unsoldierly vocations—particularly sport, and never from politics. Perhaps John Curtin came close to being a political hero, but in general Australians accord the honour to a remarkably select group of people—and animals.

Our super heroes tend to spring from the thirties when maybe we needed them most; needed someone whose life story was so extraordinary that it seemed beyond the mundane concerns of life during the Depression. In the thirties Sydneysiders used to say that they were three 'ours ahead of Melbourne ... Our Harbour, Our Bridge and Our Bradman. Don was a national demigod because he swung a cricket bat better than anyone on earth. Nellie Melba simply sang like an angel, and Kingsford Smith conquered the heaven that was left ... the first man to fly the Pacific. But surely, only in Australia could our greatest national hero have been a racehorse? Certainly it had something to do with his mysterious demise at the height of a young and brilliant career. And certainly the legend of Phar Lap remains intact because only he, of all the heroes, did not have feet of clay. Unlike the stories of other Australian heroes there are no scandals, no chinks in his wonderful armour. The legend of Phar Lap is unassailable.

INSEPARABLES *Phar Lap playing with his devoted attendant, Tommy Woodcock a few months before their departure for America.*

EVERYONE LOVES A WINNER *Jockey Billy Elliott (right) surrounded by well-wishers after riding Phar Lap to victory in the 1932 Agua Caliente Handicap—the great horse's first and last race overseas.*

Phar Lap

Dawn in America on Tuesday, 5 April 1932; a grey light floating through Australian eucalypts growing on a Californian ranch. In the stables devoted trainer Tommy Woodcock was sleeping, as he often did, beside his pet horse 'Bobby', a giant red gelding known to the rest of the world as Phar Lap.

Soon after midday, Phar Lap was dead. The horse collapsed and died in the arms of young Tommy Woodcock who, at the age of seventy-five, still talked about it with tears in his eyes:

> I woke up about a quarter to five and when I went to hand up the sugar to him I felt he was hot. The vet came down and said he might have a slight touch of colic and his temperature was starting to rise. It was over a hundred. I led him around and I thought he was going to die. I thought—you know, I didn't know what to do. I just led him in the box and he gave one squeal and he haemorrhaged and just dropped dead.

The news was relayed from America by wireless and newspapers to the thousands of people who had followed the spectacular, three year career of 'The Mighty Conqueror'. Many claimed Phar Lap had been 'nobbled by the Yanks—like Les Darcy', the Australian boxing champ who had died in Memphis back in 1917. It was the beginning of a legend.

Phar Lap—Siamese for lightning—has enjoyed the reputation of being one of Australia's national heroes for fifty years, which isn't bad for a horse, especially one that was not even an Australian. Like so many Melbourne Cup champions, Phar Lap was bred in New Zealand. There was little in the stud book to show that he would be perhaps the greatest horse of all. Nothing about this ugly, ungainly colt suggested that he would go on to win thirty-seven out of his fifty-one starts and rank favourite in forty-one out of forty-two consecutive races.

Harry Telford, a trainer from Sydney, didn't have the money to buy him, but persuaded a wealthy racing enthusiast, David J. Davis, to

PHAR LAP'S FRIEND *Melbourne racehorse trainer Tommy Woodcock, the devoted handler and companion to Australia's greatest racehorse —Phar Lap. Woodcock accompanied the horse to America in 1932, where Phar Lap died in his arms.*

THE BEST *Even in death, Australians revered Phar Lap as if he were an equine god.*

THE MIGHTY CONQUEROR *The immortal racehorse Phar Lap with favourite jockey Jim Pike in the saddle—a study in motion beloved by hundreds of thousands of Australian punters.*

put up the auction bid—a paltry 160 guineas. At that price, Phar Lap must have been the biggest bargain in turf history. Yet when the horse reached Australia, Davis thought so little of him that he agreed to lease him to Telford for three years.

Phar Lap was unplaced in most of his early races and it seemed the playful two-year-old would never find form. The horse was a clown, playing tricks with his track rider Tommy Woodcock, pulling the jockey's hair with his teeth and ripping stableboys' shirts. He ran track work at half pace with his feet hardly off the ground, and he was always tripping himself.

Then, in September 1929, Phar Lap won his first race. A taste of victory—and soon he was off on a series of winning runs that made him the favourite for that year's Melbourne Cup. The November classic, which had started with a prize of a few hundred pounds in 1861, was now worth £9000 to the winner. Phar Lap carried only 7 st 6 lb (about 47 kg), but he was headstrong and the horse and jockey fought each other from the start. Finally, the jockey gave up trying to hold him and let him have his head. Phar Lap tired in the straight and finished

the race a close third.

After a summer spell, the 'Red Terror', as they called him, went on another winning rampage, at times winning by fifty lengths. He was favourite four months before the 1930 Melbourne Cup, even though he was to carry 9 st 12 lb (about 62.5 kg), a massive 15 lb (about 7 kg) over weight-for-age. His win was, in fact, so certain that turf rivals tried to kill him. Two men in a car, with a rifle wrapped up in newspaper, fired at the horse. But Tommy Woodcock, riding the white pony that always travelled with the champion, shielded Phar Lap against a fence and no one was harmed. From then on Phar Lap's movements were kept secret. He won the 1930 Melbourne Cup at 11 to 8 on, making him the first 'odds on' favourite in the history of the event.

Phar Lap earned £12 429 at the Melbourne carnival, winning five major races in fourteen days. His proud jockey, Jim Pike, in the now famous red, white and black silks, told the newsreel cameraman: 'They can breed 'em with wings on and get Kingsford Smith to ride 'em, and I doubt whether they'll beat him then.'

Telford's lease expired at the end of 1930 and Davis agreed to sell him a share of Phar Lap for £4000. From then on the two men worked in a partnership marked by many differences of opinion. By 1931, Phar Lap had grown to a gigantic 17.1 hands, standing 6 ft 10 in (208 cm) from the ground to the top of his head. That year, the Victoria Racing Club decided the only way to curb him was to introduce special handicapping. He was to carry an incredible 10 st 10 lb (about 68 kg) in the Melbourne Cup, and Telford was strongly against him starting. His partner overruled him and Phar Lap came in eighth.

This was to be his last race in Australia. His owners wanted him to take on the world, and in January 1932 Phar Lap was hoisted aboard a steamship on his way to Tijuana in Mexico. The target was the Agua Caliente ('hot water') Handicap, then the richest horse race in the world. Phar Lap romped home first, with the race commentator at Tijuana calling:

... a great debut for the Australian beauty Phar Lap, one of the handsomest horses seen on an American track—a little temperamental but what star isn't? In one race he's proved himself, and how the fans love it.

The triumphant Australians returned to their base camp, a training ranch outside San Francisco. Sixteen days later Phar Lap was dead, and to this day there has not been a satisfactory explanation of the fatal illness, although it seems most likely to have been 'intestinal tymphany'

THE LAST 'THEY'RE OFF!' *The start of the Agua Caliente ('hot water') Handicap raced at Tijuana, New Mexico. Phar Lap won easily, but sixteen days later he was dead.*

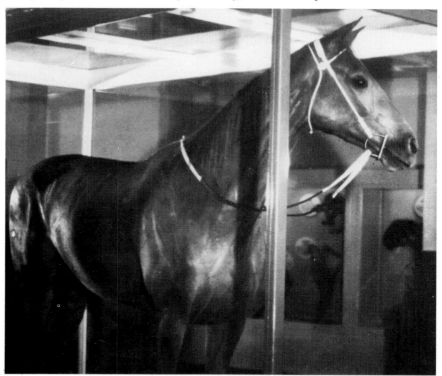

MUSEUM PIECE *Phar Lap's stuffed hide, shipped back from the United States, was too big to fit inside the show case. Carpenters had to raise the lid a little.*

caused by highly fermentable green pasture.

Phar Lap's body was dissected for autopsy and the organs studied by scientists in America and Australia. It was found the champion's heart weighed 14 lb (over 6 kg), twice the normal size. That heart is now preserved at the Institute of Anatomy in Canberra. Phar Lap's skeleton is mounted in a New Zealand museum and his stuffed hide stands in the Melbourne museum. In fond memory, a headstone has been placed in the lawns at Randwick Racecourse in Sydney.

Nellie Melba

In 1861, the year the first Melbourne Cup was run, a girl was born at Richmond, Melbourne, and christened Helen Porter Mitchell. Later, in a manner peculiar to Australian stars of the opera, she would change her name to Melba, in honour of her home city. Others who underwent similar patriotic name changes were Florence Austral, Elsa Stralia, and more recently June Bronhill, but none made such an impact on the musical world as Nellie Melba.

Madame Melba became the singing sensation of the century and dominated international music for nearly forty years. Perhaps more importantly, she was the first Australian to be well known as an Australian outside her own country. By the end of the First World War Melba had been created a Dame of the British Empire for her contributions to music and for her charity concerts and fund drives in Australia, which raised more than £60 000 for the war effort.

Gounod coached her in the role of Juliet for his *Romeo and Juliet.* Puccini acclaimed her as his ideal Mimi for *La Bohème,* and it is said he created the role of Madame Butterfly especially for Melba, although she never publicly sang it.

Melba's early life was not a happy one. Although she had a wealthy father whom she adored, she began an unhappy marriage which took her to a sugar plantation in Queensland. The role of wife of the manager of a mill in the steamy tropics did not suit her, and soon after the birth of her son she left Queensland and her husband behind. She was turning her back on marriage.

In 1886, she took her young son, George, to London. She had collected a clutch of letters of introduction but they seemed to lead nowhere. However, one letter was from the wife of the Austro-Hungarian consul in Melbourne to Madame Mathilde Marchesi in Paris, then the world's most famous singing teacher. After Melba had sung just one line it was said that Marchesi announced: 'I have found a star.'

THE GREAT DAME *Rupert Bunny's imperious portrait of Nellie Melba at the height of her international career. She had risen to become the greatest opera singer in the world and the best known Australian outside her own country.*

THERE'S NO PLACE LIKE HOME *When Helen Porter Mitchell and Armstrong were married they moved to this modest bungalow near Mackay. Eighteen months later she had left, and within a few years she was Nellie Melba, the toast of London and New York.*

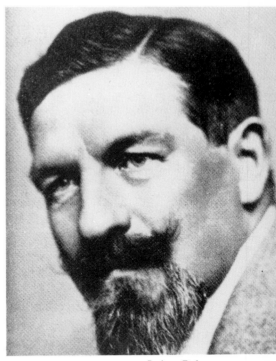

THE INDISCREET DUKE *Luis Robert Phillipe, whose torrid affair with Melba almost cost the singer her career.*

Melba's first operatic performance took Brussels by storm. She was called to the royal box after her first performance in *Rigoletto*. Soon afterwards she was singing at London's Covent Garden. The British critics, however, chose to ignore the newcomer, and the young star, already seeing herself as a prima donna, swore never to return. A personal invitation from the Princess of Wales soon changed her mind.

Now there were invitations to sing for Queen Victoria at Windsor, and for Czar Alexander III in Russia. Melba conquered all, even the notoriously critical audience at La Scala Opera House in Milan. After she had sung the famous 'mad scene' from *Lucia di Lammermoor*, the frenzied applause lasted ten minutes. Melba quickly rose to an exalted position among European high society. She entertained royalty at her sumptuous mansion in London, which she had decorated after the style of the palace at Versailles.

A stately, domineering woman, Melba was always intolerant of imperfection. She preferred the company of men, and political debate to the 'idle chat of women'. Once in Germany after the Kaiser had criticised her singing, she told him she would never dream of criticising his government. The Kaiser turned on his heel and walked away.

At thirty, Melba fell in love with the suave, wealthy Duke of Orleans, the 22-year-old Bourbon pretender to the French throne. They were constant companions for many years, and the resulting scandal almost ruined her career. Marriage was impossible for the Catholic prince and the commoner who was already married. The scandal spread to Australia where Melba's husband, Queensland sugar producer Charles

THAT'S MY SON *Nellie Melba with her only child, Mr G. Armstrong. He was the issue of a short unhappy marriage between Nellie and Charles Armstrong, an Irish aristocrat who managed a sugar mill in the tropics of North Queensland.*

Armstrong, began divorce proceedings. Finally, British diplomatic influence was brought to bear and the whole affair died down.

There were to be many more liaisons and friendships, including that with the legendary tenor, Enrico Caruso. Like Melba, the 'Great Caruso' enjoyed playing practical jokes and one night, while he sang the aria 'Thy Tiny Hand is Frozen' during *La Bohème*, he pressed a hot sausage into her hand. Furious, Melba flung it across the stage into the wings.

But Melba was herself a practical joker. Early one April Fool's Day she ordered a bathtub to be delivered every quarter of an hour to the composer Bemberg. By midday he was begging her to stop. To add insult to injury he had to pay for the baths and organise their removal.

Aloof and imperious, Melba made enemies, and there were many prepared to invent scandalous stories about her style of life. She ignored most, but she always vehemently denied reports that she once advised British singer Dame Clara Butt, while touring Australia, to 'Sing 'em muck. That's all they understand.'

Dame Clara's autobiography was recalled to the printers so that pages referring to this incident could be removed.

When Australia's most famous daughter returned to Melbourne in 1902 it was a triumphant 'royal tour'. Tens of thousands of people lined the streets, and at Lilydale, outside Melbourne, where she later bought Coombe Cottage, Melba was welcomed by a special edition of the local newspaper printed in gold ink on blue paper.

By 1926 Melba had started her famous 'farewell' tours. Yet the legend that led to the phrase 'more farewells than Melba' was unjustified according to Melba's piano accompanist, Lindley Evans:

The whole point about a farewell was that she was leaving this city to go somewhere else, but people took up this word 'farewell' as if she was saying: 'This is my final concert. I'm never going to sing again', which is stupid.

Melba came home for the last time in November 1930. After falling ill on the ship, she was taken to St Vincent's hospital in Sydney where she died on 23 February 1931. She was sixty-nine years old.

For a woman who brought whole

Melba's Interest In Australia

SING 'EM MUCK *Melba was one of Australia's greatest heroines, yet she too had her critics as this cartoon shows. She was accused of making tours which were 'bank raids'. She caused a controversy when she was reported to have said that Australians understood only basic music and one should 'sing 'em muck'. The truth of this report has never been proven.*

THE SINGER NOT THE SONG *The advent of gramophone recordings helped make Nellie Melba the first truly international operatic superstar. Her command of the music-loving public was so great that people were prepared to pay one shilling more than the standard price for her records.*

AGEING DIVA *Her face now showing the strain of a long and strenuous career, Dame Nellie Melba waits on the steps of Parliament House, Canberra, before stepping forward to sing the National Anthem as part of the 1927 opening celebrations.*

SEND SOME FLOWERS *Dame Nellie Melba, over sixty years old, at one of her many farewell concerts. The magnitude of the floral tributes emphasises the impression that Melba was more than simply a great singer—to Australians she was a national heroine.*

cities to a standstill there is little to perpetuate her memory. Her recordings, made on primitive apparatus, give no real indication of how great her voice must have been. As a memorial there is the Melba auditorium in Melbourne and, at her suggestion, the great Escoffier created the Peach Melba dessert for her. But perhaps her most lasting monument will be the suburb of Melba in Canberra. With its rows of brick veneer houses it is a far cry from her sumptuous home at Great Cumberland Place in London. But there is no doubt that the naming of part of our national capital was an honour which Melba, an intense patriot, would have taken deeply to heart.

Donald Bradman

In the 1930s it was said that Bradman made more records than a gramophone company, and that wasn't far wrong. In a career that spanned more than twenty years, Don Bradman scored an incredible 271 centuries.

He captained Australia for twelve years with a test match average of 99.94 runs. Just one more six over the fence and he would have brought up the amazing average of a century for every test innings he played.

Donald George Bradman, born in Cootamundra on 27 August 1908, was to be labelled the Phar Lap of cricket. The now hackneyed phrase 'a run-getting machine' was invented for him. At one stage the English press seriously suggested the rules of cricket be changed to put a limit on Bradman's runs. A smart entrepreneur even persuaded Bradman to make a gramophone record. Thousands of fans heard 'the Don' playing the piano on one side and teaching cricket on the other.

The young batsman was the idol of Australians from the day in 1927 when he scored a century in his first Sheffield Shield match. He was just nineteen years old. Then, in 1930, he piled up a world record 452 not out in 415 minutes against Queensland.

Off to England with the Australian team that year, Bradman became a national hero, amassing a score of 334 in one day (including

'HE'S IN' *Don Bradman, later Sir Donald, was the most famous Australian of his time. The newspaper posters said simply 'HE'S IN' and every Australian knew what it meant. What few people realised about this great cricketer, however, was that as a young* *man he had developed his unique eye using a highly unorthodox practice method. Revisiting his childhood home Bradman demonstrates his practice technique: bouncing a golf ball against the tankstand and stroking it back with a cricket stump.*

ONCE MORE WITH FEELING *When 'The Don' took the field, it changed the whole climate of a cricket match. The moment when he pulled on his batting gloves was the signal that another devastating display of aggressive artistry was about to begin. One of the surprising features of this photograph is the number of young women spectators who attended the game.*

105 before lunch) in the Third Test at Leeds. His boots, still preserved behind glass in the Long Room at Lord's, commemorate that epic innings.

Bradman's tour aggregate for that year was 2960 runs from thirty-six innings—more than many batsmen make in a lifetime—and it was his massive scores against the English Eleven that led the British bowlers to invent 'bodyline', perhaps the most infamous weapon in the history of cricket. Bodyline, a style of bowling which intimidated and even injured batsmen was used to demoralise the Australians in the 1932-33 Test series. While Bradman did adapt to the bowling, he was able to notch up only one century against the bodyline attack.

Just why Bradman was unique is still a mystery, although there are some clues. As a boy, in the New South Wales country town of Bowral, he spent hours in the backyard of his home hitting a golf ball with a cricket stump against the brick base of the tank stand. Who knows whether this practice made Bradman see the ball just that much bigger than other cricketers?

Bradman's contemporaries tend to speak about him not so much with affection, but with some awe. Bill O'Reilly, the incomparable test bowler, gives some idea of the Bradman determination:

This man, Don Bradman, was born to be king as far as the game of cricket was concerned. He fell into it like a duck falls into water, and God help anybody who tried to take it from him.

As stirring as Bradman, the cricketer, was on the pitch, in his personal life he was always quiet and careful to preserve his privacy. Another Australian test cricketer, Jack Fingleton, said of Bradman:

He didn't seek the friendship of other chaps. He was quite happy to be on his own. He was such an intent businessman. He was tied up in all manner of things so that I don't think he had time to think about mateship, and that, to most of us, meant a lot.

And Bradman, still in his twenties, told an English interviewer:

THE CLASSIC SWING *Don Bradman was not considered the most attractive batsman of his time, but his strong, reliable swing earned him a test average of 99.94 runs.*

A REGAL ENCOUNTER *Donald Bradman chats with his King at Balmoral Castle in 1948. Later the press criticized him for having his hands in his pockets.*

I think one of the main reasons why I am able to carry on so long is the fact that I don't drink and I don't smoke. I really don't do anything to get myself out of condition. Consequently, I haven't got to train to get myself into condition to play a match.

Bradman, who led Australia's test teams from the thirties through to the late forties, was consistently the best batsman in the world. According to a later test captain, Bobby Simpson:

Bradman saw the ball a lot quicker and he was able to transfer that thought to movement. He could make a success of any sport or business he took up—he had so much natural intelligence.

The 1948 tour of England, when Australia won the Ashes undefeated, is remembered as the Don's farewell.

THE IDOL *Don Bradman (with a policeman guarding his rear) fights his way out through the adoring crowds to play his last innings at the Sydney Cricket Ground.*

THE BATSMAN BROADCASTER *A young Donald Bradman, already a national hero after his remarkable batting performances during the 1929-30 Test season, turns the tables on the commentators by making a radio broadcast himself. Later he even recorded his own piano playing for commercial release.*

In one of the great anti-climaxes of the game, he went for a 'duck' in his last innings.

Bradman was knighted in 1949. After his retirement from cricket, he was a stockbroker and company director in Adelaide and served until recently as a selector for the Australian Cricket Board. Having been lionised, analysed and criticised all his life, he now shuns public appearances; in the last few years he has broken his silence only to criticise the new World Series Cricket.

The reason for his success is simple. He was uncannily good. In fact, on paper, his figures show he was about fifty per cent better than any player in history. But that still does not explain the slightly unreal aura which surrounds his name. It was a time of economic depression, a time of depression in body and spirit, a time when just some of the worries could be forgotten under the glorious arch of a red ball sailing into the crowds. Perhaps his kind of heroism was needed in the thirties when they literally sang his praises.

Who is it that all Australia raves
    about?
Who is it deserves our very highest
    praise?
Our Don Bradman, now I ask you
    is he any good?
Our Don Bradman, as a batsman
    he certainly is plum pud.

AND GIANTS WALKED THE EARTH *Perhaps the two most famous Knights in modern Australian history—Sir Robert Menzies and Sir Donald Bradman.*

A MEETING OF THE MASTERS *At a social match in Canberra, two unchallenged supremos in their field take their ease in the grandstand. Robert Menzies, Prime Minister of the nation and the outstanding politician of his era, in the middle, his wife Pattie, and on the right, Sir Donald Bradman, perhaps the greatest cricketer of all time.*

Charles Kingsford Smith

On 3 December 1906, the newly formed Bondi Lifesaving Association gave its first demonstration of rescue using the line and reel. Just eleven days later, two young boys who had been swept out to sea were rescued by the novel method. One of them, who had almost drowned, gave his name as Charlie Smith. He had gone just that little bit too far past the breakers and almost paid dearly for his taste of risk and adventure.

But it didn't teach Charlie Smith any lessons. Thirty years later he would still be pushing his luck to the limit. Only by this time he would not be Charlie but Sir Charles Kingsford Smith, 'Smithy', described by some flying experts as the world's greatest aviator.

After his flirtation with death on Bondi beach as a child, there would be many more near misses for Smithy even before he was twenty. As a teenager he served at Gallipoli, and, as a pilot in the Royal Flying Corps, he had three toes shot off.

Immediately the war ended, Smithy suffered one of his greatest disappointments. He was refused permission to enter the £10 000 competition to fly from England to Australia. The Australian Prime Minister of the time, Billy Hughes, told the young flier that he lacked the experience and the backing. To rub salt in the wound, the competition was won by two other young adventurers, also called Smith—Ross and Keith—from Adelaide.

Smithy continued his life of adventure and, for a while, was barnstorming for the silent movies in Hollywood. At one stage he almost lost his life in a trick which called for him to hang upside-down from the undercarriage of a plane. He underestimated the strength of the slipstream and only managed to climb back into the cockpit with the utmost difficulty.

But, in 1928, Smithy was planning a feat more serious and more daring—in fact, the most audacious flight of all time. Lindbergh had just flown the Atlantic, but Smithy and his mate Charles Ulm wanted to be the first to fly across the Pacific from America to Australia. For £3000

PER ARDUA AD ASTRA *A dramatic studio portrait of Charles Kingsford Smith at the height of his fame as a pioneering aviator.*

A TOAST IN KAVA *Before taking off on the final leg of his epic 1928 crossing of the Pacific, Kingsford Smith toasts the Fiji natives who helped him prepare for a daring takeoff along an island beach.*

IN THE GRAND COLONIAL MANNER *Smithy and Ulm were both carried ashore in Fiji shortly before takeoff so their flying boots would not get wet and cold. Thirty-five hours later they landed in Brisbane. The first aerial crossing of the Pacific was over.*

TRIUMPHANT PARTNERS *Smithy (right) and Charles Ulm, just a few seconds after their triumphant landing at Brisbane in 1928 at the conclusion of the first aerial crossing of the Pacific.*

SMITHY *Forever squinting over new horizons and dreaming of challenges just out of reach. The strong face of Charles Kingsford Smith, first man to fly the mighty Pacific Ocean.*

they bought a Fokker tri-motor monoplane, an enormous aircraft for its day. The plane had to be specially rebuilt for the flight. Smithy and Ulm recruited two Americans, Harry Lyon, a navigator, and Jim Warner, an experienced radio operator.

Smithy was at the controls on 31 May 1928 when the *Southern Cross* left San Francisco: ahead of the enthusiastic crew were 8000 nautical miles of flying. Conditions on board the Fokker were almost unbearable. The vibration rattled their teeth. The constant thunder of the engines made

it impossible to speak, and all communication was by handwritten note.

Smithy and Ulm flew up front in the semi-open cockpit exposed to wind, rain and biting cold. After twenty-seven hours, they arrived in Honolulu to be greeted by a battery of questions and welcoming speeches. They heard nothing: all four were temporarily deafened from the roar of the engines. By this time, the whole world was beginning to hear about their progress. They flew through heavy storms to Fiji, then on to Brisbane. Smithy had achieved his dream in just eighty-three hours.

In Sydney 300 000 people turned out to watch them land. They had tamed the Pacific with their epoch-making flight. This was only the beginning of a warm partnership that would attempt to set more records.

But the adulation that welcomed Smithy home was soon to change to animosity. He would even be cursed in the streets. The troubles started within a year of the trans-Pacific flight. This time Kingsford Smith and Ulm were heading for England on yet another attempt to break a long-distance flying record, and also to buy aircraft for a new airline venture. They were farewelled by huge crowds. However, in the far northwest of Australia, they landed on a mud flat. They said later there had been a violent sandstorm and they had lost radio contact.

Smithy was missing and Australia's first big air search was launched. The lost crew were found after thirteen days on the mud flat they called 'Coffee Royal', after their coffee and brandy rations. But two of Smithy's friends, who went searching for him in a little plane called the *Kookaburra*, were forced down and suffered horrible deaths from thirst and starvation. A Sydney newspaper suggested that Smith and Ulm had staged the whole air drama as a publicity stunt, and by the time Smithy and Ulm got back to Sydney 'Coffee Royal' had become the dirtiest tag in Australia.

Eventually the affair became such a *cause célèbre* that the Prime Minister called for a public enquiry. During the hearing Smith and Ulm found their business acumen mildly criticised, but nothing was proved that cast doubt on their motives. Smithy's reputation was gradually restored, but he was plagued by rumour and gossip for the rest of his life.

TRAGIC HEROES *Pilot Keith Anderson and his navigator Bob Hitchcock were old friends of Smithy. When the* Southern Cross *was reported lost during a flight to England in early 1929, the two men set out in their tiny plane* Kookaburra *to search for their missing mates. Forced down by a dust storm in desert country, Anderson and Hitchcock perished.*

ON STICKY GROUND *Smithy and Ulm attempt to rig a generator using the starboard wheel of the* Southern Cross *which had been forced down on a mud-flat.*

THE BUSH GIVES UP ITS SECRET *Twenty-seven years after the airliner* Southern Cloud *disappeared on a flight from Sydney to Melbourne, the remains of the aircraft were discovered by a bushwalker in the rugged country of the Snowy Mountains. This disaster helped bring on the collapse of the ANA company, founded by Smithy and Ulm.*

THE CONQUERORS RETURN *Smithy and Ulm went on to set further flight records. Here the two airmen (right) acknowledge a heroes' welcome on their return from a trans-Tasman flight in 1929. With them are navigator H. A. Litchfield and radio operator T. H. McWilliams.*

To many Australians, though, Smithy was still the ultimate hero. He was dashing and good looking with a confident, yet somehow self-effacing, personality. He made the headlines again after an amazing incident during the trans-Tasman mail run. Part of the propeller on the *Southern Cross* broke off and carried away part of an engine. While Smithy fought to keep the plane aloft, his co-pilot, P. G. Taylor, walked out on to a wing strut, drained oil from the damaged engine into a thermos flask, and transferred it to a second engine which was overheating. The operation, which had to be repeated many times, won Taylor the George Cross for bravery.

These were Smithy's lucky days. With his cheeky grin and his deeds of bravado, he was a much sought-after prize for the Sydney social set. He disappointed them by marrying a Melbourne girl, Mary Powell. They had a son, Charles Arthur, who was born in 1933.

But Smithy suffered more setbacks. It was a sign of his failing fortunes that the passenger airline company he and Ulm started, Australian National Airways, collapsed after the pride of their fleet *Southern Cloud* disappeared in the Snowy Mountains. The wreckage of the plane was not found until twenty years after Smithy's death.

ON A WING AND A PRAYER ... *Safe on the ground Bill Taylor re-enacts the transfer of oil from a disabled engine on the* Southern Cross *to the faltering motor on the other wing. Note the thermos in his hand and the damaged propellor which at one stage threatened to vibrate the engine to pieces.*

Smithy ran into more trouble during preliminaries for the 1934 centenary air race, firstly because he proposed using an American plane. The authorities refused to let him name it *Anzac*. They need not have worried; Smithy was forced to withdraw from the race because of technical problems. Then, as if his worries had not been great enough, he was sent abusive letters and even white feathers for being 'too cowardly' to compete.

By 1935 Smithy had sold his all but immortal aircraft *Southern Cross* to the government. He was disappointed in the price, which he considered an insult, and now in his thirty-eighth year he seemed generally tired and dispirited. Ulm was now dead, killed in a crash. Close to bankruptcy, Smithy decided to make one last record attempt in the plane he had bought for the great air race. In a letter to a friend just two weeks before take off, he confided: 'The pressures are becoming too great.'

On 25 October 1935, with Tommy Pethybridge as co-pilot, he set off in the *Lady Southern Cross* in his last race against time. His aim

BEHIND EVERY GREAT MAN *Sharing the podium . . . and the newsreel microphones with flyer Sir Charles Kingsford Smith was a pretty young girl called Mary . . . his fiancee. Their marriage was brief, and ended when Smithy was lost during an air race.*

FATAL LADY *Smithy at Sydney airport in 1934, sporting the familiar grin and flashy two-tone shoes. Behind him his last plane, the Lockheed Altair* Lady Southern Cross *in which he was soon to disappear.*

A HERO AND A HERO'S SON *In the cockpit of the legendary* Southern Cross, *Sir Charles Kingsford Smith talks with the son of Charles Ulm, Smithy's co-pilot on so many of his record-breaking flights. Ulm had just died in an air crash.*

was to lower the record of seventy-one hours for the trip between England and Australia. Somewhere between Rangoon and Singapore the plane disappeared. A huge search was led by Australian pilots, and backed by British bombers and flying boats from Rangoon. Leaflets printed in local dialects were dropped to villagers living along the coast.

By the end of November, the search was called off. Not a trace of the pilots or their plane was found. Nothing, until eighteen months later when the port wheel from the *Lady Southern Cross* was washed up on an island in the Bay of Bengal.

Smithy's widow later married an English businessman and moved with her son to Canada. Now Mrs Mary Tully, she still remembers vividly the horror when she heard of her husband's death:

It just didn't seem possible to me that he wouldn't come back. He always did. He used to say to me: 'Just don't worry, because Poppa is going to die in bed with his socks on.'

In some ways Smithy had all the makings of a tragic hero in the Greek sense. But he had something which endeared him especially to Australians—a touch of 'Sydney or the bush' about him. He could walk with kings and princes and he did, but he could also drink a glass of beer standing on his head. His plane was grandly named *Southern Cross*, but to him it was always 'the old bus'. It took smart planners and accountants to make a business out of the routes Smithy pioneered. It took science and technology to transform the paddock which Smithy used to approach with a wing and a prayer. But when it came to a name for Sydney's first major international airport, it could only ever have been Kingsford Smith.

HOW DADDY DID IT *At the handing over of the* Southern Cross *to the Australian Government, Sir Charles Kingsford Smith's son Charles looks out the cockpit which his father had made the most famous command post in Australian aviation history.*

SIR DOUGLAS MAWSON *All rugged up in his favourite cold weather woollens, Australia's most celebrated Antarctic explorer and the man who survived an epic struggle against misfortune during his first expedition. Mawson showed great powers of endurance during his return to the base camp.*

Douglas Mawson

In November 1912, the bodies of British polar explorer Robert Scott and his companions were found, entombed in snow just 18 kilometres from a food and fuel depot which could have saved their lives. The story of how they died after reaching the South Pole, to find they had just been beaten to first place by the Norwegian, Roald Amundsen, is a classic saga in Antarctic history.

But at the same time, on the ice 1600 kilometres away, the bizarre and tragic story of Dr Douglas Mawson was unfolding. Mawson, then thirty, was making a scientific expedition which would end in madness and death. As the only survivor Mawson, after many weeks, struggled back to base only to see his rescue ship steaming off over the horizon.

Half mad from eating the livers of husky dogs, with his skin falling off, his hair gone, no soles on his feet, and weighing half his normal 95 kilograms, Mawson would have to wait another year for the ship to return to the remote base. But he went back later—providing more scientific knowledge of the Antarctic than any man of his time.

Mawson left on his fateful journey with Xavier Mertz, a young German aristocrat and champion skier, and a handsome young Englishman, Lieutenant Belgrave Ninnis of the British Royal Fusiliers. With other teams they planned to explore the land in a fan pattern, working over 2400 kilometres of coast and inland.

About 515 kilometres from base, Mertz signalled a crevasse ahead. This was not unusual, and Ninnis guided his dogs and his sled over a snow bridge. As he touched the snow bridge it collapsed and Ninnis dropped straight through into a black abyss, the sled and dogs falling after him.

The two survivors stayed at the hole, shocked and sickened, for three hours before taking stock of their situation. The lost sled carried all the dog food, some of their food, and vital equipment. They decided as each dog became weak from hunger, it would have to be killed for food.

Within a day of Ninnis' death, the men ate their first meal of dog, unaware of the horrendous consequences.

As the weeks passed, they were surprised to find the dogs' livers fairly appetising. What they did not know was that husky liver contained toxic doses of vitamin A. Indeed, it was only in that year that the term 'vitamin' was coined. The poison had horrifying effects, stripping their skin, swelling their spleens, and causing severe disorientation. But the men did not know why. The dogs were dying out, one of the last being Pavlova, the husky that had been patted on a wharf in London by the great ballerina herself. Pavlova, who had been sent to see Mawson by none other than Nellie Melba, had said to the tall, handsome young Mawson: 'Take it with you, instead of me.' Mawson ate Pavlova's paws in a stew.

DR. MAWSON BACK FROM THE ANTARCTIC

Dr. Mawson.   Dr. Mertz.   Lieutenant Ninnis.

After two years of Antarctic exploration in Adelie Land, Dr. Mawson has reached Port Adelaide. He returned on the Aurora, the ship of the expedition. Lieu-

MAWSON AND HIS COMPANIONS *Mawson and his two companions who died in their terrible Antarctic journey of 1912. Ninnis fell into a crevasse and Mertz died, debilitated and driven mad from the effects of eating the livers of the husky dogs. Mawson, with the soles of his feet tied on with lamp wick, managed to walk over 160 kilometres back to his base camp.*

PAINFUL PROGRESS *The laborious method of traversing polar ice. It was through savage, featureless terrain like this that Mawson struggled alone, on foot, for more than 160 kilometres.*

NINNIS PLUNGES TO HIS DEATH *Young Lieutenant Ninnis fell to his death in a crevasse like this one. Later Mertz died. Mawson alone managed to make his way back to base camp only to find that his ship had just left that day. Mawson would be trapped in the land of the blizzard for another year.*

XAVIER MERTZ *The aristocrat who became a tragic victim of the desperate journey across the Antarctic. Vitamin poisoning contracted from eating dog meat sent him insane.*

ALONE IN THE ICE WORLD

VIVID NARRATIVE FROM DR. MAWSON.

DISCOVERY OF NEW LANDS.

A FIGHT WITH STARVATION.

HOW LIEUT. NINNIS VANISHED.

NEWS TO THE WORLD *The story of Mawson's epic Antarctic journey as it was reported in the London newspaper the* **Daily Mail.**

Mertz slowly became insane, even biting off one of his fingers. When he died Mawson was left with only the instinct to survive. He planned to travel 5 miles (8 kilometres) a day, often against headwinds of 80 miles per hour (about 130 kilometres per hour). The soles of his feet fell off

completely. He fell down a crevasse, hanging from his sled. He was saved by his harness and, after numerous attempts to climb out, somehow made it to the top. He woke from unconsciousness in the snow, unable to remember getting out.

Then a miracle occurred. Mawson

stumbled across a cairn of stores which had been left by one of the parties out searching for him. This gave him the strength and encouragement to reach a small depot called Aladdin's cave, where Mawson made a new pair of wooden shoes with nail spikes for the final treacherous walk down to the main base. The soles of his feet, which had completely come away, were tied back on with lamp wick.

When at last he staggered into the base camp, the men did not recognise him. As they peered at what seemed like a living skull, one of the men cried out: 'My God, which one are you?' Mawson was then greeted with some numbing news. His ship *Aurora*, the one contact with civilisation, had left that very day and could not return for ten months. In hindsight, Mawson felt it may have been a blessing. He did not feel he would have survived the journey. Yet his days as a scientist and Antarctic explorer were far from over. While he never completely recovered from his ordeal, he managed more scientific work on that trip before returning to Australia.

Mawson joined up for the First World War and later resumed his geological work. He was, in fact, the first man to find uranium in Australia. During the 1920s and 1930s he returned to the Antarctic, and is said to have contributed more to Antarctic research than any man before or since.

In his later life, Sir Douglas Mawson became an ardent campaigner against the slaughter of whales.

ANTARCTIC HERO *Twenty years before this picture was taken, the man was going through an almost unbelievable series of tragedies and hardships at the South Pole. His name was Douglas Mawson, and the story of his polar expeditions is one of the great epics of Australian heroism.*

VIVID STORY OF DR. MAWSON.

TRAGIC JOURNEY.

HOW HIS TWO COMRADES DIED.

TERRIBLE PRIVATIONS.

YORKSHIRE EXPLORER'S STRUGGLE FOR LIFE.

MAWSON'S TERRIBLE JOURNEY *The headlines in no way exaggerated. After Mawson's companions died he walked over 160 kilometres back to his base camp.*

WITH MAWSON TO THE LAND OF THE BLIZZARD *The handful of men who survived early Antarctic expeditions considered themselves lucky to see the Australian mainland again, but Captain Moreton Moyes has done better than that. Now 94, Captain Moyes was a member of the epic first Mawson expedition of 1912.*

3

HUMOUR

What makes Australians laugh?

Is our humour really so special, or are we much the same as anyone else? Here's a joke, and if you laugh you probably are Australian.

There's an old swaggie walking along a road about a hundred miles back o' Bourke. It's 110 degrees in the shade and the dust and flies are really crook. As he's trudging along in the heat a ute pulls up and a grazier sticks his head out the window and says: 'Would you like a lift?' The swaggie looks at him for a while and then says with a slow smile: 'No thanks, mate, you can open your own bloody gates.'

If there is something special about Australian humour then it is perhaps the lazy, ironic, 'Well, I'll be buggered' feeling about it. As Melbourne's humorous columnist Keith Dunstan says: 'There's a feeling of hardship and toughness ... funny lines like "The harvest was so crook that the sparrows had to get down on their hands and knees to get at the wheat".'

For most of its history the Australian comic tradition has been rooted in the bush. It's the kind of grim comedy which comes from adversity, the constant struggle to survive and eke out a decent living in a vast, tough land. 'What else can any Australian do but laugh?' says

another Melbourne wit, Phillip Adams. 'You're drowning in floods one minute and being cooked in bushfires the next.'

Our preoccupation with the humour of the bush has lasted well into this century. 'Dad and Dave' is still probably our best known radio serial and no less than sixteen feature films were made about the exploits of these rustic yobbos. But even at the turn of the century Australia was becoming a nation of city slickers. In 1900 about half our population lived in towns and the capital cities, and we were rapidly becoming one of the most urban nations on earth. Not surprisingly, our humour started moving in the same direction.

AW, GEE DAVE ... *Dave and his girl Lil, the durable hicks from Steele Rudd's classic* On Our Selection *stories. The 'Dad and Dave' yarns were filmed many times during the silent era, and remained firm favourites with the audience.*

OUR MOST FAMOUS CARTOON *Stan Cross drew this legendary cartoon for* Smith's Weekly *in 1933, captioned 'For gorsake stop laughing—this is serious!.'*

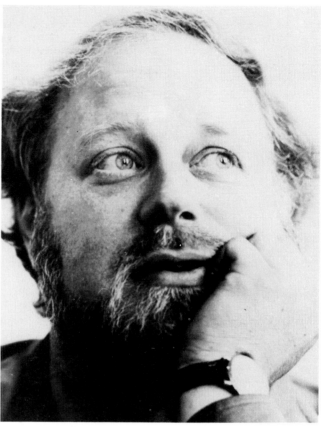

PHILLIP ADAMS *Melbourne advertising executive and writer whose satires of Australian society continue the great 'knocking' traditions of our humorous prose.*

Our doyen of comedians, Barry Humphries:

> We have a rich vein of deeply sardonic humour in Australia. The custodians of it are largely taxi drivers ... and homosexuals ... and homosexual taxi drivers, and black-and-white cartoonists.

Around the turn of the century our black-and-white artists had tired of gags about knowing graziers, stupid farmhands, lazy Aborigines and evil Chinese, and began to explore the comic possibilities of city life. In *Smith's Weekly* Stan Cross gave us easily our most famous cartoon with the caption: 'For Gorsake stop laughing—this is serious.' It was a joke built on a modern phenomenon, what we used to call 'skyscrapers', but it still used the classic device of Australian humour—laughter in adversity. Below the rigger is certain death, but above him is the scrawny nakedness of his mate, whose pants he's clinging to.

Films, too, now reflected our awareness that we were no longer a nation of 'bushies'. *The Sentimental Bloke,* the classic working class ballad by C. J. Dennis had sold 100 000 copies before the end of the First World War, and Raymond Longford's marvellous film was just as popular. The Bloke, and his mate, Ginger Mick, who spoke 'wiv ixprissions thick' were the 'ockers' of yesteryear. Certainly the Bloke himself was a little Aussie battler—a boozy, brawling bard, putty in the hands of his girl, Doreen, and embarrassed to the extreme by anything that smacked of culture. 'Put in the boot,' he cries during the duelling scene from Shakespeare's *Romeo and Juliet,* which Doreen has persuaded him to attend.

Like Mo McCackie, George Wallace, Barry Humphries, Paul Hogan and Norman Gunston after him, the Bloke and his language were criticised for being grotesque

GENTEEL MALE CHAUVINISM Her: *'Do you approve of clubs for women, Uncle?'* Him: *'Ye-e-es, but only after every way of quietening them has failed.'*

STEALING ALL THE BEST LINES *A publicity photograph for one of the hundreds of great radio comedy shows of the pre-television era. On the right, Roy 'Mo' Rene is trying to draw Jack Davey's attention back to his own script.*

BACK LANE CUPIDS *One of Hal Gye's extraordinary illustrations for the most popular edition of the C. J. Dennis folk classic* The Sentimental Bloke.

and embarrassing caricatures. But C. J. Dennis, for one, had a very good ear, and he certainly summed us up with his anthem 'The Austral-aise' which he entered anonymously in a competition run by the *Bulletin* in 1915:

> Fellers of Australia, blokes and coves and coots,
> Shift your — carcasses, move your — boots,
> Get a — move on, get some — sense,
> Learn the — art of, self de — fence.

Most assumed that there was a 'bloody' for every dash, but in the trenches in the First World War the poetic 'ixprissions' were somewhat richer.

Author and columnist Max Harris has a theory that Australians have an innate verbal humour which descends from

> . . . a lot of garrulous Irishmen in the nineteenth century. Fortunately, most of them never took to the stage, never became professionals, and never relied on the lavatory innuendo and the 'prawns and beer' syndrome, but basically on their quick verbal wit. That is, if we're busy, we're 'flat out like a lizard drinking'.

Now that's not uproariously funny, that's a metaphoric poetic usage which brings the element of wit into what would otherwise be a pedestrian statement. 'Flat out like a lizard drinking' goes back to the 1890s, but at this moment people are saying, when something is not very active or is boring: 'You'd find more life in Harry Butler's beard.'

Even if we are slightly crude it's very delicate and gentle. For instance if a horse starts off first from a barrier a race commentator is likely to say: 'He's off like a bride's nightie'—it's got a certain amount of innuendo about it, but nonetheless you get a sense of speed.

Keith Dunstan agrees that we have a great tradition of spoken humour, but maintains that we are not very good at writing it down. 'Graffiti, however, are an exception,' he says. 'There's the famous one which apparently happened in Melbourne where someone had put a sign outside the Hawthorn church.

What would you do if Christ came to Hawthorn?
And somebody wrote underneath:
Shift Peter Hudson to centre-half forward.'

According to Dunstan there's 'great exaggeration and also a waspish cynicism in our humour, like this famous convict joke:

A convict was out on a property at Parramatta, and his boss told him he wanted him to deliver a letter to the magistrate. The convict knew damn well what was in that letter—he was to get twenty-five lashes. So he goes all around the district and finally pleads with a nice young fellow to deliver the letter for him to the magistrate. And the magistrate reads the letter, sees the nice young fellow, promptly puts him up on the pole and gives him twenty-five lashes.

Of course, to the convict, that's an immensely funny joke. There's an earthy contempt for authority in Australian humour. It helps you hate the magistrate.'

Dunstan notes the Australian preoccupation for rhyming slang and the love of the metaphor for the impossible situation. 'A line they love to use is: "It hasn't happened since Christ played full-back for Jerusalem."'

'Australian humour has become a bit more subtle in the twentieth century, but it also has a nice twist. My favourite joke concerns the Digger and, of course, it's a war joke.'

There's a wounded Digger and he's being carried across No Man's Land by another Digger, and there are bullets coming from everywhere. The fellow that's on the other fellow's back says: 'How about turning round and going backwards? You're copping the VC and I'm getting all the bullets.'

But perhaps the most droll summary

FATHER OF 'THE BLOKE' *The author C. J. Dennis at work in December 1922, still using the desk at which* The Sentimental Bloke *was written. A classic working class ballad,* The Sentimental Bloke *had sold 100 000 copies by the end of the First World War. Dennis' use of the Australian language and 'ixprissions' (demonstrated so ably in 'The Austral-aise') endeared him to his public.*

of Australian humour comes from one of Australia's wittiest writers, Phillip Adams. Adams' almost jaundiced views are in themselves part of the Australian comic tradition.

Is not Australia one great big joke? Now I see the map of Australia looking like a great pair of buttocks spreading across the wrong end of the world—the bum of the world—you've got Perth as a hip and Adelaide as a sphincter, Sydney as a hip. And, of course, all the animals in Australia have great big bums. Have you ever noticed that in the coat of arms you've got this great big fat bummed kangaroo and on the other side this enormously bummed emu?

But the whole country is a joke—a great piece of irony surrounded by water. You get dumped here—'Against the Wind' extras that's how everyone got here to Australia—you're sort of dumped on this forlorn continent. Great humour comes out of misery. The more Draconian the context, the funnier the response. It's no joke that the world's greatest comedians are Jews.

IS SHE ANY GOOD? *Roy Rene—without the trademark 'Mo' makeup—with his young wife Sadie Gale, a soubrette on the Tivoli Circuit. Unlike those of many of their showbusiness friends, the marriage lasted until Mo's death in 1954.*

STIFFY AND MO *Still the most famous comedy partnership in Australian history, even though their eighteen-year teaming ended half a century ago. Old timers can still remember lines from their more outrageous routines.*

Roy Rene

Roy Rene, 'Mo', Australia's most famous comic, had an act no other Jewish comedian could compete with. His grotesque stage character, a sort of lewd leering Shylock who slobbered over the sheilas, upset the Jewish press to the point where they recommended that readers avoid his shows. But Mo loved upsetting people, and the more he called them 'mugs' the more they came. He was everybody's favourite mug lair, the eternal prankster and lurk merchant. Dame Sybil Thorndike called him 'the greatest living clown'. Jack Benny watched him again and again to learn the secrets of his timing.

Roy was born Harry van der Sluice in Adelaide in 1892, the son of a Jewish Dutch cigar manufacturer. He began his career as a boy soprano and was 'Boy Roy' as long as he could get away with it. When his voice broke, he took the name of the famous French clown, Rene. Everyone was amused by his talents, except his own family. Sadie Gale, the pretty young vaudeville soubrette Mo married in 1929, says his own family planted stooges in the audience 'to give him the Richard the Third—the bird. They wanted to break his heart. They wanted him out of show business.'

But Mo was unstoppable. By 1914 he had perfected the Roy Rene character with black and white stage paint mask and painted moustache, and when he teamed with comedian Nat Phillips the 'Stiffy and Mo' double became the most successful comedy act on the Australian stage. The partnership had tremendous ups and downs but it lasted a total of eighteen years, and by that time Harry van der Sluice was the biggest thing in the business.

Stiffy and Mo were experts in innuendo, an art later exploited just as successfully by his admirer Graham Kennedy. In one celebrated Mo routine there's a large blackboard and Mo writes the letter 'F'.

Mo: 'What's that?'

Stiffy: 'K'.

Mo: 'How come every time I write "F", you see "K"?'

And Mo laid the mugs in the aisles with the simple ones:

Woman: 'Do you have the time?'
Mo: 'Yes, but I don't have anyone to hold my rifle.'

Even though Mo looked a bit like a sly Al Jolson, his humour was one hundred per cent Australian. Mo invented his own language and to the dismay of 'correctly spoken' citizens many 'Mo-isms' became popular slang. Mo's 'mots' included expressions such as 'coming the raw prawn', 'cop this', 'you beaut', 'mug lair', 'strewth', 'strike me lucky', 'you little trimmer', 'cheeky possum', 'one of my mob' and 'suck it and see'.

Mo made just one film, *Strike Me Lucky*. It was unsuccessful because the producers failed to come to grips with his distinctive style and because the comedian himself found it hard to work without a live audience. Nevertheless, it has its moments of brilliance and some surprisingly bold lines. 'I know who you are,' says Mo as he stumbles upon Robinson Crusoe and his pet goat. 'Cat Whittington and his dick (splutter, splutter) no, I mean Dick Whittington and his cat.'

For all of his adult life, Mo was troubled by ill health. An unbroken stage career of thirty years took its toll. Yet, against all advice, he took on even more work; this time on radio. The legendary 'McCackie Mansions' show was born and Mo conquered a whole new generation who had never seen him perform in the great old days of vaudeville. Freddie Parsons wrote much of his material, but he recalls that Mo had some marvellously witty observations of his own:

He was insanely jealous of anyone else who did well on the show, and when Larry Adler was here—Adler was one of the greatest harmonica players in the world and he was doing very well—somebody said to him: 'That Larry Adler is a great performer, isn't he, Roy?' and Mo said: 'I can't see it. Take away his mouth organ and he wouldn't be worth a zac.'

Mo was such a giant on the Australian comedy scene that he probably could have become an international star. He was tempted by overseas offers, but declined them, usually with the same words:

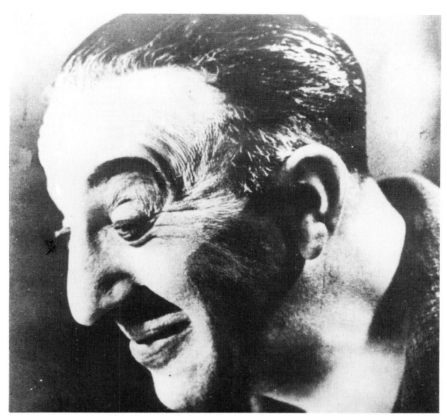

IMMORTAL CLOWN *The characteristic makeup and profile of Roy 'Mo' Rene, perhaps the one original comic genius Australia produced in the first half of the century.*

'The people here understand me. I work in their language. My stuff is folklore stuff. I don't think I'd go over anywhere else.' And he once told his sister, who came to visit him after twenty-three years in New York: 'Break it down, love. Look what happened to Les Darcy and Phar Lap when they went to America.' He was content to be the big fish in a little pond, and he was undismayed by the fact that the big overseas stars who appeared on the same stage as him were earning thousands of pounds; his only concern was that he was getting £10 a week more than anyone else on the Tivoli circuit.

He was a man of modest ambitions, but his legacy was enormous. By the time he died in 1954 his unique style had influenced the course of Australian humour. The former Governor of New South Wales, Lord Beauchamp, once wrote to him and said: 'Your art is an important expression of the Australian ethos.' With typical cheek Mo cracked back: 'Gorblimey, I hope that's a compliment.'

YOU LITTLE TRIMMER *Mo as he appeared in his only feature film,* Strike Me Lucky *made by Cinesound in 1934. The half-leering grin and the fag-end cradled in a cupped hand were Mo trademarks.*

ARTIST AT WORK *George Wallace shows his stagecraft in the 1938 feature film* Let George Do It. *After attempting suicide by poison, Wallace decided to have a quiet smoke while waiting for the potion to work. He accepts a light from his cobber...*

George Wallace

Like Mo, the other great star of Australian comedy, George Wallace, ascended from a vaudeville double act, 'Dinks and Onkus'. But, apart from that, Wallace and Mo had little in common. While Mo could be quite blue on stage he was reserved, even something of a prude, in private life. Wallace, on the other hand, was never smutty in his act but he could be quite risque off stage. And, while Mo made only one unsuccessful film to pass on to posterity, Wallace made five major movies, all of them hilarious.

Wallace's greatness lay in his movement. With his uncanny timing and sublime sense of motion, he was the closest Australia ever had to Chaplin. Most Australians remember him as the fat bloke with the hat half on and a few grogs under his belt, and even when it seemed he could hardly scratch himself, his feet barely touched the floor as he improvised his eccentric dances. His impressions of the 'Great Russian ballet dancer Palmolive' laid his audiences in the aisles.

In films like *Harmony Row, Let George Do It*, and *Gone to the Dogs* he was the classic Aussie battler, but with a nice sense of the absurd. Accused by his boss of sleeping on the job, he responds: 'We weren't sleeping, Mr Austin; we were unconscious.' Being questioned by the inevitable police sergeant:

Now then, what's your name?
Wallace.
Wallace? . . . What initial?
S.
S for Samuel?
Tom.
S for Tom?
Yeah.
How do you get S for Tom?
I don't know. I just don't care, that's what it is.

And, after one of his thousands of brilliant pratfalls, he picks a bloke for deliberately pushing him: 'Listen, I've had seventy-eight fights and seventy-eight losses, but me luck's liable to change any minute.'

It was Wallace's endless supply of gags, his musical skill and superb stagecraft that allowed him first to compete with Mo and then eclipse him, but in fact George Wallace got his start, indirectly, through Stiffy and Mo. Wallace's family had been in show business and George was a would-be comedian. But he had not had much luck and, to support his family, he'd been cane cutting in his home state of Queensland. In 1919, he was in Sydney, and one night he was sitting in the car park of the Tivoli theatre with another would-be comedian, Dinks Paterson, listening to the audience roaring with laughter at Stiffy and Mo. In Paterson's words: 'George said suddenly, "There's the opportunity for us. Why don't we team up and start a double act too?"'

The 'Dinks and Onkus' partnership got its first laugh in 1919 and ran for the next five years in four Sydney theatres. But Wallace was clearly a huge individual talent, and he evolved out of the partnership to create a whole range of characters: 'Sophie the Sort', 'The Drongo from the Congo' and 'Fanny Shovelbottom's Friend'. They brought him fame and fortune, and he was ear-

... more than the fag ignites ...

... and a thunderstruck Wallace thinks maybe life would be safer if he were already dead. Joe Valli played his terrified mate in Let George Do It.

ning £90 a week in the middle of the Depression.

He had a dazzling array of talents. He wrote a good deal of the scripts for his films as well as a score of radio plays and more than thirty songs. He exhibited watercolour paintings, sculpted, made novelty dolls, played five musical instruments, ran a chicken farm outside Sydney and performed on stage six days a week for more than forty years.

The best known of his songs was the digger's favourite, 'Brown Slouch Hat' which Wallace wrote at a moment's notice for one of his co-stars, British singer Jenny Howard. It is forty years since the two met, but Miss Howard still has vivid recollections of their introduction:

I arrived at a producer's office in 1940 to meet Wallace, and I can honestly say I have never seen such an apparition. I think he'd been out the night before and, having never seen anyone keep their pants up under a big fat stomach without braces, I was fascinated. They stayed up all that morning, much to my amazement.

He had a tie spotted with tomato juice and orange. And he had stains and all kinds of things down his suit. Having just arrived from England, and being a little bit British, I was stunned. Then he spoke to me in a very hoarse croaky voice. He said: 'I'm a natural lair.' Well, I thought that must be an aborigine of some kind, I'd never heard the expression 'natural lair'. We don't have such a thing in England as lair.

Jenny Howard and George Wallace played together for the first of many performances in a sketch called 'The Love Burglar'. This is the story of a happily married couple who find someone is stealing pictures of the wife (Jenny) from their bedroom. So the husband (George) decides to come home unexpectedly one night. Jenny recalls:

I'm on stage in this lovely bed and there's two French windows and through them you can hear clippity clop—you know, coconut shells like horses' hooves—and I know it's not in the script. The next moment, George throws back the glass doors, he's rushed across the room, he's looked down into the bed, pulled back the sheet, and said: 'You've done it again.'

Well I died with embarrassment. I thought what have I done? There's this hush in the audience, and as quick as a flash, he's said: 'Eating biscuits in bed—how many more times have I to tell you?'

That was just too much for them. The audience fell off their seats. I loved Wallace from that moment—what a comedian!

By the time Wallace died in 1960, aged sixty-six, he had carved a career through vaudeville, then radio with the Macquarie Network, and he was one of the first people to appear on television in Australia.

All the Onkus stories could never be told in one sitting, and a great many cannot be repeated in polite company, but there's one which shows how the country bumpkin and sometime amateur fighter from Queensland always enjoyed a chat.

A backstage visitor at the Tivoli one night reminded Wallace that he had once been time-keeper when Wallace took on a blacksmith in the boxing ring at Walkerston, near Mackay. That was all the urging Wallace needed to invite the man for a drink. They talked about the old days in Queensland and the visitor commented: 'Well, George, you've come a long way from the canefields.' Wallace thanked him and added, as an afterthought: 'By the way, what are you doing these days?' His visitor grinned and said: 'Oh, struggling along. They've just made me Prime Minister.' He was Arthur Fadden.

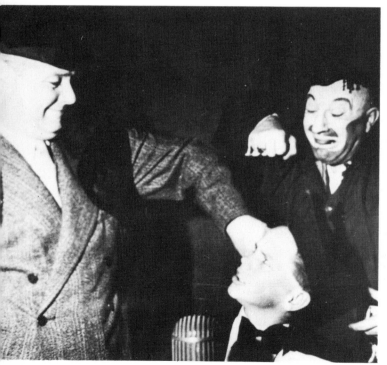

COMEDY SCHOOLROOM *Masters Davey (left) and Rene (right) extracting the last twist of the ear from a terrified pupil. With 'live' audiences in the auditorium, dressing up for radio shows didn't seem at all strange. With his radio shows Mo conquered a whole new generation.*

STOP ME IF YOU'VE HEARD IT . . . *In the twilight of their respective careers, George Wallace (left) tries to sell Roy Rene a joke—one of the thousands they've heard a thousand times before.*

Jack Davey and Bob Dyer

The two big 'D's'—Davey and Dyer—were the biggest names in local radio for twenty years. Yet, ironically, neither was an Australian.

The second son of a steamer captain, John Andrew Davey was born in New Zealand. When he breezed ashore in Sydney in 1931 at the age of twenty, he had already failed as a signwriter and used car salesman. Within two hours he had found himself a flat with a harbour view in fashionable McLeay Street, and borrowed £2 from his landlady.

The year was 1931, and somehow he talked Radio 2GB into giving him a job as a singer. In the words of his lifetime friend, aide and biographer, Lew Wright:

They said: 'Oh, yes, you can sing for us, Mr Davey, at three guineas.' So he said 'OK.' He had to sing three times a week. But even at three guineas, it's an actual factual story, which I have from a person who knew him all his life, that he went into Park Street in the city and he bought three suits, ties, shoes and a motor car, within an hour of getting a job at three guineas.

But when the end of the week came, he received a cheque for nine guineas. He said: 'Lew, if they're that careless with their money, they could have had me for three. I knew this is where I belonged.'

Three months later Davey had his own breakfast show, and within two years he added a daytime quiz programme, a music and variety show in the evenings, and another job compering Movietone newsreels. Jack Davey was here to stay.

At the same time a poor white boy from Nashville, Tennessee, was carving out a name in show business the hard way. His name was Bob Dyer and he had come to Australia with a vaudeville group as a banjo-strumming comedian. His star turn was an act called 'The Death of Willie'. This was a send-up of the craze for singing cowboys. Harry Griffiths, 'Young Harry' of the Mo McCackie days, recalls:

Bob could stamp his foot and

THE VERY BEST OF FRIENDS *The two 'Big Ds' of Australian radio—Davey and Dyer. For a generation these two effervescent personalities dominated the nation's airwaves like no other stars before or since. Despite their continuing public rivalry, Jack Davey and Bob Dyer were close friends, sharing a common passion for big game fishing. But for the cameras they were careful to preserve the gimmick of their feuds.*

THE LADIES' MAN *In an era when the great stars were heard and not seen, the distinctive voice of Jack Davey stood out from the crowd. Despite two marriages, he managed to keep his family away from the publicity spotlight which followed his every move.*

sing—The Martins and McCoys they were reckless mountain boys—there was no doubt about it when he told a gag—whack! You know, there was no uncertainty about anything he ever did.

We had a big variety show once; Dick Bentley, Roy Rene—all these people were in the show—and Dyer was on and he did his bit. When he came off the boys were all sitting there in the chairs looking at him, and as he walked toward them through the curtains he said: 'Well, I may not be the funniest comedian in Australia, but I'm the loudest.'

And Roy Rene said: 'Yeth, you thed it, pal.'

Dyer liked Australia, stayed, and was soon into radio. In those frenetic early days he relied heavily on the comedy tricks he had learned in vaudeville. It was 'slapstick radio', designed as much for the eye as the ear; and the reason was that the audience was there in the auditorium to see those radio shows being made. And when they didn't cram the auditoriums they would jam the streets to watch crazy stunts for shown like 'Can You Take It?' long before Bob Dyer had asked his first quiz question, he could pull literally thousands of people into the streets to watch a Mr Ray Mitchell wheel a pram carrying a midget dressed as a baby through the streets for the princely prize of £50.

THE MAN WITH THE GOLDEN TONSILS *Jack Davey's unique voice was in constant demand for radio advertising.*

OH NO, EVERYBODY *Jack Davey at the peak of his career was ready to try anything—even the violin. To entertain troops during the war, he picked up a fiddle and played the easy parts of 'Night and Day'. Davey was a compulsive worker who made his reputation with quiz programmes, but he also produced variety shows, serials, plays and newsreel commentaries.*

I JUSH BIN HIT BY A BONDI TRAM *Jack Davey delighted in the opportunities his association with the Fox-Movietone newsreels gave for constructing short comedy items. In this scene he staggers on-screen somewhat the worse for wear after a night of self-indulgence. In real life, Davey often spent the small hours in similar fashion.*

The Jack Davey style was almost the opposite to Dyer's. Davey's strength was in his verbal wit, and his optimistic, ad-libbed humour was the most familiar sound on radio for nearly twenty years. There are numerous Davey stories, many of them no doubt apocryphal, but this one from Lew Wright perhaps sums him up.

The local radio station, Victory Moree, sent of all things a cub reporter to interview him, and he said to Jack: 'You're here for the football match against Glen Innes, aren't you?'

Jack looked up at the ceiling and said: 'Glen Innes, Glen Innes . . .' I knew what he was up to. He was thinking of putting £100 on Glen Innes at say 6 to 4.

But the cub reporter thought that Jack wasn't too good on his geography and he said: 'Glen Innes, Mr Davey, you must have heard of Glen Innes.'

And Jack said: 'Oh yes, Glen Innes is next to Godliness.'

Davey headed his own radio production unit; writing, producing, directing and starring. At the same time the American radio king, Art Linkletter, boasted of making thirty-two shows a year, Davey had made six hundred and eighty.

Davey had his enemies, but his friends loved him dearly, and it is said that while his quick wit went straight to the point, it rarely hurt anyone. He was a master at extracting humour from other people, turning the joke away from them, and yet somehow scoring points for the result. Another typical exchange is recalled by Lew Wright:

He said to a boy contestant: 'What is a brazier?' (A brazier is a pot with glowing coals in it which is used for a soldering iron, and making morning and afternoon tea.)

The boy thought for a minute and said: 'Have I got to answer that one, Mr Davey?' And Jack said: 'If you don't, you don't get the pound!' It was 'Snatch and Grab'.

The boy said: 'I'll cop hell when I get home, but it's that thing that holds a woman together.' Jack said: 'Together, or apart?' And away they went again, you see? The audience loved it. But he turned the humour back to people themselves. He had an innate confidence in people themselves.

BREAKFAST WITH THE STARS *Before television came along to snatch the media spotlight from radio, listeners followed the lives of their favourite personalities with intense interest. Jack Davey's waterfront apartment in Sydney was often the location for impromptu breakfast shows. Here with Davey are Dyer with ukelele, pianist Wilbur Kentwell and a young Graham Kennedy.*

. . . AND TWO TONNES OF CHIPS *At Cairns, Bob and Dolly Dyer pose beside the massive black marlin they caught off the North Queensland coast in December 1967. Game fishing has been a favourite with Bob and Dolly for many years. Also, fishing was a hobby which Bob shared with Jack Davey. Bob and Dolly have now retired to the Gold Coast.*

Davey's mark was entertainment, making people laugh. And his golden voice was money in the bank. At his peak he commanded five million listeners a week, and even if you missed his shows the voice was there in commercials for everything from electric shavers, to aspirin and radio valves. He commanded a healthy income, but his personal extravagances cost more. Big boats like *Sea Mist,* and fast cars like his famous D-type Jaguar became his trade mark. He gave away huge sums of money to people in need, and some not so desperate. While he was known to buy silk pyjamas for all the patients in a pensioners' home, he might also tip a drink waiter £40 at a time.

For himself he gambled heavily, entertained in lavish style and generally seemed hell-bent on trying to out-do his own playboy image. In the book *The Jack Davey Story* there are dozens of 'Daveydotes' and this is typical:

He always thought and acted big. Like the time he was going to do a show for the Wool Bureau and he haggled with the Macquarie Network for six months about how much he was worth. He wanted £500 a week and he fought and fought until he got it. When they finally agreed, he charged them £5 a week, but he'd had to establish that he was worth £500 before he'd agree to it.

Davey's personal motto was: 'Bite off

more than you can chew, and chew like buggery.' He rationed himself to four hours sleep a day. He used to say: 'If Napoleon could do it, then why can't I?' He'd work until three or four o'clock in the morning, often in the car, concocting gags or maybe cutting thirty-two seconds from last night's Persil show; always on the move and always with a cigarette in his hand.

Stories of the hell-raising Davey abound; this one is from a former programme manager of 2GB, Percy Campbell:

The company provided Jack with a brand new Chrysler car, and they were hard to get in those days. Anyway, Jack drove it around happily for months. He was a great gambler as you know, and he drove it into the 2GB Macquarie garage every day, and there came a week when it didn't turn up. So we said: 'What's happened to the car, Jack?' He said: 'It's sold, mate.' And the managing director, a gentleman of the name of S. R. I. Clarke, said to him: 'But Jack, that wasn't yours to sell; that was a company car.' He said: 'Oh, I thought you gave it to me.' Anyhow we got him around to seeing the wisdom of it and he said: 'I'll pay you back every penny.' So the following day he walked into the managing director's office and he emptied out his pockets. He'd been to baccarat the night before, and out tumbled a couple of thousand pounds. He said: 'There you are

boss, that squares it all up.'

But if Davey was the gallivanting bachelor, Dyer was the devoted married man. In fact, his life has really been a double act with the ubiquitous Dolly. He met her when she was the lovely young showgirl Dolly Mack. They honeymooned at the infant Surfers Paradise, and ever since she has been his perfect foil.

By the 1950s Davey and the Dyers controlled the airwaves, and they revelled in it. They were so unassailable they could indulge themselves in friendly public rivalry; playing practical jokes on each other, putting each other down, even appearing on each other's shows. The first of the post-war superstars, they became great friends and fishing buddies.

But while Davey was keeping up his playboy image all over town, it

was really Bob and Dolly who were having the good time. Davey was now a sick man, and while the Dyers travelled the world chasing sharks and marlin, Davey was in and out of hospital. The combination of 'cigarettes, whisky and wild, wild women' were taking their toll, and Davey was hospitalised nine times in the next seven years.

By the time Davey's sponsors took him into television he was fading fast. With its cumbersome trappings and technological problems, television did not allow quick editing out of an ad-lib that might be a little too blue. It restricted him and made him somewhat uncomfortable. The greatest star of Australian radio was little more than a grey ghost on television, and the end was near. At the age of forty-nine, the doctors confirmed that he was dying of cancer.

He told Lew Wright: 'I'm at the top of the tree. I haven't got all those young fellows like Bobby Limb trying to push me off the pedestal. So it's a good time to go.'

Towards the end he said to his old friend: 'What are you crying for? I'm the one that's going to die. I have had a hundred years of living. I can show you people walking up Pitt Street a hundred years old, who haven't lived fifty of them. I'm lucky, I can say goodbye to all my friends.'

He said: 'By the way, I'd like to go to dinner at Romano's.' So I asked the chief medical officer at St Vincent's if it was alright if he was back by nine o'clock. I dropped him at Romano's and I went back at nine o'clock. The commissionaire said: 'Don't you dare come in here, trying to serve a summons on a man like Jack Davey. You know he's not a well man.' And of course, Jack came home at half-past twelve. That was his attitude; he was going to die and he was going to enjoy every last minute of it, and he did.

He lived it right up to the end. The born showman went out in customary style. More than 150 000 fans packed the streets to watch the cortège pass by; the biggest funeral Sydney had seen since the death of Billy Hughes.

THE VERY LAST SCENE *Jack Davey, pictured in his Sydney hospital bed just a few days before he died of cancer at the age of forty-nine. Literally, at death's door, he still managed to extract humour from his plight by posing with a prophetic card sent by well-wishers.*

Bob Dyer's career, on the other hand, still had a decade to run. Whereas Davey had failed on television, Bob and Dolly took to the new medium like marlin to water. Dyer understood television. He had the voice, the stagecraft and, above all, an astute business brain. Bob and Dolly owned everything they ever did, and they knew how to sell it. And, unlike Davey, Dyer knew how to pace himself. Having quickly made his mark in television, he decided to change his style almost immediately.

I ceased being an entertainer after the first year of television. I found that being an entertainer was too much, too much of a demand. It ate up too many people and put too many people in their graves and insane asylums, so I started being myself and became what I would call an entrepreneur. I'm not an entrepreneur, I'm a showman. And being a showman is being myself; engineering things and deciding situations such as a quiz show, which I used to look down my nose at. Quiz shows in vaudeville? I wouldn't be in it. I thought anybody can ask questions and give money for correct answers, but there's more to it than meets the eye.

THAT'S ALL FOLKS *Bob and Dolly Dyer on the patio of their Sydney home after announcing the end of their long-running radio and TV quiz show 'Pick-a-Box'.*

IS MY TIE STRAIGHT? *Quizmaster Bob Dyer checks his attire in the lens of the camera before going out 'live'. 'Pick-a-Box' was consistently the most popular Australian programme for more than a decade.*

THAT'S MY GAL *When Tivoli showgirl Dolly Mack married Bob Dyer in the 1940s, she entered into a partnership that was to become the most successful husband-and-wife team in the history of Australian showbusiness.*

Dyer was an entrepreneur, an electronic circus ring-master, and now and again he discovered a star who would help carry him through yet another year of his many years at the top of the tree. One was Barry Jones, now MHR for Lalor, whose bumptious mastery of the quizzes kept millions of Australians spellbound. Here's a typical exchange:

Dyer: 'Who was the first British Governor-General of India?'
Jones: 'Now there are two . . .'
Dyer: 'His name?'
Jones: 'Now it could be either Canning or Mountbatten, because Canning was Governor-General of India in 1858 and Mountbatten was Governor-General of India in 1948. Now it could be either of these two.'
Dyer: 'One of those two, ah?'
Jones: 'Mmmm.'

Dyer: 'Ah, the first . . .'
Jones: 'You mean with the actual title of Governor-General of India? The former Governor-Generals were called Governor-General of Bengal, and earlier of course the first Governor-General of Bengal was Warren Hastings. But he was only Governor-General of Bengal. He was in effect (laughter) Governor-General of India. He only held the title of Governor-General of Bengal . . .'
Dyer: 'Customers, I find myself in a dilemma.'

While Dyer may have been the loudest stage comedian, on television he knew how to hang back. He played straight man to the waspish Barry Jones, who left the show with more than $58 000 in cash and 'Pick-a-Box' prizes and left his hosts that much wiser and richer.

Dyer's work in the 'Pick-a-Box' and 'BP Super' shows earned him an OBE in the Queen's honours, and in 1971 the television industry honoured him with its highest award, a gold Logie.

'I'm flabber-bloody-gasted,' Bob said on receiving his gold Logie. 'But I have one thing to say all of you who are assembled here would probably appreciate, I promise you this won't happen again.'

With a wardrobe full of Logies, Bob and Dolly retired quietly to the Gold Coast, the place where they first went for their honeymoon forty years ago. Recently, they moved even further north to Cairns. Their only address is a post office box, and the telephone has an unlisted number. Their old friend Davey kept performing to his last gasp, but Bob and Dolly said: 'That's it.' And it was.

OLD DROOPY DRAWERS *Bob Dyer (left) and Al Thomas, all dressed up for one of the outrageous stunt routines which peppered Dyer's legendary radio show 'Can You Take It?'*

MR KNOW-IT-ALL *With Bob Dyer, the most famous of all the 'Pick-a-Box' contestants, Melbourne schoolteacher Barry Jones, now MHR for Lalor.*

Norman, Hoges and Edna

Of all the comedians who have graced the stage since the war, only one seems ready to take his place in the Australian comics' hall of fame alongside the illustrious Roy Rene and George Wallace. He is, of course, Barry Humphries; perhaps the cleverest of them all. Humphries is both uproariously funny, and at the same time acerbic. A deadly, viperish wit whose characters punish the audience as much as they amuse and entertain it.

For decades now Australian audiences have queued up to be knocked down, to have their own failings and pretensions thrown back at them—even down to the colour of the water in their toilets, which in this country is invariably royal blue.

Humphries' most successful character, 'Dame Edna', is a combination of everyone's mother and mother-in-law. She envelops her audience, confides in it and scolds it … a mixture of mum and malevolence.

A typical exchange with Barry Humphries:

Question: 'Is there anything of your mother in Edna?'

Answer: 'Well, that depends what you mean (pause) I suppose there is something of my mother in Edna (longer pause) I used to think there was a lot of my mother in Edna (wicked pause) that was until I met your mother.'

Edna, who was made a 'Dame' by the Australian Prime Minister Gough Whitlam during his cameo appearance in the movie *The Adventures of Barry McKenzie,* is Humphries' most durable and most successful character. Some have come and gone, but among the other notables is 'Bazza' himself, who was actually created for a comic strip in the English satirical magazine *Private Eye*; Sandy Stone, the suburban returned soldier in the twilight of his repatriated years; and Les Paterson, former Labor Minister for The Yarts, and Australia's roving cultural attaché.

Dame Edna, the matriarch for all Australians, is really a little over twenty years old. Humphries tells how she was born:

Well, Edna began not as a monologue, but a very real character with whom I feel very little personal affinity at all, except that from time to time I find traces of Edna's make-up on my collar in the mornings.

But Edna started as one half of a dialogue, a two-handed sketch that was written in 1956 at the time of the Olympic Games in Melbourne. At that time, I was

STOLEN MOMENT *When full-time actor and part-time Housewife Superstar Barry Humphries settled down to talk with Peter Luck about the history of humour in this country, he seized any object that happened to be lying around in the room to help illustrate his points. The end results were often quite bizarre.*

KULCHA VULCHA *One of the most inspired and caustic of Barry Humphries' satirical creations, Senator Doug Manton—a mixture of a well-known ABC General Manager and lesser known Labor politician?*

working in a repertory company in Melbourne. The director was Ray Lawler, who, in his spare time, was hatching *The Summer of the Seventeenth Doll*, which was presented later that year. Ray suggested that for the Melbourne Theatre Company's presentation of the Christmas pantomime, or review, Noel Ferrier and I do a sketch together in which Noel interviewed me disguised as an Australian housewife.

The reason they decided that I would be good as an Australian housewife was because we'd been on tour with *Twelfth Night* early in that year and, between country towns, each member of the cast tended to improvise, sing songs, recite, just to while away the boring hours on the bus. One of the things I did rather well was a falsetto, and my falsetto could frequently be heard from the back seat of the bus imitating the lady mayoress of the next country town

ORIGINAL OCKER *The repulsive Barry McKenzie, a character created by Barry Humphries to symbolise the 'Ugly Australian' overseas. Bazza McKenzie introduced the world to modern colloquial Australian speech, and has been accused of setting back the English language at least twenty years.*

PLAYWRIGHT *Ray Lawler, few people realise that the author who wrote the most famous Australian play* The Summer of the Seventeenth Doll *also helped create the notorious 'Dame Edna'.*

THIS IS A RECORDING . . . *The cult ocker hero of the 1970s, Paul Hogan, aided and abetted by his good mate 'Strop' (John Cornell) during the videotaping of a segment for 'The Paul Hogan Show'.*

HOUSEWIFE SUPERSTAR *Humourist Barry Humphries in the guise of Edna Everage—a character which evolved from a routine Humphries used to amuse friends during long bus journeys.*

PSYCHIC COMEDY WITH HOGAN *As the clumsy stage magician Luigi the Magnificent, comedian Paul Hogan tries to summon Uri Geller-like powers in an attempt to bend Mum's rice pudding spoon.*

we were going to. She would invariably make a speech over the lamingtons, thanking everyone for 'doing' Shakespeare so wonderfully and bringing culture to their country town.

Ray said: 'You know, you ought to do that character on stage,' and I said: 'I could do the voice from the wings and one of the girls could act it, you know.' He said: 'Oh, no, you ought to do it yourself. We'll dress you up as a housewife.'

Edna became such an overwhelming character that she has at times almost threatened to submerge her creator. The media have often come away from an interview with Humphries still not quite sure to whom they've spoken. Dame Edna may be a figure of fun, but she does not tolerate fools gladly. She has helped Humphries take a firm hold of British theatre and television, and more recently the Australian comedian tried to make his mark in New York. So far, the reviewers have tended to be interested but wary, and some of the American audiences do not seem to understand this strange man in down-under drag.

But Humphries could well conquer the American market. He is a comic genius, well aware of the roots of his art, and no doubt capable of turning his devastating wit to suit almost any audience. He has this to say about the current climate for local humour:

I think audiences in Australia enjoy what is called 'a bit of stick'. So much of our entertainment is soft, without any real bristle. Everything has to be censored, and approved of, and filtered like baby cereal for television and radio. People are actually frightened of giving offence.

However, as long as Humphries creates the kind of characters who continue to give offence, his success is assured. His audiences actually love to be offended by him, and his style is now so assured that no one would dare step into his stiletto-heeled shoes to challenge his position as the doyen of our comedians.

But there are other modern Australians who make us laugh, and have made fortunes doing it. Paul Hogan, 'Hoges', has achieved wealth and success on television by reviving the stock comic cliché of the brash

OUR 'OGES *The embodiment of the ocker humour of the 1970s—comedian and ex-Harbour Bridge painter Paul Hogan lays it on the line in a television sketch.*

battler—the ocker working-class hero with a modicum of guile and wit. Hogan had been a rigger on the Sydney Harbour Bridge and was discovered through a 'New Faces' talent quest. His act has never lost its orig-

inal home-grown feel but, although he is now as much a fixture in comedy as Wallace or Mo must have been, he has not managed to attract the same warmth of affection from his audiences.

A MEETING OF GREAT MINDS *Ocker comedian Paul Hogan shares the stage with Norman Gunston (Garry MacDonald) in a toe-to-toe slugout of contemporary Australian humour.*

AND HERE I AM WITH MY VERY SPECIAL GUEST . . . *Norman Gunston tickles the national funnybone with his comedy-of-embarrassment style. Australia's gift to suburban gaucherie braves an interview with ageing Hollywood siren Zsa Zsa Gabor.*

Humour today means television; a monster which lets an audience of millions chew up a year's material in a single night. Television destroyed more comedians than it made, and brought with it new demands. One of the medium's most original and successful new talents is actor Garry MacDonald, who created a unique comic character in 'Norman Gunston'.

Gunston, the little Aussie bleeder, revives an area of humour which has lain dormant since the twenties: the 'theatre of embarrassment'. He's been described as a symbol for the inspired amateurism of Australia as a whole: a naive walking disaster who doesn't even know it. As an audience, we catch ourselves thinking: 'No, he wouldn't dare.' But he

TOGETHERNESS *The cast of 'The Mavis Bramston Show', the satirical revue which dominated Australian television in the mid-sixties and gave a host of comedy actors the chance to dress up in drag.*

THE GREAT TRADITION *In a brilliant re-creation of Australian vaudeville comedy of the 1930s, actor Garry MacDonald takes the role of Roy Rene in the classic 'Mo, the Lifesaver' sketch.*

does, and his deliberately awkward interviews with any of the world's leading figures have us aching with laughter. But, as Garry MacDonald explains, not everyone quite understands the dividing line between the actor and the character he has created:

I was in a shopping plaza the other day signing autographs when a girl said: 'I want it for my mother.' A woman came up, you know, very heavily made up, very pale with big rosy cheeks. She came over and I thought it was the girl's mother. She said: 'I've always wanted to meet you,' and I said: 'Oh . . .' And she said: 'To tell you how rude you are!' And she stormed off.

Many of the world's great comedians have embarrassment in their repertoire. It's often our funny men who show us the worst side of our society. There is something of Norman Gunston in all of us, something too of Paul Hogan, certainly something of us in at least one of Barry Humphries' remarkable array of characters. Many of them make us squirm but when we cannot laugh at them the chances are we're taking ourselves too seriously.

ROCKING THE BABY WITH THE VISITING EXPERTS *Norman Gunston tangles his string into spaghetti during a demonstration of yo-yo pyrotechnics by three visiting South American virtuosi.*

119

4

WAR

WELCOME HOME *A rare moment of happiness for a wounded Australian digger as he is reunited with his family. By the end of the war over 90 000 soldiers had been disabled by wounds.*

Australians at war

If it wasn't for the terrible cost in human lives, an outside observer could almost be excused for thinking that Australians actually like going off to war. Every generation since Federation has had its own war to fight and die in—we were even at war before the loose collection of colonies was unified as a nation in 1901. Not surprisingly, the exploits of Australians at war have formed a major part of our international reputation.

Counting the cost

It has been said that Australia came of age through war; that although we became a nation in 1901, we did not gain international status until we signed up for the 'Big One' in 1914. That may be true, but at what cost? At the Australian War Memorial in Canberra, the roll of honour lists 102 389 names of Australian men and women who died in our many wars, from the Sudan in 1885 to 1972 when we left Vietnam. That's a pretty high price to pay for taking our place amongst nations.

The loss of life during the First World War was staggering. Of the 330 000 who embarked for overseas service, more than 200 000 were killed or wounded; a casualty rate of sixty-six per cent compared with fifty-one per cent for the British Isles.

In August 1914 Australia responded to the news that the Empire was at war with a spontaneous out-

BOXERS AND BOERS *As Australia prepared to become a nation in 1900 it was already at war — against the Boers in South Africa (because Britain was) and against the Boxers in China (because Christian foreigners were). This contingent of dashing Australian riflemen was photographed before embarkation to South Africa.*

PATRIOTIC CANNON FODDER *Proudly showing their artillery, the Victorian Volunteers ready for action outside their bivouac. Before nationhood in 1901, Australian soldiers fought as part of the British army.*

burst of patriotism. Today, we tend to forget that the original 'Diggers' were an entirely volunteer army. Around Australia, converted passenger liners were packed to the gunwales with cocky young soldiers ready to steam across the equator. For weeks those ships were their parade ground, horse stables and barracks.

Patsy Adam-Smith, author of *The Anzacs:*
At first they thought they were off to an armed version of the Olympic Games. You stood on the sidelines and you cheered and you called out: 'You're going to your baptism of fire.' They didn't know until then that a baptism of fire took off an arm and a leg, and

sent a man mad.
You see, Gallipoli didn't really stop them. The casualty lists—well, they expected it and it showed what Australia could do. But France was different. Those hideous casualty lists—and by this time the men were writing back and telling them what war was like.

EYES RIGHT *Officers of the Australian Cavalry proudly parade in Sydney's Centennial Park before embarking for action in the Middle East. Many of them travelled in converted passenger ships which were to act as parade ground, stables and barracks for the weeks of the voyage.*

WAR

"I'LL HAVE YOU!"

THE OGRE *Anti-conscription cartoon of the period portrayed Prime Minister Billy Hughes as a simian maniac intent on enslaving Australia's youth.*

THE BUGLE SOUNDS *Amongst the atmosphere of the conscription referendums the 'Call to Arms' was made at fever pitch. This recruiting poster was designed by Norman Lindsay.*

OUTBACK PATRIOTS *This First World War poster attempted to equate enlisting in the army with the spirit of bush mateship.*

POLITICAL PRIEST *Archbishop Daniel Mannix who was in the forefront of a conscription battle during the First World War.*

BILLY BOY *If Billy Hughes had support from a single group above all others, then it was his beloved Diggers. He supported them through thick and thin, and they loved him for it. In London, he was chaired through the streets by them, but back home, Australians were not so impressed. The conscription referendums were both lost . . . despite Billy's vociferous support.*

Conscription

By 1916 most of the young men who wanted to fight, and who were old enough, were already overseas. After the horrifying death toll at the Somme in France, Great Britain was demanding that we supply even more men for the war. In England, Australia's new Prime Minister, Billy Hughes, agreed to send more troops. But the only way to swell the army's ranks now was to introduce conscription. Back home, Billy Hughes faced two hurdles. The trade unions and his Labor Party were implacably opposed to conscription. Hughes decided to take the issue direct to the people in the form of a referendum. With the Establishment press behind him, he was absolutely confident of victory.

The 'Little Digger' launched his Vote Yes campaign, fighting his opponents in typical style. Hughes branded them 'scabs' and 'blacklegs'. He ordered soldiers to break up anti-conscription meetings, often sparking violent street fights. This heady period of Australian politics culminated in the celebrated 'Warwick eggs' incident in the town of Warwick in Queensland, where the Prime Minister was campaigning for the Yes vote. From Melbourne *Argus* writer, Lloyd (later Sir Lloyd) Dumas:

The moment the Prime Minister stepped from his carriage, he was surrounded by a mob. They commenced hooting and groaning and hurling vile epithets at him. An egg thrown from the crowd just missed him. A second one, better aimed, broke upon the Prime Minister's hat and knocked it off.

Fists were flying everywhere, and the Prime Minister was in the thick of it striving to get at the man who had assaulted him. Mr Hughes was hustled and jostled by men twice his size ... but the Prime Minister was daunted by nothing.

He demanded assistance from the police in apprehending the man. Although Mr Hughes demanded in his capacity as Attorney-General of the Commonwealth that they should take action against his assailant, Senior-Sergeant Kenny declined to do so, declaring that he recognised the laws of Queensland and would act under no other.

This particular incident led Hughes to form Australia's Commonwealth Police Force. For half a century, until a shot was fired at Opposition Leader Arthur Calwell lacerating his chin, during another conscription row, the 'Warwick eggs' represented the summit of political violence in Australia.

Through two referendums, Hughes fought tooth and nail to convince the people to vote Yes. But he met his match in the fiery Irish Catholic Archbishop of Melbourne, Dr Daniel Mannix. The anti-British Dr Mannix addressed public meetings attended by hundreds of thousands of people throughout the country. He attacked Hughes at every opportunity, arguing that the European conflict was in reality a 'sordid trade war', and that Australia should not conscript her sons for 'cannon fodder'.

Hughes had the entire establishment press on his side, and used propaganda material including cartoons depicting Belgian women with their breasts cut off by the 'filthy Hun'. He also invoked the Defence Act to suppress the huge flow of anti-conscription pamphlets, magazines and newspapers.

One of the most effective weapons for the No voters turned out to be a melodramatic poem. This ballad persuaded most women, and many men, to vote No. It was called 'The Blood Vote':

THE DIGGER SPIRIT *Amidst the carnage of the Western Front, the Australian soldier still found time to display his characteristic sense of humour. An aid station was transformed into the local pub, complete with sandbagged billiards outhouse.*

'EMDEN BEACHED AND DONE FOR' *This signal flashed from the Australian cruiser* Sydney *after she had defeated the German cruiser* Emden *on 9 November 1914 after a firefight off the Cocos Islands.*

AFTERMATH OF VICTORY *A view of some of the 4 500 prisoners taken by the 2nd Australian Light Horse Brigade during their operations in Syria. Every generation since Federation has had a war to fight.*

FRAGRANT WEED *Amongst the spoils captured by weary Diggers near the Bois de Crepy during the First World War was a case of choice cigars. The celebration smoko went unseen by the dead German soldier in the foreground.*

Why is your face so white, Mother?
Why do you choke for breath?
O I have dreamt in the night, my son,
That I doomed a man to death . . .
They gave me the ballot paper,
The grim death-warrant of doom.
And I smugly sentenced the man to death
In that dreadful little room . . .

Perhaps the poem tipped the balance. On 28 October 1916, Billy Hughes' conscription proposal was defeated by a narrow margin. Undeterred, he mounted a second referendum in 1917. He lost yet again, this time by a more substantial majority.

Twenty-five years later, John Curtin, the young anti-conscriptionist who had authorised publication of 'The Blood Vote' in 1916, became the Labor Prime Minister of Australia. By a strange irony he would in fact be the man who would eventually introduce conscription to Australia.

In the Pacific campaigns of the Second World War, Australian forces looked pitifully small along-side the massive US armies led by General Douglas MacArthur. As the war came closer to home, to New Guinea and then to Darwin, John Curtin began to believe that our purely volunteer army was no longer adequate. Curtin spoke to the nation:

Clearly and specifically every human being in this country is now, whether he or she likes it, at the service of the Government to work in the defence of Australia. For no longer shall this Government appeal, it shall order and direct.

Behind Curtin's aggressive oratory was the message that Australian men were to be conscripted for military service.

Australian law allows for the compulsory enlistment of men into the army only in the event of a direct threat to Australia. Curtin interpreted this to include the Pacific war zone. With the Japanese closing in, Australians this time accepted conscription without quarrel.

In 1964, when Sir Robert Menzies

PROFILES OF POWER *Douglas MacArthur and John Curtin—during the Second World War two most powerful men. The American General ran the entire Allied armies south of the equator; John Curtin was Australia's Prime Minister.*

127

re-introduced a form of conscription he brought in new legislation and renamed it 'national service'. There was some criticism from the Labor Party and the trade unions, but to most Australians it seemed that 'a dose of army discipline' would not hurt our young men. Within a few months the Australian army, conscripts included, had joined the Americans in Vietnam.

But not every young Australian was prepared to accept that fate. Simon Townsend was the most prominent of a small band of people who decided to take their opposition to conscription before the courts. As a conscientious objector Townsend refused to obey his call-up orders. He quickly found himself a prisoner in solitary confinement living on bread and water in an army prison. It took three years, one court-martial and five civil court cases before a Sydney magistrate in June 1968 finally decided that Simon Townsend's objections to military service were indeed conscientious. Townsend says that amongst the 'tea chest' of letters he received was a selection of venomous correspondence:

In a small bundle there were twenty-two hate letters. They were quite extraordinary: white feathers, a silver bullet with my name scratched on it. Really vile letters that made me realise that people, who'd never met me, hated me so much they would have preferred to see me dead.

It was November 1972 before conscription and Australia's involvement in Vietnam was finally halted by the incoming Labor government. But it was too late to save the lives of young men like twenty-one-year-old Private Errol Noack. Private Noack, who had been in Vietnam only ten days, became the first of 187 National Servicemen to die. Ironically, we had managed to win the First World War without conscription, then lose Vietnam with it.

Australian Diggers have always volunteered to fight against nations that they believed have threatened freedom, but Australians have shown that over more than fifty years they will not easily accept the concept of compulsory enlistment. Future governments will surely think twice before introducing conscription again.

THE FIGUREHEAD *During the bitter anti-Vietnam war confrontations Labor MP Dr Jim Cairns emerged as a spokesman of the Moratorium movement. Subsequently he rose to Deputy Prime Minister in the Labor Government, but then fell from power after a succession of scandals.*

A FOREST OF PLACARDS *Almost everywhere he went during his brief tour of Australia, American President L. B. Johnson was confronted with bands of anti-war protestors. It was 1972 before Australia's involvement in the war ended.*

A CONSCRIPT'S GRAVE *The plaque on this modest memorial in Centennial Park Cemetery, Adelaide, simply tells the passer-by that this is the grave of Private Errol Wayne Noack, who was killed on active service with the Australian army in Vietnam. He had been in Vietnam just ten days.*

The Diggers

Australia's most enduring hero of the First World War was not an Australian. He didn't win a Victoria Cross, and he didn't even carry a gun. By today's military standards, he might even have been court-martialled for desertion. John Simpson Kirkpatrick was a young British adventurer, sailing the world on a steamship. When war was declared, he went ashore in Western Australia and joined the Australian forces to fight overseas. At training camp, Simpson, as he called himself, proved a bit of a larrikin. He played jokes on the other men, and made friends with the camp dogs. He loved animals and even carried a possum on board the troop ship.

Simpson was assigned to the Third Australian Field Ambulance. When he stepped ashore at Gallipoli on 25 April 1915, he was the second man off his boat. The first and third were killed beside him. That initial confrontation with death in the Dardanelles had an immediate effect on the young man: he disappeared and was reported missing.

By the next day, Simpson had been found. He was walking through Turkish sniper fire leading a donkey that carried wounded men from the front-line carnage back to the medical team on Anzac Beach. He had

MENIAL DUTIES *These German prisoners of war captured by the French during the 1914-18 conflict were pressed into service, under guard, cleaning the barrel of antiquated French horse-drawn artillery.*

CURLY-HEADED HERO *One of the few authenticated photographs of Simpson (centre) and his donkey. It was on an errand similar to the one shown here—bringing a wounded soldier down from the front line—that the great Anzac hero was fatally wounded.*

not even bothered to join his unit. In just twenty-five days the 'bloke with the donkey' became a legend.

Simpson had found his first donkey 'Duffy' on the beach. They defied death to run their one-man ambulance service, working all day and half the night. Simpson straddled the wounded who couldn't walk across Duffy's back, while he helped other Diggers limp to safety.

Another stretcher-bearer at Gallipoli, Mr N. W. Faulkner of Melbourne, remembers him:

> He was a law unto himself. He just did it on his own. He got killed eventually. He was an absolute target for the snipers. It was bad enough when you had to get yourself under cover, but you can't put a donkey under cover very well.

By 19 May Simpson had rescued scores of men and acquired a second donkey. That day, he stopped for breakfast before starting his trek through 'Shrapnel Gully'. Breakfast wasn't ready, so Simpson said: 'Never mind, get me a good dinner when I come back.' He was returning through the gully with the two donkeys and two wounded men when he was shot through the heart by a Turkish sniper. Simpson was only twenty-two years old. The next day, Colonel John Monash wrote from Anzac Beach to the Australia-New Zealand headquarters:

> I desire to bring under special notice the case of Private Simpson. Private Simpson and his little beast earned the admiration of everyone. Simpson knew no fear and moved unconcernedly amid shrapnel and rifle fire, steadily carrying out his self-imposed task.
>
> Enquiry solicited that he had belonged to none of the units of this brigade. He had become separated from his own unit, and had carried on his own perilous work on his own initiative.

There were sixty-six Victoria Crosses awarded for service in the First World War, but nothing for Simpson. Yet, his story of heroism has lived longer than any other. Today, Anzacs march with the image of the man and his donkey on their medals. To them, Simpson *is* Gallipoli.

Easing the tedium

NAVAL MANOEUVRES AT BERRIMA War creates some bizarre sidetracks in a nation's history, and few could be more peculiar than the fate of the German-speaking males who were interned at Berrima Jail in NSW during the First World War. They improvised elaborate schemes to keep themselves amused, including concerts and these quaint aquatic escapades on the local river.

IMPRISONED CELEBRATIONS *The elaborate title page to the program of a concert staged by German internees held at Berrima in NSW during the First World War. The extravaganza was held in honour of the birthday of the German Crown Prince.*

A QUIET WAR *A group photograph of German prisoners held at the Berrima Camp during the First World War.*

BERRIMA BLIMP *A model Zeppelin made by internees.*

BERRIMA RIVER *German internees enjoying the water.*

THE GONDOLIERS *Memories of Venice.*

THE FLEET SAILS BY *German internees on the Berrima River.*

SWASTIKAS IN BRISBANE *In the late thirties, in the calm before the storm that would soon engulf the world, German gymnasts proudly took part in a parade through Brisbane streets, and displayed the Nazi emblem.*

WE'LL MEET AGAIN *An intense mixture of emotions coloured each troopship as it left Australian docks for the war in the northern hemisphere — the sorrow of separation blended with pride in serving one's country and the anticipated excitement of battle.*

THE LONG GOODBYE *The wives and sweethearts of Second World War soldiers optimistically expected their boys home soon. The war dragged on to many times its expected length, but most of the men who went returned.*

The 1914-18 conflict was the 'war to end all wars' but, less than a generation later, the courage of thousands of Australians was tested again, sometimes on the same battlefields. More than 750 000 Australians enlisted for the Second World War and only twenty received the Victoria Cross. Of these, just ten lived to tell the tale.

Sydney newsreel cameras filmed one of the heroes, Lieutenant Roden Cutler, twenty-five years old, when he arrived home on crutches after the 1941 campaign against the Vichy-French forces in Syria. The young officer had, on a number of occasions, distinguished himself by 'remarkable acts of gallantry', and saved the lives of the men who served under him. Lieutenant Cutler's Victoria Cross citation reads:

This gallant artillery officer inspired the infantry to press on and his name became a byword amongst the forward troops with which he worked. At Merdjayoun on 19 June an infantry attack was checked after suffering heavy casualties from an enemy counterattack with tanks. Enemy machine-gun fire swept the ground, but Lieutenant Cutler pressed a continuation of the attack. With another artillery officer and a small party he pushed ahead of the infantry and established an outpost in a house. The telephone line was cut. He mended this line under machinegun fire and returned to the house. The enemy then attacked this house with infantry and tanks, killing Bren gunners and mortally wounding other officers. Lieutenant Cutler and another manned an anti-tank rifle and a Bren gun and fought back driving the enemy infantry away ...

Lieutenant Cutler then personally supervised the evacuation of wounded members of his party. Undaunted he pressed for a further advance ... With a small party of volunteers he pressed on until finally, with one other, he succeeded in establishing an outpost right in the town which was occupied by the Foreign Legion

LAST LOOK *A Digger takes his last eyeful of Australian 'terra firma' before shipping out for the Second World War which was to last until 1945 — much longer than at first expected.*

WE SHALL REMEMBER THEM *Sir Roden Cutler, VC, receives a sprig of rosemary from a young Legatee. Sir Roden distinguished himself during the 1941 campaign against Syria.*

... The enemy attacked and he was cut off ... He was forced to go to ground but after dark succeeded in making his way through enemy lines ... On the night of 23-24 June he was in charge of a twenty-five pounder sent forward to silence an enemy anti-tank gun and post, which held up our attack. This he did ...

Later at Damour on 6 July, when our forward infantry were pinned to the ground by hostile machine gun fire, Lieutenant Cutler, regardless of all danger, went to bring a line to his outpost when he was seriously wounded and twenty-six hours elapsed before it was possible to rescue him. His wounds at the time had become septic, necessitating amputation of his leg.

Today Sir Roden Cutler, thirty-second Governor of New South Wales, and now the longest serving state Governor in Australian history, describes his moments of personal heroism:

I was damn frightened, if you want to know. I think everyone is. If there is a dangerous situation and you can see some way you might rescue the people with you, then you act pretty quickly. You don't have time to sit and think. But, by jove, when it's getting pretty close to you, you're very frightened; and it's overcoming fear that really matters.

133

War at home

It was morning tea time on 19 February 1942 when Australians at home had their first real taste of war. Darwin's telegraphist, Archibald Halls, was telling his counterpart in Adelaide: 'Wait a sec, there's another air raid alarm. I'll see you shortly . . .' He never did. Halls was one of ten people killed in the post office when the Japanese bombed Darwin, just three months after Pearl Harbour.

The Darwin attack was Australia's first experience of war on the home front, and, like the Americans at Pearl Harbour, we didn't exactly distinguish ourselves with our preparedness. Despite a warning received at 9.30 a.m. the alarm wasn't sounded for another twenty-eight minutes. By then Japanese bombs were ripping apart the large naval and merchant fleet anchored in Darwin Harbour. Two hours later, the bombers returned to attack the airfield. It was all over by lunchtime.

The toll was 238 dead, 320 wounded, eight ships sunk and

JILLY'S GOT HER GUN *To help the effort to raise money for the War Loan, these Tivoli Show Girls manned an ack-ack gun in Sydney's Martin Place to attract the lunchtime crowds. They did.*

twenty-three aircraft destroyed. And, after the raid—panic. By mid-afternoon, the main road out of town was crowded with cars, trucks, horses, bicycles, people on foot, and even a sanitary cart, as Darwin's population fled inland. Local wags dubbed the whole affair the 'Adelaide River Stakes', but to the authorities it was a matter of serious concern, which would lead ultimately to a Royal Commission. Many of those who did not flee, including service personnel and police, took to looting. An air-raid officer in Darwin at the time, Mr Ray Fosky,

THE DESTRUCTION OF CHINATOWN *During the repeated Japanese air attacks on Darwin, one of the areas to suffer most was the long-established Chinatown district. Because no accurate population figures were ever collected, losses amongst the Chinese and Aboriginal communities of Darwin will never be known.*

THE VICTIM *An official Navy photograph of HMAS* Sydney, *the cruiser which was ignominiously sunk without trace by the German raider* Kormoran *on 19 November 1941.*

THE WAR COMES HOME *Darwin Harbour in February 1942. Darwin was bombed fifty-nine times before effective anti-aircraft defences deterred any further attacks.*

described the confusion:

> We were delegated to go and collect some rations, and we ran up against the police. They were more or less helping themselves. We couldn't challenge them. They had authority over us because everyone assumed it was martial law, although it was never made very clear at the time. It wasn't until three or four days after that before things settled down.

Prime Minister John Curtin announced the Japanese raid on Darwin with the words: 'The government has told you the truth. Face it like Australians.' In fact, what we were told was often far from the truth.

Wartime censorship suppressed the horrifying casualty figures, and the panic which followed. Detailed newspaper reports of the raid were banned by the Federal government and the full story of the Darwin raid would not be known until many years later.

A Royal Commission later investigated reaction to the raid. It discovered that groups of airmen were found up to 110 kilometres away, while one was 640 kilometres away and another covered 4500 kilometres to Melbourne in thirteen days.

Darwin was bombed fifty-eight more times and, during that period, the city of Sydney had its own visit from the Japanese Imperial Forces.

A BIT OF A LAUGH, REALLY *The first time the Japanese bombed Darwin in 1942, more than two hundred people were killed ... still the largest loss of life in Australia on a single day. After a while, the people of Darwin and the soldiers stationed there became accustomed to the raids, and could even extract a laugh from it all.*

KUTTABUL *The sight which faced Sydneysiders the morning after the Japanese midget submarine raid. Nineteen young naval ratings died when the ferry sank at its wharf at Garden Island.*

THEY DIED SO YOUNG *The funeral of nineteen naval ratings who were killed when a torpedo from a Japanese midget submarine sank the ferry boat* Kuttabul *which had been converted into a dormitory. These young men died when the war came home to them before they'd a chance to go out and confront it.*

On Sunday night, 31 May 1942, three months after the first Darwin raid, the calm of Sydney Harbour was shattered by the sound of warfare. Searchlights swept the waters seeking a target. Shells whistled overhead and the crack of machine-gun fire was mixed with the muffled explosion of depth charges. Patrol boats criss-crossed the harbour trying to locate the enemy and co-ordinate a defence.

It was dawn before most people realised what had happened. During the night, three Japanese midget submarines had sneaked into the harbour. One became entangled in the submarine boom just inside the Heads and the crew blew it, and themselves, up. Another submarine was destroyed by depth charges. The third fired two torpedoes at the US cruiser, *Chicago*, moored near Garden Island naval base. The torpedoes missed, but one blew up beneath the ferryboat, *Kuttabul*, converted to a dormitory for naval ratings. Nineteen young men asleep on board were killed. Sydneysiders can count themselves lucky that the attack wasn't more successful.

It was soon established that the eighty-foot (twenty-five-metre) long midget submarines were launched

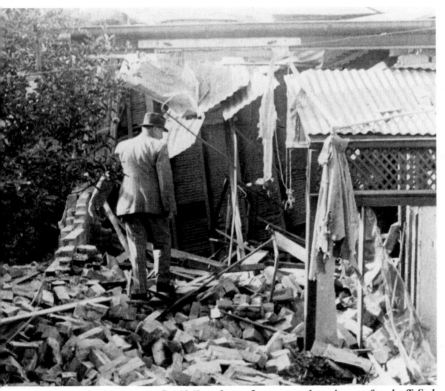

PLEASANT NORTHERLY ASPECT *In 1942, a large Japanese submarine surfaced off Sydney's Bondi Beach and calmly shelled the eastern suburbs. The worst injury was a sprained ankle, but a few buildings were damaged. Property values plummeted.*

A RATHER LARGE FISH *Harbour salvage workers recover the hull of one of the Japanese midget submarines which entered Sydney Harbour in 1942 and threatened the US fleet at anchor.*

from a convoy of 'mother' submarines. Now there were embarrassing questions for the defence chiefs to answer: How did these larger ships cruise so close to our coastline, undetected and unchallenged? How adequate was the harbour's submarine boom if two of the three invaders could get through? While these questions were still being pondered, one of the mother submarines surfaced off Bondi Beach and calmly shelled the suburbs of Bellevue Hill and Rose Bay. Property values plummeted, but no one was hurt.

After the war, Australian journalist Richard Hughes interviewed Iso Susumo, a Japanese pilot who flew over Sydney the night before the midget submarine raid. The Melbourne *Herald* published Hughes' report on 2 April 1949:

. . . a pack of six long range 3330-ton Japanese submarines surfaced 35 miles north-east of North Head (at the entrance to Sydney Harbour). Three submarines carried a midget two-man submarine each. The other three carried a tiny scouting plane. Ito and his observer took off from their submarine at 3 a.m., just before moonrise . . .

'I flew in over North Head and descended to 600 feet to fly up the harbour while my observer sketched the position of the boom and its entrance,' Ito told me. He came down and flew over Farm Cove, skimmed towards the bridge, climbed again and circled over Cockatoo Island naval base.

Trying to get his bearings, he sought Mascot aerodrome. Mascot apparently mistook him for a friendly plane and turned on the landing lights.

He flew back towards Farm Cove, observed a ship on the north side of the harbour and flew out towards the sea. He had been over Sydney for about ten minutes . . .

The midget submarine that blew up the *Kuttabul* was never found, but wrecked parts from the other two submarines were later assembled as one complete vessel. Today the 'submarine' is installed at the War Memorial in Canberra: the last relic of Sydney's night to remember.

The war brides

SMILE AND SHOW A LEG *An American sailor makes the most of his shore leave during the War. The footpath photographers did a great trade during the war snapping sailor boys with their new conquests.*

BRAVE NEW WORLD *English War Brides — women who married Australian servicemen stationed in the United Kingdom during the War — arrive in Australia to start a new life.*

OFF TO THE USA *Reverse traffic War Brides embarked from Australia to journey to the United States where they would settle down with the American boys who'd won their hearts during the war.*

Prisoners of war

In the Second World War thousands of soldiers saw only a fleeting glimpse of tanks and machine-gun fire. Their war became a battle of personal survival of another kind. They were the prisoners of war, who spent years 'behind the wire' often subjected to torture, starvation and disease.

There were many tales of utter horror. The last members of the Australian Army Nursing Service to leave Singapore embarked on the *Vyner Brooke*, which was bombed by aircraft and sank. Twelve sisters were

ONE MAN'S WAR *Gerald Carroll enlisted because of a broken romance. He spent most of the war behind barbed wire as a prisoner of war. A cab driver, he left his cab at the Melbourne depot when he went. Five and a half years later he returned, picked up the keys, and drove the same cab out of the garage and back to work.*

'ROOM INTERIOR - SAGAN'.

d'après BEAR 44.

FUN AND GAMES IN STALAG LUFT 3 *Carefully recorded in this exuberant caricature are pen portraits of all the major 'characters' of the infamous prison camp. The cartoon is part of the collection of Gerald Carroll, who ran a laundry service 'behind the wire'.*

lost at sea and twenty-two who surrendered to the Japanese were ordered to walk into the sea. They were machine-gunned, and all but one of them was killed. Thirty-two surviving nurses from the *Vyner Brooke* became prisoners of war in the Netherlands East Indies, where they suffered greatly in captivity. Eight more died before the war ended.

And yet, while the Second World War was responsible for twenty million violent deaths, some of its participants experienced miraculous good luck. Melbourne taxi driver, Gerald Carroll, was one.

He went to the war on a whim. After a broken love affair he decided, on the spur of the moment, to leave his taxi and keys at his depot, told the boss to look after his cab until he got back, and enlisted. After three months in Crete, Private Carroll was taken prisoner and eventually sent to Stalag Luft 3, site of the famous 'wooden horse' escape. He was determined not to waste the time he knew he had to spend in the

prison camp, so he set up a laundry service for well-off British officers too lazy to do their own washing. With no money on hand, Carroll operated on credit. He explained the method:

The officers made out a slip of paper like a bank cheque and I gave it to the postal authorities. Through the German authorities, the letter would go to the Red Cross in Switzerland and then to the Commonwealth Bank in Australia House in London. They processed it through the officers' bank accounts.

After the war, Gerald Carroll went to London. 'I just fronted the teller and introduced myself. The bank account was there, and the figures were satisfactory.' Before he left London, Gerald Carroll met and married an English girl. When he returned to Australia, five years after he'd left, Gerald Carroll walked back into his old taxi depot, picked up his keys and went back to work.

Not many POW stories had such

PRIVATE ENTERPRISE BEHIND THE WIRE ... *while a prisoner at Stalag Luft 3 (the 'great escape' and 'wooden horse' camp) Gerald Carroll went into business washing the laundry of other men.*

THE HUNGRY YEARS *Those Australian POWs lucky enough to survive the notorious Japanese camps could hardly have been blamed for harbouring hatred for their captors. These men, from a prison on the island of Ambon, were taking the sun on the troopship back to Australia.*

TOJO'S MATES *Notorious for their brutality, these Japanese prison camp officers had themselves pictured as benevolent caretakers in the propaganda film* Calling Australia. *The mystery of the origins of this film has never been solved.*

a happy ending. However, if the Japanese had it their way, we'd have believed their cruel camps were run like luxury hotels. In late 1942 or 1943 the Japanese made a propaganda film titled *Calling Australia.* It showed Australian POWs eating hearty meals and drinking beer, sunning themselves beside swimming pools and playing golf on the island of Batavia, site of one of the harshest POW camps in the war. No one knows exactly why the film was made, or how a copy came to end up in Australia after the war. But the most curious question is: Why did Australian soldiers co-operate with the Japanese to apparently misrepresent their treatment? As yet, there is no official answer. With Australian voices used throughout the film, the script reads in part:

Necessary commodities are supplied to us, not plentiful, but rationed enough to keep everybody going on a normal scale. Nevertheless, the boys need the extras such as cigarette lighters, a pack of cards or a bottle of beer. And in another scene, two officers are playing golf:

First Officer: 'Perfect! How do you do it?'

Second Officer: 'Constant practice still keeps me fit, sir.'

Warrant Officer Adrian Knowles of Melbourne acted as an interpreter between the Japanese soldiers and the other Australian prisoners on Batavia. Mr Knowles said of a scene in *Calling Australia*, which shows Australians apparently relaxing at a mountain holiday resort:

To get the people to go, the Japs said they were having a holiday camp for officers and they called for volunteers. On the face of it, it looked reasonable and some of the officers went. A meal was set forward, and before they could eat it, it was taken away. They would have become suspicious of course, but they'd committed themselves. What could they do? I imagine a lot of what they did and said was to reassure people back in Australia.

The film, which incorporates a background of 'Waltzing Matilda' and other familiar Australian sounds and voices, goes on to show officers sunning themselves in deck-chairs at the 'cool mountain sanatorium'. 'You are not looking at a bungalow in Rose Bay,' the Australian voice says, 'though it is very much like it, but a real home for officers. This privilege, as stated in international law, is given only to officers who have pledged their word of honour.'

Overall the film is frightening in its persuasiveness. But for the fact that its Australian cast all have shaved heads, one might be excused for thinking that life in prison camps on Batavia was indeed 'all beer and skittles'.

But we know it wasn't, so how this film was made remains a mystery. But there is an even greater imponderable. Why was the film made at all? What purpose was gained in showing Japanese captors as noble and kindly souls? Was it made for audiences in Australia or Nippon? Only the Japanese who conceived and made the film know the answers.

WISH YOU WERE HERE *As depicted in the Japanese propaganda film* Calling Australia, *Australian POWs relaxed in prison camp games' parlours complete with bars and billiard tables.*

MANY MEMORIES *Warrant Officer Adrian Knowles, an Australian prisoner of war who acted as an interpreter for fellow prisoners held captive by the Japanese on the island of Batavia.*

GATEWAY TO HELL *The entrance to the infamous Changi Prison, Singapore, where the Japanese held thousands of Australian prisoners of war in appalling conditions for more than three years.*

Shooting with cameras

Australians at home watched the bloody battles of the Second World War through the eyes of newsreel cameramen. Much of our understanding of war was framed by the action films we saw in the picture theatres. They were shot by men like Damien Parer, one of the greatest war cameramen of modern times, who went bravely to the front lines carrying film instead of bullets. Parer's famous documentary film, *Kokoda Front Line*, won Australia's first Academy Award. Tragically, Parer never lived to see the 'Oscar'.

Damien Parer was born in 1912 in Melbourne, and grew up on the barren landscape of King Island off the Tasmanian coast. His father was a Spaniard, an artistic man who ran the local store and hotel to support his large family. His mother was an Australian of strong Irish 'gold-digging' stock, and deeply religious. This volatile mixture produced a man of extraordinary character.

By 1941, Parer was with the Australians at Tobruk as an official war cameraman for the Australian Government. In Libya, Greece and Syria he built a reputation for his films and the risks he was prepared to take. War correspondent Maslyn Williams was Parer's friend and colleague. They covered most of their war assignments together:

He browned me off, I can tell you. You'd say: 'Well, Damien, we're going—you know such-and-such has happened today and we've talked to the Intelligence Officer and the General and so forth,' and he'd say: 'Well, the best place to shoot· this is there.' I'd say: 'But Christ, you'll get your head shot off if you do that,' and he'd say: 'No, where else would you go?' Just as simple as that. 'I've got to get the shots. I've got to be there.'

MAN WITH THE CAMERA *Parer, perhaps the most remarkable combat cameraman in the world, was an Australian who eventually worked for the Americans. His* Kokoda Front Line *won our first Oscar.*

While *Kokoda Front Line* won Australia's first Oscar, the cameraman was never really happy with the final film. Within weeks he was back in New Guinea with his camera and the Australian soldiers he admired so much.

Parer prayed often, sometimes loudly, under fire. Yet the man's intense religiosity blended easily with his coarse army 'language', and the soldier's 'vices' he loved so much. It is said of Parer that he never drank liquor before the war, and

NEW GUINEA RIVER CROSSING *If there's one scene which sums up the Second World War for Australians then this is it — Damien Parer's famous shot of a Digger helping his blinded mate across a New Guinea river. Parer's stunning newsreel coverage of the war was both a booster to morale and a gritty picture of the war as it really was. Parer was killed while filming an American assault on the island of Pelelieu.*

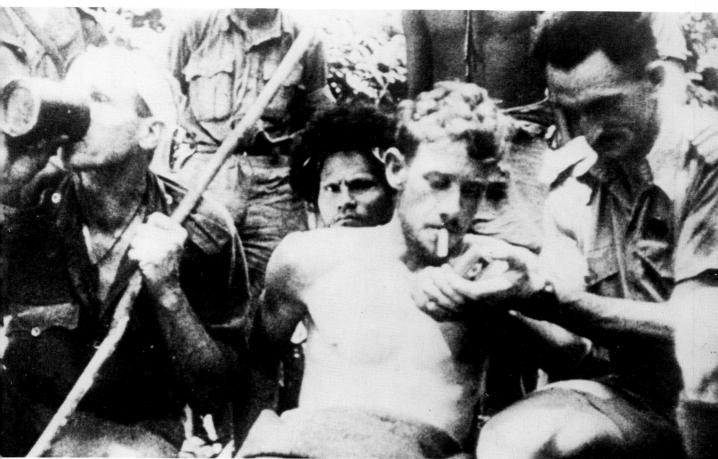

MATESHIP *One of the many classic shots from the films of famous wartime photographer, Damien Parer. Diggers, some wounded, some completely exhausted, take a respite from the fighting in New Guinea. From Parer's film* The Road to Salamua.

then, he never learned how. He poured himself anything from the bar and drank it in double time, which didn't help his gambling around the 'Slippery Sam' tables.

In New Guinea, Parer covered the slow retreat down the Kokoda Trail. Like the soldiers, he had to throw away his personal belongings to lighten the load. He even threw away one of his cameras but he held on to the precious film which won the 1943 prize.

As much as Parer loved filming the war, he hated the more mundane propaganda assignments back in Australia which were also part of his official work. His handsome, tanned face and his encouraging speeches in the newsreels were familiar to most Australians, so when he decided to join the Americans there was wide criticism.

Moslyn Williams agreed with Parer that he should have been allowed to keep his talents for the battlefield. Williams said:

He loved the Australian Digger. Quite frankly, I'm a snob and I don't like the Australian Digger.

A MAN AND HIS MEDIUM *Damien Parer with the material which helped him portray the bravery of Australian soldiers in the Pacific war—35-mm black and white newsreel film.*

THE PICTURE MAKERS *Cameraman Damien Parer, with tripod slung on his shoulder, pauses to watch official war artist Julian Ashton sketching the Diggers at work during the Second World War.*

THE YANKS ARE COMING *American paratroopers float silently into the beach landing place of the Allied offensive to occupy the island of Noemfoor off the coast of Dutch New Guinea in July 1944.*

FREEDOM OF THE PRESS *In 1944, with Australia locked in war with the Japanese, the Government exercised its power to censor newspapers. In April, editions of some papers were actually seized before distribution.*

But Parer literally loved Australians, those boozy fellows with a can of beer.

He said what great men they were, and it broke his heart to work with the Americans. He did it because the peanuts who were running our organisation would not let him do what he had to do. The Americans literally had more cameramen than they could use, but they could see Parer was in a class of his own and they offered him complete editorial freedom. He was with the marines when they invaded the island of Guam. He followed the tanks in their advance from the beach, filming the infantry in amazing close-up. Four American cameramen were killed in that bloody combat, but it did nothing to stop Parer.

Often he filmed from ahead of the American lines and, in getting those scenes, he was more exposed than the men he was filming. Parer wanted to be in front of the front line, to have the soldier's face on film, a technique he'd discussed with Maslyn Williams. Williams said:

I wouldn't have a bar of it. He said the best way to film a war was to get between the two combatants and get the reaction from both sides. A nice idea, but . . .

Just before Parer left to join the Americans in the Pacific, he confided to one of his brothers:

I think that before the war ends I will die if I continue taking photographs the way I am doing. I feel that it my duty to try to portray the truth and the honesty, the justice and the beauty in the soul of every soldier that dedicates his life to fight and, if necessary, die for his country. I will go on taking photographs the way I know I should, even though I die taking them.

Parer died just two weeks later on 17 September 1944, when the marines landed on the island of Pelelieu. He was racing across open ground when a machine-gun opened fire from a Japanese pillbox about eighteen metres away. Bullets ripped through his chest, killing him instantly. He was thirty-two years old, and had been married just six months.

READ ALL ABOUT IT *The news of the Japanese surrender was greeted with amazing scenes of joy. On 15 August 1945 the Sun published the front page everyone had been waiting for.*

OUR LONGEST PARTY *When the announcement of peace in the Pacific was made by Prime Minister Ben Chifley in September 1945, Sydney went mad. Ticker tape fights raged for hours.*

Australians have been at war for about a quarter of the past century: the Sudan, the Maori wars, the First and Second World Wars, Malaya, Korea, Vietnam, and who knows where in the future? It is impossible to say through the stories of just a few individuals what war has meant to us as a nation, how it has affected the collective psyche. It would be encouraging to think that this young nation would not find itself embroiled in another war this century, but, even with just two decades to go, it seems too much to hope for. Nevertheless, our attitudes to war have changed; our feelings are summed up by one of the nation's heroes, Roden Cutler, VC:

Most of us have reacted against war. We don't like it. We think it's senseless, and I think people express this view in many ways, one of which is this changed attitude towards what we were brought up on; deeds of derring-do—you know, the 'thin red line' and all that sort of stuff. That's gone out of fashion long ago, and I think rightly so.

EVERYONE LOVES A SOLDIER *Especially on the day peace was announced, any man in khaki or navy could get a kiss from as many girls as he could corner. It was a day of rejoicing . . . and no inhibitions.*

5

SPORT

'HE'S IN' *Australians only had to hear these words to know that Don Bradman, the brilliant batsman of the 1930s was batting. Later to become Sir Donald, Bradman is seen here with S. J. McCabe resuming their third wicket stand against England in Melbourne 1936–37. Bradman scored 169, McCabe 112 of Australia's 604.*

The Australian obsession

In 1971 an English observer, Jonathan Aitken, wrote: 'Sport is the religion of Australia, and Saturday is the day of worship. Gallup Polls indicate that two-fifths of the population play some sport regularly, and that three-quarters of the population watch it.' That may have astounded an Englishman, but most Australians are more likely to be wondering what the remaining quarter have managed to find to do with themselves.

Swimming

As a race, we Australians are so besotted with our swimming prowess it's a wonder we haven't started to grow fins. Yet it was an Englishman who introduced us to the art of social swimming, and a Solomon Islander who taught us the 'Australian crawl'.

The history of swimming in this country is in part the story of the amazing Cavill family. Fred Cavill, a former British Navy man, was a self-styled 'professor' of swimming, whose list of distinguished pupils included the future Queen Mary.

In the early 1900s he came to Australia and set up baths at Lavender Bay in Sydney Harbour. On a trip home soon after, he won his fourth medal for bravery—leaping into the sea to rescue a woman passenger who tried to drown herself. Cavill also had the dubious honour of posing as the torso for a statue of King Edward VII before coming

BATHE BETWEEN THE FLAGS *The inaugural surf carnival of the Manly Club — 6 January 1912. Twenty thousand people attended the spectacular that Saturday, and a seventy-year tradition had begun.*

THE FIRST OF MANY *Australian swimmer Freddie Lane who won our first Olympic swimming gold medal by stroking up and down the River Seine in Paris faster than his 1900 rivals.*

THE NATATORIUM *The Cavill family swimming centre at Rushcutter's Bay, Sydney, pictured just before the turn of the Century. Annette Kellerman learned to swim here, and it was 'Professor' Cavill who pioneered water safety techniques.*

back to Australia to continue his remarkable career.

Cavill had nine children, most of whom became Australian or world swimming champions. Two of his sons died in strange circumstances: one was frozen to death while trying to swim Seattle Harbour, the other was killed by poisonous gas during an underwater demonstration in baths in California. Dick Cavill, another son, was the first man in the world to swim a hundred yards in less than a minute, and Sydney St Leonards Cavill invented the butterfly stroke. A grandson, Dick Eve, was the only Australian to win an Olympic gold medal for diving.

Australia's first Olympic gold medal for swimming was in fact won by Freddie Lane in Paris in 1900. Lane was an exponent of a stroke called the 'trudgeon kick', which would soon be swept aside by the Australian crawl.

SURFING IS AN OFFENCE: PENALTY £1 *Bondi Beach, Sydney in 1901. Forbidden to enter the water during daylight hours, the crowd sat sunning themselves, watched the children paddling at the water's edge, or promenaded.*

The crawl was introduced to Australia by Prince Wickyama, a teenage schoolboy from the Solomon Islands. As Alick Whickham, he thrilled Australians with his daring aquatic displays, including '200 foot dives'. Wickyama beat all rivals with his islander's style of crawling across the water. The stroke caused a sensation and was quickly adopted by other swimmers including Arthur 'tums' Cavill, who introduced it to the Americans.

At the 1912 Stockholm Olympics, Australia's Fanny Durack became the first woman in the world to win an Olympic gold medal. By 1920 the swimming hero was Frank Beaurepaire, who held every Australian title from 200 yards to a mile. Beaurepaire is better remembered

THE ORIGINAL CRAWL *Solomon Islander Alick Whickham amazed Sydney clubs by winning races by twenty metres with his overarm 'crawl' stroke. This style soon became the standard racing stroke.*

SWIMMING SENSATION *Australian Fanny Durack was world swimming champion over a score of distances, but her reputation overseas rested more on her attire than her aquatic exploits. In this 1918 picture Fanny models the one-piece costume.*

for the tyre company which still bears his name.

In 1924, the great Swedish swimmer, Arne Borg, was brought out to Sydney, at the age of twenty-two, to swim against Australia's new champion. He was Andrew 'Boy' Charlton, only sixteen and already a giant, blond lifesaver. He seemed to swim mostly with his arms which were more powerful than other men's legs were.

SAFETY FIRST *These ladies of Wollongong formed the first women's rescue and resuscitation team in the world. But in 1912, the restrictive dress requirements seemed to make the girls themselves likely candidates for drowning.*

AT THE TURN *Swimming idol Andrew 'Boy' Charlton turning during an exhibition swim at Sydney's Domain Baths. Forty years later, the re-built baths would be named in his honour.*

THE BIG BOY *Charlton (right), the Australian distance swimmer who dominated international competition throughout the twenties and early thirties. He is seen here with his coach Harry Hay.*

The organisers of the Borg-Charlton clash packed 7000 fans into the old Domain baths. Moss Christie, a 1924 Olympic swimmer, recalled Charlton's victory over the Swede:

After the race, Borg put Charlton in a boat and rowed him up and down the baths calling: 'Boy is champion.' Of course, the crowd just cheered and cheered. It was fantastic.

When Charlton got on the Manly ferry to go home, he couldn't get off. All the people were on the wharf at Manly. They crowded around so much, they had to get the police.

At the Paris Olympics that year, Charlton proved his potential by winning a gold and bronze medal from older, more experienced champions like Borg, Johnny 'Tarzan' Weissmuller and Duke Kahanamoku, the Hawaiian who introduced surfboard riding to Australia.

Despite his success, Charlton was often a reluctant racer. He never won an Australian title because, at the time of the championships each year, he was jackarooing up near Gundagai. After the 1932 Olympics in Los Angeles, Charlton 'retired' to live on a sheep property. He died in 1975, aged sixty-eight.

It was thirty years before

THE 'BOY' FRIEND *Although he represented Australia at the 1926 Olympics, Moss Christie's main claim to fame was that he was a friend of 'Boy' Charlton.*

BIRTH OF A LIFESTYLE *Duke Kahanamoku, the champion Hawaiian swimmer who introduced Australians to the sport of surfboard riding during a visit in 1915. This pastime eventually became a whole way of life for thousands of Australians.*

PROTOTYPE HERO *At the height of his fame, in 1924, Andrew 'Boy' Charlton embodied the great heroic image of the bronzed Aussie. A world champion swimmer, he still found time to do his duty as a Manly Beach surf lifesaver.*

THE FIRST SURFIE *Duke Kahanamoku, (centre, arms folded), the visiting Hawaiian swimming champion who introduced surfboard riding to Australia. On the Duke's right, in a dashing string tie, is Freddie Williams, the young Manly boy who pioneered riding the breakers, to local swimmers. The photograph was taken on the verandah of the then Freshwater Surf Lifesaving Club.*

RESCUE BY BELT AND HAGGIS *The Bondi Surf Lifesaving Club led by bagpipes during the march past event of a surf carnival held at Manly in 1909. The Australian lifesaver was already something of a superhero, and was even allowed to break the dress regulations which required the body to be covered from the 'neck to the knee', including the upper arms.*

Australians saw a new breed of swimming champions, and always one length ahead of them was Dawn Fraser; a 'tomboy' of the fifties who could thrash all the boys at the local pool. When coach Harry Gallagher saw her, he commented that her swimming style was 'rough' and so were her manners. Gallagher took two years to persuade the 'wild kid' to join his squad. Dawn began training early in 1955. In just twenty months she was ready for the Olympics.

The Fraser legend began when the swimmer was a teenager, before a delirious home crowd in Melbourne in 1956. Dawn, then seventeen, won the hundred metres freestyle in world record time. She won it again in Rome in 1960 and again in Tokyo in 1964. Dawn Fraser is the only swimmer to win three Olympic gold medals for the same event.

LEGENDARY PARTNERSHIP *Dawn Fraser in discussion with her coach, Harry Gallagher. This twosome broke scores of world records and captured three Olympic gold medals.*

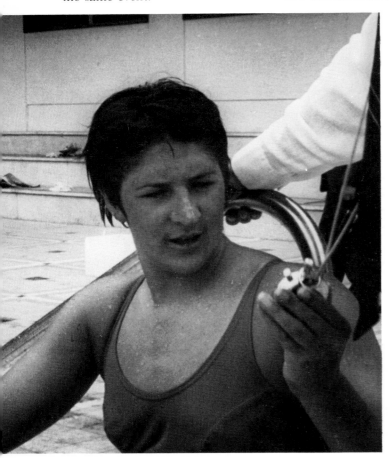

THE FIRST SUPERFISH *Dawn Fraser had set herself the target of breaking the 60-second barrier for the hundred metres freestyle swim. The world record mark of 58.9 which she set at the North Sydney pool in 1964 stood until 1971.*

A FAMILIAR SMILE *The slightly shy, but still confident grin of our greatest 'Golden Girl', swimmer Dawn Fraser who won three successive gold medals in the hundred metres freestyle at the 1956, 1960 and 1964 Olympic Games.*

But, behind the scenes, trouble was brewing. In Rome, Dawn fought with officials, refusing their dress and swimming instructions. Her subsequent ban from touring (despite a written apology) left her in tears. Then, in Tokyo, she was caught 'souveniring' an Olympic flag from the Emperor's palace, an incident which made world-wide headlines. The Australian Swimming Union took revenge on the 'unruly' champion, and banned Dawn from competitive swimming for ten years.

Today, Dawn Fraser is more than just a name to Australians. She represents qualities many of us would like to claim: sporting prowess, a healthy disregard for officialdom and, above all, the courage to say what she believes. No swimmer since has generated quite such public affection. The fact that for ten years she swam faster than any woman, and most men, in the world, is merely icing on the cake.

HEROINE'S RETURN *On her arrival back in Australia, Dawn Fraser is wheeled across the tarmac at Sydney Airport following her famous after-hours escapade in Emperor Hirohito's palace gardens.*

THE WONDER SEAWEED EATER *Murray Rose won three gold medals at the 1956 Olympics in Melbourne yet unlike most Australian sporting heroes, he was a vegetarian. While his team-mates downed steak, Rose trained on a diet which included dried seaweed.*

THE KONRADS KIDS *Born in Latvia, these two children astonished Australia by both breaking their first world record while only fifteen years old. Between them they held records between two hundred and fifteen hundred metres, and we were quick to claim them as our own.*

PROUD HERITAGE *Sydney teenager Shane Gould who joined a long line of Australian Olympic champions with her powerful style. Shane retired from competitive swimming while at the peak of her career, to become a minister's wife.*

MENTOR OF CHAMPIONS *Forbes Carlisle Olympic Swimming Coach who dropped out of the 1980 Moscow Olympics. He resigned in protest over the Russian-Afghanistan conflict.*

MASSED BACKHANDS *Between the wars, Australia was proud of its sporting prowess, particularly in tennis. These schoolgirls in their tunics and stockings had to practice their groundstrokes every sportsday.*

Tennis

In 1899 a young Harvard student called Dwight Davis asked his wealthy father for a silver cup as the trophy for a tennis match he was organising between his American friends and some visiting Englishmen. Davis won his first cup in 1900. But by 1907 a combined Australasian team had joined the contest, and that year the 'Davis Cup' made the first of many visits 'down under'. Young Dwight said later, had he known how his idea would grow he would have asked his father for a gold trophy.

Norman Brookes, the first Australian to win Wimbledon, helped win the 1907 Davis Cup, and captained five more winning sides. He was called 'the fox' because of his uncanny anticipation. Brookes successfully played forehand and backhand strokes on the same side of his racquet, using what the British called the 'colonial grip'.

Brookes was a sombre, poker-faced fellow who played even on scorching

THEY CALLED HIM 'THE FOX' *Still Australia's most successful tennis player, Sir Norman Brookes dominated the game for almost twenty years, and established the tradition of Australian eminence in the sport.*

ANYONE FOR TENNIS? *Lawn tennis was one of the few sports in which women were accepted as competitors almost from the beginning. With hardly an inch of flesh exposed, these Sydney ladies stroked the balls back and forth at White City while preserving as much female decorum as possible.*

157

hot days dressed in long trousers and heavy woollen cap, dabbing away with his flat-topped racquet, which he continued to use long after they were out of fashion. Legend has it that he sipped champagne between particularly gruelling sets to keep up his strength.

Brookes' international acclaim started a frenzy of tennis playing at home. Australian 'liberated' women in full Edwardian costume came out in the mid-summer heat, to play one of the few games they were allowed to play against men. The tennis court became as familiar as Ayers Rock, and often the surface wasn't much better.

MAESTRO IN CREAMS *Sir Norman Brookes, nicknamed 'the fox' because of his uncanny sense of anticipation. He persisted with square-topped racquets long after they'd fallen into disfavour, and used a club-like grip on his forehand side.*

ON THE BACKHAND *Brookes shows his curious 'paddle shot' style. By turning his wrist through almost 180 degrees, Brookes played the backhand and forehand with the same side of the racquet. The slower pace of tennis then allowed for such idiosyncrasies.*

But Australia's dominance of the tennis world early in the century did not continue. Dozens of other countries became just as passionate about the sport, and just as skilled. It wasn't until the 1930s that Australia produced another enduring international great, 'Gentleman' Jack Crawford, a beautiful stylist on and off the court. In 1933 shorts were all the rage at Wimbledon. But Gentleman Jack wasn't the favourite of Queen Mary for nothing. Aged a mere twenty-five, he announced he would have none of the new-fangled fashion, and in long 'creams' he stepped on to the court to win the title before the Queen.

Crawford was the great champion of his time, but it was Harry Hopman, another player of the thirties, who would influence Australian tennis perhaps more than anyone else. During the next twenty years the canny tennis genius coached fourteen Davis Cup teams, discovering, urging and orchestrating talents like the 'terrific twins' of the fifties, Lew Hoad and Ken Rosewall.

DAPPER JACK *Jack Crawford, who won the 1933 Wimbledon title in his customary elegant style. His demeanour and clothing were as refined on the court as off.*

PILLARS OF AUSTRALIAN TENNIS *The 1932 Australian Davis Cup side with team manager J. Clemenger (left) before their departure for Cuba. The team members (left to right) became long-serving contributors to the cause of Australian tennis. Jack Crawford was the greatest stylist of his era. He won Wimbledon and now owns a Sydney sports store. Harry Hopman became our most successful Davis Cup coach, before moving to the US. Cliff Sproule became the longest-serving tournament referee in Australian tennis history.*

GENESIS OF A GROUNDSTROKE *The legendary Ken Rosewall back-hand as it looked when he was twelve years old. Thirty years later, it still swings as sweetly.*

BLOND BOMBSHELL *Lew Hoad at fourteen demonstrates the characteristic, powerful serve which helped him become the most devastating attacking player in the game.*

Hoad and Rosewall first played each other when they were ten years old in an exhibition match in Sydney. An old newsreel film of the match shows Rosewall wearing the little 'security' cap that was his trademark for many years. The score in that first clash was Rosewall d.

Hoad 6-0, 6-0. The 'twins' as the press called them later, were nothing alike. Hoad was built like a locomotive. Rosewall was tiny but, in one of those nice Australian ironies, it was Ken who was always called 'muscles'.

Hoad and Rosewall won a

Wimbledon doubles final by the time they were seventeen, and they were clearly Australia's hope to win back the Davis Cup. On the eve of the 1953 challenge the two juniors beat the Americans Vic Seixas and Tony Trabert in the New South Wales championships. But the Cup

CANNONBALL DIGGER *Lew Hoad as he looked as a National Serviceman. The sight of Hoad in khaki represented a pinnacle of post-war national pride.*

TO THE VICTOR, THE SMILES *A triumphant but exhausted Lew Hoad waves to the jubilant crowd after defeating American Tony Trabert in a marathon five-set Davis Cup tie played at Kooyong in 1953. Hoad's victory levelled the Cup at two matches all.*

challenge matches would not be so easy. After three rubbers, Australia was down 2-1. On a treacherous, rain-sodden court at windy Kooyong, Lew Hoad, the kid from Glebe, played the match of his life to equal the score. It was a heart-stopping affair. Hoad, playing for the first time with spikes, fell over often, broke strings on his racquet, and generally had the crowd on the edge of their seats. He eventually beat Trabert in five sets. Rain stopped further play and Rosewall had a sleepless night waiting to play Seixas. He won brilliantly the next day. It was a victory even the laconic Rosewall will never forget:

> When the match was finished, after four days, to see all those cushions being thrown into the centre of Kooyong stadium was really something.

And then the inevitable. The Americans were turning professional and if Hoad and Rosewall could beat the best of the Americans, then they must be worth money too. Within weeks the lucrative cash offers were flowing in; yet they both declined.

Lew went into the army and the newspapers and newsreels followed the all-Australian boy in khaki. The cameras were out again in 1956 for

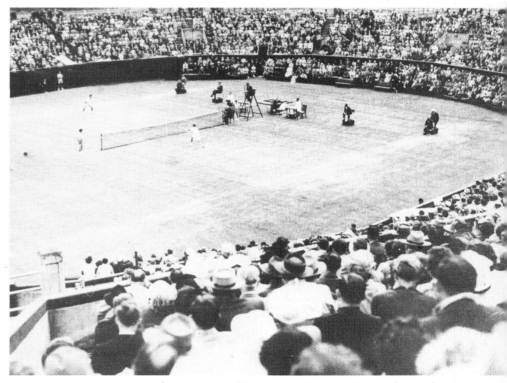

THE SACRED SQUARE OF GRASS *Centre court at Kooyong in Melbourne, the premier tennis location in this country. The experts say that if you can win here, you can win anywhere in the world.*

Ken Rosewall's marriage to Wilma McIver. With his new responsibilities, Rosewall decided to turn 'pro'. Hoad joined the professional ranks too and played in epic series like the 100-match tourney against Pancho Gonzales before trouble with his back forced him out of the professional game. Ken, however, looked as though he would go on forever. Hoad says of Rosewall:

I used to think it was an ego thing with Ken—to prove that he could beat all the up-and-coming guys. But now I think that he just basically loves tennis.

In reply, Rosewall said:

Well, I think everybody has got to have some kind of ego. It helps you keep pushing yourself along. Both Hoad and Rosewall are a credit to tennis. In the fifties, they were criticised for letting the amateur side down, but they bore the 'name calling' with dignity. They had their futures to consider and it paid off.

Today Rosewall is still hero to younger players and a god for any man who's over forty and still playing. Lew has carved himself out a very comfortable living with a picturesque tennis ranch in Spain. Harry Hopman, their Svengali, lives and coaches in America.

In 1961 another Australian tennis legend began when Mr Bill Kurtzman, president of the tennis club at a small Riverina town called Barellan in New South Wales, told some talent scouts for Sydney coach Vic Edwards about a promising nine-year-old part-Aboriginal girl who seemed something of a prodigy. The little girl, named Evonne Goolagong, started her tennis training by seeing how many times she could hit a ball against a brick wall.

THE FAIRYTALE ROMANCE *Lew Hoad with his fiancée Jenny. She had been an usherette at the Kooyong stadium in Melbourne and had watched Lew Hoad and Ken Rosewall capture the Davis Cup for Australia.*

THE ARTISTRY OF AN OLD MASTER *Ken Rosewall, the most enduring legend of Australian tennis, played his first international match at seventeen and was still playing at that same level twenty-five years later.*

VIVA NEWCOMBE! *The unmistakeable drooping moustache and electric physical presence of John Newcombe, twice Wimbledon champion and still one of the best-known names in Australian tennis. Eyes riveted on the ball, he lunges for an awkward backhand volley. Bewdy Newk.*

EYES ON THE BALL *Evonne Goolagong, twelve, practises her serve under the critical eye of her coach and guardian Vic Edwards. The Edwards family virtually adopted Evonne into their Sydney home when she moved from the New South Wales country town of Barellan to start on the long road to Wimbledon.*

With parents who were not too well off, Evonne had to borrow her racquets, but after she had become the most improved player in the club, Mr Kurtzman gave her her own. Edwards was delighted with his find. In his words:

All I could see with the girl was the keenness and the movement and the rhythm. Stroking is quite easy to build if you have all that and she seemed to have that. Also there was another reason. Evonne was part-Aboriginal, and I had in my early days been in the back country, and I always felt that if you could find somebody like this in that race, with their natural movement and so on, you could develop. I think that had quite a bit to do with it.

In a move which brought him some criticism over the years, Edwards virtually adopted the little girl from the country and soon she was making headlines. The press was amazingly prophetic, predicting even when she was twelve that she seemed set for a Wimbledon victory in 1970. Another glimpse into the future came when Evonne could barely see over the net. She met and had her photograph taken with the great Australian tennis champion Margaret Smith (later Court).

In 1971, only a year after the papers had predicted it, Evonne met Margaret in the most prestigious tennis event in the world, the Wimbledon singles final. Goolagong defeated Court 6-4, 6-1. Evonne went on to become the darling of the tennis world and eventually, Mrs Evonne Cawley.

RETURN OF SERVICE *When Margaret Smith (now Court) was Wimbledon Champion and Evonne Goolagong a talented thirteen-year-old, there can't have been much rivalry involved when Margaret showed the Aboriginal girl the secrets of her forehand grip. In 1971 Evonne thrilled the world by defeating Margaret in the Wimbledon final.*

MASTER AND PUPIL *Vic Edwards acted not only as Evonne Goolagong's coach, but also as her guardian.*

The only criticism ever made of her has been that she lacks the 'killer instinct'. But many find that makes her even more endearing.

Evonne both elevates the sport and puts it in its place. It is, after all, not a business and not warfare, and Evonne thrills the world by just doing something wonderfully well.

TEN MILLION BACKHANDS *Evonne Goolagong aged sixteen practising her distinctive underspin backhand on the court of her coach and guardian.*

LITTLE EVONNE *The Aboriginal girl from Barellan, New South Wales, listens to coach Vic Edwards explain the subtleties of tennis technique.*

Boxing

Boxing is one of the more bizarre sports still with us, a mixture of ballet and battery, blood and big money. The idea of 'a good stoush' has always appealed to Australians, but it wasn't until 1908 that we had our first real taste of the boxing big time. The Canadian heavyweight champion of the world, Tommy Burns, was challenged for the title in Sydney by the American Jack Johnson. Burns refused the fight on the grounds that Johnson was a Negro, but an offer of £6000, win or lose, helped Burns overcome his racial objections and he was soon in training at Rushcutters Bay in Sydney.

Sydney promoter, Hugh D. McIntosh, who had turned a Chinese market garden into an outdoor stadium, sold 30 000 tickets, and hundreds who had paid ten shillings or £1 for seats were turned away. McIntosh billed it as 'the fight of the century' and, considering the century had barely begun, this seemed like a safe prediction. But in truth it was a farce. Johnson stood six inches over the champion and was almost two stone heavier. He knew he was to get only £1500, so it must have given him some satisfaction to humiliate the champion.

Jack London, the novelist, who was in Sydney to cover the fight for an American newspaper, described it as 'an Armenian massacre':

> The fight, if it can be called a fight, was like unto that between a colossus and a toy automaton, and had all the seeming of a playful Ethiopian at loggerheads with a small and futile white man.

Eventually police had to stop the fight. Before Jack London left Australia he called on the white race to provide a champion to 'wipe the smile off Johnson's face.' But Australians wanted better than that, they wanted a home grown champion. And soon they had one.

Les Darcy has often been described as the greatest fighter Australia produced. Gene Tunney called him the greatest middleweight of all time. But he was more than a boxer. He was this country's first real martyr of the twentieth century.

Darcy was born in East Maitland,

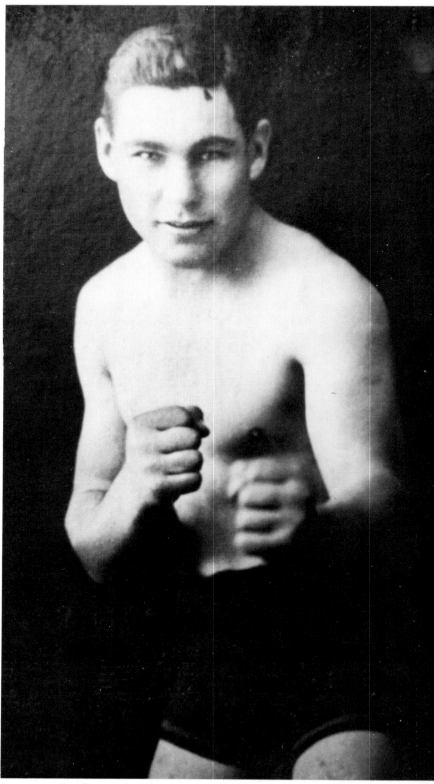

THE CHAMP *Les Darcy . . . the man many people believe should have been boxing champion of the world. A product of the tough mining district of Maitland, Les Darcy was little more than a boy when he died tragically in the US. Darcy beat all comers, but on the eve of the conscription referendum in 1917, he slipped out of the country. Controversy raged, but before the issue was resolved, Australia's finest boxer was dead.*

New South Wales, in 1895, the second of eleven children. His parents were poor and he helped support the family, working as a blacksmith. By 1914 his spare-time boxing career had developed so quickly that his first fight in Sydney was the biggest event since the Burns-Johnson fight. He fought Fritz Holland, one of America's most skilled boxers, and when he lost after a controversial points decision Darcy's followers tried to burn the stadium down.

Darcy went on to beat all comers but he had one tragic flaw in his timing: the time he chose to be champion. Just when he was ready to take on the world, it was falling apart. Australia was at war and as Darcy fought and made money with gloves on, some of his critics were asking what a strapping young man like Les was doing at home when many young men were laying down their lives for practically nothing at Gallipoli and the Somme.

From then on the Darcy story has been clouded with emotion and mystery. He became a hero to many, particularly the Roman Catholic community, while others branded him a shirker and a coward. It must be remembered that the whole nation was split on the issue of conscription, and two referendums would barely resolve the argument.

'AN ARMENIAN MASSACRE' *Jack London's description of the World Heavyweight title fight between Burns and Johnson in Sydney, 1908. Johnson won easily. The temporary stadium at Rushcutter's Bay was eventually covered and became the Sydney Stadium.*

Darcy was on the verge of greatness and some thought he should be allowed to 'have a crack at a real title'. He had beaten anyone they could send to Sydney but he knew the real champions were overseas.

THE END *Amongst the crowd who watched Darcy's funeral were many who'd criticised his refusal to volunteer for military service.*

According to Darcy's defenders he had 'tried to do the right thing by his country'. He had tried to enlist, but his mother had refused on the grounds that he was still a minor. Whatever the truth, in the midst of bitter argument about Darcy's motives, he made a rash decision. On the eve of his twenty-first birthday, and in defiance of the War Precautions Act which forbade people from leaving the country, he stowed away on a ship for America. The press, particularly the British press, were incensed. Their headlines screamed 'Darcy Bolts', but there were many Australians who cheered him on.

One who will defend Les Darcy until his dying breath is his younger brother Joe, who maintains that Les had become a political football even before he left.

Others were getting passports to go overseas at the time— sportsmen, business people, vaudeville acts, but the government refused Les repeatedly. He offered to go for six months and deposit £1000 here. He would return in six months and enlist. But this was refused.

He became a political football, more or less . . . they offered him a captain's commission to go straight in as a captain in a recruiting campaign to go around the country as 'Les Darcy in uniform' and in this way get the youth to enlist. Now he didn't want this, he didn't want to feel he was being in any way used just as bullet bait, as he said, for the war.

At first, Darcy was greeted enthusiastically by the Americans, and headlines predicted spectacular bouts with huge purses. But soon the doubts crept in. Where were the promised fights? Months passed, until Darcy was even forced to join a vaudeville troupe to make money. There is little doubt strings were pulled to prevent him fighting. The Australian government could not afford to let him become a hero.

Then at last, in late 1917, it seemed that a fight had been arranged. Darcy went into training in the American deep south. There was ex-

cited speculation in the press. But Les Darcy never made it to the ring. Just days before the fight, he was taken to hospital in Memphis, Tennessee, where he died aged only twenty-one.

The rumours of foul play and poisoning still persist, but the death

MEMENTOES OF A HERO *When Les Darcy died, they even wrote songs about him. On the sheet music of one of these musicals 'In Memoriums' lies the gold watch and ingot Darcy's supporters gave him after he defeated the American heavyweight McGoorty.*

certificate stated 'septicaemia' (and pneumonia), thought to have been caused by infected teeth loosened in an earlier bout. Darcy's cortège resembled a state funeral by the time it reached San Francisco. In Australia 100 000 people viewed his embalmed body.

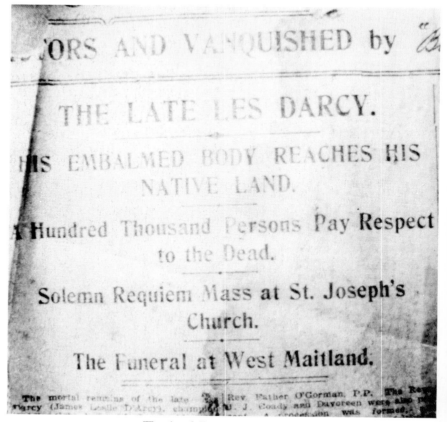

SPEAK NO ILL OF THE DEAD *The rise, fall, and rise again of an Australian sporting hero. When Les Darcy stowed away on a ship bound for America, the press and public were quick to condemn him as a slacker and a coward . . . ready to fight for money but not for his country. But when he died of blood poisoning in America, he returned a hero.*

FISTIC WHIRLWIND *Jimmy Carruthers versus Vic Toweel for the world bantamweight title, in South Africa in 1952. The Australian exploded from his corner to unleash a withering barrage* *of punches which caught the defender literally off guard. Toweel crumples under a Carruthers uppercut halfway through the first round.*

In many ways, Darcy's dilemma parallels that of Cassius Clay so much later: whether to choose his own destiny or run with the mob to fight a distant war. Like Clay, Darcy decided to be his own man and like Clay he was left with an unofficial title. After Darcy's tragic death, it was nearly half a century before Australia had a boxer who could claim to be the undisputed champion of the world.

Jimmy Carruthers was the first Australian boxer to win a world title this century. In the fight that won him the crown, he threw 147 punches in 139 seconds for one of the fastest knock-outs in boxing history.

Like thousands of boys in the thirties, Carruthers started boxing in the Police Boys' Clubs. By 1946, young Jimmy was New South Wales Amateur Bantamweight Champion, and two years later he won the Australian title. Jimmy was going right to the top, but he would go right down again too.

In the amazing world title knockout of 1952, South Africa's Vic

CARRUTHER'S OPPONENT TAKES A TUMBLE *Carruthers stands in centre ring watching his opponent crash through the ropes and out of the fight. Toweel had taken one swing, which missed. Carruthers landed 147 punches in the 139 seconds the bout lasted.*

NOT A MARK ON HIM *After his victory over Toweel, Carruthers' smiling face looks far from the image of a professional fighter.*

HAIL THE CONQUERING HERO *Jimmy Carruthers waves the hands that pummelled South African titleholder Vic Toweel into submission within the space of a single round.*

Toweel responded to the Australian's 147 blows with just one punch, and it missed. In one of the great Australian understatements, Carruthers said: 'I visited him in hospital later and tried to mag with him, but he was a bit browned off with me.'

Carruthers went on to defend his title, including an exotic bout fought barefoot in heavy rain in Thailand. Then he retired and put his money into a pub. It was a financial flop, and ten years after his big fight Carruthers tried to make a comeback. He put in some creditable performances, but never regained any of his former championships.

Jimmy Carruthers is a tough character and he bounced back again, this time to share his 'secret of success'. Natural foods had served him well in the good days; today, Jimmy Carruthers' vegetable juices and health sandwich counter opposite Hyde Park is a landmark in Sydney.

CELEBRITY BARMAN *After his retirement from the ring, World Champion bantamweight champion Jimmy Carruthers bought a pub on Sydney's waterfront and pulled beers for the admiring regulars. A few years later, he attempted an unsuccessful comeback.*

Cycling

In 1928 more than one and a half million readers of a French magazine voted a young Australian cyclist, Hubert Opperman, twenty-four, as the most popular sportsman in Europe. They loved his endurance, his loyalty and his eternal smile, although Australians at home joked that he had to smile because he didn't know what the French were saying.

On endless back tracks around Australia, 'Oppy' trained for the thousand-mile (about 1600 kilometres) cycling championships he won in Europe. His greatest victory was the Paris-Brest-Paris marathon in 1931. Oppy kept himself awake on the 726-mile (1168-kilometre) non-stop race by slapping his face and singing. In sight of the finishing line, he pedalled past the field leaders and won by a length.

The name Opperman is synonymous with Malvern Star, a bike Oppy found in a one-man Melbourne cycle shop. The young man behind Malvern Star was Bruce Small. They soon formed a partnership and became lifelong friends.

PEDAL POWER *The young man in the woollen jersey broadcasting for Melbourne radio station 3LO was at the time (the 1920s) perhaps the best known Australian outside his own country. His name was Hubert Opperman, and he was a competition cyclist. Opperman went on to become a Minister in the Menzies Government, but back in the 1920s true stardom was 'going over the wireless'.*

MALVERN STAR FOREVER *Australia's most famous cycle promoted by Australia's most famous cyclist. A youthful Hubert Opperman awaits the silver trophy about to be presented by Joe Lyons (far left), soon to become the nation's Prime Minister.*

THE RECORD BREAKER *Part of the Opperman legend was built on a seemingly endless series of long-distance record-breaking rides across Australia. It was a lonely and back-breaking way to make a name for yourself, but the rewards of money, publicity and fame made it all worthwhile for the young Oppy.*

But that was only one of Bruce Small's business coups. Even in retirement, Sir Bruce Small was making millions, buying land on the south coast of Queensland to build Australia's richest playground, the Gold Coast. If Small and Opperman had anything in common it was energy. Sir Bruce told us:

Once from Perth to Sydney, I found (Opperman) so exhausted I told him to have four hours rest. Then I tricked him. I put the coffee on and timed him for ten minutes, then woke him. He thought he'd lost four hours, and he rode away as if he was just starting fresh in a sprint race.

Opperman's self-discipline served him well when he retired from competitive cycling. In 1949, he entered federal politics and served as a cabinet minister. Sir Hubert Opperman was later appointed Australian High

THE HERO AND HIS MENTOR *Hubert Opperman, the smiling cyclist, was a hero to most Australians and half the world for twenty years. The man behind the Opperman fame was businessman Bruce Small (right, with glasses), who through his Malvern Star bicycle company, made himself a fortune while making Oppy a legend.*

Commissioner to Malta, where he served until his retirement in 1972.

Another of Australia's most famous cyclists, Russell Mockridge, proved bike-racers and runners should share the same training techniques. It did not really matter whether your feet were on the ground or pedals, as long as they kept on turning. Mockridge rode Australian bike circuits in the fifties, in the days when thousands of spectators turned out to watch cycling championships in Australia. Before a big race Mockridge used to go down to the beach at Portsea, near Melbourne, where he joined athletic coach Percy Cerutty's merciless sandhill sprints. Cerutty's spartan sandhill runs helped Mockridge win a gold medal at the 1952 Helsinki Olympics. Soon after, Mockridge was killed in a collision with a bus during a bike race.

LEGS OF STEEL *Hubert Opperman ('Oppy') powering his way to yet another long distance cycling record across Australia. Opperman went on to become a Cabinet Minister under Menzies.*

PEDALS AND POLITICS *As a young Australian cyclist Opperman swept all before him, establishing himself as a sporting superstar. Opperman eventually went into politics. His last official post was as High Commissioner to Malta.*

RUSSELL MOCKRIDGE *Smiling shyly through his spectacles, the young Australian cyclist whose incredible strength and stamina helped him win a gold medal at the 1952 Olympics. Soon after he was killed during a road race.*

Running

Not long before he died, Mockridge ran up Percy Cerutty's so-called 'killer sand dune' and established a time that would never be beaten by the world's finest athletes. It was on this torturous, almost vertical sandhill in the Portsea dunes that Cerutty developed his intense physical and psychological conditioning of athletes like John Landy and Herb Elliott. Cerutty's sandhills helped cut more than twelve seconds off Landy's time for a mile (about 1.6 kilometres). Landy broke the four-minute mile forty-six days after England's Roger Bannister in 1954.

Australians also remember John Landy for another incident, which reveals his personality as much as it demonstrates his track performance.

DEVASTATING DUO *Herb Elliott (right) and his new coach, Percy Cerutty. Elliott was to smash world records and earn a gold medal in the 1500 metre race in the 1960 Olympics.*

THE FAMOUS FLAME *Sixteen-year-old Australian runner Ron Clarke bore the Olympic Flame into the Melbourne Stadium for the opening ceremony of the 1956 Olympic Games.*

ELEGANT ENIGMA *University student John Landy could run the mile faster than any of his contemporaries, but found it difficult to win races against top international competition.*

GLORIOUS RELIEF *Australian runner Herb Elliott one stride past the finishing line after winning the gold medal for the 1500 metres at the Rome Olympics in 1960. A lifetime of effort and sacrifice culminates in a single moment of total relief.*

THE WONDER MILER *Stylish runner Herb Elliott held a handful of world records, but to Australians it was his sub-four minute miles that made him special. Elliott broke his own world 1500 metre time to win the gold medal at the 1960 Olympics.*

Before a crowd of 22 000 at Melbourne's Olympic Stadium in 1956, Landy was running behind team mate Ron Clarke, when Clarke fell and was spiked by Landy's shoe. Already further down the track, Landy turned back. When Clarke convinced him to keep running, Landy was sixty yards (about fifty-five metres) behind the field. He started off again and, in one of the most spectacular feats in athletic history, he ran to the lead and won the Australian Mile Championship. Clarke got up and ran in fifth.

At Rome in 1960, it was Herb Elliott's turn to put Cerutty's sandhill training into practice. As Elliott started to run in the 1500 metres event, the eccentric old coach, then in his sixties, jumped the barrier and ran on to the arena, waving a yellow cloth to spur Elliott forward. The Italian police had to forcibly remove the coach.

Elliott won the gold medal eighteen metres ahead of his nearest contender. His time of 3 minutes 35.6 seconds remained the world record for seven years. Elliott later described his victory:

I planned in the race to go from the half-mile mark. I remember getting there and some mad bloody Frenchman had got out in front, and he set almost a world record pace for 800 metres.

I recall thinking, 'I'm buggered'. I then had the split-second decision: will I stick to my plan or take the rest of the race as it comes? I stuck to my plan. It was probably one of the most courageous decisions I have made in my life. It wasn't easy.

I remember the fear once I actually hit the front. If some guy passed me I was gone. I can remember very well the absolute relief when I got to the finishing line. There is a photograph of me like an animal ready to pounce, all aggressive and mean and attacking. Probably that is just the big sigh I was letting out at the end.

In the next two weeks, Elliott broke the four-minute mile three times.

Then, only a month after the Olympics, he announced his retirement from competitive running and moved with his wife and child to England to study science at Cambridge.

A CLOUD OF SAIL *In 1932, these eighteen-foot sailing skiffs racing on Sydney Harbour were the fastest things afloat. Nowadays, a modern eighteen-footer would be right around the course before these old skiffs had reached the first rounding mark.*

Sailing

The America's Cup seems such an impossible prize to capture that some Australians wonder if it's even worth our while trying. One imagines the entire New York Yacht Club might commit collective suicide if the Cup was finally taken from them after 130 years. Americans have done almost everything short of piracy to keep the old, dilapidated mug which did not belong to them in the first place.

It was originally called the Hundred Guineas Cup, and its contenders sailed in England off the Isle of Wight. When the US schooner *America* won the Cup in 1851, the crew handed it over to the New York Yacht Club. Its name was changed and the race rules revised unashamedly in America's favour. It was those rules that stopped Australia's first challenge for the America's Cup in 1887 by Walter Reeks, a Sydney businessman. Reeks was told he would have to sail his yacht to America before he could qualify to race. So Australia's first challenge fizzled out. That left the racing to Canadian and British sailors, including the famous English tea baron, Sir Thomas Lipton. He spent £6 000 000 in five attempts, but never succeeded in winning the Cup back for England.

AND THERE THEY GO *The majestic massed fleet of yachts surging towards the Heads at the start of the Sydney-to-Hobart Yacht Race. This sailing sight has become a regular holiday jaunt for sightseers on Boxing Day.*

THE FIRST SYDNEY TO HOBART RACE *In 1945, a motley collection of sailing boats started the first 650-mile rush from Sydney to Hobart. Some were trapped in storms for days, and the race was won by the smallest boat in the fleet.*

Australia, meanwhile, was breeding generations of tough sailors aboard the legendary eighteen-footers. First built near the turn of the century by Charles Messenger for the Sydney retailer Mark Foy, they carried so many crew they were called 'troop ships'. A favourite trick when the wind dropped was to unload half the crew on the nearest buoy to lighten the boat for the final run home.

At the end of the Second World War some bright spark had an idea of a yacht race from Sydney to Hobart. At first it seemed a bit ambitious, but the 1050-kilometre ocean classic soon became an institution, eventually attracting even the Americans to the other side of the world. One of the men who owned a Sydney-Hobart yacht was Sir Frank Packer, a Sydney newspaper buccaneer who knew a thing or two about cut-throat competition. He wanted a new boat for harbour racing, but by the time he'd commissioned Alan Payne to design a

yacht he'd changed his mind and decided to 'go the whole hog and have a crack at the America's Cup'.

It was now seventy years since the Americans had sent Walter Reeks and his crew packing, but by 1962 Australia was ready to challenge the invincible Americans again. Public excitement, nudged along considerably by Sir Frank's newspaper, the *Telegraph*, was intense when the twelve-metre yacht *Gretel*, named after Lady Packer, was launched. She was shipped off to America and, with Jock Sturrock at the helm, promptly lost her first race to America's *Weatherly*. While *Gretel* had fared much better than the British yacht *Sceptre* had done in the previous challenge, it seemed that we were going to get a nice pat on the head for trying, and be sent home empty-handed. But the second race was to provide one of the most exciting moments in the history of Australian sport. What happened that day would help explain why twenty years later Australians would still be

HAVE A GO *Walter Reeks, the yachtsman who tried to mount the first Australian challenge for the America's Cup.*

plotting, still arguing, still spending millions, in their quest for 'the Cup'. Jock Sturrock tells the story:

It was the second race where it blew up to twenty-five knots and *Gretel* sort of came into her own in those conditions. It was a thrilling race. We were eight seconds behind after racing for eight miles, and then our crew did an excellent job. They set their spinnaker faster than what the crew on *Weatherly* did, and just as the spinnaker set, we managed to catch a wave which carried us past. As *Weatherly* behind tried to sort of luff up to do the same thing to us, to take our wind, her spinnaker pole bent and that made it very difficult for her to catch us for the rest of the race.

It was just one wave—and the spinnaker set and the boat just seemed to fit into that particular wave, and away she went. She kept on the wave for maybe two or three hundred yards which was enough to drop us off about two hundred yards ahead of *Weatherly.*

In fact, *Gretel* won no more races but it was enough to give the Australians a taste for victory. Next time it was Australia's *Dame Pattie,* defeated 4-0 by the Americans in 1967. By 1970, Sir Frank took *Gretel II* to Newport for what was the most controversial race in the Cup's history.

At the start of the second race the American *Intrepid* cut across in front of *Gretel* and the two boats collided. Consequently, the Australians were left about 90 metres behind at the start. *Gretel* caught up on the last leg, winning by just sixty-seven seconds. Then *Intrepid* lodged a protest claiming that *Gretel* had caused the collision. The New York Yacht Club

THE CHALLENGER *Australia's first twelve-metre yacht — and our first challenger for the America's Cup — slips gently into the water outside the yard in which she was built. Later to be christened* Gretel, *the yacht would win one race of the 1962 series and lose the next by the close margin of 26 seconds.*

declared *Intrepid* the winner and *Gretel* lost the race, on a protest over a starting incident which had put her a hundred metres behind!

Sir Frank Packer can take the credit for launching Australia as the toughest modern competitor for the America's Cup. Since his time, *Southern Cross* and *Australia* have tried and failed and, like Sir Frank, their owner, Alan Bond, has poured millions of dollars into his attempts to capture the 'auld mug', as the British used to call it.

A challenge for the America's Cup requires almost unlimited financial backing. As Alan Payne, designer of the *Gretel* challengers, says:

In the two times I tried to win the America's Cup for Sir Frank, he never once asked me what anything would cost. I think that's a wonderful quality in an America's Cup sponsor.

MONEY NO OBJECT *An extremely rare photograph of Sydney media baron Sir Frank Packer actually giving away money. The coins were to be placed under the mast of his America's Cup challenger* Gretel *— a traditional seafaring observance intended to bring the new yacht good luck.*

SHEETS EASED *After a testing workout off Sydney Heads,* Gretel *slips back into the Harbour to pick up her mooring and await shipment to Newport, Rhode Island, for the 1962 America's Cup series.*

WE'VE DONE IT! *The magic moment during the second race of the 1962 America's Cup challenge when* Gretel *caught a wave and surged past the American defender* Weatherly *to record our first win in the event.*

Cricket

It is a sight unique to Australia—the vision of a man in shorts, towelling hat and thongs, lugging his Esky of beer and leading his friends or family to the cricket.

We played our first official game of cricket back in 1826, a match between the Military Club and the Australian Club on the Turnpike cow paddock, which later became the Sydney Domain. Those early matches on the cow paddock soon became an institution in the new colony. A respectable picket boundary fence was erected and games were played on a semi-regular basis.

The original habitués of the 'hill' were not so regular. Wagers were placed at every turn, and there are reports of bets laid in livestock, grain, rum and even lumber. Unconventional crowds notwithstanding, the game continued at the Outer Domain, the cradle of Australian cricket, until the 1850s when someone burnt the boundary fence down. It seems that with the colony just

'AVA GO, YA MUG! *The classic Sydneysider's view of Test Cricket—as seen from over the top of a cold tinnie being consumed amongst convivial company on the 'Hill'.*

SLOW RIGHT ARM, AROUND THE WICKET ... *A match between Victoria and James Lillywhite's British Eleven played at Richmond Paddock in 1876. The first test match between England and Australia was played here a year later, and the Paddock soon became the Melbourne Cricket Ground.*

two generations old, some people still thought cows more important than cricket. They quickly became the minority.

Just thirty years later we were making our mark in international cricket, beating the English at their own game and on their home grounds. To rub salt into the wound, a death notice was published in the *Sporting Times* of London:

In affectionate memory of English Cricket which died at The Oval, 29th August, 1882. Deeply lamented by a large circle of sorrowing friends and acquaintances. R.I.P.

N.B. The body will be cremated and the ashes taken to Australia. In Sydney the next year, an urn containing the ashes of a burned cricket stump was handed over to a victorious English team. The 'Ashes' now stay permanently in the Members' Pavilion at Lord's and the word has come to mean the ultimate prize in cricket: victory, in England versus Australia Test matches.

In Affectionate Remembrance
OF
ENGLISH CRICKET,
WHICH DIED AT THE OVAL
ON
29th AUGUST, 1882,
Deeply lamented by a large circle of sorrowing friends and acquaintances.

R.I.P.

N.B.—The body will be cremated and the ashes taken to Australia.

ORIGIN OF THE ASHES *The death notice for English Cricket placed in the London* Sporting Times *after a celebrated MCC defeat. The following year, a small urn containing the ashes of a stump was presented to the victorious English team.*

WOT? NO HELMETS? *The 1905 Australian test side felt safe enough practising in the most meagre protective equipment. The demon pace attack of Thompson and Lillee was fifty years off. Still, they looked graceful then . . .*

Since the Ashes began no event in the history of cricket has been as controversial as the English plan to use 'bodyline' bowling to 'get Bradman', the Australian wonder batsman of the 1930s. The principle 'bodyline' worked on was simple: outright fear. At the Third Test in Adelaide in 1933, the English bowlers Bill Voce and Harold Larwood bombarded the Australian batsmen with short-pitched deliveries down the leg side. The close infield was lined with men in catching positions. Playing the ball meant the risk of being caught. *Not* playing the ball meant the even greater risk of being hit.

The Australian captain, Bill Woodfull, was struck by a speeding ball near his heart. Then Bert Oldfield landed one on the temple. When the English team offered sympathy, Woodfull made his famous comment: 'There are two teams out there on the oval. One is playing cricket, the other is not. This game is too good to be spoilt. It is time some people got out of it.'

As furious telegrams flew between the cricket officials in Australia and London, bodyline was revolution-

ising Australian batting. The batsmen were padding their bodies against the onslaught, and traditional footwork was replaced by evasive ducking and swaying. Australia lost the Ashes that year, but bounced back in the next series under Bradman's brilliant leadership. In fact, since Test matches between the two senior cricketing nations began in 1877, Australia still retains a comfortable margin of wins over their traditional enemy, the MCC.

Much of the animosity between the two nations can be traced to

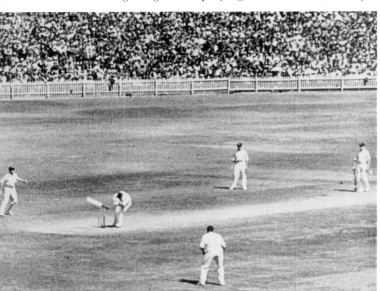

FELLED *Australian wicket-keeper W. A. Oldfield on the receiving end of a Larwood bumper bowled during the Adelaide Test of the 1932-33 series. Oldfield had to be supported off the field and was unable to resume his innings.*

VENOMOUS ACTION *The classic fast bowling delivery stride of Harold Larwood, spearhead of the English attack during the notorious series of 1932-33.*

GENTLEMAN BILL *Bill Woodfull, Australian Test cricket captain during the savage 'bodyline' series.*

subtle differences in their approach to the game. Until the rise of Kerry Packer's 'World Series Cricket' there was no real professionalism in Australian cricket. Good players emerged from Saturday club competition and gradually worked their way through the state side until they were chosen for Australia.

During the same period, England always had two kinds of cricketers: 'gentlemen' and 'players'. The gentlemen were the amateurs, usually selected from the strong university sides of Oxford and Cambridge. The players were the professionals: talented working class lads who turned their ability to play the game well into their meal-ticket. The class distinctions were maintained until well after the Second World War. Although playing in the same side, gentlemen and players entered and left the field through separate gates, and, although a player might be the finest cricketer in the side, the captain of England was *always* a gentleman. These relics of aristocratic snobbery incensed the Australians, and helped fuel the special animosity which has coloured England versus Australia matches.

MOST HATED PLAYER *A rare portrait of MCC Test captain Douglas Jardine. He masterminded the infamous 'bodyline' attack of the 1932-33 season.*

NEVER BEFORE *The dramatic last moment of a memorable Test match. This splendid run-out created the first-ever tie in Test Cricket history. The match was the First Test in the West Indies v. Australia series of 1960-61. The scoreboard at the Brisbane Cricket Ground showed the visitors ahead by one run, but the official score was a tie.*

OWZAT? *Amiss, bowled Greg Chappell, during the Centenary Test at the MCG, 1977. Australia won the match by exactly the same margin as they had won the first Test Match a century before.*

POETRY OFF THE FRONT FOOT *Australian captain Greg Chappell completing a majestic straight drive during a recent England v. Australia Test match at the MCG.*

Yet strangely, the most exciting cricket of the international calendar has always been that played when Australia and the West Indies take the field. These Test matches are played in exceptionally good spirit, and have yielded both the most amusing and heart-stopping moments in recent cricket history.

During the legendary West Indies tour of Australia in 1960-61, the electric atmosphere of the series generated two moments unique in the long saga of the 'flanelled fools'.

The first Test in Brisbane ended in a dramatic draw, the only such result in Test history. The second encounter in Melbourne drew more than 90 000 people to the MCG in a single day, still the largest crowd ever to attend a cricket match.

In 1977, exactly a hundred years after the very first Test match played between England and Australia, a special commemorative Test was played in Melbourne between the two modern descendants of those first sides. In a hair-raising finish, which could not have been stage-managed better, Australia won in the dying moments of the game by just forty-five runs. The result was an exact repeat of the outcome when the same match had been played a century before — amazing.

SWORN ENEMIES *Australian batsman Ian Chappell forces England spin bowler Derek Underwood away on the leg side during the Second Test, January 1980. Nothing quite matches the 'spirit' in which England v. Australia series are played.*

Football

Australian Rules, according to the experts, evolved from Gaelic football, influenced by the large Irish population in Victoria last century. The game is uniquely Australian, with its own cult following in all states except New South Wales and Queensland. Like all cults, it has bred 'super-heroes', players such as the high-leaping Roy Cazaly. It is said that in wartime Australian infantrymen from Melbourne shouted: 'Up there, Cazaly' as they began bayonet charges.

Today's super-hero is coach Ron Barassi, who has contributed more to the game than anybody. Barassi even took an Australian Rules team to Ireland to beat the Irish at gaelic football. But there is no Irish influence in Australian Rules today. As Barassi said:

ANCIENT RUCKMANSHIP *A contemporary engraving showing the Melbourne versus Carlton match of 1876, an epic colonial struggle in the pre-history of Australian Rules.*

FOOTY FEVER *A special Melbourne tram service in 1908 which took footy-mad fans to the Essendon v. South Melbourne clash of 20 June. The one woman on board peeps coyly out from behind a stanchion.*

UP THERE, CAZALY! *The legendary Australian Rules footballer Roy Cazaly, whose high marking gave rise to such a well-known catchcry that troops even shouted it as they went 'over the top' during the Second World War.*

You call it Australian Rules. Who are the Australians? Think of all the star names ... Kekovitch, Schimmelbusch, Barassi, Jesaulenko, Ditterich ... take out all the foreigners, and what are you left with? The donkeys—that's from Sam Kekovitch.

It is a measure of the sporting distance between Melbourne and Sydney that Australian Rules is unfamiliar to most people living north of the Victoria-New South Wales border. There you say 'Eadie' or 'Cronin', and you're speaking the football language of New South Wales: Rugby League.

Rugby was one code until, in 1907, a player called Alec Burdon broke his arm and had to pay his own medical expenses. That led a team of players to break away and professional Rugby League was born. In those days, footballers like Dally 'the Boot' Messenger were 'brought over' from Union for £150. Today, rugby union players are wooed with 'confidential' payments and gifts totalling tens of thousands of dollars.

After the Second World War, thousands of migrants arriving from Europe introduced Australian cities

PLAY ON *The umpire trails behind play in the first VFL Grand Final ever filmed — the clash between Carlton and South Melbourne in 1909.*

to soccer, a game previously played mostly in the coalfields of New South Wales. By the mid-seventies, Australia had made respectable attempts at gaining Olympic and

World Cup honours. Our emergence as a soccer nation is reflected in the fact that in the 1980s more Australian children will play soccer than any other football code.

KANGAROO HOP *The sight that all Australian Rugby League fans relish — Australia's national side, the Kangaroos, scoring a try against their arch-rivals the British Lions.*

THE GLADIATORS *Rival Rugby League captains Norm Provan (left) and Arthur Summons leave the field after the 1963 Grand Final. The match was played at the Sydney Cricket Ground in what were described as 'far from ideal conditions'.*

Motor sport

As soon as cars began travelling as fast as race horses it was pretty clear that they could be used for some sort of sport. It's believed that the first actual motor race was held at the Maribyrnong gymkhana in Victoria in 1903.

But the sight of cars thundering along at 20 miles per hour (about 32 kilometres per hour) was not exactly soul stirring. Before long a host of other events became popular—hill climbs, rallies, inter-city record breaking attempts and one particular event which was to eventually become an Australian mania, the reliability trial.

In 1905 the Dunlop Rubber Company conducted two events which were in fact the nation's first reliability events. Both of them involved routes between Sydney and Melbourne. In those days reliability was fairly easily defined—a reliable car was the one that finished. The problem with those first rallies was that even though most of the field was eliminated half a dozen of the vehicles kept going. Even when the course was lengthened considerably some of the infernal mechanical beasts refused to be cowed. So, by the mutual consent of five surviving drivers the Dunlop Cup was inscribed with the performance of all the cars that finished. The *Daily Telegraph* in Sydney was moved to comment:

> The keen interest taken in the motor contest is something more than a sporting interest. It is the recognition that in the development of the motor lies the solution of many transit problems of the future, and among these the problems of our great dry spaces West and South West. The fascinations of speed are already irresistible once they have been tasted, but what is really wanted for outback conditions is a car that will be modestly capable of twenty miles per hour with engine and tyres warranted to withstand the roughest bush tracks.

Australia is often credited with the invention of motor-cycle speedway racing and so far no one seems to have contested the claim. According to legend a group of young blades from the Maitland district in NSW were bored with the prospect of hacking around the rough country roads, so one day they took their machines on to the local trotting track. One thing led to another, and in 1925 J. S. Hoskins organised the first official races at the Maitland Agricultural Show. Within a few years the sport had developed from a national to an international sport

VICTOR'S RETURN *Unvanquished by the countryside, dust, bald tyres or sunstroke, our intrepid duo, seen setting off from Sydney on page 19, flash through the finish line of the 1905 Dunlop Rally. The mechanic seems to have managed to keep the same cigarette going for the whole reliability trial!*

climaxed by the famous test matches between England and Australia at Wembley Stadium.

The twenties also saw a boom in the sport of motor racing and a thrill seeking public demanded more and more excitement from the competitors. At one stage a favourite contest was between a motor car and an aeroplane which, in the twenties, were capable of about the same speed. It must have been hair raising stuff, because in the earlier days a racing car wasn't much more than the biggest motor a driver could find, bolted to the strongest chassis.

A favourite machine was the Brooklands Riley and one of these cars, driven by Billy Thompson, won Australia's first grand prix, a 200-mile (about 320-kilometre) handicap event.

The most popular New South Wales track was at Penrith outside Sydney, and it was the site of many accidents. Three spectators in the crowd were killed during a race in 1938. The car, a MacKellar Special, was hardly damaged. Its co-driver, Warren Brown, remembers the crash:

We had come around the corner and the car went into a slide and it wouldn't come out, just stopped in the slide right up the straight and the crowd was very much thicker there. Everything happened so quickly. We didn't realise what happened until the car

THE QUIET MASTER *Jack Brabham won world racing championships both as a driver and designer. While the other Grand Prix stars led flamboyant and dangerous lives, Brabham stayed cool, calm — and alive.*

pulled up right on the safety fence. By that time a tremendous number of people had been injured and there were people lying all over the place, including us.

I've never stopped thinking about it. You would like to forget it but human nature won't let you forget certain incidents in your life, especially a thing like this.

AND THE BIG CARS FLY *In the thirties, the Australian racing championships were held on Phillip Island, near Melbourne, and the cars were so big and powerful they needed a driver and a mechanic to keep them on the track.*

THE MAN WITH A BANG *'Gelignite' Jack Murray, who won the 1954 Redex Trial in his beloved 'Grey Ghost', a Ford Mercury. Murray earned the nickname from his habit of punctuating the outback silence with the odd stick of gelignite.*

UNHAPPY STARTER *Filling in for the official starter, radio star Jack Davey flags away the famous 'Grey Ghost' of Jack Murray, the best known of all the Redex Reliability Trial contestants. Davey, who had driven in earlier trials, was too ill to compete.*

OFF AND RUNNING *A Peugot driven by the New Zealand team, sets off from the Sydney Showground on the 1954 Redex Trial. These tests of reliability were restricted to production model cars, and a victory assured that 'marque' of a sudden boost in sales.*

But no matter how many lives it claimed, Australians were hooked on the quest for more speed. In 1964, we played host to the world's most celebrated land-speed record attempt. Englishman Donald Campbell, in his futuristic *Bluebird*, flashed across the salt flats of South Australia's Lake Eyre, setting an incredible new world record of 403 miles an hour (almost 650 kilometres an hour). The enormous cost and danger of Campbell's exercise was justified by the claim that the technical knowledge gained by his challenge would be used in the design of cars for the general public. But it all seemed a long way from a Sunday afternoon spin with the family. Most Australians were driving compact six-cylinder cars like the Holden and Falcon, and we were more interested in how reliable these cars were than how fast they could go in a straight line.

The Redex Trials, the legendary tests of men and machines over outback roads, were run between 1953 and 1955. Redex itself was a petrol additive, and through the spectacular publicity the trials received, it quickly became the best known petroleum product in the country. The three round-Australia car trials organised by the Redex Company brought whole towns out to line the highways as car after car flashed through the dust or limped into the next checkpoint.

The contests were a typically Australian mixture of shocking roads, rugged conditions, cheery improvisation, all mixed together with a generous helping of larrikinism. But what the Redex Trial did test, and in merciless style, was whether an ordinary family saloon could stand up to the punishment of 10 000 terrible miles (about 16 000 kilometres).

The acknowledged master of those early reliability trials was Jack Murray, affectionately known as 'Gelignite' Jack because of his quaint habit of punctuating the outback silence with the odd stick of explosive. Murray won the 1954 Redex Trial, and twenty-five years later, he is still an inexhaustible source of great Redex yarns:

We came over the top of a hill about a hundred miles out of Alice, and there's this Volkswagen sitting in the sand. They had hit a big 'roo, an old bloke about twenty years old. So they said, 'Will you take a picture of it?' They propped the 'roo up and one of them took his coat off. I said, 'Why don't you put it on the 'roo because they're easy to dress up.'

I got the box Brownie and I'm taking the picture but the 'roo was only stunned. The 'roo leapt about twenty feet, just missed me and shot off.

I roared out laughing and this fellow said, 'What are you laughing at? That coat's got £200 of mine in it, and me bloody licence!'

ANYONE SEEN THE ROAD? *A competitor in the 1954 Redex Trial struggles through a typically muddy stretch of the course between Townsville and Cloncurry.*

GO NORTH, YOUNG MAN *The first car to cross into the Tropics in the 1954 Redex Trial was the intrepid Vanguard Spacemaster of Eric Nelson and Brian Simpson.*

6

LEADERS

GRIM IRONY *When Gough Whitlam appointed Sir John Kerr as his Governor-General in 1974, he could have had no idea the appointment would backfire so disastrously. Within a matter of months Kerr had sacked Whitlam, who in a bitter speech on the steps of Parliament House in Canberra, said the new Prime Minister, Malcolm Fraser, would be remembered in history as 'Kerr's Cur'.*

The delicate balance of power

Australia has two kinds of leaders: those elected by the people and those given to us by decree of the Crown. And disputes between the two are nothing new. From the time we first became a nation our chosen leaders and our appointed ones have been involved in skirmishes, and usually it's the politicians who have lost.

The names Barton, Lang and Whitlam span this century in Australian politics, and there is a common thread in the stories of these men. Each was the victim of an extraordinary political decision taken on high, each was a leader with a tremendous following, and yet each was thwarted by the supreme authority in this country, the vice-regal representative.

Only days before Australia became a nation on 1 January 1901 our first Governor-General, Lord Hopetoun, ignored the obvious and popular choice for Prime Minister and with a vice-regal bungle chose instead a man who could not even muster a handful of men to form a government.

Thirty years later, during the Depression, the Governor of New South Wales, Sir Philip Game, de-manded the resignation of the state's dynamic Premier, Jack Lang, and got it.

In 1975 the Governor-General removed the Prime Minister, Gough Whitlam, from office while his party still held a majority in the Federal Parliament.

Edmund Barton

In 1900 Edmund Barton was the man most Australians wanted, or at least expected, to be the first Prime Minister of the new Commonwealth of Australia. Barton, a protégé of Sir Henry Parkes, was the acknowledged leader of the Federation Movement

EDMUND BARTON *The New South Wales barrister and politician who became Australia's first Prime Minister. Barton resigned through ill-health in 1903 and took up a place on the bench of the newly-created High Court of Australia. He died in 1920.*

FATHER OF FEDERATION *Henry Parkes, the chief advocate of a federated Australia gazes majestically into the future in this 1896 portrait. The first Prime Minister, Edmund Barton, was a protégé of Parkes.*

—almost symbolic of the new spirit of national unity.

The nation's first Governor-General, Lord Hopetoun, a British aristocrat, arrived in Sydney ill from typhoid just two weeks before Federation. It was his task to choose a Prime Minister who, in turn, would choose a government until the first elections could be held. Hopetoun could in fact appoint whoever he liked, but he had been well briefed in England about the political climate in the colonies, and it was expected that he would make the popular choice. But Hopetoun, after consulting the Chief Justice of New South Wales, Sir Frederick Darley, astonished the country by inviting Sir William Lyne, the Premier of New South Wales, to form Australia's first federal government. Lyne had been an arch enemy of the whole idea of Federation. He accepted the commission but was unable to find the necessary ten men to govern with him.

HERE WE ARE IN VENICE *Edmund Barton, in the dark suit in the nearer gondola, with a party who visited Venice in 1902.*

So Australia's history as a nation began with a vice-regal 'bungle'. Hopetoun had to go, feathered cap in hand, to Barton and, on the eve of the birth of modern Australia, Barton secured his government. To help save face for the Governor-General, and generally diminish the embarrassment all round, he included Lyne in his government.

SYDNEY ON THE EVE OF FEDERATION *This drawing by Percy Spence shows the face of Sydney at the turn of the century, a romantic time of fine fashion and horse drawn transport.*

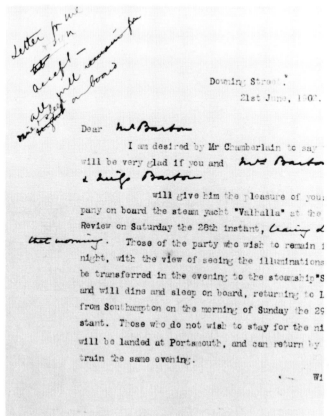

ALL ABOARD *During their visit to Europe in 1902 Edmund Barton and his family were invited aboard the* Valhalla *to watch a Naval Review. Barton scribbled his reply on the invitation.*

John Thomas Lang

J. T. Lang was 'the Big Feller', loved by the working class, hated by the Establishment and a good deal of the press, and even by his Labor colleagues in Canberra.

He was called 'the people's champion' and he earned the title. He would have made the history books for his legislation alone. In the late twenties his government was the first in the world to introduce widows' pensions. He brought in child endowment, reduced the working week from forty-eight to forty-four hours, and improved workers' compensation.

His government was defeated in 1927 but he came back into power two years later to face the task of governing New South Wales for the most difficult period in its history, the Great Depression.

Lang opposed even his own colleagues in the federal Labor Party in their philosophy that the economic burden should be shared equally by the community. In 1930 he introduced an anti-eviction law to help unemployed tenants keep their homes. The Moratorium Act allowed house buyers more time to pay off their mortgages.

By 1931 Lang was embroiled in bitter conflicts with the federal Labor government. He was refusing to pay interest on funds New South Wales had borrowed from Britain, claiming his state needed the money more than those 'bowler hatted bastards' in London. Lang dropped New South Wales' domestic interest rates to three per cent to help people borrowing money. He continually refused federal government demands to cut wages, pensions or social benefits.

The depressed workers all but worshipped their champion. He could be a snarling tub-thumping orator, and they turned out in their thousands to hear him speak at rallies. But the conservatives, and especially the extreme right wing, detested Lang with a vehemence uncharacteristic in Australia.

THE BIG FELLER *Loved by the working class and hated by the establishment, John Lang was disliked by the press and even by his colleagues in Canberra.*

TIGER BY THE TAIL *NSW Premier Jack Lang was often caricatured as a frenzied, irrational madman. He could be a snarling tub-thumping orator.*

In 1932 a certain Captain Francis De Groot, a member of an extreme group called the New Guard, stole Lang's thunder at the opening of the Sydney Harbour Bridge by riding up on his horse and slashing the ceremonial ribbon.

But Lang had greater problems to concern him than this embarrassing incident. By now he had completely polarised the electorate. Sections of the press were calling him the 'mad dog'. Finally the federal government honoured the New South Wales interest debt to London, intending to make Lang repay it. True to character, he refused.

In the meantime, in the tranquil oasis that is Government House, Sir Philip Game, a small, pert and somewhat nervous man, knew that, as the King's representative, he would soon have to intervene. But in his remote sandstone castle he was cut off from the goings-on outside, and, according to his daughter, Rosemary, who was then thirteen, the family employed some extraordinary methods to find out what was happening.

Well, Mr Lang held a rally in the Domain during the period before the dismissal and my mother wanted to go and hear what he was going to say—dress up incognito—but my father really wouldn't allow her. He didn't think it was very wise, and anyway she wouldn't get past the police all round the house. And so the butler went—Mr Turner—and he came back very upset, and very fussed, and said that Mr Lang had had a crowd of 50 000 there, and he had asked the people: 'Do you want to be governed by the people you've elected to represent you, or do you want to be governed by the Governor?' They shouted back: 'We want to be governed by you!' And poor old Turner was very upset at this and came back and reported it to my father.

Nearly half a century after this tense period in Australian politics another vice-regal representative, Sir John Kerr, would be severely criticised for taking and making public the advice of the Chief Justice of the High Court and former Liberal lawyer, Sir

REPAIRING THE RIBBON *After Captain De Groot had slashed the ribbon before Premier Jack Lang had a chance to cut it at the official opening of the Sydney Harbour Bridge in 1932, embarrassed officials hurriedly joined it together again.*

'DADDY MAY HAVE TO TAKE US HOME' *This little girl is Rosemary Game, daughter of the late Sir Philip Game, former Governor of NSW. As such she was privy to some of the secrets of one of the most extraordinary periods of Australian politics. In 1932 Game took the unprecedented step of sacking the Premier of the State, Jack Lang. Rosemary remembered her mother saying 'Daddy may have to take us all home'.*

Garfield Barwick. But in 1932 it seems that Sir Philip Game was not averse to taking a little backroom legal advice. As his daughter recounts:

Mr Lang said that he couldn't pay the interest due to the British bondholders. Of course, that was a terrible thing to do, because it was a debt that he couldn't honour. So my father thought that he should ask a lawyer about this, and he got my brother to drive him to New South Head Road and told him: 'Drop me at the house of this lawyer and go away and come back for me in about an hour. I don't want the car standing outside.' Because, with the crown on it, the people would know whose it was.

If that clandestine meeting had been made public all those years ago it might have created a sensation. But it wasn't, and while the identity of Game's Double Bay lawyer is a secret of history, it seems fairly clear what his advice must have been.

By May 1932 the federal government had introduced new economic measures for the nation. Lang hit back with his own legislation, negating them in New South Wales. Game then made his move, withholding the Royal Assent from the 'illegal' New South Wales Act introduced by Lang. Game demanded an assurance that Lang would not disobey federal law. Lang refused. On 13 May 1932 the Governor called the Premier to his office at Government House and asked for his resignation. To the amazement of Lang's supporters their hero surrendered. Lang said many years later:

What would I have fought—the entire military forces of Australia? Who would I have fought with—the flesh and blood of the men and women of New South Wales, people of peace, order and goodwill? It's always been my unchangeable principle, something I have never changed, and please God I never will, the Labor Movement doesn't need to disobey laws; the Labor Movement has the power when it will to change the law and change the power peacefully, without bloodshed, without murder, without death.

Lang's days as a political leader were over. But 'the Big Feller' would hover in the political wings for the rest of his long life.

At the age of ninety-nine, he was still catching the train to work each day and publishing his own newspaper, the *Century*.

CALM BEFORE THE STORM *Governor of NSW, Sir Philip Game, at the helm of his yacht at the first regatta of the season in 1932. Just a few weeks later, he would sack the Labor Premier in one of the most dramatic events in Australian political history.*

ANOTHER RIBBON *Thirty five years after Captain De Groot, brandishing a sword, had stolen his thunder at the opening of the Sydney Harbour Bridge, Jack Lang cuts another ribbon to open a new nursing home in the Blue Mountains.*

Edward Gough Whitlam

Gough Whitlam was impressed by the irony of the date when he was dismissed by the Governor-General, Sir John Kerr, in 1975. It was 11 November, Remembrance Day, the national day of mourning. His speech, made to a stunned nation from the steps of Parliament House, Canberra, is now famous to some, infamous to others:

> Well may we say 'God save the Queen' because nothing will save the Governor-General. The proclamation which you have just heard read by the Governor-General's official secretary was countersigned 'Malcolm Fraser', who will undoubtedly go down in Australian history from Remembrance Day 1975 as 'Kerr's cur'.

The previous days had been ones of Machiavellian high drama. Just a few hours earlier, Malcolm Fraser had been in one room of Government House—his car parked out of sight around a corner—while the Governor-General, Sir John Kerr, informed the Prime Minister, Mr Whitlam, that his commission had been withdrawn. Minutes later Fraser, was sworn in as caretaker Prime Minister.

It was a remarkable climax to a period of government which had started out so buoyantly. Before the 1972 election, Labor had been in power only sixteen of the seventy-two years since Federation. The Liberals, on the other hand, had been in office for twenty-three straight years, and the government was starting to fall into a state of decay. The Liberal Party had seen a couple of leaders since the retirement of its founder, Sir Robert Menzies, and the crown had finally fallen on the head of the most unlikely pretender, William McMahon.

It was clearly time for a change, and using just this theme, 'It's Time', in a massive media campaign, Gough Whitlam had little trouble pushing his weak opponent aside.

But the new Labor Government quickly ran into difficulties. Fired with a zealous urge to reform, the changes came too thick and too fast for much of the electorate. The shift in emphasis from the private to the

BUOYANT START *Wild enthusiasm greets Edward Gough Whitlam at an election rally in the Opera House. Great hopes for the Labor leadership were soon dashed as the Government began to fall into decay, eroded by inflation, unemployment and scandal.*

public sector caused considerable heartburn. The government's economic measures exacerbated the effects of a general international recession, and the problems of inflation and unemployment became major preoccupations.

The Whitlam Government suffered further from public scandals which resulted in a series of sackings and resignations. The relationship between the Deputy Prime Minister, Jim Cairns, and his assistant, Junie Morosi, caused a furore, and the complex and mysterious series of events which became known as the Loans Affair, led eventually to the demise of the Government.

GOOD FRIENDS *When Junie Morosi worked for Jim Cairns the Deputy Prime Minister it caused a furore. She was employed as an office co-ordinator.*

MOURNING *Gough Whitlam was impressed by the irony of the date when he was dismissed by the Governor-General Sir John Kerr, in 1975. It was Remembrance Day.*

By 1975 the Liberal Opposition had managed to create such a public controversy about the Labor Government's proposals to borrow huge sums of money from untraditional sources in the Middle East, that the conservatives felt confident enough to try to bring the government down. Even though Whitlam had a working majority in the House of Representatives, the Liberals had a slender advantage in the Senate. In September 1975 the Senate blocked the Appropriation Bills, effectively cutting off the money supply to all government departments and authorities.

The rest of what happened is dramatic history which most Australians will never forget. As the nation became bogged down in what seemed to many as an almost tedious Constitutional crisis, Kerr made his sudden and sensational move. Still reeling from the shock of his sacking, Whitlam told a stunned nation that such an event had not happened since the days of King George III. But he had to go no further than the days of Jack Lang for proof that Australia is not so much a democracy but a monarchy, where the ultimate law is the Queen's man.

IT WAS THAT BIG! *Prime Minister Gough Whitlam may, or may not, have been swapping fishing yarns with Chinese leader Chou-en-Lai during his 1973 tour of China. Either way, his audience seems suitably impressed.*

Whitlam asked his supporters to 'maintain the rage', but despite talk of a coup d'état the conservative status quo of Australian politics was soon restored. Once again, the Labor Party gathered its tattered remnants to face the future in its almost traditional role as opposition.

Despite the conservative promises, five years after the most significant single event in Australian politics, inflation, unemployment and industrial unrest were still the major problems. In the long run, little had changed except the names, and the drastically thinned group of Labor men in Parliament House were living testimony to what happens if you rock the political boat just that little bit too much.

ANTI-KERR DEMONSTRATIONS *A stunned nation turned to demonstrating against the sacking of the Prime Minister.*

THE EMPEROR'S NEW CLOTHES *Bruce Petty's classic cartoon comment on the dramatic resolution of the constitutional crisis of November, 1975. Tailor Kerr shows Caretaker Prime Minister Fraser the way to the throne.*

Hughes and Bruce

If Barton and Hopetoun, Lang and Game, Kerr and Whitlam were studies in contrasts, then Hughes and Bruce were the Laurel and Hardy of Australian politics—so different, yet so alike.

William Morris Hughes and Stanley Melbourne Bruce were two prime ministers who showed just how fragile power can be, and just what strange bedfellows politics can make. As 'Billy and Stanley' they could have been in vaudeville, except that they basically couldn't stand each other. Hughes was a tough, rough diamond. Bruce was the sort who wore them in his tie clip—all class, right down to his spats. They spent years fighting each other; sometimes in the same party, sometimes in rival ones. They got each other into power and out of it again. They made one of the most intriguing double acts in politics.

Hughes said to the Australian people just before he died in 1952:

Many of you will remember me. Some of you will know me quite well. You should. I have been in public life a very great while. In fact, I've been there over half a century.

In fact, Hughes was a member of parliament for a total of fifty-eight years. Even at the turn of the century, this wrinkled, gnome-like little man never looked young.

Hughes was born in Wales in 1864 and emigrated to Australia when he was twenty. He tried his hand at dozens of different jobs, from bound-

LONG DISTANCE PARLIAMENTARIAN *William Morris Hughes was in parliament for a total of fifty-eight years. This portrait claims to show him at the time of his first Prime Ministership in 1915.*

UNLIKELY ALLIES *No two Australian political leaders held each other in quite the same mutual contempt as Billy Hughes (left) and S. M. Bruce. This handshake was strictly for the newspaper photographers.*

ary riding to umbrella repairing. In Sydney he became involved in the hurly burly of Labor politics and, as secretary of the wharfies' union, he sat in the New South Wales Parliament.

Hughes used his backroom connections to gain a seat in the first federal government in 1901. By 1915 he was Prime Minister, and his carefully cultivated image as the little 'Aussie battler' and patriotic wartime leader served him well. Author Donald Horne, who wrote a biography of Hughes, said:

> Hughes is seen by some people as a symbol of national unity. He was, I think, probably the greatest symbol of national disunity we had. He was either, at best, a true blue koala bear patriot or, at worst, a very devious unprincipled little character.

Hughes was always like that—a bit of both. He'd been a staunch unionist, yet he beat unions into submission and persecuted socialists. Those of the working class who actively opposed him were sometimes jailed, yet he called himself the working man's friend.

Although his party was against it, Hughes wanted to introduce conscription. He broke away from his own men to fight two unsuccess-

BILLY THE UNDERTAKER *At the height of the conscription debate, Billy Hughes was pictured as the murderer of the Labor Party, content to be the coffinmaker for his old political allies.*

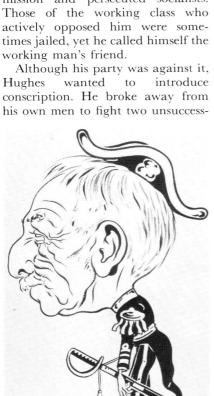

OLD SEA DOG *A 1941 cartoon lampoons Billy Hughes, then Federal Attorney-General and Minister for the Navy.*

THREE INTO ONE STILL GOES *Never a person to do things by halves, if Billy Hughes had to be seen kissing a baby, it might as well be triplets.*

ful referendums on the issue. Each time the alliance of Catholic church and trade unions combined to defeat him. Somehow, Hughes survived the referendum losses, a split in the Labor Party, and endless internal squabbling. Always the campaigner, he used his fierce rhetoric and political cunning to cling to the Prime Minister's job from 1915 to 1923.

But his days as leader had been numbered. While Labor saw him as a traitor, the Establishment believed he was 'dangerously socialist'. In an attempt to placate big business,

Hughes appointed the well-heeled S. M. Bruce his Treasurer. As a political move, it backfired completely. Within a short time Bruce, in harness with the Country Party's Earle Page, was the nation's new leader.

Stanley Melbourne Bruce was everything 'the Little Digger' was not. Aloof and imperious, he cut a smart figure in pin-striped suits and spats. While Hughes had literally dragged himself up from the back streets, Bruce lived in stately luxury. His grand home stood on 500 acres (about 200 hectares) of land in Mel-

bourne. Designed by Walter Burley Griffin and built in 1926 for £26 000, it reflected a lifestyle despised by the working class.

Bruce tumbled into parliament almost by accident. Educated at Cambridge, where he took a 'blue' for rowing, young Stanley quickly made a mark for himself at the London Bar. He served at Gallipoli with the Royal Fusiliers. On his return to Australia to manage the family firm, he represented success, wealth and class—the epitome of the Melbourne Establishment.

READ ME ANOTHER ONE *Quiet evenings at home must have been a rarity for Billy Hughes, who entered politics before the turn of the century and remained there until his death in 1952.*

I THOUGHT YOU HAD THE TICKETS *Former Australian Prime Minister Stanley Bruce and Mrs Bruce (centre) among eminent guests at an Australia Day Dinner at the Savoy Hotel, London.*

KEEP UP THE GOOD WORK LADS *During World War II Stanley Bruce visited Australian units stationed in Britain. Here he is addressing the men of the Australian Forestry Company.*

AUSTRALIA AT WAR *Australian High Commissioner to London, Stanley Bruce, is pictured here chatting with Australian servicemen at an exhibition entitled 'Australia at War' in London in November 1944.*

Victoria's business community drafted young Bruce to stand for the seat of Flinders, and the campaign was organised for him. He won easily, but Bruce had taken so little interest he maintained he wasn't quite sure whether he had gained entry into the Victorian or Federal Parliament. Five years later he was Prime Minister, aged just thirty-nine.

Bruce led, perhaps ruled, Australia for most of the 1920s. In terms of his legislative record he introduced compulsory voting, established the Loans Council (to bargain state-federal finances) and specialised in the economy. In 1927 he moved the seat of the Federal Parliament from Melbourne to Canberra. He cut a smart figure in tails at the opening of the new Parliament House, which he presided over with such notables as the Duke of York and Nellie Melba.

Underlying his suave exterior, however, Bruce could be a tough, even savage, Prime Minister. The trade union movement, with its demands for an eight-hour day, its protests and processions, was growing in militancy. Bruce responded with 'the big stick'. He provoked union leaders and in turn blamed 'the Bolsheviks' for industrial unrest, demanding in his propaganda films that 'the Reds' be kept out of 'white Australia'.

On the eve of the Depression, Bruce tried to gain more power over industrial workers, and then virtually set about dismantling the arbitration system. For his old rival, Billy Hughes, who had been a pioneer of the arbitration idea, it was time for a killing. In 1929, on a motion introduced by Hughes, the Bruce Government was brought down by just one vote.

For Bruce the ensuing election was a personal and political debacle. He could claim the dubious honour of being the only Australian Prime Minister to lose not just an election, but his seat in parliament as well. Perhaps only a man of Bruce's independent means and superior attitude could have survived such a defeat. He was back at his office in Flinders Lane on the following Monday, for the first time in ten years.

He got back into parliament in 1931 but, stripped of his old rank, he was happy to accept the post of Australian Commissioner to London. In the tense diplomatic negotiations before the Second World War, he emerged as one of the Empire's most distinguished ambassadors.

Bruce's friend and diplomatic colleague, Alfred Stirling, says of him: He worked terribly hard before the war trying to avert the disaster, and then trying to ensure that Italy didn't come in, and above all, that Japan didn't come in. He galvanised the Australian War Cabinet into more aircraft production and he was involved in keeping Turkey and Spain neutral as buffers to prevent Germany breaking through into North Africa. Either of them would have been a terrible disaster and Bruce, almost more than anybody in London, saw the need for keeping Spain and Turkey neutral, and worked very hard at it.

After Billy Hughes had toppled

RALLY ROUND THE FLAG *Billy Hughes, in full rhetoric at a recruiting rally in 1941. The crowd does not appear to be fired with enthusiasm to enlist.*

Bruce from the leadership, his own days as leader were also over. In the same year as Bruce took the London job, Hughes suffered a great personal tragedy. His private life had revolved around his daughter, Helen. But in 1931, soon after she turned twenty-one, she died following an operation. Hughes was greatly affected by the loss, but the ingrained fire and ambition of the born politician never died. He held a number of portfolios; he served in the Menzies War Cabinet; he even came within a whisker of snatching back the leadership. He was the idol of the fighting man, and every Anzac Day his failures and excesses

PATER BILLY *Billy Hughes and his daughter, Helen (who died tragically at the age of twenty-one) pictured together in the garden of their Sydney home.*

BILLY AND ROSEMARY *Forever the idol of the fighting man, Billy Hughes, 'The Little Digger', could always count on nostalgic affection on Anzac Day.*

were forgotten under the sheer weight of affectionate nostalgia. When he died in 1952, at the age of eighty-eight, he was still a member of parliament.

His funeral was the biggest in Sydney's history, with 150 000 people lining the streets to see the cortège, and the newsreels tapping a well of almost mawkish sentiment. And Stanley Melbourne Bruce, who would survive the Little Digger by fifteen years, showed that even in his dotage he could look back on his old enemy with a wry affection:

He had indomitable courage. It was no fun for Billy to annihilate some half-wit on the back benches of parliament. Billy liked a foeman worthy of his steel. And I may be peculiar, but I'd say there's nothing dirty he hasn't done, or didn't do in his day, but when he died I had a certain regard and affection for him.

DOG DAY AFTERNOON *Still a parliamentarian but no longer a leader, Billy Hughes relaxes in the garden of his Sydney home with the family dog.*

THERE HE GOES *150 000 people turned out for the funeral of Billy Hughes — often called 'The Little Digger' — and still the most loved, and most hated leader Australia ever produced.*

Robert Gordon Menzies

When Sir Robert Menzies left the Canberra stage in 1966, he was more than our longest-serving Prime Minister. For half of the population, he was the only Prime Minister they'd known. When Menzies spoke on television to the nation for the last time as leader, it was in his usual indulgent manner:

There are very many people who are looking in tonight. I'm told it's almost compulsory, this. It's not an ordinary decision. It's something that doesn't happen very frequently for a man to go out of office under his own steam. I've gone out of office before today under somebody else's steam, but this time—under my own.

Sir Robert Menzies was a father figure to the modern generation of Australians. He was, after all, the man who had led us through the fifties and sixties, and somehow it had all turned out pretty well. A large man, with ego to match, he manipulated others in and out of government, ignored his critics and spun words in wondrous webs of oratory.

He was a master of the meandering, often witty, speech. But often told us nothing, for example, in this interview after one of his frequent visits to London:

There are matters to consider, and therefore they won't be considered in a light-hearted way. But I quite agree that the people of Australia are entitled, at the first possible opportunity, to be told what we want to do and how we would like to do it and what proposals we have, if any, for achieving it.

Needless to say, they never were. Australian political writer, Rob Chalmers, says of Menzies:

He knew in the fifties and sixties,

LOOKING OVER THE SHOULDER *When the Defence Council met just before the outbreak of war, Menzies seemed intent on reading over Richard Casey's shoulder. Casey was soon appointed Ambassador to Washington and eventually was the Governor-General who received Menzies' resignation as Prime Minister twenty-five years later.*

what was required to govern. It was to do nothing. That was the Menzies' masterpiece.

He was regarded as a great political leader by the average Australian who then, much as now, wanted his Holden and his television set. In the Menzies era he got it. Menzies knew what he had to deliver, and he delivered it.

He wasn't a man of innovative turn of mind. If you look back at his domestic policies, at the real achievements of the Menzies era, there are only two.

The first is Canberra. It was Menzies who took the bit between his teeth and decided that he was going to force the public service and the service brass out of Melbourne, and build this place as the national capital, instead of 'the old bush capital' as Jack Lang derisively called it.

His other achievement was to realise that the universities were about to be strangled of all funds in the mid-fifties. He set up the Australian Universities Commission, which saved the day.

The Snowy Mountains project was the initiative of the Chifley Labor Government. Certainly, the Menzies Government carried it through. It's hard to think of any other concrete achievements.

Robert Gordon Menzies was born in the small country town of Jeparit, in the Victorian shire of Dimboola. He was a chubby, happy little boy, bright and ambitious from the start, learning to read as soon as he could hold a book. His parents could not afford an expensive education for their son, so he sat for and won a scholarship to Melbourne's exclusive Wesley College. At seventeen, he won a scholarship to Melbourne University where he edited the university magazine and was president of the Students' Council. His writings at that time reflect his conservatism.

POISED, CONFIDENT, AMBITIOUS *Robert Menzies, the boy from Jeparit who became our longest-serving Prime Minister. A brilliant scholar and lawyer, he led the nation for longer than the terms of all the Labor Prime Ministers combined.*

After a shining academic and legal career and a spectacular rise in politics, Menzies was just into his forties when he began challenging the leadership of the ailing Prime Minister, Joe Lyons, and was accused of disloyalty. Then in 1939, in the midst of a bitter party struggle, Lyons died. The Country Party leader, Earle Page, fought to keep Menzies out of the Prime Minister's chair, but to no avail. Menzies was sworn in as Prime Minister on 26 April 1939. Page attacked him at every opportunity. Yet it was typical of each man's pragmatism that they could work together in the same Cabinet ten years later.

After only six months at the helm, Menzies addressed the nation to announce the outbreak of war; and he took on the role of war leader with energy and oratory using these words to inspire:

We can't be beaten except by ourselves. We can't be beaten except by disunity within our ranks, by the occasional ugly acts of treachery within our own ranks.

THE TWO OF US *Few married couples have ever been more closely linked with Australian politics than Joe and Enid Lyons. He was Prime Minister in the 1930s, while she was destined to become the first female member of the House of Representatives.*

THE AMATEUR CAMERAMAN *Sporting his home movie camera, and in the company of Australian commander Thomas Blamey, Menzies inspects ANZAC troops in the Middle East in 1940.*

DON'T FALL IN *Prime Minister Menzies inspects Australia's first nuclear reactor at Lucas Heights, near Sydney. Before nuclear power became a political issue, Lucas Heights was seen as the dawn of an age of clean, limitless fuel.*

The following year, the Prime Minister was overseas supporting the Diggers. With his home movie camera, double-breasted suit and trilby hat, he made an incongruous figure beside the troops in the hundred degrees heat of the Middle East. But the real enemy for Robert Menzies was waiting at home. Menzies was away four months, including eight successive weekends as a guest of Churchill, staying at Chequers. In Australia, the Queensland 'bush boy', Arthur Fadden, was Acting Prime Minister, and to most of the party he seemed easier to get along with than the imperious Menzies.

When Menzies arrived home, colleagues in the United Australia Party turned on him and, in the upheaval that followed, Menzies was forced to resign and Arthur Fadden became Prime Minister. It was a short reign. In 1941 the Labor Party and its forceful leader, John Curtin, were elected to government. Curtin's charismatic leadership, combined with the total disarray of the opposition, gave Labor another victory in the 1943 elections.

Chastened by the defeat, Menzies made his master stroke. At a conference in Albury in November 1944, the Liberal Party of Australia was born, with Menzies as both mother and midwife.

WE DARE NOT FAIL! *One of the continued supports to flagging Australian morale during the Second World War was the inspiring oratory of Prime Minister John Curtin. Here he is exhorting a Sydney lunchtime crowd to buy War Loan Bonds.*

P.M. WITH A PROBLEM *When Ben Chifley became Prime Minister in 1945 he faced the enormous problem of rebuilding the economy after six years of war.*

THE PRIME MINISTER RETURNS *When Menzies arrived in Australia after his visit to London and the Middle East in 1940, he found the political climate had changed. Artie Fadden (right) had run the country in his absence, and the country liked the change. Within a year, Menzies was toppled.*

"GOING MY WAY—ON A FULL PETROL-TANK?"

PREPARING FOR THE FRAY.

THE PICK-UP *Menzies brought his Liberal Party to power in 1949 on a slogan of 'Tip out the Socialists and Fill up the Bowsers'. Many political analysts consider the simple promise to end post-war petrol rationing as the masterstroke of the campaign.*

THE BLACK KNIGHT *Menzies' return to power in 1949 was largely based on his promises to tackle the forces of socialism and communism. Yet after three years of legislation, referendum and denunciations, Australians would not make communism illegal.*

The strain of the war years literally killed Curtin. He died just five weeks before peace was announced on 15 August 1945. The new Prime Minister, Ben Chifley, inherited the problems of economic reconstruction and was forced to extend wartime austerity measures, such as petrol rationing.

When the Labor leader tried to nationalise the banks, the press and public reacted strongly. By 1949, with the war over four years, people resented not being able to keep their petrol tanks filled, and the general hangovers of austerity. In the elections that year, Menzies' campaign of promises was based on the issues of rationing and the growing international fear of communism. His simple slogan 'Tip out the socialists

and fill up the bowsers' worked. The Liberal Party was swept into office on 10 December 1949 and Robert Gordon Menzies again became Prime Minister of Australia.

When Menzies and his wife, Pattie, moved into the Lodge in Canberra, no one could have predicted they would stay for such an incredibly long time. Menzies 'ruled' for a record term of seventeen years. So long, in fact, that by the end Australians were calling it the 'Ming Dynasty'.

This second term as Prime Minister saw a marked shift in the Menzies' style. His hectic first twenty years in politics had taught him how to survive, and he determined not to make the same mistakes again. Menzies' emphasis now moved from

simply gaining power to making sure he held it. Any danger from inside his own ranks could be solved with an occasional Cabinet reshuffle or an inspired diplomatic appointment. He even learned to live with old enemies, including Earle Page. He needed Page in his 1949 ministry, and Page went in with him.

The new government was quickly blooded in a tremendous struggle over the issue of communism. No Australian leader has realised the electoral potential of 'Red-baiting' more acutely than Menzies. By the fifties, Australia was embroiled in a local version of America's McCarthyist war against the 'Reds'. Menzies wanted to outlaw the Communist Party and ban its followers from trade union and government

This rough, dirty job of loading ingots of pig iron from rail heads onto ships bound for Japan became one of the most fiery political issues in our modern history. Menzies refused to bend to his opponents who claimed the iron would become Japanese bombs and bullets. The nickname 'Pig Iron Bob' stuck for the next twenty years.

positions. But in 1951 the Party went to the High Court of Australia and Menzies' Communist Party Dissolution Bill was voted unconstitutional.

But Menzies was undeterred. As Hughes had done with conscription, Menzies flew in the face of even his own colleagues, and put the communist question to the people in the form of a referendum. Australians—traditional No voters anyway—once again preserved the status quo and Menzies' so-called 'Red Bill' was vetoed by a slender majority of 52 000.

Taking a personal interest in the court case against Menzies' Red Bill, and campaigning against the referendum question was the new Labor leader, Dr Herbert Vere Evatt. Evatt's popularity was increasing towards the 1954 elections and, with unemployment high, it was clear Menzies might need another magician's trick to win. He found it just forty-six days before the votes were cast. The central character of the drama, and the man who would give his name to the whole affair, was Vladimir Michailovich Petrov. On Friday, 11 April 1954, Petrov left work at the Russian Embassy in Canberra with a sheaf of papers

VOTE NO! *Menzies' legislative attempts to outlaw communism eventually drew the nation into a divisive referendum. The defeat of this last attempt to 'get rid of the Reds' owed much to trade union opposition. This banner led a May Day March in 1951.*

under his arm. On 13 April Menzies announced in parliament:

It is my unpleasant duty to convey to the House (that) Mr Vladimir Petrov voluntarily left his diplomatic employment and made to the Australian government a request for political asylum. The request has been granted.

Petrov's 'defection' was ideal election ammunition, but not even the imaginative mind of Robert Menzies could have dreamed up the melodramatic spy scenes that followed. Australians were told how Petrov used his Third Secretary's appointment at the embassy as a cover for espionage activities for the Russian secret service, the MVD (later called the KGB). He had turned over documents to the Australian Security Intelligence Organisation (ASIO), although the importance of these was later questioned.

As election day drew nearer, Petrov was seen as a 'cold war' ally for Australia—a Russian communist who had seen the light, and Menzies was his valiant rescuer. In fact, Petrov, a weak, heavy-drinking man, had been persuaded to defect after a two-and-a-half year campaign by ASIO.

POLITICAL DUPE OR MASTER SPY? *Vladimir Petrov, the Russian diplomat based in Canberra who defected to the Australian intelligence authorities for £5000. Pictured here outside the Melbourne chambers of the Royal Commission into Espionage, 1954.*

Evdokia Petrov, Vladimir's wife, also an MVD agent, had been held incommunicado at the Russian Embassy since her husband's defection. On 19 April two Russian couriers escorted Evdokia to a commercial air flight leaving Sydney's international airport. In a demonstration of emotional hysteria, more than a thousand shouting people, mostly migrants from 'Iron Curtain' countries, crowded on to the tarmac trying to pull Mrs Petrov back from the aircraft door.

On board the aircraft the drama continued. An air hostess, briefed by ASIO, approached Mrs Petrov in the ladies' toilet. Mrs Petrov was persuaded to defect and, on stopover in Darwin, she was taken from the helpless Russians by Northern Territory police and returned to Sydney to join her husband who was being carefully hidden.

DIPLOMATIC FLASHPOINT *A week after the defection of Vladimir Petrov, his wife Evdokia was escorted across the tarmac at Sydney airport to board a flight to Moscow. At the extreme right was cadet radio journalist Gary O'Callaghan.*

The carefully stage-managed Royal Commission which followed was a mixture of fact and farce worthy of a B-grade movie. Journalist John Stubbs, who with Gough Whitlam's son Nicholas later wrote a book on the whole affair called *Nest of Traitors*, tells of an extraordinary incident involving Petrov and another celebrated figure at the hearing, Dr Michael Bialoguski:

Well, what happened was that Bialoguski, who was the host, was entertaining Petrov at his home. He knew that Petrov drank to excess when given the opportunity. Bialoguski was pretending to be a communist sympathiser and went to a demonstration for clemency for the Rosenbergs, some people caught up in the McCarthy era persecutions in America and, in fact, later executed.

When he returned Petrov had drunk himself unconscious, and he went through his pockets and went to the lavatory and copied them down on the only paper that was available. By the time he had finished copying the entire contents of his pockets he'd got to the core of the toilet roll, and the core of the toilet roll was in fact produced at the Royal Commission. A translator looked at what these secrets were on the document and they were some very rude words written by Petrov who was trying to teach himself Australian swear words.

A lot of other documents were just as irrelevant, probably more irrelevant, but that incident did prove that Petrov had been thinking of coming over, jumping the wall, defecting to Australia, for some time.

It also says a couple of other things—that he did like drinking, that he was an unreliable sort of personality, that he was in trouble with people in Russia. He wasn't terribly interested in going back to Russia and was looking for a way out.

Menzies used the Petrov sensation to his advantage to win the 1954 election, and in the months following, the right and left wings of the Labor

THE DRAMA OF DOCUMENT J *Prize exhibit in the Petrov Espionage Royal Commission investigation was 'Document J', purportedly the work of communist journalist Rupert Lockwood (left). Lockwood responded to his summons to appear before the Royal Commission, but refused to answer any questions.*

THE DISILLUSIONED COMRADE *Today, journalist Rupert Lockwood has split with the official Communist Party over the issue of Soviet intervention in Czechoslovakia, but his dramatic involvement in the Petrov spy scandal is still remembered.*

Party split—largely over the issue of communist influence in the unions. In 1955, the Catholic right wing helped found a new party, the Democratic Labor Party (DLP). The DLP directed its second preference votes to the Liberals, helping consolidate Menzies' position for the next decade.

The Petrovs, after giving evidence at the Royal Commission set up by Menzies, faded into obscurity. Today they are official residents of Australia protected by a special 'D' notice, a gentlemen's agreement between the government and the media not to disclose their whereabouts.

The 1961 'credit squeeze' election was Menzies' closest brush with defeat. Even with the help of the DLP, Menzies scraped back into government by just thirty-two votes. But for most of the time Menzies ran the country with consummate ease, almost as if it was an enjoyable hobby.

Outside politics, Menzies worshipped cricket and the Queen. He was Australia's most vocal royalist, and in 1963 during a royal visit to Canberra, the Prime Minister made the young Queen of England blush, when he recited poet Thomas Ford's sentimental stanza

There is a lady sweet and kind,
Was never face so pleased my mind;
I did but see her passing by
And yet I love her till I die.

When Menzies retired as Prime Minister on Australia Day, 26 January 1966, the country had never been richer or stronger. But sadly, all his legacies to Australia were not so kind. Before he left he had committed Australia to conscription and Vietnam, and there were hard times ahead.

LORD WARDEN OF THE CINQUE PORTS *Sir Robert Gordon Menzies strode the Australian political stage like a colossus and he seemed to revel in the trappings of his office. When he was installed as a Knight of the Order of the Thistle at St Giles Cathedral, Edinburgh and became Lord Warden of the Cinque ports most Australians could barely comprehend what it all meant.*

GRAVEN IMAGES *When news of his impending retirement spread, plaster busts of the distinctive Menzies image, complete with windswept eyebrows, sold briskly. When he retired the country had never been stronger or richer.*

HER MAJESTY AND HER LOYAL SUBJECT *Prime Minister Robert Menzies proudly follows his Queen into a State dinner in her honour to be held inside Parliament House, Canberra. It was during his speech that night that Menzies quoted the celebrated 'I did but see her passing by' lines.*

215

Arthur Calwell

On a cold winter's night in June 1966, Arthur Calwell was deep in conservative country campaigning against Australia's involvement in the Vietnam war. If Labor won the next election, he told the staunch upper-class residents of Mosman in Sydney, he'd bring the conscripts home. It was an orderly meeting, with just a few Liberal hecklers. When he was leaving, Mr Calwell, contrary to his usual fashion, left the car window wound up. The cold night helped save his life.

A few seconds later, a young man walked up to the car, pointed a rifle at Mr Calwell's face and pulled the trigger. For the first few moments there was confusion. Calwell was rushed to hospital but it was revealed that the only damage done was to the massive chin so beloved by cartoonists. It was lacerated by glass fragments. Arthur Calwell left hospital the same day. But the frightening impact of this first attempted political assassination in Australia, coming less than three years after the death of John F. Kennedy, was felt across the country.

The morning after the shooting, a twenty-year-old youth, Peter Kocan, appeared briefly in court. Kocan later pleaded guilty and was given a life sentence. He was released in 1977 after serving ten years.

Today Peter Kocan is well regarded in Australian literary circles. He has published pamphlets of poetry and has received a government grant to write a book. Explaining the assassination attempt, he says:

> It was an act springing out of profound mental confusion. It was a process of probably three or four years during which time I was becoming more isolated and more alienated, more filled with this peculiar notion that this was a way to make oneself somebody. You know, the old hackneyed thing about identity crisis. I wanted to make myself feel real.

Now for anyone who hasn't experienced the kind of psychologi-

WOULD-BE ASSASSIN *Peter Kocan, who in 1966 attempted Australia's first political assassination when he fired at Labor leader Arthur Calwell.*

BLOODIED BUT UNBOWED *The massive Calwell chin shows where glass fragments were embedded in the skin as a result of the bungled assassination attempt.*

POLICE ESCORT *The leader of the opposition, Arthur Calwell is heavily guarded by police and Commonwealth Security men as he is discharged from Royal North Shore hospital after an attempt on his life in June 1966.*

cal confusion that I experienced prior to the attack on Mr Calwell, that may sound a bit peculiar. But my problem really was that I didn't feel like a real person. I felt like some sort of shadow or ghost or disembodied wraith wandering the streets.

And the significant thing about an act like that, the shooting, to me, was that at one stroke it would prove my realness. After all, you have to be real to pull a trigger, to set in motion the whole process of the media, and the headlines and so on.

While Kocan was in Morisset Psychiatric Hospital, Arthur Calwell kept in touch with the young man's mother to follow his progress. Just before he died, Calwell told Kocan he was planning to visit him at the hospital.

It had been a remarkable episode in Australian politics—a story of high drama, compassion and some hope.

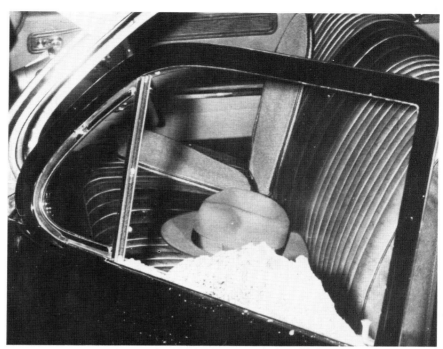

WHERE DID I LEAVE MY HAT? *The lonely aftermath of the shooting. Arthur Calwell's hat lies amid the shattered glass of his car window.*

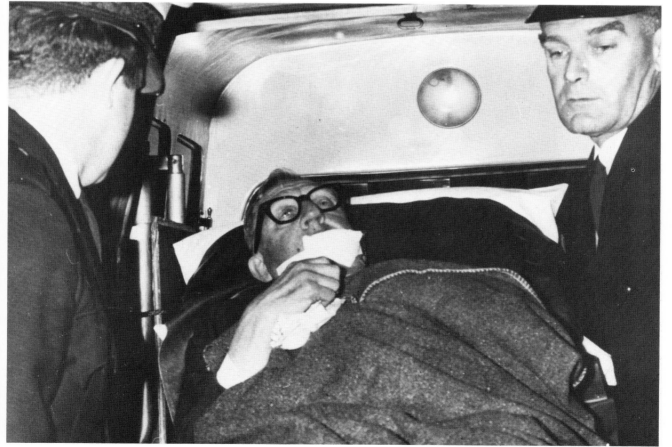

WOUNDED POLITICIAN *Arthur Calwell nurses his injured chin as he is assisted from the ambulance which took him to Royal North Shore Hospital after the dramatic shooting incident at Mosman.*

WEEKEND PRIME MINISTER *Harold Holt's hobby of skindiving was well known to the Australian public. The thought of their Prime Minister slipping into a wetsuit was faintly amusing. Ironically, it was Holt's love of the water which would eventually lead to his mysterious disappearance.*

Harold Holt

The new Liberal Party leader, Harold Holt, won the 1966 election which saw the removal of Arthur Calwell from the opposition leader's chair to be replaced by Gough Whitlam. Holt 'ruled' until 17 December 1967 – then he disappeared.

Holt was Menzies' faithful, hard-working lieutenant; a handsome, popular man with a vivacious wife, who immediately set about redecorating the conservative Prime Minister's Lodge in what was an avant-garde style for the sixties.

Holt's hobby of skin-diving was well known, and Australians looked on his enthusiasm for the sport with some humour. The thought of their Prime Minister slipping into a wetsuit had a faintly whimsical air. But why not? We all have our weekend relaxations.

Harold Holt loved his freedom and he was an experienced swimmer. At fifty-nine, he was fit and knew the waters around Portsea, on the Victorian coast, as well as the best divers. But surely it could only happen in Australia that the leader of a nation could walk on the beach with friends without security protection? In what other country could the head of government walk into dangerous surf and swim out to sea alone?

The alarm was raised at 12.40 p.m. on a summer Sunday, and within minutes a massive search operation was under way. The Prime Minister was missing, presumed drowned. Melbourne's police, navy, army and air force were thrown into the hunt. When the search was abandoned in the failing light that evening, it was obvious the exercise was futile.

Artist Clifton Pugh, an experienced skin-diver, frequently swam with the Prime Minister. He described Holt's last day on Cheviot Beach:

I think he probably wanted to show off a little bit. I believe there was a young bloke and his young girl there and I think it was the story of the old bull and the young bull. You know, out he goes without his wetsuit. He'd had a few drinks and you get puffed very quickly. The young bloke had much more sense. He went a little way and came back. Apparently, right at that time, the tide changed and the water became an absolute millrace. And then, in that water is a lot of debris and kelp up to thirty feet long whipping about. He might have just got a bit exhausted. He could have been hit on the head by a bit of debris, or caught by a bit of kelp. It's all holes there and rock caverns. I think he probably just got pulled under.

Holt's death upset the whole future of the Liberal Party, which had been so carefully planned by Menzies. The stately order of leadership was thrown into turmoil. There was a series of coups and counter-coups, four Liberal leaders and an election defeat before the Liberals could discover their new strong man. As the former British Prime Minister, Harold Wilson, once declared so accurately: 'A week in politics is a very long time.'

THE HAPPY HOLTS *Unaware of the impending tragedy which was to take his life, Prime Minister of Australia Harold Holt and his wife Zara smile radiantly for the camera on a State occasion.*

A PRESIDENT MOURNS *U.S. President L. B. Johnson was deeply moved by the funeral service for Harold Holt. He is seen here with Australian Prime Minister John McEwen.*

TRIBUTE TO A PRIME MINISTER *Among the world leaders who flew to Australia to attend the funeral service for Harold Holt were Prince Charles and U.K. Prime Minister Harold Wilson.*

7

FADS, FASHION AND FEMINISM

BESIDE THE SEASIDE *So many Australians live close to the sea that beachwear fashions have always been extremely popular. This happy pair model what girls, big and small, were wearing in the early fifties.*

Australian fads and crazes

No doubt even the first-fleeters found something to amuse themselves on their less than pleasant cruise to the colony, even if it was telling Irish jokes. Australians have always loved fads, fashions and crazes, and while we've borrowed most of them from overseas, just occasionally we've invented some of our own.

Fads

In a country where the national dress is jeans, the national food is a McDonalds hamburger or Kentucky Fried Chicken, and the national drink is Coke, it's not always easy to find a distinctively Australian pastime. But now and then, in amongst a sea of weird activities ranging from the fandango to phone box stuffing, there is a genuine home-grown fad.

While America had its drug stores and soda fountains, the milk bar was an exclusively Australian invention. The first 'strawberry malted' was poured at Australia's first milk bar which opened in Martin Place, Sydney, in 1933. The same year, milk

ON A SESAME SEED BUN *The invasion of Australia by the American drive-in, take-away, fast-food concept elevated the humble hamburger to haute cuisine — with tomato sauce. Chains of restaurants sprang up all over the country to cater for this new trend.*

bars began opening in Melbourne and Brisbane, and it soon became the sport for milkmaids across the country to fill their tumblers by stretching the milk out at arm's length in front of them, in a sort of liquid milky way. How and why this sort of long-distance decanting

AIN'T GOT NO DISTRACTIONS *Like many many previous American craze imports, the pinball machine, with its flashing lights and pinging bells, quickly became a fixture of Australian pubs and milkbars.*

PASSPORT TO TRACTION *For the young and supple, the fad for hula-hoops was energetic fun, but for many adults who tried it, the result was sometimes lengthy periods of physiotherapy.*

LIFTS AND SEPARATES *Most of our crazes were both useless and imported — the pogo stick was no exception. These ladies seemed set to bounce from Sydney to Melbourne .*

caught the public imagination is a mystery. But then most fads are.

Sydney's first milk bar had an electric cow as decoration in the front window. Milkshakes were sold for fourpence each, extra if an egg was added. An American ice-cream soda cost sixpence and sundaes, dripping with chocolate syrup and topped with nuts and shiny green cherries, were ninepence, to be ordered only on special occasions.

Many fads pioneered by children are often taken up by their parents. In the 1950s Australian children and adults were crazy about bamboo hula-hoops, another Australian invention. We whirled them around our necks, hips, arms and legs in backyards, at exercise classes, even at parties, and the nation was alive with the sound of slipping discs.

In 1958, when two Californian toymakers heard about Australia's hoop craze, they made their own version out of plastic. Within six months, with the help of the Wham-O Company, American children were spinning thirty million hoops across the United States, setting records of up to 3000 twists without stopping.

In the early 1930s mini-golf was all the rage in towns and cities across our nation. At weekends we spent

leisure hours with backs bent, putting a golf ball around a concrete obstacle course of fairytale mediaeval castles and miniature Sydney

Harbour Bridges.

In Sydney, one of the most popular courses was built in a temple overlooking picturesque Middle

AND HE KEEPETH ME BELOW PAR *And on the seventh day, he putted. In the 1930s, Sydneysiders played mini-golf in the remains of a Theosophist temple overlooking Middle Harbour. The incongruous setting no doubt gave added interest to the game.*

223

Harbour. This mock Grecian edifice was, in fact, all that remained of a previous fad. It was built during the 1920s by members of Sydney's Theosophist Society purportedly to watch the 'second coming' of Christ, who, some were led to expect, would walk across the water through Sydney Heads and up the harbour. These people were in fact victims of a persuasive Indian mystic, and while they were disappointed, the subsequent tenants of the temple were delighted with their spectacular venue for mini-golf.

The craze blossomed with 'links springing up like mushrooms', according to a newspaper report. There has been a revival of the mini-golf craze recently, but in today's rushed society, it's mainly become a place for Mum to dump Dad and the kids while she does the shopping.

To the kids of the fifties, the 'drive-in' was as modern as

AS MODERN AS TOMORROW *FJ Holdens, Chevs, Vanguards and Consuls line up for their Friday night dose of drive-in movies. If what was happening on the screen lacked interest, there were always the gymnastics in the car beside you.*

1960s GOTHIC *The high-contrast imagery of a gleaming new Holden, steaming asphalt and a giant steel screen captured the spirit of waiting for sunset and the beginning of a drive-in show.*

ROLL THAT BALL *Despite the massive promotion and capital investment, the post-war introduction of the American game of ten-pin bowling never really captured the public imagination.*

tomorrow. Families often arrived while the sun was still up to get a good spot. Dad tried to get the front wheels perfectly on top of the bitumen mound, and then there was always that familiar crash as the loud-speaker was hooked on to the glass window. Somehow the knob always either stuck or came off. At interval everyone rushed out of the car and tried to be first to the hot dog counter. On the way back you couldn't find your car in the dark, and when you finally got there the main feature had invariably started. If it got boring, there was always the chance of some fun and games in the back seat; if not in your own, in the car beside you. At worst, it rained and you had to sit peering through the windscreen wipers at Charlton Heston building the pyramids.

Close behind drive-ins came another American family fad. In 1960 the first ten-pin bowling alley was opened at Hurstville, Sydney. Scores more followed, each decorated in the early sixties American style, with snack bars and garish plastic furnishings.

America also gave us the pogo-stick and the urge to break crazy records like phone box stuffing, a sport almost exclusively confined to university students.

And then there was that hardy perennial, the yo-yo! Yo-yos might seem as American as Coca-Cola, but the US can't claim to have invented this fad. Prehistoric man used yo-yos as hunting weapons. King George IV of England played with one when it was called the 'bandalore'. And history tells us that aristocrats distracted themselves with yo-yos on their way to the guillotine during the French Revolution.

Yo-yos have been launched on to the Australian market on at least seven occasions, and every time this simple device with no moving parts has always become a giant fad. During 1978 more than a million were sold just in the suburbs of Sydney.

At right: THE KNACK *Either you've got it or you haven't. But when the yo-yo craze swept Australia, as it did several times, everyone got all strung up about it.*

PADDED ROOM *A 'dream home' interior of the early 1950s, complete with padded bar, floral carpet and indoor gardening.*

For most of this century dance crazes have been a favourite target for wowsers. In 1903, the Reverend Dr Torrey in Melbourne warned women in his congregation that if a girl knew what a man was thinking while he was dancing with her, she would never dance again. But that's exactly why she did dance again, and again. In 1914 the New South Wales Presbyterian Assembly denounced Sydney women for their shameful 'sleeveless' evening gowns and daring new dances. Waltzing was barely acceptable, and any other dance that brought young people close together was 'shocking'. But the ballrooms were as crowded as ever. It seemed there was no stopping the modern wave of sinful dancing. After the austerity of life during the First World War years, Australians were dancing the Foxtrot and Pride of Erin, often at musical evenings in homes where the loungeroom carpet and chairs were pushed back to make a dance floor.

With the introduction of radio in 1923 came the hits of the 'golden twenties'. Australian flappers danced the American Charleston to the beat

JITTERBUG, LINDY HOP AND BOOGIE WOOGIE *Artie Smith and Eileen Joyce jitterbug their way to a £25 first prize in the NSW Championships of 1945. Jitterbugging was a huge craze and attracted crowds of thousands. The highlight of Artie and Eileen's act was a throw which saw Eileen drop from 10 feet in the air into the splits.*

of 'jazz' music that reflected the gay affluence of the times. A generation later we were copying the Americans again, this time dancing the Jit-terbug in the merry-making days after the Second World War. The Jitterbug was the maddest dance of all. Not many people could do it

HEP CATS HOP *The 'with it' post war 'cats' brought the American jitterbug craze to Australia with a vengeance. Dance Palais that had been used to the foxtrot and Pride of Erin suddenly had their floorboards pounded by athletic exponents of the Lindy Hop and the Boogie Woogie. Until Rock 'n' roll came along, Bop Till You Drop was the order of the day.*

well, and so just watching the experts became a craze. The Jitterbug's popularity produced teams of professionals who performed their acrobatic displays of dancing in front of huge crowds.

Eileen Joyce and Artie Smith won the New South Wales Jitterbug Championship at the Bondi Pavilion in 1945. They also danced the Lindy Hop and the Boogie Woogie, plus dozens more variations of their own invention. Eileen remembers:

We used to dance to 'In the Mood', 'Twelfth Street Rag'—anything that was really jazzy. The music really got into us. When the music was on, you could see Artie just drift away. He just loved music. You know once you've got the music you can just keep on going. It was very strenuous and entailed a lot of training. We used to train three days a week—like a racehorse. I think we were the only jitterbuggers where the woman threw her partner.

And according to Artie Smith:

We had precision. There was one routine where I used to put Eileen up on my shoulders and I'd throw her to the ground and she'd go into a complete split. We had a unique set of double throws. My footwork was pretty fast and my partner was double-jointed. She could twist herself any way.

CUTTING A RUG *One thing you could say about jitterbugging, it was hardly dignified. But for Eileen and Artie Joyce, it was a professional passion. Moves like the above gyrations earned them the NSW Championship of 1945.*

YOU PUT YOUR LEFT LEG IN... *Lunatic song-and-dance craze of the early 1950s — the Hokey Pokey. The strange dance and hand movement rituals defied description but claimed Polynesian origins.*

ARTHUR MURRAY IN A HURRY *In the safety (and privacy) of a dance studio, customers learn the Twist, the dance craze of the 1960s that brought as much joy to orthopeadic surgeons as it did to those wishing to twist the light-fantastic.*

STOMPIE WOMPIES *Enthusiastic exponents of the only dance craze ever to originate in Australia — the Stomp — these teenagers, wearing their regulation stomping gear, pound out the relentless beat at the Bilgola Surf Club, Sydney.*

Being dropped six feet on to the floor in the splits was not to the taste of every Australian matron, and soon we were looking for a modern step we could all do. After a decade of rock 'n' roll, we discovered the 'Twist', a dance so simple that anybody could do it. For the first time since the Charleston, dancing partners actually let go of each other permanently and moved around the dance floor in separate motion. The Twist went up-and-down and round-and-round and just about any way you wanted to go. If you tired of your partner you could twist off and dance with someone else. The Twist lasted only a few years, but in the meantime Australia was already inventing its own dance craze, the 'Stomp'.

To do the Stomp in regulation style, you needed a special uniform of rubber sneakers, jeans and extra-outsize jumper. It started on the Sydney beaches, and Sunday nights soon saw thousands of teenage 'surfies' flocking to the Avalon or Bronte Stomp to stamp their feet to the music of young bands like the Bee Gees, who played the surf club circuit.

The dance spread west to Kings Cross in Sydney to a stomp hall called Surf City, which became something of a battleground for Sydney's rival teenage gangs, the stomping surfies and the 'rockers', who were mainly bike riders and their mates from the western suburbs. But apart from that parents could stop worrying. The Stomp had

LIKE WE DID LAST SUMMER *Australians in 1962 — right down to formally dressed mannequins — dutifully aped the latest American dance craze, the Twist.*

SATURDAY NIGHT STOMP *By the time the Twist had gyrated its way into oblivion, the Stomp had taken over Australian dance floors. No one knows where it started, but at the Bilgola Surf Club it went on all night.*

no sex appeal whatsoever. No one is even sure where it started, but one little girl came to be identified with it more than anyone. Patricia Amphlett was just into her teens when she climbed on to the stage at her local surf club to sing 'Stomping at Maroubra'. Today Little Pattie is a successful singer on the Australian club circuit. She remembers well the days of the Stomp:

> Anybody could do it. It was less complicated than rock 'n' roll and even less complicated than the Twist. I mean, overweight people couldn't twist very well, but anybody could do the Stomp. It stayed for a little while, and it is Australian.

It seems that dancing, like sex, is here to stay. It still does not always meet with the older generation's approval. But tripping the light-fantastic is certainly not the picture of debauchery predicted by another Melbourne cleric, the Reverend Wallis of Fitzroy, who forty years ago denounced meeting on the dance floor as 'The nursery of divorce, the training ship of prostitution and a modern ulcer threatening public morality.'

REAL GONE SURFER BOY *The girl who first put the Stomp really on the map with her song 'Stomping at Maroubra', pop singer Little Pattie, joins forces with political hero of the early 1970s, Gough Whitlam.*

Fashion

> When you went to town in the fifties, you wore a hat and gloves. You wouldn't dream of going to town without a hat and gloves.

So says Australian fashion historian, Norma Martyn. Not until we dropped the old English customs, including the hat and gloves uniform, did Australians begin to develop a fashion style of their own.

In the early 1900s 'a woman walked in beauty and in pain', as Norman Lindsay's wife, Rose, once said. She wore steel-ribbed corsets that cupped the breasts and layers of padding below a tiny waspish waist. Stiff necklines choked her lily-white neck.

Men's fashion too made no attempt to suit Australia's hot, humid summers. Gentlemen went to the office dressed in three-piece tweed suits, more suited to the cold English climate. Even if, very occasionally, they took their coats off, the waistcoat was *never* removed. Hats were also compulsory, and most men wore Australia's version of the English bowler, which we called 'the boxer'.

Women wore large hats feathered with fancy plumes plucked from ostriches, which were bred on farms especially set up to supply the fashion. The sale or possession of ostrich feathers was banned in 1918.

MELBOURNE CUP DAY — 1915 *The Members' Enclosure at Flemington was the place to be seen if one wanted to be amongst the leaders of fashion. In 1915 the 'in' outfit was a top hat and cutaway jacket.*

TOPPERS AND PLUMES *In 1910, elegant headwear was a compulsory fashion accessory for the high-class racegoer, male or female.*

The first breakthrough in modern fashion came soon after the turn of the century. Quite simply, the ankle was revealed. It was the most dramatic happening in fashion. In one sense, the revelation of the ankle was the point at which we started to enter the age of 'permissive society'.

But it was some time before tightly squeezed female bodies were released from their less visible constriction of voluminous underclothing. Women still wore layered skirts and steel corsets. One Sydney retail store even advertised that corsets could be returned for refund if they showed signs of rust.

In 1914, the first 'brassiere' was patented in America by a young heiress with the appropriate name of Caresse Crosby. There is much dispute among fashion historians as to whether this was, in fact, the first bra invented. Bust garments had been worn in Australia earlier this century at first by 'stout' women only. But by 1918 they were popular with all women and soon became a moral 'must' for all modest ladies. Ironically, many of today's grandmothers, who seem so disgusted at the modern trend to go 'braless', were themselves without support in their younger years.

As skirt lengths inched upwards from the ankle towards the knee after the First World War, compulsory sleeves and high necklines also disappeared. The war years had brought a new, simple fashion. Tight waists and flared skirts gave way to soft, uninhibited styles that left a woman able to breathe and move freely.

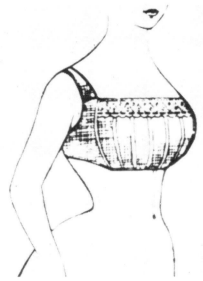

IN HARNESS *This 1910 forerunner of the bra seemed to combine support, containment and defense. It was probably as uncomfortable as it looks.*

CRICKET CROWD — 1919 *In the Ladies Stand, a microcosm of the relaxed lifestyle of the Australian middle class in summer. Every face tells a story — and every hat shades a pretty face in an age when ribbons and veils were the essence of femininity.*

At left: 1924 SUPER COUTURE *The perfect woman of the 1920s had no bust, no waist, no hips and was preferably as slim as a poplar. But she could, for the first time, show her ankles.*

A MERE SLIP OF A GIRL *This fashion show of ladies lingerie was about as daring as the newsreels companies ever got when it came to showing the female form. The scene is from a Mark Foys fashion parade in 1934.*

TOP COSSIE *For more than a generation, Speedo dominated the swimwear market. This bathing costume would have been a familiar sight in the 1930s.*

By the 1920s fashion conscious women were aligning their clothing tastes with the prevailing mood of feminism. Skirts took a sudden leap to the knees and black wool and lisle stockings gave way to skin-tone sheer silk. 'Fast' young ladies openly smoked cigarettes in public and even made personal calls on the telephone without being formally introduced.

The flappers, with their new found freedom, began wearing straight 'tubular' dresses that showed no bust, waist or hipline. Bobbed-cut hair, introduced as a practical measure for women doing war work during 1914-18, now became the fashion, and by the late twenties bobbed curls had given way to a more boyish cut, the Eton crop.

These boyish fashions eventually led to a return of femininity in the thirties and women who could afford to copied French fashion photographs on their Singer sewing machines. Bodices were shaped around padded shoulders, and emphasised the bustline. Waists were tightened and skirts curved out to the hips and bottom, then back into narrow hems.

Rayon, made from wood pulp and

HANDS ON HIPS ... SMILE! *These carefully coiffured ladies model what the well-dressed beach belle was wearing in Australia in 1932. The wristwatch and bangles, like the curls, were optional extras for those never intending to get wet.*

first exhibited by a French scientist in 1889, was woven into cheaper stockings in the thirties. The traditional white evening dress was replaced by a dramatic, brief black number called the 'cocktail dress'. Gloves were very vogue, worn up to sixteen inches long at night, and elbow length by day.

With rayon came the age of synthetics. Nylon, dacron, banlon, in fact just anything that ended in 'on'. After the Second World War, baby-doll shortie pyjamas introduced teenagers to a new American fad, the pyjama party. And, when older women went 'out' they dressed up in shiny Rita Hayworth style, or glam-orous taffetas à la Monroe.

Yet soon all this formal elegance was gone, swept aside by the most potent fashion accessory of all—bare flesh. Most of the changes had been gradual but soon the salons were set reeling by a sequence of sensational events, that started to reveal more of the female form.

SEASIDE SINFULNESS *A late-night pyjama party of Surfers Paradise holiday-makers was considered the height of permissiveness 20 years ago, and revellers were often arrested for indecency.*

At left: CLASSY LADY *This formal evening ensemble of 1927, heavily embroidered with pearls, epitomises the era between the wars when elegance was the keyword and evening wear was designed to be exquisitely eyecatching.*

Swimsuits that had started off as woollen neck-to-knees were well established as 'two piece' by the forties, and in 1946, when the United States began testing the atom bomb at Bikini Atoll in the Pacific, the first 'bikini' was launched by a French designer, Louis Reard. Bikinis gradually gained acceptance in the fifties, especially on the Gold Coast of Queensland; although they took a little longer in Sydney where council beach inspectors were still ordering bikini 'birds' off Bondi beach in 1961. Ironically, the same council was the first to sanction topless bathing on a popular public beach in 1978.

But it was during Melbourne Cup week in 1965 that a battle between European models dramatically changed the course of Australian fashion. Representing 'pure wool' was French mannequin, Christine Borge. Appearing for 'synthetics' was Great Britain's Jean (the Shrimp) Shrimpton, at that time the highest paid model in the world.

AHEAD OF HER TIME *The long arm of the Council By-Law reaches out to banish a bikini-clad bather from a Sydney beach in the early 1960s. The Beach Inspector's outfit would raise more eyebrows today than would the girl's.*

CHIC SHEIKS OF 1961 *A swimwear creation with a touch of the Arabian Nights, by Paula Stafford, the Surfers Paradise designer who pioneered the bikini costume in Australia.*

Borge had arrived in Melbourne in late October. As she stepped off the plane from Paris, she fell into an elegant faint straight into the waiting arms of the local Wool Board representative. The airport pictures made front page news. Later, Christine Borge told Melbourne columnist Keith Dunstan, 'I just can't think of anything the Shrimp can do to upstage me.'

But the Shrimp fought back in dramatic style. She arrived at the Flemington members' stand in a skirt that was four inches above her knees. Not only did she make every front page in the country, but she also had reporters flying out from London to cover the story.

To Melbourne's conservative social set, the Shrimp was a brazen hussy. Not only did she show almost a quarter of her thigh, but she wore no hat, no gloves and—horror of horrors—no stockings! To make matters worse, the cheeky little minx was wearing a man's watch. Where, they asked, would it all end? It's hard now to understand the uproar. But you have to remember that these were the first deliberately exposed human knees ever seen inside the members' enclosure at Flemington.

BRAZEN HUSSY *English model Jean Shrimpton, the Shrimp, horrified the ladies of the Members' Enclosure at Flemington during 1965 Melbourne Cup week by wearing the first mini-skirt seen in Australia. To add insult to injury, she wore no stockings!*

TRACK RECORD *What the well-dressed lady racegoer was wearing to Flemington in the 1950s. Note the identical hemlines.*

Fortunately, the next time Australia made world headlines with fashion we had learnt to admire, rather than gasp at, a shapely leg. This time, the scene was the White House in Washington and most Australians felt our First Lady had done us proud. As Sonia McMahon walked down the staircase of the White House, the skirt of her long white dress parted to reveal an arresting sun-tanned leg from ankle to thigh. The photographers and press had a field day. That one daring evening gown kept any serious discussion between Prime Minister William McMahon and President Nixon, if there was any, off the front pages.

President Nixon's problems with unsuccessful cover-ups were still to come, but for Lady McMahon it was a venture into foreign affairs she will never forget:

I never thought twice about wearing it. I actually was going to wear that dress to crown Miss Australia that year. But then President Nixon asked us to go over to the United States rather hurriedly so I took my white dress with me. Naturally if you have a new dress you think of wearing it to the White House.

You know, it's not all that daring unless you get caught by

THE THIGHS THAT BIND *While President Nixon and Prime Minister William McMahon forged bonds of international co-operation at a White House dinner, it was the PM's wife Sonia who captured the headlines with her revealing 'split' dress.*

POLKA DOTS AND PLAYSUITS *A natural bush setting for this mannequin of the 1960s, who seems about to become airborne in her delta-wing creation tastefully set off by a coral necklace, matching bangle and plastic sunglasses.*

SPLIT PERSONALITY *Remembering the 'split' dress with amusement, (and with a signed picture of Richard and Pat Nixon beside her) Sonia McMahon still exhibits the penchant for dramatic dresses that catapulted her into the headlines in 1971.*

photographers sideways walking up and down stairs.

In many ways the early seventies were the end of an era for high fashion. The harsh modernism of Dior's 'sack' look had made a mockery of the word 'style'. At last Australians began to cast a critical eye over the strange plastic, metal and modular creations that kept arriving from overseas. We were ready to try a home-grown product. Carla Zampatti, one of the first contemporary Australian designers, remembers:

Up to five years ago women used to say, 'I will buy my wardrobe in Paris or London or Italy or New York'. Today, the same people come to me and I outfit them for the trip.

Australian fashion, led by designers like Zampatti, Prue Acton and Trent Nathan, helps support the 120 000 people who work in the local fashion industry. At last, Australians have come to terms with the climate and our fashions have earned a place in international salons.

It's true that the seventies were also the age of denim: most of us like to spend a good deal of our time in jeans and T-shirts. But at least when we do dress up, we've learned to do it in a distinctly Australian way.

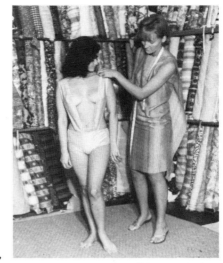

SAVING ON MATERIAL *The newspapers stirred up considerable outrage in 1964 with the appearance of the first 'topless' swimsuit.*

PROUD PRUE *Prue Acton with a sample of her 1973 collection. Prue is one of Australia's true success stories in the fashion industry, taking the country by storm with her innovative approach to fashion excellence.*

TRENDY TWOSOME *Trent Nathan and Carla Zampatti are two of Australia's leading world fashion designers, paving the way for Australia to earn a place in international salons. 120 000 people work in the local fashion industry.*

WHO IS THE FAIREST OF THEM ALL? *In 1908, the magazine* The Lone Hand *decided to respond to a challenge, issued in America, for a beauty to match the best the USA could offer. Pride swelled in the collective Australian bosom, as did the circulation of* The Lone Hand *for the nine months the competition lasted.*

BEAUTY FOR SALE *The great search for the first Miss Australia in 1926 was conducted with the hoopla and promotion of a major sales campaign.*

Miss Australia

The search for a true Australian beauty queen has always been something of a national preoccupation. In 1909 the magazine *The Lone Hand* felt it should defend our womanly honour and set off in search of an Australian entrant for the World's Beauty Contest to be held in America later that year.

The judges narrowed the field down to a handful of aspiring queens by sifting through thousands of photographs. But it wasn't a foolproof system and the magazine reported with regret the exclusion of a young Queenslander of 'classic mould' when the unfortunate girl appeared in person for the judging.

Accompanied by her sister, we met a tall girl of eighteen summers. But, alack, not quite the girl imagination and photograph had pictured for us. It may be that five years hence, after exercise has developed what at present are promises, this young lady would be acclaimed the winner of a beauty contest.

In those days marriage was not considered a handicap and Mrs Otto Wunderlich and Mrs Della Carsons were starters. Daisy Clifton was a strong runner but eventually she was pipped on the post by Alice Buckridge, a twenty-one-year-old drapery assistant who weighed in at a demure 10 stone 6 pounds (about 66 kilograms). The judges waxed lyrical about her 23-inch (58-centimetre) waist and her 'unblushing face full of the joy of life, and beautiful even in repose'. Miss Buckridge's photographs were forwarded to the Chicago *Tribune*, which by now seemed to have forgotten about the event. But the circulation of *The Lone Hand* climbed handsomely and the commercial potential of the beauty quest was established beyond doubt.

The official Miss Australia Quest, as we know it today, began in 1926 when two Sydney newspapers, the *Guardian* and the legendary *Smith's Weekly*, set about the rather costly business of choosing the most gorgeous girl in the country. Badly damaged fragments from a film of the first Miss Australia Quest are the only visual record of the event. It seems the girls were thoroughly tested for Australian conditions, parading before judges in clinging woollen swimsuits. By modern standards they were, in fact, quite bold. Miss Australia contestants today do not pose in bathers.

NOT A PRETTY SIGHT *These turn-of-the-century ladies, flaunting their bodies for the camera before plunging into a private harbour pool at Clovelly in Sydney, were forbidden to bathe in mixed company. No reports exist of men striving to break the ban.*

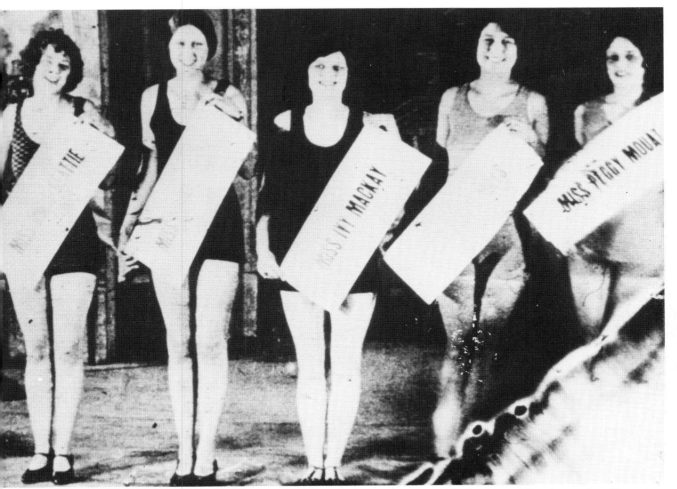

OUR FIRST BEAUTY *Fifty years before the women's libbers decried all beauty contests with the slogan 'Aint she sweet making money off her meat', Australia was gripped with the excitement of its first National Beauty competition. The first Miss Australia competition was held in 1926, and the winner was Miss Western Australia, Beryl Mills.*

SEA NYMPHS *These forward young ladies of the 1920s are representative of the freedom that the flappers had sought for so long. No explanation survives as to why their alluring forms are adorned with garlands of seaweed.*

With prizes of £1000 and two motor cars, the beauty quest caused tremendous excitement. And, when the big night finally came, it was the girl from the West, Miss Beryl Mills, who beat Monica Mack and Mascotte Rawlston to become the first official Miss Australia.

Beryl, a nineteen-year-old from Geraldton, Western Australia, was described as 'a splendid stamp of glorious Australian womanhood'. Hal Missingham, later a Miss Australia judge, recalls meeting Beryl when they lived in the same neighbourhood fifty years ago:

She was a big bird, you know. All built right, a pleasant kind of look about her face. Open. She had a big mouth, big eyes. She really was something.

After her win, Beryl went to Hollywood for a screen test in the silent movies. When she returned she was soon taken up by the local advertising industry to spruik for Australian products.

After the death of her first husband Beryl married again and went to live in America. She died in 1977 at the age of seventy. In the late twenties she was Australia's most famous girl, yet reports of her death made barely a couple of paragraphs in the papers.

There have been scores of Miss Australias since Beryl Mills. Like any other institution that is more than half a century old, the Miss Australia Quest has had its ups and downs. Outwardly it is a shiny pageant which has raised more than

THE FIRST OF MANY *Beryl Mills of Perth, Western Australia. Beryl won the inaugural Miss Australia competition in 1926, an event which became as much an Australian institution as Vegemite and two-up.*

$20 million for charity. But for many years it was a tool for commercial interest. The image of Miss Australia is as sacred as motherhood,

MISS AUSTRALIA 1947 *Judy Gainford, a pretty girl from the town of Lismore was crowned Miss Australia in 1947. Judy was lucky enough to meet the King at Buckingham Palace.*

BEAUTY AND THE DUCK *By 1954 Australia had resumed its peacetime entertainments, including the Miss Australia Quest; an Army 'Duck' paraded the new Beauty Queen through Sydney.*

VINTAGE LOVELY *As Miss Australia Judy travelled the world on a wardrobe which included 12 evening gowns, 7 cocktail dresses, 24 pairs of shoes, 12 pairs of gloves and 20 hats.*

FETCHING LASSIES *These entrants in the 1946 Miss Australia Quest are more daring than their contemporary counterparts. Today, entrants are forbidden to wear swimsuits.*

and yet in 1975 the Northern Territory withdrew from the Quest because its entrant was disqualified, she was in fact a mother.

Few people can remember one year's winner from the next. But one beauty remains firmly in the memory of millions of Australians. Ironically, she was not even born in the country she represented so successfully, not only as Miss Australia but as Miss International as well.

The progress of fashion

Early in the 1900s women wore steel ribbed corsets that cupped the breasts, and layers of padding below a tiny waspish waist. Fashion has relaxed over the years, it may not be so elegant, but it is surely more comfortable.

A DAY ON THE RIVER *Melbourne crowds in their Sunday best flock to the annual Henley-on-Yarra Regatta, the place to see and be seen in the latest fashions.*

LA DOLCE VITA, AUSTRALIAN STYLE *The good life Australian style — sunworshippers of the 1950s on Bondi Beach. Hit tune of the era:* A White Sportscoat, *hit flavour: Iced Vo-Vo.*

BUT CAN SHE TYPE? *In a Sydney 'College' designed to turn ordinary 'housewives' into women of elegance, an instructress steadies a pupil learning how to walk with a book balanced on her head. This skill proved useful for armless librarians, but did little to raise the general standard of deportment amongst Australian women.*

HIGH FASHION, LOW INTEREST *The lady in the audience at this 1950s fashion parade appears totally unimpressed by the creation being modelled.*

242

Tania Verstak was born in Shanghai. She was something of an ugly duckling as a child. She came to Australia at the age of seven with her White Russian parents who were refugees from the Communist regime in China. The family settled at Manly and by the age of sixteen Tania had begun to blossom as a beauty. She had brains as well as charm. She took an Arts degree at Sydney University and spoke several languages. In all she won five beauty quests, from Miss Movie Ball and Miss Sydney University, to Miss New South Wales, Miss Australia and finally Miss International.

The daily press followed Tania's every move for three years. Hers was the best known face in Australia. The story of the refugee child who grew up to conquer the world came to a fitting climax when she married Peter Young, a successful Australian businessman, and then retired from public life to have her baby girl. Tania was indeed the fairytale princess who lived happily ever after.

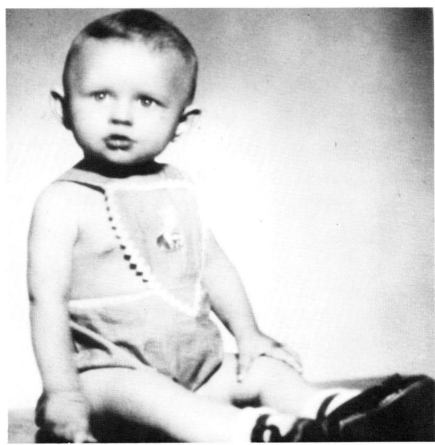

PRETTY BABY *Boy or girl? It was hard to tell then, but twenty years later, this jug-eared infant would become the most popular Miss Australia of them all.*

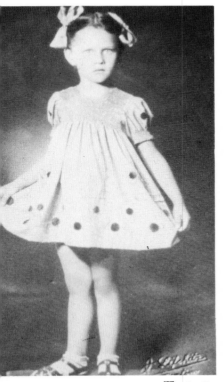

MAKINGS OF A BEAUTY QUEEN *The pretty little girl in the patterned dress is Tania Verstak. Already at five years Tania possessed the flashing good looks and self assurance of a beauty queen.*

THE NATION'S SWEETHEART *Miss Australia, 1961, Tania Verstak. Within a year, she was Miss International and the best-known face in the nation.*

243

Today, she lives in a quiet, wealthy part of Perth in a large house set amongst a spectacular garden. She describes the changes in her life since those heady days when she was the nation's sweetheart:

Tania Verstak has become Mrs Peter Young. I think she's been leading a very normal life. She has a daughter of thirteen, and a house that takes a lot of looking after. She plays sport, she takes part in a few social things and leads a normal life.

Tania rarely flicks through her scrapbooks. Now, as she approaches her forty-first birthday, the excitement of 1961 seems far away. But there are fond memories:

It was very satisfying to have given eighteen months of your life towards charity. Not many of us have a chance to do that. And I have a lasting memory of the effect my winning the Miss Australia Quest had on the New Australian community. I met girls of

PROUD MUM *Tania Verstak's baby was awaited eagerly by a nation which had taken the Miss Australia to their hearts for the previous three years. After her marriage, Tania retired from public life to care for her family.*

thirteen or fourteen who said they felt accepted because I had won the Miss Australia Quest, and that was a wonderful feeling.

The worst part was the lack of privacy and the curiosity it aroused. People wanted to know about you. I suppose that's the worst part of it. And now, with a daughter growing up, I can feel the effect on her at school— children saying your mother was a Miss Australia or Miss International , or Miss Universal.

UNFADING BEAUTY *Tania Verstak, the fairytale princess, now Mrs Peter Young, is a relaxed, confident forty-one year old Perth housewife, who can still flash a devastating smile.*

The Ladies

Chevalier Jules Lefebvre's famous painting of a nude French woman, titled simply *Chloe*, is one of Australia's most admired paintings. But instead of hanging in a gallery, *Chloe* looks down on the patrons of a Melbourne pub. She has occupied pride of place in Young and Jackson's Hotel since she was bought for four hundred guineas back in 1908.

Perhaps it says something about Australia's attitude to women that, for most of the seventy years since, only nude paintings like *Chloe* and the ever-present barmaid have been allowed in our public bars. For much of this century Australian womanhood, if it wanted to drink at all, was politely ushered into a special area quaintly called the 'ladies lounge'. It wasn't many years ago that all Australian women were expected to be much like *Chloe*, to know their place and be seen but not heard. A woman could be beautiful, fashionable, witty—but she always understood her main role in life was to 'honour and obey'.

One young Australian woman who didn't take too much notice of convention was Annette Kellerman, the daughter of a Sydney music teacher. She became an international film star and the world's first screen 'pin-up' girl.

SHADY LADY *Lefebvre's celebrated picture* Chloe *on exhibition at the Melbourne gallery in 1883. Its full-frontal nudity caused outrage amongst the moralists. Today the painting hangs on public view at Young & Jackson's Hotel.*

245

As part of her recovery from a childhood illness, Annette was encouraged to take up swimming, and while still in her teens, she was winning state championship events. By 1903, her aquatic talents were spectacular enough to warrant a special show at the Melbourne Aquarium. As *Punch* reported.

A lissome young lady gambolled fearlessly among the fishes and eels. She will become the rage of the town.

In fact, when Annette added the rather bizarre trick of eating a banana under water, she was well on the way to becoming the rage of the world.

In England, the Kellerman name shot into the headlines when she swam down the Thames, and before long she was commanding $4000 per week for her lavish aquatic 'fantasies', which were performed on

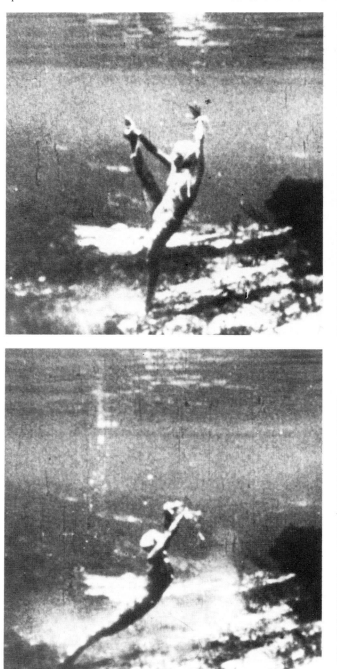

UNDERWATER BALLET *Annette Kellerman, Australia's first international film star, was an outstanding swimmer. Her ambition however, was to be a ballet dancer. Always resourceful, she combined her talents and invented underwater ballet.*

1914 **NUDE SCENE** *Australian swimming sensation Annette Kellerman took an infant Hollywood by storm in the period epic* Neptune's Daughter. *Her willingness to portray a mermaid 'déshabillé' shocked the producers but filled the cinemas.*

stage in giant tanks built especially for the purpose.

It wasn't long before Hollywood made Annette an offer to try her luck in the newly established world of celluloid fantasy, and she created a sensation with a brief 'nude' scene in the 1914 melodrama *Neptune's Daughter*. Kellerman's sister, Marcel, now ninety-two, remembers the drive and ambition that took Annette to stardom:

I think it was that tenacity that she had. She never gave way on anything at all. Nobody counted. All she wanted to do was get to the top of the tree.

As Annette grew older, she seemed to live at an even more hectic pace. She no longer staged her water ballets in public, although at sixty she could still perform amazing underwater feats for the cameras. She became famous for her views on exercise and diet, was elected to the swimming hall of fame and passed on her skills to any youngster willing to learn.

NOW YOU'LL THINK I'M AWFUL *On her return to Australia in 1934, Annette Kellerman teased the press with obtuse references to her international fame as an object of male admiration. "I wouldn't know anything about that," she said.*

When she retired to Surfers Paradise she was already a legend, and in 1975, in a fitting end to her life-long love affair with the water, her cremated remains were scattered in the seas of the Barrier Reef.

ARMS UP, TUMMY IN *At a swimming pool in Brisbane, legendary Australian swimmer and aquatic ballerina Annette Kellerman trains keen young girls in the art of water ballet. She was still capable of amazing underwater feats at the age of eighty.*

THE FIRST LADY *Enid Lyons as she appeared on state occasions as the wife of Prime Minister Joseph.*

Australian women won the right to vote in 1902. But although they made up half the electorate, a woman was not voted into parliament for another forty years. In the thirties, at the height of the Depression, one in four women was battling against unemployment, hunger and poverty just to keep their families together. The new Prime Minister, Joe Lyons, was proving a skilful politician but, in public at least, he never seemed a very forceful personality. His popularity, it was often said, was partly due to his wife, Enid, the woman behind the throne. Dame Enid, now eighty-three, described their relationship:

We were very close. We were one person really. Of course my role has often been exaggerated in this. People used to say I advised him on everything, which of course wasn't true. But all the big decisions—that affected the family, particularly—naturally he would discuss them. Especially with me having an interest in politics, as I always had. I know without my backing he probably wouldn't have done things. If I'd said I don't like it he probably would not have been able to do it.

Enid Lyons was the kind of young girl who always knew what she wanted, and usually got it. At fourteen she decided to become a school teacher. Then she met Joe Lyons, at that time Tasmanian Minister for Education. She wanted to marry Joe, and she walked him down the aisle when she was just seventeen. He was exactly twice her age.

Enid Lyons wanted a large family. She had her first child at nineteen, and by the time the Lyons household moved into the Prime Minister's Lodge in Canberra, Enid had borne twelve children, of whom eleven survived.

MUM AND THE KIDS *Enid Lyons poses informally on the front porch of her Devonport home with nine of the eleven children she mothered. ZPG was a long way off.*

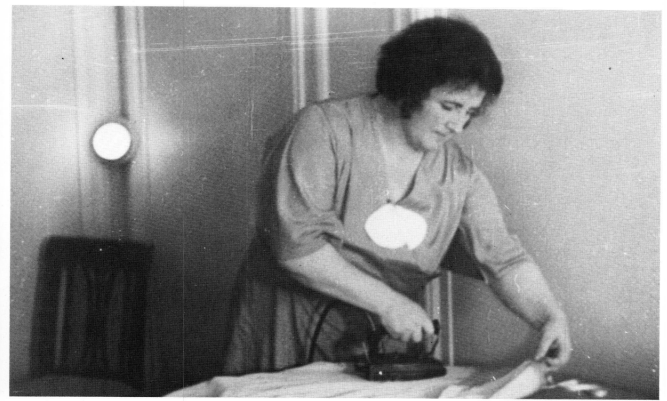

Dame Enid Lyons was both a model and an exasperation to feminists. She was a major political force in Australia, yet she maintained her belief that women are naturally subservient to men.

While Joe Lyons settled into the leader's job, Enid became a national figure in her own right, often making three speeches in a single day. But to the media at least, she was still the classic, subservient woman. The newsreels delighted in depicting her as a hard-working devoted wife who ironed Joe's pants and did the mending. Dame Enid said:

I see nothing derogatory in darning socks. I always used to say that some of my best ideas for speeches came when I was washing clothes. In those days it wasn't a washing machine, you know. You really slogged it out at the washing tub.

Joe Lyons died in April 1939. A few months later the world was plunged into war, and many Australians, particularly women, turned to Enid Lyons to raise their sinking morale. She knew enough about politics to recognise her own electoral potential and in 1943, just four years after her husband's death, she was elected to Federal Parliament—the first woman to take a seat in the House of Representatives. Dame Enid believes only a few women ever choose to enter parliament:

Women are of a different make-up from men. A man is a naturally aggressive person, and I think a woman has within her a certain desire to please. And, though I hesitate to say this because I'm sure I'll be torn to pieces by feminists, I believe they like to please men. A subservient role in certain aspects of their lives is normal.

Dame Enid Lyons was the first woman to be elected to the House of Representatives. Only a few years earlier, her husband, Joe Lyons, had served as Prime Minister.

Dame Enid Lyons, in 1976, was dubbed the 'Germaine Greer of Tasmania' after she gave her official approval to 'much of women's lib'. It seemed a strange tag for a woman who, for sixty years, had reigned as the ideal of Australian motherhood. At home in the sprawling white house where she had raised eleven children, she told reporters:

> My great-grandson brought me a box of matches. I asked him why, and he said I would find them useful for burning my bra.

The bra-burning bonfires lit by women's liberationists were already blazing brightly in 1972 when a book written by expatriate Australian, Dr Germaine Greer, became almost the bible for the international women's movement. *The Female Eunuch* was acclaimed by critics as a work of notable scholarship. By the time she returned to Australia in 1972, after seven years working in universities abroad, Germaine Greer was the biggest celebrity in feminism.

Germaine Greer was born in 1939 and came from a conservative, middle-class Melbourne family. Educated in convent schools, she went on to graduate in Arts from Melbourne University. She gained her MA with first-class honours at Sydney University, then moved on to Cambridge University for her PhD.

When she came home to launch *The Female Eunuch* in Australia, 'respectable' women were shocked by this young Australian who encouraged abortion for women who didn't want to have babies.

Thousands turned out in the streets of Sydney to march behind Dr Greer. They were protesting at discrimination against women in the home, in the workforce and in public facilities like hotels, where women were still unwelcome in most public bars. To Germaine Greer the memory of those days is still fresh:

> I can remember going into a pub in Gippsland, and I went into the public bar. The expression on the faces of the blokes drinking there was so appalled—their whole day was ruined. I mean they were standing there quietly sousing. I

THE LADY AND THE PRIME MINISTER *Dame Enid Lyons, at eighty-three, looks back on a varied life both in and out of politics. She combined the role of first lady with that of a wife and mother, and later embarked on a political career of her own.*

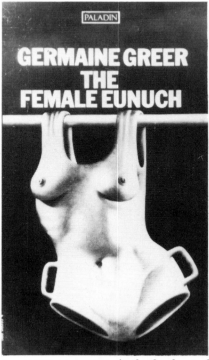

THE WOMEN STEP OUT *At the forefront of the women's movement of the 1970s was Australian writer, academic and agitator Germaine Greer. Her book* The Female Eunuch *was acclaimed as a work of considerable scholarship.*

stick my head around the door and they go. They weren't rude or anything. I just knew that if I stayed there I wouldn't do myself any good and I'd make myself uncomfortable, so I withdrew. The man I was with said, 'I didn't think you'd do that. I thought you'd be liberating the bar.' I said, 'You don't seem to get the point. I mean, why should I go somewhere where I'm unpopular? I'm not going to get anything out of it. It's obviously the place where they go to get away from the missus, and they're allowed to have it as far as I'm concerned. I'm not going to jostle for occupation of the men's lavatories.'

Many of the early liberation battles today appear to be won. But has there been any real change in men's attitudes to women? According to Dr Greer:

People can no longer abuse women as thoughtlessly as they used to. But there's still no relish in women's company for men. I mean, they make an effort to kind of get you into a group that women are part of, but I think they'd rather have it the way it was.

THE LEADER *A striking figure in her neat frock, Germaine Greer, long-legged champion of women's rights is head and shoulders above the crowd as she takes part in a women's movement protest march in Sydney, 1972. Australians either agreed or disagreed with this outspoken young woman, but they seldom ignored her.*

MEDIA MAESTROS *An unlikely alliance during a Germaine Greer visit to Australia in the mid-seventies: the feminist campaigner teamed with current affairs anchorman Mike Willesee.*

8

FEAR AND TRAGEDY

SAD SALVAGE *25-year-old Danny McIver stands amid the rubble of his Darwin home clutching his cat and the bathroom sink. Cyclone Tracy destroyed everything else.*

Environmental hazards and human error

Australia has few predatory creatures. The one we fear most is the shark, but despite our preoccupation with the dangers of the sea, we face much more of a threat from drought, flood, cyclones and, the most destructive of all in terms of human life, the bushfire. But ultimately the most dangerous element in our environment is man himself.

Sharks

To most of us sharks are terrifying creatures, and Hollywood proved recently that even if you make one out of rubber and put a motor inside it, you can still scare the swim shorts off half the world.

Shark attacks have been recorded throughout our history, and it is a

KILLER CAPTURED *By the 1930s, shark attacks were causing so much concern that a system of meshing the major Sydney beaches was introduced. 12-foot monsters were regularly caught, and there has not been a fatal attack on a meshed beach since. As the bays and inlets were not included, risk still surrounds these waterways.*

GET ANY BITES? *One shark attack that achieved notoriety is shown by an engraving featured in the popular press of 1877 simply titled: 'Fishing Party Attacked by a Shark off Long Nose Point, Parramatta River'.*

sobering thought that some of the most dangerous areas are in Sydney Harbour, just a few miles from the GPO.

In 1929, eight Australians were killed by sharks. At Bondi Beach young Colin Stewart was mauled. 'He seemed to be pushing it away,' witnesses said, 'but it came back at him.' Colin died the following day. The same year a girl was maimed by a shark at Collaroy Beach on Sydney's north side, and a youth was attacked at Maroubra to the south. Another man was killed while swimming in Sydney near the suburb of Balmain.

Sharks were causing so much concern in New South Wales that the government introduced a meshing system in 1937. There has not been a fatal shark attack at a meshed ocean beach since. But the problem in Sydney is that the busy harbour thoroughfares cannot be encumbered by nets. Swimmers bathing in

GRUESOME CURIOSITY *Oblivious to the dangers, canoeists paddle to the meshers' boat.*

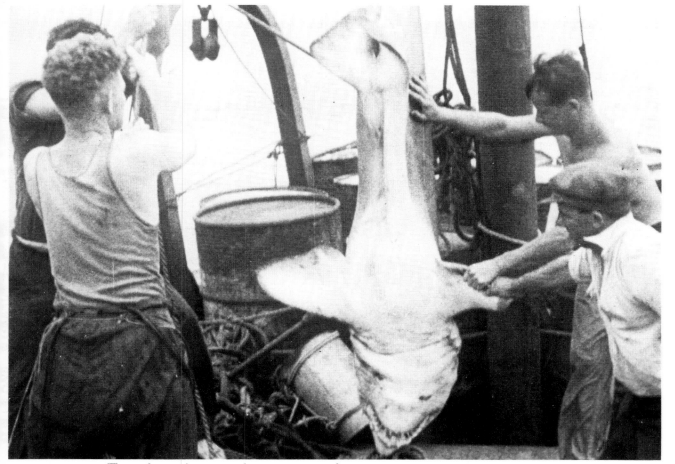

TIGER BY THE TAIL *The meshers string up one less menace to surfers.*

the inviting bays and inlets are easy bait for sharks.

Australia's most notorious location for sharks is Middle Harbour in Sydney, an idyllic stretch of placid water and picturesque beaches. Middle Harbour has seen six fatal shark attacks since 1942, the last and most horrific attack was in Sugarloaf Bay.

MARCIA HATHAWAY *The young actress who was the victim of a savage shark attack in just 75 centimetres (30 inches) of water at Sydney's Middle Harbour.*

It was the Australia Day holiday in 1963; a hot, humid, overcast day—the sort that Sydneysiders call 'good shark weather', and yet also the sort they seem to spend in the water until late afternoon when the thunderstorms break. A young actress, Marcia Hathaway, was cooling off in just seventy-five centimetres of water. Her fiance, Fred Knight, was swimming nearby when Marcia suddenly cried out, 'I've been bitten by an octopus.' But, it was no octopus. By the time her fiance and a friend had freed her from the jaws of the shark, her right leg was torn to shreds.

NASTY CUSTOMERS *Even in death, these two sharks manage to fix the spectator's eye with a defiant, ferocious and terrifying glare.*

DISABLED AMBULANCE *With shark attack victim Marcia Hathaway fading rapidly from blood loss inside, the ambulance is pushed desperately up the road away from the water. The ambulance failed to climb the hill after burning out its clutch, so a second one was called, however by the time Marcia was transferred to it and rushed to hospital, she was dead.*

Marcia Hathaway died in the most tragic circumstances. The beach where she had been swimming was inaccessible by road. She was taken by boat to the nearest landing place while her fiance dived back into the water and swam to the nearest house to call for help. An ambulance was waiting for the victim when she arrived, but as it started up the slippery slope, it began to lose traction and the clutch burnt out. A second ambulance had to be called. By the time it arrived and the girl was transferred, it was too late. Marcia Hathaway was dead on arrival at hospital.

Many shark victims don't live to tell the tale but Henri Bource, a Melbourne scuba-diver, who lost his left leg to a White Pointer shark off the coast of Victoria in 1964, is believed to be the only person whose attack was actually recorded on film.

INSTANT AMPUTATION *Skin-diver Henri Bource lost his leg to a White Pointer while studying seals off the Victorian coast. The shark caught him totally by surprise, and shook him violently, as a dog would attack a slipper. (Film re-enactment).*

257

Henri used the film in a documentary to tell the story of his terrifying experience. In Bsource's words:

At the impact I knew immediately what had happened. I was dragged under the water and shook and shook—like a dog with a slipper. In a minute and a half it was all over.

Henri Bource owes his life to an incredibly courageous young diver, Jill Ratcliffe, who grabbed a rope and went to his assistance, diving into the turbulent, bloodstained water. With the help of other divers, she brought him back to the boat.

The leg came off and I had to get to the surface to get air. Everything after that just happened automatically. Everyone went into action. They got me on board the boat and they put a tourniquet on the stump and stopped the bleeding. It took an hour and a half to get me to hospital.

If I hadn't lost the leg when I did, I would have drowned. There is no doubt about that. Although it was only a minute and a half under water, according to the lookout on board who put a time on it, that's a relatively long period of time without breath when you're under stress.

Bource was one of the lucky ones. He was soon back in his skin-diving

gear, more determined than ever to defy nature and make the sea his life. Today, Henri is a contract diver and underwater photographer.

LIFE AND DEATH *Diver Henri Bource struggles for life on the deck of a trawler after losing his left leg to a shark. (Photograph taken during actual attack).*

BLOODIED BUT UNBOWED *In a specially adapted wet-suit and wearing a flipper on what remains of his left leg, shark attack victim Henri Bource (right) returned to the water. Today he is a professional diver, and has continued in an uneasy truce with the killers of the sea. After his accident his preference was for dead sharks (above).*

Crime

Australian history has also had its share of human killers, and if ever there was a shark of the underworld it was 'Squizzy' Taylor. Taylor, who terrorised Melbourne in the twenties, was one of those criminals who somehow managed to become part of our folklore. Another was a Sydney waiter named Antonio Agostini, husband of the mysterious 'pyjama girl'. Perhaps the most infamous of all was a Hungarian migrant, Stephen Leslie Bradley, Australia's first kidnapper.

Squizzy Taylor

Joseph Leslie Theodore (Squizzy) Taylor was an evil little punk who showed that, if crime didn't exactly

pay, it wasn't a bad way of making a name for yourself. Taylor was really only a larrikin criminal, who dressed like 'Pretty Boy' Floyd, wrote doggerel like Bonnie and Clyde, and died like John Dillinger.

Taylor started his career as a pickpocket, graduating through standover tactics and blackmail to armed robbery. Unfortunately for many innocent people, most of the stories told about Squizzy Taylor were true. He was involved in at least six murders dating back to 1913, but was never convicted of any. They were mostly killings of unsuspecting law-abiding citizens.

In 1916 Taylor telephoned a Melbourne chauffeur service and ordered a car to call at an exclusive

address. Taylor and an accomplice met the car outside, planning to use it for their getaway after robbing a bank messenger. When the driver refused to co-operate, he was shot dead. By the time Taylor appeared in court, the frightened witnesses somehow 'forgot' what they had seen and Squizzy had found himself an alibi.

On another occasion, Taylor sent two of his henchmen to the Melbourne suburb of Glenferrie. At 11.00 a.m. in the busy shopping centre, Thomas Berriman, manager of the Commercial Bank, was hurrying to the railway station past women with prams and small children. In a small bag he carried £1850 in notes, surplus cash he was

SQUIZZY AND FRIEND *Squizzy Taylor, (right) perhaps the first real folk hero of crime since Ned Kelly, and fellow Melbourne criminal Bush Thompson in a study which would have done one of the old masters proud. Like many crims of his type Squizzy had great vanity, often posed for photographs and once made a film to show that he was alive and well while evading police.*

returning to the bank's head office in the city. Taylor's men confronted him on the railway ramp. Berriman pulled out his security revolver, but the thieves were quicker and a bullet ripped into the bank man's chest. Men in the crowd chased the bandits, but they escaped with the money. Berriman died in hospital soon afterwards.

In the heady days after the First World War, Melbourne was the crime capital of Australia, and Squizzy Taylor was its undisputed boss. Around the notorious slum suburbs rival gangs fought over two-up schools, racecourse rackets and cheap brothels. In the back alley area of Fitzroy, commonly called 'the narrows', the bullets flew thick and fast. The Police Department's only regret was that the criminals did not shoot straighter and wipe each other out.

Squizzy, or 'the Turk' as he was known in the underworld, stood just 5 ft 2 in (almost 158 cm) high, a diminutive spiv sporting flash clothes and flash girlfriends, including Mollie Jervis who was known as the 'decoy duck'. His loyal 'moll' was Ida Pender, a pretty teenage shoplifter. But even in their moments of privacy, Taylor was not immune from police raids. Former CIB detective Harold Saker, who broke into Taylor's home in one of the many raids, said:

I went to the back door and instead of knocking I just put the jemmy in. I dashed up the front and Squizzy Taylor was in bed with Ida Pender. I just put up my guns and told them to jump out of bed. Squizzy said, 'She can't get out, she's got nothin' on.' And I said, 'Well she won't bloody frighten me, so she can come out.' She was a good sort, too.

The raids on Taylor's various homes never gained the police much more than good publicity. But in 1921, they caught him red-handed during a warehouse robbery. Taylor skipped the £3000 bail and went into hiding. He evaded the police for a year, arrogantly teasing them with newspaper correspondence like this:

Dear Sir: I can't understand what the fuss is about. (Your story) says

SO NICE TO SEE YOU ALL *After a twelve-month chase, Melbourne hoodlum Squizzy Taylor (centre, and bottom left) gave himself up to the police. Taylor was the most notorious criminal of the first two decades of the century. He died from bullet wounds while defending the 'honour' of a prostitute.*

I was seen in St Kilda. That's a lot of rot. I haven't been there for months. Last month I went to see Johnny Get Your Gun at the Theatre Royal and had supper at the Sawdust Factory and then went home on the Toorak line. As soon as I have finished my business, I will pop up to the CIB where I'll be welcome because I know I can't keep running around much longer.

There is no doubt that the idea of a criminal skipping bail and writing to the newspapers to tell them about the shows he had seen appealed to the larrikin instinct in many Australians and, if it wasn't for Taylor's visciousness, it could have been amusing. He eventually telephoned the detectives to announce his surrender and they sent a car around to pick him up. By now Taylor's every move was front page news. Out on bail again, he was shot and wounded by a rival gangster the night before his trial was due to begin. But this time he turned up, on crutches, to hear the jury find him not guilty yet again.

Taylor was now at the peak of his career. He was perhaps the first real folk hero of Australian crime since Ned Kelly, and with more murder and armed robbery charges hanging over his head, Squizzy could not be suppressed. Warned off the race tracks, he continued to show up until one day at Caulfield the stewards threw him out into the street. That night Squizzy was back to settle the score. He took matches and fuel and burnt the members' stand to the ground. It was an effective demonstration of Taylor's power.

Undeterred by police harassment, he continued his career. He was as hated and feared by criminals as he was by the public. He was a police informer, 'sneaking' on his underworld colleagues, and there were prisoners in Pentridge Prison who had sworn to poison his food if he was put behind bars.

The fitting finale to the Taylor legend came when he died from bullet wounds received during a gunfight while defending the 'honour' of a prostitute. In October 1927 it was reported that Taylor, with his gun drawn, had burst into the home of an up-and-coming young standover man, 'Snowy' Cutmore. Cutmore was asleep when Taylor burst into his bedroom, but in a second he had woken and pulled a gun from under his pillow. The two gangsters shot each other dead.

Some historians, however, have found this climax just a little too pat. There are theories that Cutmore and Taylor were set up by rival criminals, and even that the police were somehow involved. Certainly, if they weren't, many would have liked to have been. Whatever the answer to the mystery, it was hardly a day of national mourning when Joseph Leslie (Squizzy) Taylor—'the Turk'—met his spectacular demise.

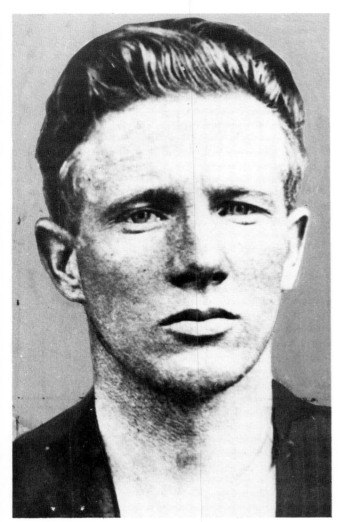

'SNOWY' CUTMORE *The Sydney gunman who is reputed to have shot Squizzy Taylor in a wild gunfight in October 1927. Cutmore also died in the duel.*

THE TURK *This police mug shot gives some support to the underworld nickname for Squizzy Taylor. Graduating from a career as a pickpocket, Taylor was notorious as a standover man.*

The 'pyjama girl' case

During the Second World War Antonio Agostini was an Italian waiter at Sydney's plush Romano's restaurant. One of his regular customers was Police Commissioner Bill MacKay. The New South Wales police force had been trying for ten years to solve what had become known as the 'pyjama girl' case. In 1944 the Police Commissioner and the waiter found themselves sitting face to face across a desk in the Commissioner's office. Suddenly one of the world's strangest murder mysteries unfolded.

It all began in 1934 on the Howlong Road, a few miles outside the New South Wales border town of Albury. A young farmer, Tom Griffiths, was leading a prize bull along the side of the road when he stumbled across the body of a young woman in a culvert. Her face was mutilated and her body badly burnt. A bag had been drawn over her head and shoulders. She was loosely clad in yellow crêpe Chinese pyjamas. When he rushed home to telephone the police, neighbours asked Tom if he had seen a ghost; he replied that he thought maybe he had.

LINDA AGOSTINI *After ten years of patient cross-checking, police finally established the 'Pyjama Girl's' identity as that of this attractive young woman . . . Linda Agostini, who was killed by her husband Antonio.*

HAPPIER TIMES *Antonio Agostini and his wife Linda the 'Pyjama Girl', relaxing on the beach shortly before the arguments which led to the killing of Linda.*

Establishing the woman's identity seemed routine enough. Missing persons' files were checked, and this description was issued by the police:

... between twenty and thirty years of age, 5 ft 2 in to 5 ft 3 in, slim to medium build, blue-grey eyes, light brown hair.

One of the women who seemed to fit that description on the missing persons' list was Linda Agostini, a young English woman who had settled in Melbourne, and her husband, Antonio, became a suspect. But when police investigated Mrs Agostini's dental chart it appeared slightly different from that of the 'pyjama girl', as the murder victim would become known—not only in Australia but around the world. A dentist had made a subtle mistake during the initial post-mortem, and his error would cost police ten years of laborious and mostly unnecessary work.

Initially the body was kept on ice, but when a newspaper reporter in Albury pointed out that it was

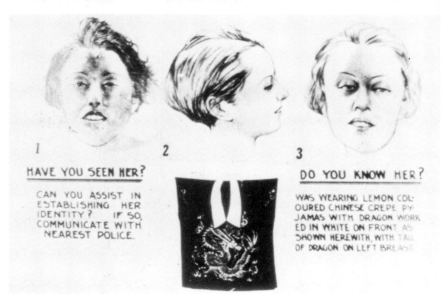

ARTIST'S IMPRESSION *An extract from the police poster circulated in the 10-year search for the identity of the 'Pyjama Girl'. The victim's husband was convicted of the killing. Later he was deported.*

developing green spots, it was decided to move the body to a mortuary at Sydney university. There the pyjama girl was placed in a bath of formalin. No one could have realised what a weird exhibit she would become or just how long she would lie in state. During the next decade, hundreds peered into the bath—noting the girl's physical peculiarities: her large hands, peroxided hair and ears with almost no lobes. They went away horrified at the ghastly sight. However, no one could identify her. At one stage police made checks on every young woman who had not voted in the federal elections. Inquiries were made in almost every country of the world.

HORRIBLE HUBBIE *Convicted of killing his wife, Antonio Agostino was later sent back to his native Italy. He remarried and died of old age in 1969.*

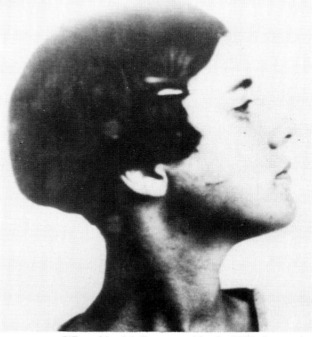

BOGUS LINDA *When this girl disappeared in the 1930s her mother and an eccentric Sydney doctor argued persuasively that she was in fact the 'Pyjama Girl' ... the girl in the formalin bath ... the victim of Australia's most famous killing. The 'Pyjama Girl' case took ten years to solve and Anna Philhomena Morgan was yet another 'red herring'.*

Determined to solve the murder, Police Commissioner Bill MacKay decided to put a fresh team of detectives on the case every few months in the hope that someone would come up with new evidence.

In 1944, a team of three dentists were asked to make yet another examination of the pyjama girl. This time the dentists noticed a tiny gap in an upper bicuspid not previously recorded. After all that time in the formalin bath, a porcelain filling had fallen out. It had been overlooked in the original dental reports. Then the dentists found another porcelain filling. The dental comparisons were made again. This time the pyjama girl's modified dental chart matched that of Linda Agostini in every detail.

With the mystery solved at last, police were ready to arrest Agostini. Commissioner MacKay spoke to Antonio at Romano's and suggested the waiter 'drop into headquarters for a chat'. He did, and within a few minutes had confessed to the murder. It was now the best part of a decade since he had been taken by police to see the body of his wife in the formalin bath, and had expressed no signs of recognition.

Time was much kinder to Agostini than it had been to his wife. After the drawn out search to establish the pyjama girl's identity, the inquest and trial were almost an anti-climax. The inquest was complicated enormously by the claims of a certain Dr Benbow who, with the mother of another missing girl, Anna Philhomena Morgan, almost persuaded the authorities that they had been mistaken and that the cadaver was in fact Anna Morgan's and not that of Linda Agostini.

At the trial, with the evidence now confused and blurred, Agostini was convicted only of the manslaughter of his wife. In 1948, after serving less than four years of his sentence in Pentridge Prison, he was deported to Italy where he re-married. He died in 1969.

The pyjama girl was the most famous corpse in our history. By the time the case was over, she had been reconstructed, put on public display, and even made up with lipstick and

THE WITNESSES *March, 1944 — ten years after the scorched and battered body of the 'Pyjama Girl' had been discovered. At the inquest were Mr Tom Griffiths (left) who found the remains, with Sergeant W. Kelly, the photographer.*

THE WAITER WHO KILLED *Antonio Agostini, (right), was the man who killed the 'Pyjama Girl'. For ten years the body lay unidentified in a bath of formalin. Once the police established her identity, Agostini confessed to the killing.*

rouge in the hope that someone might identify her. Today, she is all but forgotten. Her body lies in plot 8341 at Preston Cemetery in Melbourne. The government spent hundreds of thousands of dollars trying to find out who she was. Yet, when she was finally laid to rest, there was not enough money in the coffers to put a headstone on her grave.

The Thorne kidnapping

Stephen Leslie Bradley picked up a newspaper one day in 1960 and read that Bazil and Freda Thorne had won first prize in the £100 000 Opera House lottery. The Thornes, who had a daughter, Belinda, aged three, and an eight-year-old son, Graeme, lived in a modest Bondi flat. They were ecstatic about their windfall. But the joy in the Thorne household lasted exactly one week. On 7 July Freda Thorne answered the telephone and a voice said, 'I have your son.' It was the beginning of a nightmare.

The Thornes had been determined that the lottery win would not affect Graeme's school life. Every morning he left home at the same time and walked down the street to the corner shop where he bought himself a packet of chips. He ate them while he waited for the mother of one of his school friends to pick him up and drive him to Scots College. On the morning of 7 July he stood outside the shop as usual. An older boy who knew him told police he had seen Graeme from a car as he went past. It was the last time he was seen alive.

Graeme's mother was convinced her son's disappearance had something to do with the lottery win. But when Sergeant Laurence O'Shea of Bondi police was sent to the Thorne's flat to take down a detailed description of the missing boy, he knew nothing about the large amount of money the family had won. By sad coincidence, while the policeman was in the flat the phone rang again. O'Shea took the receiver from Mrs Thorne and a man spoke in a foreign accent:

I want £25 000. If you don't pay the money I'll feed him to the sharks.

O'Shea responded with the question, 'Where would I get that sort of money?' Immediately suspicious, the caller hung up. It would be the only contact Bradley would make with Thorne's parents.

A reward of £15 000 was immediately offered for information leading

BITTER RICHES *Bazil Thorne, a Sydney travelling salesman, waves to reporters after learning of his first prize win in the Opera House Lottery. A month later, his son was kidnapped and killed. A Hungarian-born migrant was convicted of the crime.*

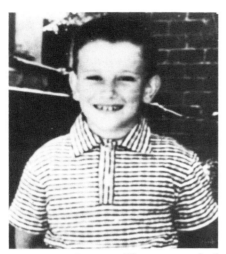

SAD SMILE *Graeme Thorne was dead within a few hours of his kidnapping. This picture smiled out at the nation from millions of newspapers and posters.*

to the boy's return. His heartbroken father spoke on the newsreels, appealing to the kidnapper to return his son:

All I can say to this person—if he's a father, and has children of his own—well, for God's sake, send him back to us in one piece.

The search quickly moved to Frenchs Forest where the missing boy's schoolcase was found a few days after he disappeared. With it were Graeme's school cap marked with his name, a maths book and an apple from his packed lunch.

Five weeks after he disappeared, Graeme Thorne's body was found by two small boys playing in a patch of scrub in the northern suburb of Seaforth. The body, wrapped in a travelling rug, was jammed into a

rock crevice. A post-mortem showed Graeme Thorne had suffered a fractured skull. A silk scarf was knotted around his neck.

Police were convinced that forensic examination of the plant clippings that had stuck to the rug would help them find Graeme Thorne's murderer. They consulted a botanist who specialised in Australian grasses; a quiet woman scientist who worked in a laboratory in a corner of Sydney's Botanic Gardens. Finally, she gave them the much-needed lead. Dr Joyce Vickery found two peculiar plants on the blanket. She said later:

We knew the two plants were garden plants, but they were not present at the site where Graeme Thorne's body was found. There-

IN EVERY POLICE STATION *As the desperate manhunt for Graeme Thorne's kidnappers slowed down, police advertised the large reward being offered for information. A Sydney-based newspaper group offered £10 000 and the NSW Government £5 000.*

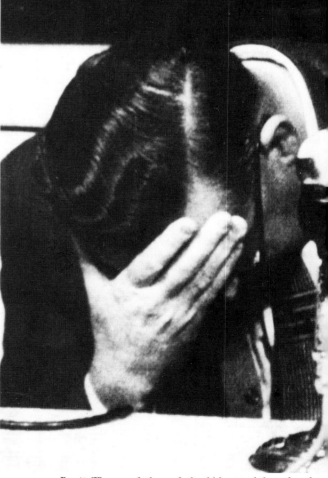

OVERCOME *Bazil Thorne, father of the kidnapped boy, breaks down while making an appeal for the release of his kidnapped son. A commercial traveller, Thorne had returned to Sydney airport to face a national press conference.*

FRONT PAGE THREATS *Australia's first kidnapping case dominated the nation's front pages for weeks. The kidnapper's chilling threat that he would feed Graeme Thorne to the sharks was splashed across the entire width of the* Daily Mirror.

fore, they must have become attached to the rug somewhere else.

In the course of identification, one of my colleagues went out into the Botanic Gardens and brought in a twig of each. When Detective Sergeant Alan Clarke came to get our report, I showed him these. He looked at them with intense interest and asked if he could keep them.

Those two innocuous cuttings helped seal Bradley's fate. One was an uncommon plant and, as Dr Vickery explained to the police, it would be unusual to find the two shrubs growing together. Another detective working on the case suggested pink powder found on the boy's clothing might be mortar like that used in housing foundations some years earlier. This was also confirmed.

Then began weeks of laborious

TRAGIC ADDRESS *The block of flats in the Sydney suburb of Bondi where the Thorne family lived at the time of their Lottery win and the subsequent kidnapping and murder of their son.*

searching. As Sydney crime reporter Bill Archibald later described in his book, *The Bradley Case:*

> Detective Sergeant Clarke had been able to tell the searchers ... that they should look for a building with high foundations. They should look also for the shrubs. The type of building had been deduced from observation that most places in which pink mortar had been used were built at ground level and had well-kept gardens around them. Grains of mortar were not likely to lie undisturbed in these places. The most probable place for the boy's body to have lain so that it would collect the mortar was under a house or in a garage.

It was a Clontarf postman working his rounds just a few miles from Seaforth who finally found the house the police were seeking. The house was empty, but the police soon established the name of the previous tenant. It was Stephen Leslie Bradley, who had already fled Australia aboard the passenger ship *Himalaya* with his wife, Magda, and their three children. Mrs Magda Bradley later told police they were

THE LONG WAY HOME *Bradley under arrest as he embarked for the journey back to Australia, trial, and life imprisonment.*

taking their youngest child, Robert, five years old, to England where he was to have specialist treatment for deafness. Bradley was arrested aboard the *Himalaya* at Colombo in Ceylon (now Sri Lanka) and extradited to Australia to face a charge of murder.

Bradley's trial was conducted amid public demonstrations of outrage and hatred. When the jury handed down its inevitable verdict,

nine months of accumulated anger was unleashed. People in the court screamed abuse. One woman called out, 'Feed him to the sharks.' Bradley was sentenced to life imprisonment. In October 1968, Stephen Leslie Bradley suffered a heart attack and died after playing a game of tennis with the prison governor. There were many who believed he should not have been allowed to live that long.

BAD BRADLEY *Stephen Bradley the Hungarian who was convicted of the kidnap and murder of Graeme Thorne.*

THE VENGEFUL *Crowds trying to force their way into the trial of Stephen Bradley at the Central Criminal Court in Sydney. When the kidnapper was found guilty, a voice cried out from the public gallery: 'Feed him to the sharks!' Bradley died in prison.*

Disasters

Australia has suffered relatively few natural disasters, and perhaps because of this the nation has been deeply traumatised when a major tragedy has occurred. The city which has suffered most is Darwin, which has been through three major cyclones in living memory and was almost bombed out of existence during the war.

For the most part, however, the nation has been shocked by 'man-made' disasters; in particular an extraordinary series of bridge collapses, and a bizarre chain of tragic circumstances which involved a ship of Her Majesty's Australian navy.

The *Melbourne-Voyager* Collision

HMAS *Melbourne* must be the only ship in history unlucky enough to have sunk two destroyers in peace time and none in war.

In 1964, Australians were becoming increasingly conscious of the country's defences. We'd had a taste of confrontation with Indonesia and were getting involved in Vietnam. Our army, navy and air force were being strengthened, and military manoeuvres and joint exercises with the allies were popular subjects for newspapers and television.

It was against this background of 'war games' that in February 1964 the Australian navy was training off the coast of New South Wales. The aircraft carrier *Melbourne* and the destroyer *Voyager* were cruising together at night about 30 kilometres southeast of Jervis Bay.

On receipt of *Melbourne's* signal to take up a 'plane-guard' position, *Voyager* moved from behind so that she was about 1800 metres to the right and ahead of the carrier. She turned further to starboard and headed away from *Melbourne*, which was steaming straight ahead. Then the situation changed drastically.

SAD DOCKING **HMAS** Melbourne *inches into dock for repairs to her bow after the collision with* **HMAS** Voyager *1964. It was the beginning of a tragic run of luck for the Australian Navy flagship. In 1969 the* Melbourne *was involved in an almost identical collision with an American destroyer* Frank E. Evans.

THE FATAL IMPACT *The bow of the Australian aircraft carrier* HMAS Melbourne, *the morning after her fatal collision with the destroyer escort* Voyager, *a naval tragedy which claimed over 80 lives. Just a few years later the ill-fated ship would sink another destroyer, the American ship* Frank E. Evans.

LONELY AT THE TOP *Commander of the* Melbourne, *Captain John Robertson (left), with Rear Admiral Becher on the bridge of the aircraft carrier when she berthed.*

A few minutes before 10.00 p.m. Captain John Robertson was on the bridge of *Melbourne* when he noticed *Voyager* had swung back to port. He assumed she was 'fishtailing' or zig-zagging to reduce speed while *Melbourne* overtook her. When the two ships were about 1800 metres apart again, Captain Robertson moved across to the compass platform just as the navigator looked up to see *Voyager* crossing towards them. Instantly alarmed, the navigator ordered, 'Stop both engines. Half astern both engines.'

A second later Captain Robertson issued the order, 'Full astern both engines.' Later Captain Robertson said:

It all happened so quickly. One minute all was well, and one minute all was not well. There was a collision. It was too late to do anything then. I guess you just wait for the crash. I don't know how quickly one thinks in those situations. The whole thing from start to finish was over in just over one minute. I think it struck me in a flash of lightning that this was probably the end of my naval career.

JAWS OF DEATH *Workmen begin repairs to the gashed bows of the aircraft carrier* Melbourne — *the bows which ripped apart the destroyer escort* Voyager *with the loss of 82 seamen. Another similar accident with an American destroyer, while on joint exercises in the South China Seas earned the* Melbourne *a sad reputation.*

By the time the situation was realised, *Voyager* was sinking fast. She plunged to the bottom in two sections with eighty-two seamen dead, either crushed or drowned. *Melbourne* rescued one hundred and ninety-seven. Among the bodies of the dead was *Voyager*'s captain, Duncan Stevens.

Melbourne, with its bows gaping like the jaws of a wounded shark, arrived back in Sydney the following morning. The scene, as the injured and the bodies of the dead were unloaded, was reminiscent of war.

In March 1964 a Royal Commission was set up to hear the complex evidence surrounding our worst naval disaster. After fifty-five days, it was found that *Voyager* was largely to blame. But *Melbourne's* officers were criticised for not warning *Voyager* of the impending danger.

By now, it was clear that Robertson's days as captain of an aircraft carrier were over. Under his command another ship, HMAS *Vendetta* had earlier been involved in a collision with a dry dock. Captain Robertson was transferred to a shore position soon after the Royal Commission ended. He resigned and for-feited a large pension.

Meanwhile, Lieutenant Commander Peter Cabban, an officer aboard *Voyager* at the time of the collision, alleged in certain documents that Captain Stevens had 'a reputation for drunkenness'. Ironically, the documents containing the evidence were in the hands of Liberal politicians, who faced the choice of remaining quiet or embarrassing their own government. In his very first speech in parliament the new Liberal Member for Warringah, Sydney barrister Edward St John, questioned the government about the evidence, and at one stage even the Prime Minister interjected. St John says in retrospect:

I felt sorry for Robertson. I think he had been made a scapegoat. I was appalled really that the government ministers and public servants should cover up the truth the way they did. They had obtained statements from naval officers on board *Voyager* which clearly corroborated what Cabban said, and they were still maintaining in parliament that there was no corroboration of Cabban, in fact, they had it in their hands.

SCAPEGOAT *Captain Robertson leaves a hearing of the first* Voyager *Inquiry.*

BEACHED *John Robertson who was the Captain of* HMAS Melbourne *when it collided with the destroyer* Voyager. *Later he ran a Sydney hotel.*

By 1968, the attacks by Edward St John and other politicians forced a second Royal Commission into the *Voyager-Melbourne* collision. The official finding this time was that Stevens was not a drunkard, but the whole responsibility for the accident was placed on *Voyager*.

Captain Robertson received a payment of £30 000 as an 'act of grace'. He became a businessman, ran a charter yacht service in New Guinea for some years, and now owns a hotel in Sydney's Surry Hills district. He says on reflection:

A big organisation tends to be very impersonal when it comes to an individual being. If you face the facts of life, however good a captain you are, if you're the captain of a ship and it has a collision, whether you're right or wrong, then there's going to be a reluctance to employ you again at sea. It's happened to other captains who've been involved in collisions—it's one of those facts of life you know!

Then, in 1969, the incredible happened. HMAS *Melbourne* was involved in an almost identical collision with the United States destroyer *Frank E. Evans*. Both ships were taking part in a joint exercise in the South China Sea. This time, seventy-four American sailors were killed and, once again, it was found that *Melbourne* was not responsible.

But *Melbourne*'s problems were still not over. In 1974, the passenger liner *Australis* bumped the aircraft carrier while she was moored at Garden Island naval dockyard in Sydney Harbour, causing minor damage.

THE DESTROYER DESTROYER *The luckless* Melbourne *steams into Singapore Harbour after its collision with the American destroyer* Frank E. Evans *in the South China Sea, 1969.*

MEASURING THE COST *Naval workmen use a painted yardstick to gauge the damage to the bow of the* **Melbourne** *after its collision with the* **Frank E. Evans.**

The following year, four crewmen were rescued from the sea off the New South Wales coast when their anti-submarine aircraft overshot *Melbourne*'s landing deck. In 1976, a Japanese freighter, *Blue Andromeda*, sideswiped *Melbourne* when she was moored at Garden Island. In early 1979, eight crewmen were injured aboard *Melbourne*, again while she was moored at Garden Island. A nylon tie-line snapped, whipping into the sailors. Seven crewmen were admitted to hospital. Then in May, *Melbourne* was the scene of yet another drama when two costly air force aircraft both, on the same day, overshot their landings and were sunk. The crew were rescued by the carrier. Another aircraft was lost overboard in 1979.

It is said that *Melbourne* is 'the unluckiest boat in the navy', an idea that the public relations men for the navy like to deny. All ships have accidents and running an aircraft carrier is something like driving a block of flats. But, with two major disasters on her log, there is little doubt that this is how the best known ship in the Australian navy will be remembered.

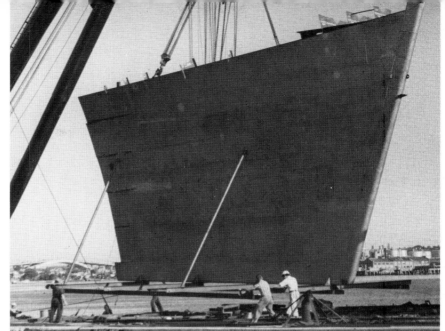

ONE MORE TIME *Shipyard workers with the new bow section fabricated for the* **Melbourne** *after her collision with* **Voyager** *during 'war games' off Jervis Bay.*

ABORTED TAKEOFF *The pilot still in his ejector seat can be seen blasting clear of his Skyhawk jet as it plunges into the sea.*

LEFTOVERS *With the pilot safely on board, the rescue team begin their salvage of the remains of the Skyhawk.*

TERRIBLE IMPACT *Thirty-five men died in October 1970 when the incomplete West Gate Bridge, crashed to the ground. This photograph was taken by a 10-year old boy.*

AWESOME GRAVITY *The scene at the site of Melbourne's West Gate Bridge project after a 2,000 ton concrete span had broken loose and plunged 150 feet to the ground. Thirty-five workmen were killed on or under the span, more were injured.*

At left: **YARRA CROSSING** *The West Gate Bridge as it appeared from the North East after the tragic crash in 1970.*

Three bridge tragedies

The West Gate bridge collapsed on 15 October 1970. Thirty-five workmen were killed on, or under, the 2000-tonne concrete span when it broke loose and plunged about 45 metres to the ground below. Many more workmen were seriously injured.

In the bitter aftermath that followed, two contracting companies were dismissed, and work on the bridge was delayed for two years. By the time it was finished, the price had soared to $200 million.

Since the tragedy of West Gate, two other Australian cities have witnessed shocking bridge disasters.

On the morning of 6 January 1975, commuters travelling to work in Hobart were greeted by an amazing scene. Two cars were perched on the brink of the new bridge, which had just been scissored open in a weird accident. During the night the bridge's long sweeping span, like a sleeping dinosaur, had been nearly

FATEFUL WARNING *A victim of the West Gate Bridge collapse awaits help. Behind him, a grimly prophetic warning sign in four languages.*

ON THE BRINK *Inches from destruction, two cars hang perched on the edge of the severed Tasman Bridge, facing down to the stretch of water that had already claimed twelve lives.*

WHOOPSIE *The embarrassing dip in Melbourne's new King Street Bridge. The defect closed the bridge for two years in 1962 and kept Sydneysiders in jokes for the rest of the decade.*

split in two when it was struck by the ship, *Lake Illawarra.* A fisherman, who saw it from his boat, described the incident:

The two sections of the roadway collapsed and the debris of the roadway just collapsed on to the ship. It started going down front first almost immediately. I saw a

car, and it careered straight off the end in a swallow dive.

At least four cars plunged into 27 metres of water drowning their trapped occupants. In all, twelve people died. The subsequent inquiry revealed that *Lake Illawarra* had been off course and had sailed between the wrong pair of pylons under

the Bridge.

Australia's bridges seemed to be 'jinxed' throughout the 1970s. Just two years after the Tasmanian incident, the nation was shocked by the most gruesome bridge disaster in our history. On 18 January 1977, Granville's Bold Street bridge was carrying early morning peak hour traffic across Sydney's western railway line. As the 6.09 a.m. train from Mount Victoria passed underneath, the engine ran off the lines and struck the bridge supports. The 170-tonne concrete span collapsed on the packed passenger carriages below.

The final horrific toll of Granville was 83 people dead. Another 213 passengers were injured, many psychologically and physically crippled for life. At the scene of the accident, where crushed carriages lay flattened under the slabs of concrete, one of the many rescuers said:

We were nine hours cutting those girders out. Of course, we got a few surprises—like people speaking to us that later died. One old fellow said, 'Don't worry any more about me. I'm done for. You rescue the young people.' Eventually he died. Imagine that.

The Coroner found six causes for the catastrophe, including the poor condition of the track, and wear on the leading wheels of the engine. The New South Wales Public Transport Commission accepted liability and expressed its deep regret. But the promise to upgrade the system must have meant little to the hundreds of people whose lives where shattered when locomotive 4620 went off the rails on that terrible Tuesday.

TERRIBLE TUESDAY *A passenger train lies crushed beneath the collapsed Bold Street Bridge at Granville, Sydney. 83 people were killed in the January 1977 catastrophe, and another 213 injured, many psychologically and physically injured for life.*

FLATTENED *The awesome power of Cyclone Tracy, Darwin, Christmas Day, 1974. The official toll was 65 people dead, 140 badly injured, thousands homeless.*

Cyclone Tracy

Darwin today is 'the town that Tracy built', a rising landscape of specially engineered strong cyclone-proofed houses.

On Christmas Eve 1974, Darwin residents waited for the cyclone they knew was coming. They had survived these storms every summer. This one would come and go like all the rest. It took cyclone Tracy just a few hours to prove them wrong and flatten the entire city.

The eye of the cyclone arrived at 3.00 a.m. on Christmas morning. By then, people were literally praying for their lives. The official toll was 65 people dead, 140 badly injured, and thousands left homeless.

Broken glass and sheets of jagged metal flew through the air as roofs were lifted off houses and walls smashed to the ground. Parents shielded their children as whole families lay cut and bleeding in the hot, furious rainstorm of that awful Christmas night.

The noise of the cyclone was as terrifying as the wind and rain. It was, according to a person who witnessed the cyclone, 'the sound of a

THE FACE OF TRAGEDY *Major-General Alan Stretton comforts a weeping resident of Darwin after Cyclone Tracy.*

million sheets of corrugated iron being scraped across the ground at 200 miles an hour'. Mr Ron Bell is one of Darwin's residents whose family still suffers from the shock of cyclone Tracy. He said:

> The noise—I think the noise is what caused my boy to have sleepless nights. A couple of years afterwards he wouldn't sleep at all without the light on. But the daughter, she was different. She had a wild outburst of crying, nearly all day. Then it was gone and over with—finished.

When the Bell family rebuilt their Darwin home, they spent another $4000 to have a steel and concrete cyclone shelter built within easy reach in their front yard.

THE HOUSE THAT TRACY BUILT *On Christmas Eve 1974 Cyclone* Tracy *devastated the city of Darwin and some people said 'never again'. After a night of terror Mr and Mrs Ron Bell bought this 'crash house' and if there is another cyclone like* Tracy *they'll spend life in a six ton concrete cocoon.*

THE GRIM REAPER *Bushfires still claim more lives than any other natural disaster in Australia. More than 250 people have died as a result of the 'Black Death' since 1900. Australia has suffered relatively few natural disasters, and, perhaps because of this, the nation is deeply traumatised when a tragedy does occur.*

CHOPPED OFF AT THE KNEES *Darwin after Cyclone Tracy was like a city with the lid sliced off. Beneath the jumble of corrugated iron, broken glass and buildings lay 65 dead.*

Another Darwin man described how, two minutes after the cyclone struck, his house—the floor, roof and walls—all disappeared. He said:

We spent four hours huddled in the yard where the house was. We had no protection. My wife was killed by flying debris.

And a little boy, who later received hospital treatment for his injuries, told how his badly injured father sought help:

All I can remember is my Dad saying, 'Keep down, keep down.' When it got a bit lighter we went over to our car where my brother was and my Dad was nearly fainting from loss of blood. He started to beep the horn and our neighbours came and helped us.

On Christmas Eve, Darwin had a population of 47 000. In the next few days, 35 000 people were flown to cities in the south in the biggest peace time airlift the nation has known.

Darwin today bears remarkably few scars of that night that shocked the nation. Within six months of the cyclone most of the population was preparing to go back home, and Darwin residents held their first 'Back to Darwin' celebration to thank the millions of Australians who donated clothing, food and more than $15 million to the city.

FLIGHT TO NOWHERE *The scene at Darwin Airport the morning after Cyclone Tracy. Following the cyclone mercy flights airlifted thousands to cities in the south.*

The *Greycliffe* and the *Rodney*

Sydney Harbour is one of the busiest waterways in the world and the traffic at peak hour can be just about as hair-raising as a drive through the city. On the whole our most famous body of seawater has a remarkable safety record, but in the days before radar and radio control, the harbour saw two major disasters in the decade. The first involved the ferry *Greycliffe*.

On 3 November 1927, Sydney was stunned by the news that the ferry *Greycliffe* which, because of its departure time of 4.15 p.m. carried dozens of schoolchildren, had been run down by the steamer *Tahiti*. The 7000-tonne ship sliced through the smaller craft like butter and the people on board had no time to panic. One passenger, John Pfeiffer, remembers:

I was upstairs on the *Greycliffe* doing my homework on the starboard side when the deckhand we all knew as 'Curly' came running up the stairs and said there was going to be a crash. I looked upwards and saw the green bows of a boat crashing into the side of the *Greycliffe*, so I don't know what made me do it. I acted on impulse, just ran outside on to the port side,

took off my shoes and I dived overboard. I don't know what made me take off my shoes but I just took them off.

The next thing I can remember was the *Tahiti* passing very quickly and I was looking up at a lot of faces staring down at me when I was sucked under by the ship as she passed. And I can remember being quite frightened of being injured—cut up by the propellers. John Pfeiffer escaped with barely a scratch but many were mutilated by the propellers, and in all forty died. Many of them were children, and the Taronga Zoo wharf resembled a

SCHOOL RUN DISASTER *Forty people died when the steamer* Tahiti *ran down and sank the ferry* Greycliffe *in November 1927. The ferry was on the afternoon 'school run', and many children were among those who perished. At a later enquiry three-fifths of the blame were apportioned to the* Greycliffe, *two-fifths to the* Tahiti. *Three years later the* Tahiti *sank in mid-Pacific.*

TRAGIC FLOTSAM *A rescue launch stationary on Sydney Harbour directly over the sunken remains of the ferry* Greycliffe. *Wreckage from the collision with the* Tahiti *floats in the foreground.*

STATE OF SHOCK *An ashen-faced woman survivor of the* Greycliffe *tragedy is helped ashore to the ambulances.*

SALVAGE *The forward half of* Greycliffe *was lifted from the bottom of Sydney Harbour and slowly dragged ashore at Whiting Beach, near the Taronga Zoo Park. The sheer force of the* Tahiti's *impact can be seen from the cut through the deck.*

pit head after a mine explosion as relatives waited anxiously for news.

When the *Tahiti* left Australia on the very night of the accident there were complaints about her 'indecent haste'. In Sydney her pilot, Captain Carlson, faced a long ordeal in the inquiries which followed. He was dismissed and had to wait until the *Tahiti* returned from America seven

months later before hearing the official conclusions about the accident. Eventually, after a long and bitter argument between the owners of the ferry and the steamship company, the judge apportioned three-fifths blame to *Greycliffe* and two-fifths to *Tahiti*.

But fate had its own penalty for the steamer. Three years later

workers on the new Harbour Bridge watched as she steamed under them for the last time. In mid-Pacific a propeller shaft carried away and put a gaping hole in the side of the ship. The crew tried to bail her dry, but it was a futile battle. The passengers and crew were picked up by a Norwegian freighter, and a few hours later *Tahiti* sank.

SECONDS TO DOOM *The packed ferry* Rodney *as it appeared on Sydney Harbour in 1938, with the passengers waving to sailors on the USS* Louisville. *Seconds later, the* Rodney *capsized. There was a long inquiry, and savage accusations about the number allowed on the top deck.*

THE LUCKY FEW *Still shocked, these survivors of the* Rodney *capsize could summon a shy smile for the newsreel cameras which rushed to film the aftermath of the tragedy. Nineteen drowned when the boat capsized.*

Ten years later the memories of the *Tahiti* and *Greycliffe* had faded. There was plenty of excitement on Sydney Harbour. The fleet was in, and it was time to farewell the American warship *Louisville*. People in little boats crowded to get a glimpse of her, and on the small ferry *Rodney* it was standing room only. But suddenly, as people crowded to one side to wave to the American sailors, the *Rodney* gave a sickening lurch and rolled over.

For Sydneysiders it seemed like history repeating itself. Only this time most trapped in the stricken craft were women, some of whom had made boyfriends among the crew and were getting a last glimpse of their new beaux. Sailors from the *Louisville* jumped over the side and rescued those who managed to get clear of the ferry. Members of a police band on another boat also dived into the water and rescued others, but a number of people were trapped inside the ferry and those on the outside literally heard their death throes. Two survivors remembered:

The panic was dreadful ... We heard the noise, that was most harrowing, of them trying to scratch to get out from the bottom of the boat. You could hear this thumping with their hands on the upturned hull.

The aftermath was just as sad as that which had followed the *Greycliffe* incident. There was a long inquiry and savage accusations about the number of people who had been al-lowed on the top deck. The boat was salvaged and quickly renamed *Regis,* and later *Regalia.*

She still plies the harbour trade, few realise the little craft spent some of its life as a coffin.

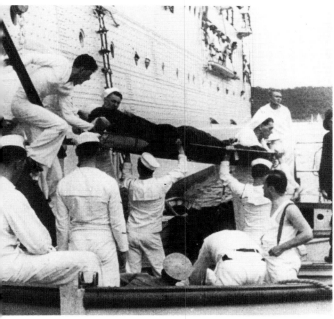

HARBOUR TRAGEDY *A triumphant day on Sydney Harbour turned into tragedy when the ferry boat* Rodney *capsized with a cargo of well-wishers farewelling a US Navy cruiser.*

STILL GOING STRONG *The ill-fated ferry* Rodney, *now renamed* Regalia *still working on Sydney Harbour, forty years after the tragic capsize.*

RIGHT SIDE UP *The launch* Rodney *afloat again after the capsize which cost so many young lives in 1938. As people crowded to the side of the boat to wave farewell to an American warship, the little craft rolled over.*

9

STAGE AND SCREEN

TEACHER AND PUPIL *The young Nellie Melba (right) and her teacher and European 'discoverer' Mathilde Marchesi. 'I have found a star' she exclaimed on first hearing the Australian . Marchesi also encouraged her to change her name from Armstrong .*

The entertainment of a nation

The twentieth century differs from all others in that it is the first to have been recorded on film. While we enjoy quite a distinguished recent history in the theatre, it is in the cinema that Australia can claim to have led the world. In radio and television we followed America, although occasionally there were typically Australian moments, from 'Blue Hills' to 'The Mavis Bramston Show'. And perhaps most memorable are the great stars: Snowy Baker, Errol Flynn, Peter Finch and Chips Rafferty.

On stage

In the past decade or so, Australian theatre has enjoyed something of a nationalistic boom. Plays written, acted and produced by Australians have done well at the local box office and made a significant impact overseas. But for most of this century, the flow has been all the other way. Australians waited breathlessly for each new shipload of culture to arrive from Europe.

In 1948 England sent us the legendary Old Vic Theatre Company headed by two of the truly 'big guns' of the international stage: Laurence Olivier and his wife Vivien Leigh. They were fêted wherever they went—the newsreel cameras even followed them on a visit to Taronga Park Zoo in Sydney. Olivier exploited this media attention, repeatedly urging Australia to set up its own national theatre.

Yet it took another six years and a royal visit by Queen Elizabeth before the Elizabethan Theatre Trust came into being. Its first play, *The Sleeping Prince,* opened on 27 July 1955 at the Trust's Elizabethan

BEST SEATS IN THE HOUSE *Squeezed in between a Canadian company selling 'Novelties and Notions' and Thomas Taunton's grog shop, the stall entrance to the Theatre Royal, Sydney in 1882.*

Theatre in Newtown, Sydney. It starred Dame Sybil Thorndike, Meriel Forbes and her husband, Sir Ralph Richardson. The critics were quick to point out that Australia's National Theatre had begun with an English play, an English cast and an English director.

The former Governor of the Reserve Bank, Dr H. C. Coombs, was a co-founder of the Elizabethan Theatre Trust. Dr Coombs remembers:

> Australian creative effort in drama was thought to be a pretty ambitious idea. Some of us believed that it would come, but I don't think you can get creative effort in as organised an art form as the theatre until you have a vigorous institution of theatre. Frankly, I am astonished, when I look back on it, at how quickly Australia has produced genuine creative artists of real quality in the theatre.

The Summer of the Seventeenth Doll was our first successful post-war indigenous play. Sumner Locke-Elliot's

S. L. ELLIOT *Elliot's spectacular* Rusty Bugles *created a big impact when first produced in 1948, so much so, that it was banned for a short time.*

DYING SWAN *The Russian ballerina Anna Pavlova. Her graceful dancing during her Australian tours of 1926 and 29 captivated audiences starved of world-class dancing. She also inspired the pavlova desert, which carries her name.*

ACTOR, ACTRESS AND BORED EXTRA *In 1948, when the great English actor Laurence Olivier visited Australia with his beautiful wife, Vivien Leigh, the least amused audience was the sleepy koala at Taronga Zoo. That's showbiz!*

Rusty Bugles, produced in 1948, had made a spectacular impact, but mostly because it was banned for a short period by an over-zealous New South Wales Chief Secretary's Department.

From its première in 1955 'The Doll' burst upon Australian audiences with almost embarrassing impact. Packed theatres around the country felt the shock of recognition, seeing the language and emotions of their own lives portrayed on stage. Author Ray Lawler said of the time:

There was a growing awareness of Australia as an identity. Certainly after the war, one could feel it in many fields, and I think theatre was one of them. It was a lucky play. There was sufficient awareness of Australian identity to make people go and see it, and it just happened to strike a note at the time. I've never felt it was more than that.

THE DOLL *Scenes from* The Summer of the Seventeenth Doll, *Ray Lawler's hit play about two cane cutters and their girlfriends in Melbourne. "The Doll" was the sensation of the post-war Australian stage, and was later made into a Hollywood feature film. The dolls were given by the cane cutters to their girlfriends every summer.*

SHATTERED DOLL *At the end of* **The Summer of the Seventeenth Doll,** *the play's theme of shattered illusion is symbolised when the 17th Kewpie Doll is smashed in a fight.*

The Australian theatre today still relies heavily on British and American writing, and we continue to import overseas celebrities. But there has been a growing acceptance of Australian plays, and the large numbers of small theatre companies in the capital cities are evidence of a continuing interest in 'live' drama.

Of the playwrights, perhaps David Williamson has had the greatest impact. Four of his successful plays, *The Coming of Stork, The Removalists, Don's Party* and *The Club,* have been filmed, and Williamson himself has written screenplays for a number of recent Australian films.

Plays by Alex Buzo, Jim McNeil, Ron Blair, Jack Hibberd, Dorothy Hewett and Steve Spears have all attracted critical acclaim, and the international success of Barry Humphries' shows has done much to encourage original work throughout the Australian theatrical world.

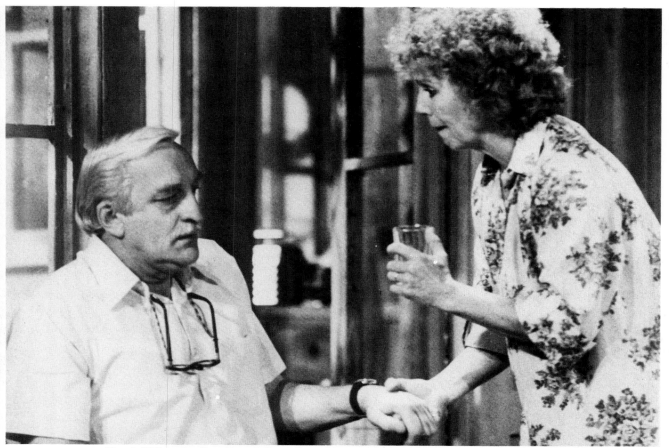

TRAVELLING NORTH *Frank Wilson (as Frank) and Carol Raye (Frances) in David Williamson's play* Travelling North *performed at the Nimrod in 1979. Four of David Williamson's works have so far been filmed.*

The big screen

Australia can claim two firsts in world cinematic history. *Soldiers of the Cross*, a religious epic made in 1900, was 3000 feet long, cost £600 to make and is believed to be the world's first full-length dramatic presentation including film. Unfortunately, the film itself has been lost, although glass slides and photographs still survive to give an impression of the lavish sets and costumes.

The Story of the Kelly Gang made in 1906, was 4000 feet long and took

THE PICTURE SHOW MEN *In the first years of the century, a picture show was more like a travelling carnival. Companies travelled from town to town with a collapsible screen, a limelight projector and a few reels of celluloid. These three showmen from Anderson's Pictures took their wares from town to town by horsepower, and made a healthy living.*

MAD DOGS AND CAMERAMEN *Only a determined cinematographer would brave the mid-day sun to film nothing happening in an outback town. For Cook's Picture Company, this employee recorded another sleepy town for posterity.*

six months to make. It is claimed to be the world's first full-length feature film and a recent discovery of three scenes would seem to support this claim.

Soldiers of the Cross was a grand presentation of film, slides and music put together by the Salvation Army's Limelight Division, probably the earliest regular film production unit in history.

The religious epic turned out to be an enormous box office success. On a rainy night in 1900, 4000 people braved the elements to attend the première. The newspapers hailed the novelty with unrestrained enthusiasm. The *Age* said:

To have some of the most tragic episodes of Christian history carried out in all savage but soul-stirring realism is an accomplishment essentially of today. It is a thrilling, novel and instructive lecture.

In the following years, Australians became fascinated with the new marvel of cinematography. They flocked to theatres that sprang up in the cities showing film of Australian scenery and people. Commercial feature films were a logical development and it's not surprising that for its first attempt Australia should choose the popular legend of Ned Kelly.

FIRST TINSELTOWN *Belgrave House — a Salvation Army Home for Girls. In 1900, the property was used for* Soldiers of the Cross, *our first (and possibly the world's first) feature-length film. The building still stands in Melbourne.*

EVERYONE CAPTIVATED FROM START TO FINISH *A publicity dodger circulated by the Salvation Army to generate audiences for their epic combination of a film, magic lantern slides and theatrical address. It was mistakenly claimed to be the world's first full-length film.*

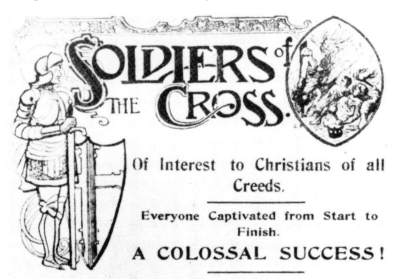

WILL YOU FOLLOW CHRIST? *Well, will you? The brilliantly executed glass slides which illustrated the 'live' sections of the Soldiers of the Cross presentation in 1900. The slides are kept at the National Film Archive in Canberra.*

CAST OF THOUSANDS *A selection of the meticulously painted magic lantern slides which were projected onto the screen while the 'live' sections of* Soldiers of the Cross *were in progress. These were seen while the reels were changed.*

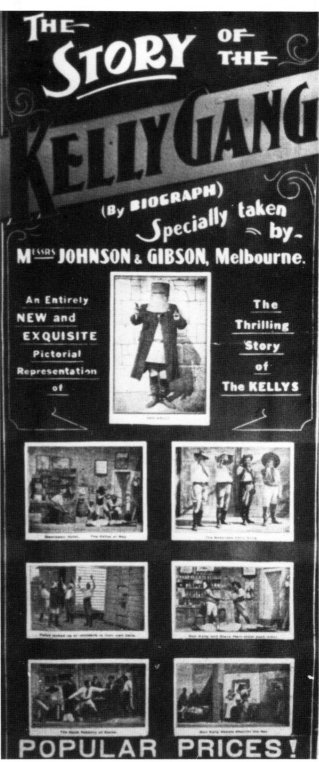

ENTIRELY NEW AND EXQUISITE *The modest poster proclaiming Johnson & Gibson's film presentation* The Story of the Kelly Gang, *which was filmed on a dairy farm near Melbourne.*

FIRST FLICK OF THEM ALL *Brochure cover for* The Story of the Kelly Gang, *an all-film dramatic feature made in Australia in 1906. Only one small section of the film survives.*

The Story of the Kelly Gang was produced on weekends by two theatrical entrepreneurs, John and Charles Tait. A dairy farm at Heidelberg on the outskirts of Melbourne was transformed into the village of Glenrowan.

The film was shown with voices and sound effects supplied by stand-ins behind the screen. The acting was outrageously overdone by modern standards, and the scene which showed Kate Kelly's set-to with the policeman could go down in history as the first blending of sex and violence on screen.

While still photographs taken from the film have been preserved, the original print was lost years ago. But in 1979 a section was discovered under a bed in an empty house. It was sent to 'This Fabulous Century' by a Melbourne collector, Mr Ken Robb, and has since been authenticated at the Film Archive of the National Library.

The film cost the Taits just £1000 to make, but grossed a colossal £25 000 at the box office. So, Australia began churning out bushranger pictures, including the first *Robbery Under Arms*. Bushranger pictures became to the Australian film industry what Westerns represented to Hollywood, and were made just as fast.

OVERACTING EVERYWHERE *From* The Story of the Kelly Gang, *Kate Kelly and Constable Fitzpatrick.*

KATE KELLY LAYS DOWN THE LAW *For this scene from* The Story of the Kelly Gang, *the script called for a considerable amount of physical violence. To avoid 'unpleasantness', the part of Kate was temporarily taken over by a man.*

SURPRISED AT STRINGYBARK *A still frame taken from* The Story of the Kelly Gang, *showing the gang surprised by troopers at their camp beside Stringybark Creek.*

THEY WENT THATAWAY! *Decision at the crossroads for the plain-clothes police posse chasing bold Ned and his gang in a scene from* The Story of the Kelly Gang.

BANG! BANG! YOU'RE DEAD! *Scenes from* The Story of the Kelly Gang, *as re-published in the sixpenny brochure was sold at the picture show, and until recently remained the only reliable source of information regarding the film. Claimed to be the world's first feature, the film was believed lost until a 3-minute sequence came to light in 1979.*

DEATH OF DAN KELLY & STEVE HAR

CAPTURE OF NED KELLY

C. J. DENNIS *Author of* The Sentimental Bloke *the classic silent movie. The verse-tale of working class romance was ideally suited for the silent screen.*

SILENT MOVIE KING *Raymond Longford (right) who began as a sailor, then music-hall artist and film actor, before becoming a scenarist and top director of his era with classics such as* The Sentimental Bloke.

But the important question is: Did Australia produce a work of lasting merit during the silent film era? Ray Edmondson, director of film for the National Film Archive, says:

The obvious answer to that is *The Sentimental Bloke*, although it's possible that other films made before that which don't survive now would have had similar significance. Certainly 'The Bloke' is our first claim to a true international classic. It had enormous impact in England and it was released in America. It's a very fine piece of film from anybody's point of view and, as a piece of silent film art, it typifies the best characteristics of the medium.

C. J. Dennis, author of *The Sentimental Bloke* verses, said of the film (made in 1919), 'It could not have been pictured better.' The classic verse-tale of working class romance in the slums of Sydney was ideally suited for the silent screen, and the written title cards which helped the story along retained the charming flavour of the slang language employed in the original book.

To add to the authentic feel of the film, all the exterior scenes were shot on actual locations around the dock areas of Sydney. There was even a scene filmed on the Manly ferry.

Its director, Raymond Longford, was the leading film maker of his day. Longford's story is, in many ways, as sentimental as that of 'the Bloke' himself. He should have been acclaimed as a genius and, in any other film producing country, he might have been. Despite the popularity of *The Sentimental Bloke*, Long-

ford never raised the money he needed for other films.

By the time the 'talkies' came along, he was reduced to playing bit parts in films which weren't nearly as good as his own. His last few years were spent working as a night watchman on the Woolloomooloo wharves in Sydney, not far from the streets where *The Sentimental Bloke* was filmed. But Longford was never bitter, and before he died he spoke with optimism of the Australian film industry that had left him behind, a generation before:

I would like to see it go ahead with leaps and bounds particularly the good Australian stories, stories full of sentiment. After all's said and done, aren't we all sentimentalists? As for myself? Well, I'm the Sentimental Bloke.

WE 'AS A DING-DONG ROW *A moment of passion from* The Sentimental Bloke *the silent film made in 1919. The film is claimed to be the best made in Australia during that era.*

'ER NAME'S DOREEN *The touching Manly beach courtship scene from the 1919 silent movie classic version of* The Sentimental Bloke. *Doreen was played by Lottie Lyell, 'The Bloke' by Arthur Tauchert.*

Stars of the silent screen

In the free-wheeling days of early silent movies the Australian outback provided a dramatic setting for romantic boy meets girl stories. Producers loved to star a fine looking girl who was just as adept at riding a horse, as she was falling into the arms of her man.

Drama came with the names of the actresses, like Louise Lovely, or in their bold manner; Annette Kellerman splashed her way down the Thames in London and into the public eye. She also made sure she stayed in the public eye by revealing more of her lovely figure than was considered 'proper' in those buttoned-up days.

Newsreel cameramen too made the most of the outback. They made a good living capturing scenes in rural Australia for news hungry audiences at the early cinemas.

At right AUSTRALIA'S FIRST STAR *Striking a typically melo-dramatic pose, Annette Kellerman (right) acts one of the climactic scenes from the 1913 Hollywood silent epic* Neptune's Daughter. *The Australian swimming sensation burst to world prominence after she swam down the Thames in London.*

HAVE CINEMATOGRAPH, WILL TRAVEL *The well-dressed newsreel cameraman of the 1920's. Free-lance cameramen criss-crossed the countryside filming everything from weddings to hay-making.*

A GIRL FROM THE BUSH *Perhaps the strongest myth portrayed by the early film directors was the stereotype of the girl who could ride like a banshee, crack a good stockwhip but was putty in the hands of the straightjawed hero. These scenes are from A Girl from the Bush.*

ROMANTIC OUTBACK A Girl from the Bush *produced by Franklyn Barrett was typical of the early films made during the silent movie era which wove romantic tales around stories set in the outback. This film was made in the 20s.*

EVERYBODY SMILE *The production crew of the 1925 silent romantic adventure Jewelled Nights take a break from filming to pose for the traditional team portrait. The film was produced by its star, Louise Lovely.*

BOY MEETS GIRL *Louise Lovely (right) looking somewhat mannish for her part as the independent heroine in Jewelled Nights a film she co-produced. Make-up and hair styles almost obscured the difference between the sexes.*

The advent of the talkies brought a boom in the cinema trade, but there was no guarantee that any of the films to be shown would be locally made. Even before the thirties began, the sad truth was that the Australian film industry, so promising in the early 1900s, had already fallen into foreign hands.

But while the Americans were making the big money, a few local directors still struggled to get home-grown films on to the screen. *The Squatter's Daughter*, one of nineteen features made for the Cinesound company by Ken Hall was as Australian as two-up. Yet it still reflected the style and bally-hoo of a Hollywood production. And Ken Hall agrees:

> I was greatly influenced by American films, and I don't see anything wrong with that because they, after all, were the best in the world. If you could follow their example and have anything like their success, then you'd be doing something worthwhile for Australia.

But there was one section of Saturday night at the flicks that was always Australian: the newsreel.

TAKING THEMSELVES SERIOUSLY *In the early days of the weekly newsreel, when the 'talkies' were still a novelty, Cinesound calmly claimed that they were the 'Voice of Australia'. They filmed everything from cyclones to singing dogs.*

THE TSAR OF CINESOUND *Ken G. Hall, trail-blazing feature film director. On budgets only a fraction of the Hollywood equivalents, Hall helped develop a pool of film-making skills which survived to see in the new boom which has occurred in Australian film making*

MEET THE PRESS *Before 'Live-Eye' and 'Action-Cam' nightly television news, this forbidding phalanx of cumbersome 35mm film cameras was what confronted a visiting celebrity as he stepped off the plane into his first Australian news conference. Early newsreel was developed for the cinema by Cinesound and Movietone.*

Almost from the day the talkies started, two companies, Cinesound and Movietone, competed furiously against each other to produce the best newsreel review of the week's events.

Over the years, the newsreels developed tremendous expertise in filming everything from cyclones to singing dogs. But they suffered badly from the advent of television. In 1970, the two companies were forced to amalgamate and by 1975 they had ceased production altogether. Ironically, the men who had helped to sustain the traditions of Australian film making through forty lean years went out of business just when the local industry was on the brink of another boom.

YOU LAUGH, I SING *The great German soprano Lotte Lehmann sings a duet with a kookaburra. This novel stunt was a favourite device of the 1930 newsreels. Kookaburras appeared on the Old Fox-Movietone title card.*

OLD FOX-MOVIETONE TITLE CARD *The famous Kookaburras appeared first in the 'O' of Fox — 20th Century Fox to be exact — the American company which first supported a weekly sound newsreel service in Australia.*

After eighty years of film making, all we can say with certainty about our early film industry is that its products were all, to say the least, Australian. *Forty Thousand Horsemen*, an epic made on the eve of the Second World War was enormously successful for director, Charles Chauvel. But Chauvel, in his other films, often sacrificed box office profits by using only home-grown subjects.

Chauvel's film *Jedda* was no exception. The first full-colour feature film made in this country, *Jedda* explored a theme which would have been struggling for mass appeal even in countries with more sophisticated film audiences. Based on the book with the painfully corny title of *Eve in Ebony*, the film is about the conflict of emotions of a black girl raised in a white society—a girl who according to the film feels the 'call of the wild', the desperate urge to go walk-about.

'SAY CHEESE' *Grant Taylor as 'Red Gallagher' and Betty Bryant as Juliet Rouget who took the leads in Charles Chauvel's* Forty Thousand Horsemen *an epic made on the Eve of the Second World War.*

BEAUTY GOES TO THE WELL *Betty Bryant in a typical 'pin-up' pose for publicity shots to promote* Forty Thousand Horsemen, *a very successful film for director Charles Chauvel.*

BRILLIANT DIRECTOR *Charles Chauvel often sacrificed box office profit by using only Australian subjects, such as* Jedda. *The story of a black girl in white society.*

Ngarla Kunoth was just sixteen, a shy child with a mission education, when she was found by the Chauvels after exhaustive screen tests. And the true story behind the fantasy of the film proved to be far more traumatic and moving than anything the screenwriters could have dreamt up. The real battle of a black girl trying to come to grips with white society was behind the cameras and not in front of them. Ngarla, now Mrs Rosalie Monks, recalls:

Well, looking back on it to me it was all—the part in that film—was trauma to me. Simply because I couldn't understand being away. It was the first time I'd been away from my surroundings. It was the first time I'd been away from having some of my relatives around me, and of course my communication wasn't, you know, as good as it is now. I can communicate with you but in those days, and especially going through my teens at the same time, it was a nightmarish thing.

The film would change her life completely. The Chauvels had taken her under their wing in Sydney and the real life scenario was somewhat more fascinating and subtle than the one they'd managed to capture on celluloid. Elsa Chauvel:

ABORIGINAL ACTORS *Robert Tudawali and Ngarla Kunoth, co-stars of the epic Australian feature film* Jedda (1954). *Kunoth became a nun and is now a social worker amongst her people.*

AFTER STARDOM . . . WHERE TO? *After the movie* Jedda *Ngarla Kunoth found difficulty coping with the glare of publicity and entered a Melbourne convent where she stayed for many years.*

THE MAKING OF JEDDA *Filming the climactic scene from* Jedda. *The tribal Aborigine Marbuck (Robert Tudawali) tried to force Jedda (Ngarla Kunoth) back to the tribal way of life. They flee from white pursuers and on the brink of a huge gorge Marbuck falls to his death.*

303

She was like a little normal 16-year-old girl. I was anxious that she didn't go back to the Territory. I knew that she'd . . . after a home with us in Sydney, her own lovely little bedroom, her own pretty frocks. I was very worried and I was very keen to have her remain in Sydney and study. And she was so fond of children that I thought she would be an excellent kindergarten teacher.

Eventually Ngarla Kunoth did go back to her people. But she found it hard to return. There were new problems and expectations, and finally she sought solace in religion. She entered a convent in Melbourne where she spent the next ten years. During this time she learned that her co-star, Robert Tudawali, had failed to cope with his success. Alone and derelict, he died in a fire in Darwin.

After a decade, Sister Rosalie felt the urge to be free again. She left the convent, married a white brewery clerk and became a social worker looking after numerous Aboriginal foster children. Now forty-three, and a mother herself, Rosalie is a social worker at Alice Springs base hospital.

TRAGIC PROGRESSION *After the movie* Jedda *was made its male star Robert Tudawali travelled the sad road of disappointment and drunkenness and finally to death. But Ngarla Kunoth the Aboriginal girl who starred with Tudawali entered a convent. Alone and derelict, Tudawali died in a fire in Darwin.*

After the Second World War, there was a complete slump in the local film industry. Any other country the size of Australia might have given up years before, but against enormous competition from Hollywood, we've persisted with our dream of having a film industry.

The struggle to make successful Australian films based on Australian subjects is best symbolised by *The Summer of the Seventeenth Doll.* It was our finest drama, yet it starred English and American actors: Ernest Borgnine, John Mills, Angela Lansbury and Anne Baxter.

STAR MAKER *Charles Chauvel took a shy girl from a mission and made her a star.*

BRIEF STARDOM *Twenty-five years ago this Aboriginal woman was plucked from her quiet background and made into a film star.*

FALSE DAWN *The premiere of the Australian-based feature film* They're a Weird Mob *in 1966 was heralded as the beginning of a re-born Australian film industry. Despite the success of the movie, the renaissance didn't generate a full head of steam for another decade. The film failed to set off the long awaited and much predicted boom.*

The re-birth of the local film industry got off to a spectacular false start with the film of John O'Grady's comedy *They're a Weird Mob.* Despite its success, the film failed to set off the long-awaited boom. It was now clear that the industry would need support from Canberra.

Melbourne producer, Phillip Adams, was one of a group of Australians herded together to advise the government on film funding. Adams said:

When Harold Holt was about to appoint us, he drowned. Gorton then got the list and asked who Holt wanted to appoint, then crossed them all off. I was left over, and this is the way you have greatness thrust upon you. Barry Jones and I, with the help of some others, really worked Gorton over. We wrote him speeches and stuff and next thing we had a blank cheque. In pretty rapid succession, we set up the Experimental Film Fund, the AFDC, which is now the Australian Film Commission, and later the Film School. To my astonishment, all our fantasies came true overnight.

In the past ten years, Australia has become one of the larger film-producing countries in the world. It is a credit to the writers, directors, actors and crews and also to the governments who have been prepared to risk taxpayers' money on the big screen.

305

The list of substantial films which have been made in Australia recently is a long one. *Picnic at Hanging Rock, Caddie, The Devil's Playground, Eliza Fraser, The Last Wave, The Chant of Jimmy Blacksmith, Breaker Morant, My Brilliant Career.* There have also been some popular successes like the *Alvin Purple* and *Barry McKenzie* comedies.

After a twenty-year infatuation with television, Australians are returning to the cinema, and new multi-theatre complexes have been built in all the capital cities to accommodate the new increase in cinema-going. The current boom in the Australian film industry may yet be a flash in the pan. But at least we've had some very good years after decades of struggle.

CADDIE'S DILEMMA *Collecting her children from the babysitter, Caddie (Helen Morse), finds a wild party going on.*

CADDIE *Helen Morse who took the leading role in* Caddie, *the story of a woman's struggle for independence.*

PICNIC AT HANGING ROCK *One of a number of good films made in Australia recently to have received acclaim.*

TRAGIC HEADMISTRESS *Rachel Roberts portrayed Mrs Appleyard, in the thriller* Picnic at Hanging Rock.

The stars
Reg 'Snowy' Baker

Reg 'Snowy' Baker was Australia's first great screen hero, a fine example of Australian manhood. In the silent movie era when actions spoke louder than words, handsome Snowy was a moral to be a star.

Even before he faced his first hand-cranked movie camera, Snowy had become a legend in Australia. He excelled in no less than twenty-nine sports. He was Australia's top diver and New South Wales swimming champion. He represented Australia playing rugby union, and he went to the Olympics as a boxer. He was Australian middleweight champion and held the New South Wales heavyweight title. He breezed into the Olympic final with just four punches. Then he lost the gold medal on a points decision, perhaps,

Snowy claimed later, because the referee was the winner's father.

Snowy was also a boxing promoter and owned the Sydney Stadium. It was on a trip to California, to find boxing champions to fight local talent like the famous Les Darcy, that he became enchanted with the film industry. Being a shrewd businessman he realised the enormous potential of the new industry, and set up a film company to exploit his own talents.

The theme of his movies was always much the same. Snowy was a kind of Ocker Superman—faster than a speeding horse and dray, able to leap verandahs at a single bound. He despatched villains all over the place. He managed to do all his own stunts, despite a back injury that kept him out of service during the First World War.

Snowy's leading ladies included big-name femme fatales like Brownie Vernon and Lily Molloy. In 1919 when Australian cinema audiences were already in the millions, Snowy Baker was the biggest matinee idol of the day.

Snowy then decided to have the inevitable crack at Hollywood, but the Americans weren't too sure about accepting him as a star. After making five mediocre films, Snowy decided to use his horse riding talents to run a successful polo ranch called the Riviera Club. If you believe the legends, he taught Valentino to ride, Douglas Fairbanks to crack a stockwhip and Harold Lloyd to crack jokes. Whatever the truth, Reg 'Snowy' Baker, sound of mind and sound of body, with his faithful horse 'Boomerang', became part of the Hollywood scene.

THE ORIGINAL MACHO MAN *Reg 'Snowy' Baker, the Australian super-hero of the first two decades of the Century. He set up a film company to feature his own exploits.*

SNOWY AND STARLET *Legend has it that Snowy Baker taught Valentino to ride a horse. Here he poses with the inevitable starlet, at his Hollywood polo ranch.*

Errol Flynn

The doctors said Errol Flynn died of a combination of TB, malaria, gonorrhea and kidney disease. Hardly sound mind, sound body.

Flynn took over where Snowy Baker left off. He really was larger than life. He faced danger on and off the screen, but his greatest danger was himself. As he said in his autobiography:

My biggest problem is reconciling my gross habits with my net income.

The son of a university professor in Hobart, Flynn was a knockabout adventurer who was literally 'discovered' from a newspaper cutting. He had been skipper of a commercial schooner which was wrecked on the coast of New Guinea. The shipwreck wasn't a big story in the newspapers down in Sydney, and the pictures were small and blurred. But the report was read by Charles Chauvel, and the pictures were enough to convince Chauvel and his wife, Elsa, that they had found the star for their new film *In the Wake of the Bounty*.

Flynn knew nothing about acting, but for £10 a week he was happy to play the legendary mutineer, Fletcher Christian. It was far from a distinguished debut. His acting was wooden to say the least, but as Elsa Chauvel remembers, all he really had to do was stand on the set and the women swooned.

One of his more memorable lines in the film was, 'Where will it all end?' and the answer, before too long, was Hollywood. Emboldened by his early success in Australia, Flynn tried making a career in repertory theatre in England. But the British required their leading men to not only be handsome, but to know something about acting as well. So Flynn headed off across the Atlantic to America.

His first role in a Hollywood feature was as a corpse lying under a kitchen table in a B-grade gangster movie. But even as a 'stiff', the Flynn face and body were so appealing they demanded attention. The wife of the film's producer suggested that the unknown Australian might be star material, and before long Errol

A HORRID LITTLE BOY *Errol Flynn, gazing wistfully into the camera for this studio portrait at the age of six. His mother admitted: 'He wasn't bad he was horrid.'*

YOUNG SUPERSTAR *The young Errol Flynn was given his start in films by writer and director Charles Chauvel. Flynn was the son of a Tasmanian Professor.*

WHO'S THAT IN THE CAP? *From this photograph Errol Flynn was 'discovered'. In his first film Flynn had the memorable line 'Where will it all end.' The answer was Hollywood, and a distinguished career.*

FLETCHER CHRISTIAN ON TEN QUID A WEEK *Errol Flynn (right) in his first movie as Fletcher Christian in* In the Wake of The Bounty *(1933). Watching extras get 40 lashes proved too boring, and Flynn was off to Hollywood.*

MY GOD BUT YOU'RE BEAUTIFUL *Errol Flynn (left) as he appeared in* Captain Blood, *The part type-cast Flynn as a swashbuckling hero, an acting stereotype he was not able to escape until his last few roles.*

Flynn had been given his first leading role. *Captain Blood* (1935) was a run-away hit, and was followed by a string of similar swashbuckling epics including *The Charge of the Light Brigade* and as a dashing hero in *The Adventures of Robin Hood.*

Flynn soon became a celebrity in 'tinsel town'. He was a favourite with the tennis set, as well as being a member of the exclusive Hollywood Cricket Club. It was a time when to be an English gentleman was terribly chic in America, and Flynn and David Niven were two of the most sought after sex symbols in Hollywood, with their classic good looks and debonair manner.

But Flynn never took himself seriously. He treated Hollywood and his own legend as a joke. Behind Flynn's crisp and smiling facade, hard living was taking its toll. He appropriately called his house 'Cirrhosis by the Sea'. He was rejected for war service because of ill health and in 1942 he was involved in a celebrated morals case that led to the famous phrase 'in like Flynn', and made him a scapegoat for the Hollywood moralists and gossips.

Despite critical acclaim for some of his later movies such as *The Sun Also Rises* and *The Roots of Heaven*, Flynn became little more than an ageing ladies' man. The swash was beginning to buckle, and for the last two years of his life the dissipated actor lived with a teenage girl, and played in pathetic films such as *Cuban Rebel Girls*.

It was thirty years since Flynn had been discovered through a shipwreck, and ironically he was on his way to sell a yacht when he collapsed as a result of his lethal cock-

ENGINE DEAD AND ANCHOR DRAGGING

Between Rock and Whirlpool

A party on the auxiliary yacht Errol went shark fishing on Saturday afternoon, but nearly went to Davy Jones's Locker.

ENGINE failure in the southerly buster and the south-easterly gale was responsible for the trouble.

The adventurers were Messrs. Kenneth Kerr, C. Burt, Errol Flynn (owner), Trelawney Adams, T. H. Arrowsmith, C. Tyler, and a "Pictorial" photographer.

They had furled sail and dropped anchor outside North Head, but the

MESSRS. C. BURT, T. Adams, and E. Flynn, who are preparing for a trip to Papua in the auxiliary yacht Errol.

HIT BY 'PLANE

THE PICTURE THAT LAUNCHED A THOUSAND PARTS *This rather melodramatic newspaper clipping was seen by Australian film director Charles Chauvel and led to the beginnings of a great screen career for one of the men in the photograph. On the extreme right is one E. Flynn.*

tail of diseases. The handsome young adventurer from Australia was finally scuttled by his own crew: an uncooperative heart, rebellious lungs and mutinous kidneys. He died at the age of fifty, and the doctors expressed amazement that he had managed to live that long.

FISH FAME *Errol Flynn (left) with his father (right) and Prof Carl Hubbs studying navigational charts on Flynn's boat Zaca. During a marine expedition Flynn had a fish named after him Gibbonsia erroli.*

Chips Rafferty

For thirty years Chips Rafferty was the screen embodiment of everything the Australian male liked to think of himself—a bronzed, dinkum, all-round, true-blue ocker, cobber mate. As dry as the drought and as big as Queensland.

In fact, 'Chips' was born John Goffage in 1909 in the far-west New South Wales mining town of Broken Hill. Determined to get into the film business somehow, Chips hung around the Cinesound studios and cutting rooms until he was noticed by Charles Chauvel, the feature film director who at that time was casting his First World War epic *Forty Thousand Horsemen*. To Chauvel, the Rafferty face, voice and stature seemed perfect for a part as one of the gallant Australian light horsemen in Palestine. From that film until his last role in 1974, Chips Rafferty was a household word.

Throughout the 1940s and 1950s, hardly a film was made in Australia without Chips taking the part of some homespun, good-natured bush character. He was in the British productions *The Overlanders*, *Bitter Springs* and *Bush Christmas* as well as in the two *Smiley* features and a variety of lesser movies. His career seemed to be taking an international turn when he was cast in the Hollywood epic *Mutiny on the Bounty*, which starred Marlon Brando in the role that Errol Flynn had tried thirty years before. But Chips had a fierce pride in his Australian origins, and he particularly wanted this country to develop a film industry of its own. On his return from Hollywood, Rafferty's faith in the potential of the local industry was unshaken. He told a television interviewer:

> Give the Australian technicians a go! Give the actors a go! Give the musicians a go! Give the Australian industry the money today and we can take the world, boy. This is what I've been screaming about for fifteen years. Backed by top writers, the material they're getting on the screen at the present time, they must win!

Sadly, just at the time the local industry was beginning to get on its feet, Chips was running out of steam.

THE DROVER'S SQUAT *Indispensable Australian actor Chips Rafferty (real name John Goffage), in a pose typical of the majority of roles he portrayed for the Australian screen — the true-blue, dinkum Aussie bushman.*

For twenty years he'd been a good actor without decent films to star in. He did manage to record a finely crafted performance in his last film *Wake in Fright*, but a few months later in 1974 he collapsed and died while taking a walk near his home at Elizabeth Bay, Sydney.

THE OVERLANDERS *In 1944 a film director, Harry Watt, arrived in Australia in search of a subject for a film. After six months* The Overlanders *evolved. Here in a shot from the film are Chips Rafferty and John Hayward.*

THEY BUILD 'EM BIG *Chips Rafferty in a fast-riding sequence in Ealing's romantic adventure,* The Overlanders, *which had its world premiere in Sydney.*

AUSTRALIAN LEGEND *Chips Rafferty who achieved international fame as a film actor, looked and sounded like the typical Australian of legend.*

CLEAN-SHAVEN WHIPPERSNAPPER *Peter Finch (centre) in his first screen role in* Dad & Dave Come to Town, *in 1938. On the left is veteran character actor Bert Bailey.*

GUEST APPEARANCE *Chips Rafferty in an episode of* Spyforce, *his last television role before his death. Chips was the screen embodiment of a bronzed, dinkum, all-round, true-blue ocker, cobber mate.*

Peter Finch

The only Australian actor ever to win an 'Oscar', Peter Finch was in many ways almost the complete opposite to the Rafferty image of an Australian. He was a highly gifted and versatile actor and could play any part, from the gawkish country simpleton he portrayed in *Dad and Dave Come to Town*, his first screen role, to the demented New York television newsreader he created for *Network* nearly forty years later. His professional life was a series of triumphs and lavish praise, while his private life was usually chaos.

Born in England, Peter Finch came to Australia as a child and always considered himself an 'Aussie'. He fought as a gunner in the Australian Army during the Second World War, but soon landed in the AIF Entertainment Unit helping to produce a variety of stage presentations. When the war ended Finch was in demand as a radio actor but, after some encouragement from the great English actor Laurence Olivier during his visit here in 1948, the young Finch was ready to test his ambitions overseas.

YOU'RE IN THE ARMY NOW *Watching over a rehearsal of his production of* French Without Tears *for the Army Entertainment Unit is a very young Peter Finch.*

MR FINCH STEPS OUT *A gaunt-looking Peter Finch in the 1939 Cinesound production* Mr Chedworth Steps Out. *He was only awarded a small part.*

Allan Ashbolt, an old army comrade who also worked in the theatre with Finch during the late 1940s remembers his remarkable powers as a dramatic actor:

> ... there was that marvellous meditative stillness he had about him—those large luminous, expressive eyes and that brooding, pervasive intensity, the tightly reined emotional explosions. He was a beautifully disciplined actor.

Finch quickly established himself as one of the most accomplished screen actors in Europe and America. His list of credits is impressive: *A Town Like Alice*, *No Love for Johnnie*, and *Sunday Bloody Sunday* are just three of the contemporary dramas which confirmed his stature. He attracted critical acclaim in *Far From the Madding Crowd* and *England Made Me*, but it was his last major role in the frenetic black comedy *Network* which eventually earned him his long-overdue Academy Award.

With an almost Shakespearean touch of tragedy, Peter Finch died just a few months before he would have received the Oscar in 1977. It was accepted—to a standing ovation—by his widow Elethea.

RATS OF TOBRUK *During a break in filming of the Australian feature film, director Charles Chauvel (centre) goes over the next scene with his young stars Peter Finch (right) and Chips Rafferty (left).*

BEAUTY AND THE BROODER *During a break in the filming of* Judith, *co-stars Peter Finch and Sophia Loren rest in a shady corner. Finch was the most distinguished Australian actor to establish an international movie career.*

I'M MAD AS HELL! *Peter Finch in his Oscar-winning 1976 role as the demented newsreader in* Network. *Although born in England, Finch always considered himself an Australian.*

Radio

In early 1919, a young Englishman called Ernest Fisk set up an office at York Street, Sydney. Fisk was a friend of Marconi—the man who invented the radio—and he'd come to Australia as the representative of the Marconi Wireless Company.

On the night of 13 August, he was a few blocks down the road from his offices, addressing the conservative membership of the Royal Society of New South Wales. At a pre-arranged time, Fisk finished his talk and switched on a receiving apparatus which had been set up in front of the members. Back at the York Street office, an assistant broadcast by radio a recording of the national anthem, which the members listened to with amazement. Australia had entered the world of radio.

AND PIGS WILL FLY *Sir Ernest Fisk, head of the giant AWA company told Australians in 1954 that we would soon be able to see 'live' events from the other side of the world through magical television. Few people believed him.*

STEAM RADIO *Why did they ever call it the wireless? This maze of cables, plugs, valves and telephones is the control room of a radio station of the late 1920's. Today it has all been replaced by a tiny printed circuit.*

REXONOLA
TABLE MODELS
£3/15/-
to
£19/10/-

REXONOLA
CABINET MODELS
of beautiful design and finish
£19/10/-
to
£60

UNEQUALLED for TONE
THE PERFECT MUSICAL INSTRUMENT

Call and hear the true reproduction of the following artists on the Rexonola: Galli Curci, Caruso, McCormick, Heifetz, Kreisler, Paderewski, and our celebrated Australian Artists. Stella Power, Daisy Kennedy (violinist), John Lemmone (flautist), Peter Dawson, and others. The music of all the world when you want it if you own a REXONOLA.
WE ARE FAMED FOR OUR COMPLETE RECORD STOCKS
Specially equipped audition rooms, so that you may select records in comfort

The Talk-o-Phone Company
(GEORGE WOLLASTON)
177 George Street, Circular Quay.

The Record House

EVERY HOME SHOULD HAVE ONE *A tastefully decorative advertisement for the new-fangled gramophone. The invention promised hours of domestic bliss, and a score of companies competed for the lucrative new home-entertainment market. The gramophone spelled doom for the pianola, and to a large extent, the sturdy upright piano in the parlour.*

The earliest wireless sets were big enough to be classified as furniture. They were a status symbol, and manufacturers put as much work into designing the box and horn as they did in building the electronics inside. The public were still so suspicious of the new marvel that advertisers had to assure everyone that it was not necessary to open the windows to receive radio broadcasts. Radio broadcasting soon brought its own social revolution to Australia, and by the mid-thirties the Postmaster General's Department had sold one million licences.

Wireless was bringing news, music and laughter to a far-flung

SEEING IS BELIEVING *The advantages of television were being advertised in The Wireless Journal of Australia.*

population, and before long Australians were trying to live up to the BBC's motto that 'Nation shall speak unto nation'. The 1933 Empire broadcast caused as much excitement in its day as a satellite hook-up. Among the official broadcasters on the great day were Sir Charles Lloyd Jones, and the young man who started it all, Ernest Fisk.

Fisk was now a man of substance, and head of his own radio company, AWA. As business thrived, the company built ambitious new offices which soon became a landmark in Sydney. Today the building still stands among the skyscrapers, and the intricate AWA tower, a replica of the Eiffel tower, is a quaint reminder of the days when the wireless was as modern as tomorrow.

Radio still had a long way to go in the thirties. What people most

wanted to hear was the cricket. Don Bradman was demolishing the British bowlers at Leeds and Lord's, but live broadcasts from England would have been far too complicated and expensive. A young ABC announcer named Charlie Moses used his ingenuity to devise a coverage that almost had the nation's cricket fans fooled.

The announcer went on to become Sir Charles Moses, ABC General Manager from 1935 to 1965. He described those early broadcasts.

It was an attempt to give our listeners the impression that they were listening to a cricket match actually being broadcast from the ground, although before the broadcast we announced that it would be a simulated description done in the studio; although many people didn't believe it.

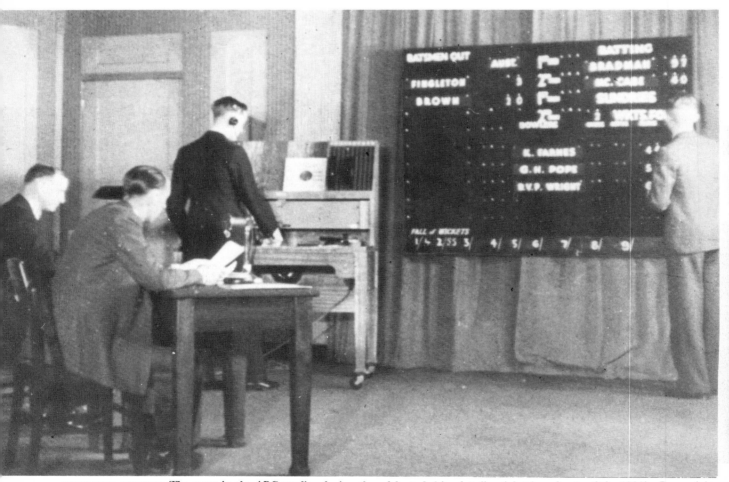

SIMULATED CRICKET *The scene in the ABC studios during the celebrated 'simulated' cricket broadcasts of the 1930's. By receiving brief telegrams from England and then improvising descriptions of the play with sound effects added, a smart studio team gave a very realistic impression of a Test match in progress.*

RADIO PIONEERS *This august gathering is a meeting of ABC commissioners who met for the first time in 1932 led by Charles Lloyd Jones but soon came under Charles Moses (standing).*

I'd arranged to get the scorer from the Sydney Cricket Ground and we had a small scoreboard and we put the scores on the scoreboard so that we could look at the board and check. The

sound effects were done by Dion Wheeler and he was very good indeed. He knew the game and he never fluffed by getting loud applause for something that was a very stodgy stroke.

One of the difficult things in this simulation was to get the sound of the ball on the bat. I tapped a pencil on a piece of wood and it made the exact sound of a full-blooded drive.

TINKLE, CRASH, BOOM! *One of the most important members of the radio drama production team was the senior sound effects man — the person who mixed together the various sounds that helped give the play or serial reality.*

THE SOUND OF LEATHER ON WILLOW *Young ABC sports announcer Alan McGilvray takes his turn for a Test Cricket broadcast. The announcers produced the sound of bat on ball by striking a wooden block with a pencil.*

STAYING HOME TO WATCH THE RADIO *Before television, the family radio was the centre of home entertainment, and many of the older models were so massive as to qualify as furniture. Settling in for a nice evening of music, serials and comedy, this middle-class family typified the broad entertainment appeal of the airwaves.*

Only twenty-five years ago, sitting down to listen to the wireless was a nightly ritual for the whole family. Today, there's a radio in every car and we flick it on mainly to ease the boredom and frustration of struggling to and from work in city traffic.

The glamour side of radio has long gone, along with the plays, serials, quiz shows, live variety and dance bands. Today, radio tends to concentrate on what it does best: news, conversation and recorded music. Old Sir Ernest Fisk would not have been amused.

So, with announcers improvising around cryptic telegrams, and the various sounds of a match in progress being concocted in the studio, the nation's cricket lovers were lulled into the belief that they were listening to the actual match 'live' from England.

KEEP YOU SMILING *In the dark days of the war, these two comic ladies . . . the legendary Ada and Elsie kept us laughing in the theatre, on radio and in hundreds of lunchtime concerts in factories.*

TUNING UP *Madcap entertainer Chico Marx tunes up the boys in a post-war recovery hospital before singing 'Waltzing Matilda', a song he thought was 'about some dame who steals a sheep'.*

TO BE OR NOT TO BE *Anzac Day, 1948, and Laurence Olivier, in Canberra made a speech of thanks to Australians for their war effort. Always the ham he made a speech about dripping sound like a Shakespearian soliloquy.*

But, as Sir Charles remembers, the days of 'simulated cricket' were not without their occasional dangers:

> The important thing was to have somebody on the other end who knew exactly what to do with telegrams. We had to have a clear understanding of what would go in the telegrams because in those days we were careful about the pennies. One had to use one's imagination and take the listeners to the ground and see it.

By the 1940s, radio was at its peak of popularity. It was the golden age of the valve wireless. Competition between the stations was fierce, and for the first time announcers were becoming celebrities. A young woman named Gwen Meredith began writing a simple serial for the ABC titled *Blue Hills*, which eventually became a legend.

TWENTY-THREE DEGREES *The frenzied activity in No. 1 studio, Radio 7ZL, Hobart. Note the regulation dinner suit and winged collar.*

Blue Hills, an inoffensive saga of country life, has been called the most successful radio serial in the world. It ran for a staggering 5795 episodes. Even grown men were known to clamber out of the sheep dip at lunchtime to find out how Dr Gordon and Granny Bishop were getting on. For thirty years, Gwen Meredith improvised her mundane country adventures straight into an office dictation machine. After the very last episode, Miss Meredith said:

I was asked on television how I felt and I said, 'A little bereft.' And the general tenor of the letters was,

'Well if you're bereft, what about us?' One letter was from North Queensland, and this woman said that when she heard it announced on the air that the serial was going off, she went around in a state of shock all day. When the shock wore off, she said perhaps I was doing her a favour because as I was getting old and tired I might have died, and then she would never have known what happened.

Blue Hills was an institution in radio, but it was never what the commercial stations called a 'commercial success'. The big money was in

advertising sponsorship. Sponsors demanded shows with plenty of action, drama and suspense. With television still decades away, the radio producers tried to create all the glamour and prestige of the theatre. The broadcasts were played on stage before packed audiences who supplied the necessary applause in return for the free entertainment. Even the sound effects men were required to dress in dinner suit and bow tie as they dashed about the stage frantically keeping up with the action, creating the sounds of door knocks, telephones, car crashes and gun shots.

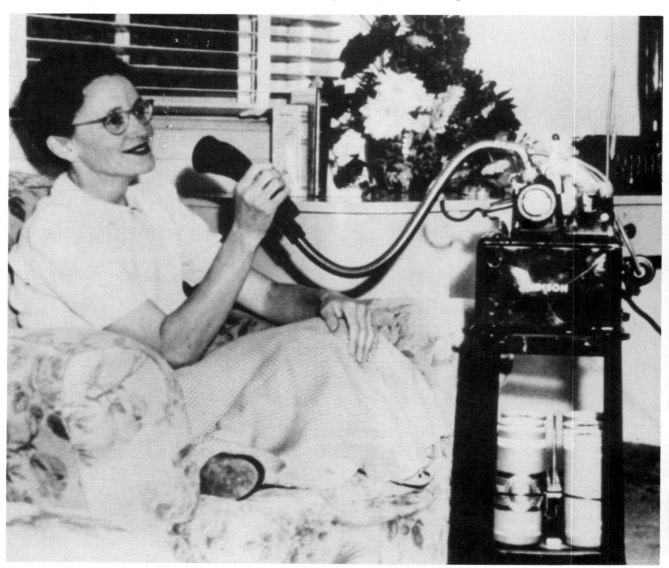

THE GREAT DICTATOR *Gwen Meredith, the quiet authoress of the epic ABC radio serial* Blue Hills *who created more than five thousand episodes, many of which were dictated into this early recording machine.* Blue Hills *was an institution on the radio. After the very last episode, Miss Meredith said she felt 'a little bereft'.*

TILL DEATH (OR THE SCRIPT) DO US PART *One of the great* Blue Hills *moments, the marriage of characters played by June Salter and Rod Taylor. Radio listeners no doubt enjoyed the sound of the confetti.*

BIG PATTIE AND OLD KING COL *From shy youngsters these two performers Little Pattie and Col Joye have become almost the General Motors of the music business. Little Pattie had to stand on a box to make her first recordings.*

THE DOOR OPENED, THE PHONE RANG . . . *In the heyday of radio, the busiest man was the sound effects assistant. Frantically, he had to keep up with the action, providing 'live' sounds from a knock on the door to a car crash.*

KEEP CLEAR! *In 1934, Doctor Val McDowall of Brisbane succeeded in transmitting a television signal the grand distance of 10 feet. He was so engrossed in his experiments the humour of the sign can't have been apparent.*

Television

The medium which eclipsed radio in popularity is now itself obsessed with its relative popularity with the viewing audience. The infamous ratings, the statistical measure which tells television executives how many people were watching a particular programme at a particular time, have come to rule the airwaves much as the ballot box rules politics. Every week a computer spits out the figures which show which television station is attracting the most viewers, and for many people within the industry these can be life or death results.

But television wasn't always such a cut-throat business. As early as 1934, Dr Val McDowell of Brisbane assembled a bizarre jumble of apparatus and with it somehow managed to transmit a television picture the grand distance of ten feet. His workshop wall sported a sign which read, 'Television. Keep clear!'

Australian electronics buffs had been fiddling with television since the twenties, but it wasn't until the world radio convention of 1938, and the visit of James Logie Baird to Australia, that we began to realise that 'radio with pictures' might soon be a reality.

VIDEO PIONEER *James Logie Baird, the British inventor who produced the first flickering television pictures. Baird visited Australia in 1938. Although his system was not the one adopted for TV transmission, his middle name lives on as the title of our television industry's top awards.*

324

Twelve years after Baird produced his first flickering television images, thousands of Londoners were watching a regular television service twice a day. As it turned out, Baird's system was not the process adopted for television transmission, although his middle name, Logie, lives on as the title of our television industry's top awards.

By the early 1950s when British and American audiences were already watching television at home, Australia was still staging experimental broadcasts in places like Sydney's Hotel Australia. Sir Ernest Fisk, poised to swing his vast AWA empire behind the production of television sets and equipment, extolled the advantages of television above radio.

Television is a new kind of radio broadcasting. You will have a set in your home with which you will see plays, variety shows, pageantries, sports and a great variety of things as they occur in your own receiving set.

TV TRY-OUT *For a closed circuit demonstration of television at the Australia Hotel, Sydney, in the early 1950's, the comedy duo Ada and Elsie performed, their quaint brand of humour.*

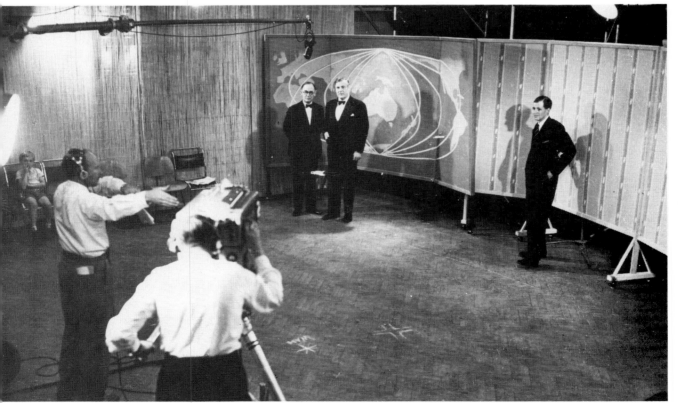

AND NOW FOR SOMETHING NEW *The official opening of ABN-2, the first ABC TV station on-air. Seen at the Sydney studios, November 5, 1956, are Mr, (now Sir) Charles Moses, General Manager of the ABC, introducing Sir Ian Jacob of the BBC. At right is Michael Charlton, who compered the programme.*

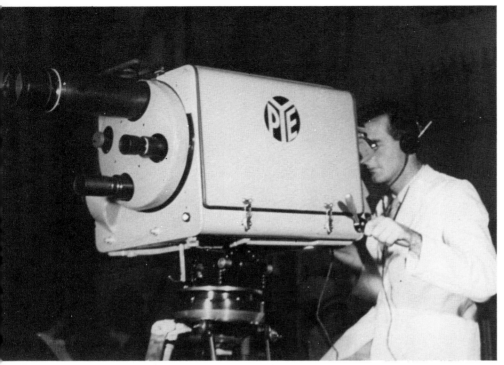

SPECIAL IMPORT *A brand new cathode-ray tube camera imported from England for a closed circuit demonstration of television in the 1950s.*

By the mid-fifties, the race to be first was hotting up. At Sydney's Channel Nine, Sir Frank Packer was so determined to win he didn't even wait for his studios to be finished.

The first Australian television programmes were produced as outside broadcasts from a tiny church hall in Surry Hills in Sydney. The dazzling variety line-up included 'The Johnny O'Connor Show', 'Accent on Strings', 'What's My Line?' and a show called 'Campfire Favourites', starring a yodeller named Ifield.

When the big day came on 16 September 1956, Bruce Gyngell, the man who now has the 'last word' on Australian television, had the dubious and uncomfortable honour of saying the first. Later to become the first Chairman of the Australian Broadcasting Tribunal and now head of the Independent Multicultural Broadcasting Corporation, he remembers the moment like this:

On the opening night I was sitting

BEDTIME BANDSTAND *The Channel 9 rock 'n roll show* Bandstand *helped bring a whole generation of young Australian entertainers to prominence. From left to right: Patsy Ann Noble, Col Joye, Judy Stone and host Brian Henderson.*

in a chair in a very small little room, in fact people commented as to why this announcer, who was unknown, appeared like this. It was because of the confinement of the space, and the only way the camera man could get the panning handle of his camera in. The chair wouldn't move any further so I sat the entire night with my left shoulder dropped and my right shoulder up saying, 'Good evening, ladies and gentlemen, welcome to television.'

Once it became established, Australian television spent most of its time transmitting English and American programmes, but we did manage to produce shows of our own. 'Consider Your Verdict', a courtroom melodrama, and 'Homicide', the legendary cops-and-robbers saga were early successes, as was Graham Kennedy, one of the few radio personalities to make a triumphant new career on television. His 'In Melbourne Tonight' shows became the longest running variety series in Australian television history, and although Kennedy has since left the new medium to try his hand at screen acting, he is still regarded as the 'king' of television.

GRA GRA *Graham Kennedy, one of the few radio personalities to make a new career on television. His* In Melbourne Tonight *had a record breaking run.*

PART OF THE FAMILY *Abigail (right), Joe Hasham and Robyn Gurney — household names while in* Number 96.

'The Mavis Bramston Show', Australia's first satirical show, kept the nation laughing through the mid-sixties, and the cast of Barry Creyton, Noeline Brown, Ron Fraser, Carol Raye and Gordon Chater all became stars in their own right.

In the seventies, 'Number 96', a sinful soap-opera, made perhaps the biggest impact of any drama series. Producer Bill Harmon has attempted to explain its amazing success:

Well, number one, it was the first of its kind. Secondly, it goes back to radio. People like to follow characters all the way through. They like to know their innermost thoughts, they like to feel they're part of the family. I think also comedy was a very big part of the success of the show. They could laugh at each other and they could laugh at the characters.

But, like every other television show except the News, the drama of 'Number 96' eventually came to an end, killed off by the ultimate judge and jury of television: the ratings.

THE LADY HERSELF *Mavis Bramston, the weird concocted femme fatale of dubious charms who gave her name to the television comedy hit of the '60s. Here she is making a personal appearance tour of South Coast change sheds.*

ISN'T SHE LOVELY *Abigail, just one of the beauties to grace the television screen in* Number 96, *a soap opera that dealt with the dubious goings on in a block of flats, and kept viewers of the '70s glued to their sets nightly.*

TOGETHER AGAIN *Noeline Brown and Barry Creyton, original cast members of the legendary Australian satirical TV programme of the '60s, the Mavis Bramston Show.*

TITILLATING TELEVISION *Providing sin and scandal for the television audiences of the '70s was* Number 96, *a soap opera which developed a huge following. It made the biggest impact of any drama series in Australia.*

10

THE SUNBURNT COUNTRY

Beyond the urban boundaries

I love a sunburnt country,
*   A land of sweeping plains,*
Of ragged mountain ranges,
*   Of droughts and flooding rains.*
I love her far horizons,
*   I love her jewel-sea,*
Her beauty and her terror,
*   The wide brown land for me!*

When Dorothea Mackellar wrote her famous verse *My Country* **at the beginning of the century, Australia was already becoming one of the** most urban nations on earth, today only ten per cent of our fourteen million people live on the land.

Dorothea Mackellar's country is a land few modern Australians have seen, the wide brown land of mirages and kangaroos, back of Bourke, back of beyond—the Never Never. Today, most of us are more likely to have tried Scandinavian smorgasbord than damper. We're more familiar with swimming pools than billabongs.

Yet the Australian ethos is still influenced by 'the bush'.

John Douglas Anthony is the leader of the National Country Party, and as such is second in charge of the nation after the Prime Minister, Malcolm Fraser, another farmer. His political rank demonstrates just how much power still lies in the land. Doug Anthony's property is among the rich, pastoral valleys on the New South Wales north coast, near Murwillumbah.

HANDYMAN'S DREAM *This desirable country property might be in need of a little attention, but to an Australian settler in 1901 it was home.*

FAR FROM THE MADDING CROWD *A far cry from the nine-to-five city desk is the life of Australians such as this sugar cane farmer. His hours, and the rewards, are uncertain.*

IT'S A GREAT LIFE *After the First World War the government launched a campaign to encourage returned soldiers to buy land. No mention was made of drought, flood and pestilence.*

THE SYDNEY Mail — PRICE — FOURPENCE

WEDNESDAY, FEBRUARY 12, 1919.

War Issue : No. 237.

Newspaper illustration publicising the Government's efforts to encourage returned soldiers to buy land

Like most men on the land, the Deputy Prime Minister sees his property as more than just a farm:

My father came back from the First World War and was given a small soldier settler's block, fourteen acres, to grow bananas. So he went and cleared the country and grew bananas. He was ravaged by bunchy-top and went broke. He tried growing sugar cane and went broke. He became an auctioneer and then went back to growing bananas. That was the beginning, and we've always had a battle.

I've got an agricultural background. I grew up on the land. And I know without any qualification this is where my love lies.

IF I DIDN'T LAUGH I'D CRY *A good sense of humour not only helps — it's essential for Australians who work the land. Farmers have more than their fair share of grief through droughts, plagues and floods. But some of our best humour has come from the land.*

"First the drought killed some of the sheep, then the flood drowned some more, and now the grass has grown so high, I can't find what's left of 'em!"

THE GRAIN OF LIFE *Farm labourers in the early 1930s sweat it out in the afternoon sun loading sacks of freshly harvested wheat onto a dray. The single Shire horse was used to help lift each sack onto the dray before joining the rest of the team in the long haul to a local silo.*

But with so much wealth in the land, how can farming, in Doug Anthony's own words, be 'a battle'?

No doubt my dress makes me look prosperous, but I happen to be a senior member of government, so you'd expect me to dress reasonably well. But because you've got cattle and because you've got land, it doesn't say you're prosperous. It can mean that you've got a substantial overdraft at the bank.

The biggest struggle on the land is not against overdrafts, but against sheer uncertainty. Even with scientific farming, mechanised war against disease, superphosphate bounties and guaranteed minimum prices, life is often still a bitter fight against the elements. One year's record crop is often followed by the next year's failure. What the Lord giveth he can also take away, even unto last year's Mercedes.

The ravages of the Australian way of life are legendary, a colourful part of our folklore, perhaps best summed up in the ironic words of the famous poem 'Said Hanrahan' by P. J. Hartigan ('John O'Brien').

Hanrahan is a bush pessimist who is first found lamenting the onset of the drought:

'If we don't get three inches, man,
Or four to break this drought,
We'll all be rooned,' said Hanrahan,
'Before the year is out.'

Then of course it rains and now he bemoans the arrival of the rain, and too much water:

And every creek a banker ran,
And dams filled overtop;
'We'll all be rooned,' said Hanrahan,
'If this rain doesn't stop.'

And, lo, after the rain, the grass grows as high as the fences, and Hanrahan gazes around the sky:

'There'll be bushfires for sure, me man,
There will, without a doubt.
We'll all be rooned,' said Hanrahan,
'Before the year is out.'

THE TIMBERGETTERS *Before Green Bans and Friends of the Earth, Australia's forests were fair game for the rugged timbergetters who were prepared to work in remote areas and steer giant trucks along makeshift mountain roads.*

Floods

The Hunter River flowing lazily past the New South Wales town of Maitland is part of a tranquil scene, typical of much of rural Australia. But when you live on the land nature can be a harsh mistress. In 1955, after weeks of heavy rain, the northern New South Wales rivers, including the Hunter, rose and broke their banks. In the floods which followed twenty-two people were killed and 10 000 homes ruined. The flooding of Maitland, the worst affected town, was fast and furious. In low lying areas houses were completely submerged beneath the muddy swirling water. Thousands fled their homes, and those who refused to go had to be removed by force. The Mayor of Maitland appealed to surf clubs on the coast, and lifesavers rowing their surf boats helped rescue more than 600 people.

At the height of the flood, hundreds of people watched as a railway signal box swayed and rocked under the force of the waters. Inside, two men struggled for their lives while a helicopter circled overhead. Within minutes, the signal box collapsed, hurling the men into the torrent. As they grabbed at a line lowered from the helicopter, the crowds cheered what seemed like an amazing rescue. The helicopter climbed to thirty metres and veered towards a nearby railway bridge where the pilot hoped to lower the two men to safety. But, as the helicopter turned to avoid power lines, the men's hold slipped. One man hit the water and disappeared, the other landed across high tension wires and was incinerated in an explosion of blue flame. Then the dangling rope tangled in the power lines and the helicopter spiralled out of control into the water. The crew of two were incredibly lucky. They survived the crash, and wearing lifejackets, were plucked from the floodwaters about three kilometres downstream by an army 'duck'.

ABSOLUTE WATERFRONT *So savage was the flooding in Maitland that at one stage 20 houses from one street were picked up by the waters and smashed against a railway bridge. In all, 10 000 homes were ruined, and 22 people were killed.*

FILMING A TORRENT *Trousers rolled and raincoat flapping, a newsreel cameraman braces himself to film the main street of Maitland at the height of the 1955 floods.*

EVERYTHING MUST GO *Even the display stock in the window of this menswear store in Maitland had to be cleared to escape the dramatic rise of flood waters.*

INLAND SURF RESCUE *Miles away from the closest beach, a life-saving crew helps rescue people and their belongings from the water. Lifesavers rowed 600 stranded people to safety.*

AIRLIFT TO MAIN STREET *When the worst of the 1955 Maitland floodwaters had receded, much of the town was totally cut off. Food supplies were parachuted in to hungry residents.*

NOTHING IN MODERATION *The Australian climate is often given to excesses. In the grip of drought, farmers pray for rain — when it comes, the result can be devastating.*

So savage was the flowing flood that at one stage twenty houses in one street were picked up by the rushing waters and smashed against a bridge. Seven people clung to the roof of one of the houses, but only three of them survived. By the time the rain finally stopped, more than ten inches had fallen in just four days. The damage was estimated at £10 million.

And as the floodwaters slowly subsided, Maitland was still cut off from the rest of the nation by water. Food and medical supplies, blankets and clothing were dropped into the town by parachute. It was weeks before

the town could return to its normal life. Since 1955, Maitland's levy banks have been strengthened and its flood warning system improved.

During the next twenty years Australia would see periodic floods in a variety of centres but none so spectacular as the torrent which submerged much of the city of Brisbane in the last week of January 1974. A freak flood, brought on by the torrential rains of cyclone Wanda overran about one-third of the entire metropolitan area of the Queensland capital, Australia's third largest city. Forty suburbs were under water, some to the amazing depth of more

than 10 metres. Fifteen people died, scores were injured and many thousands had to be evacuated from their homes. The city centre was swamped and an oil tanker broke its moorings in the Brisbane River and narrowly missed a block of flats before slamming into a wharf.

For many people, particularly the thousands who found that their insurance policies meant naught in the face of an Act of God, the Brisbane floods spelt ruin.

And the problem with the elements in this exasperating country is that they can so easily switch from one extreme to another.

Drought

'I am the master, the dread king drought, and the great west land is mine,' said Ogilvie's poem of half a century ago, and it has always been the same. Some part of Australia is always in the grip of 'the Dry' and that's why they call the drought 'the seventh state'. It's a grim, cruel fact of Australian life and it breeds its own brand of sardonic humour. It's a time when graziers tend to call clouds 'empties coming back from the coast', a time of the so-called 'darling showers' . . . three thunderclaps, two drops of rain and one dust storm.

It is impossible not to be profoundly emotionally affected when travelling into a drought-stricken area, and the desolation, death and despair have made their mark on Australia's writers. In the face of drought the doggerel which characterises so much Australian poetry, including that of Lawson and Pater-

SURVIVORS *'I am the master . . . the dread King Drought', said Ogilvie's poem of half a century ago. Herb and May Springer were devastated by drought seven years ago and when it was over the floods took the rest. Despite the odds they survive.*

TRAPPED *Where once there was water there is now only baked mud over a treacherous bog. A steer flounders helplessly, trapped by the land that betrayed him.*

THE AGONY OF DROUGHT *Sheep roam their scorched paddock, pathetically searching for a spot to graze. But for one the battle against hunger and thirst is over.*

son, is somehow elevated to a different plane. And even Australia's unknown bards have been moved to a rare eloquence.

Eerily wails the drover,
When the drought wind sweeps the sky,
And men say, 'Hear the Plover',
As he moves the ghost mob by.

And they never speak of rain,
When the blazing sun is setting,
Like a disc of shining brass,
And they wouldn't steal a copper,
But they all steal grass.

The name of the writer of this old ballad is lost to time. But many of Australia's well-known writers have been inspired by the spectacle of drought and their words, considering the circumstances of their inspiration, have an almost indecent beauty. Mary Durack linked beauty with the tragedy of drought in this passage from *Kings in Grass Castles.*

Every morning clouds piled up to the north to melt in the midday heat and evening skies were agate bright fading to amethyst. Cracks widened on the parched plains and hot winds filled them with the brittle remnants of precious grass.

MAN OF THE LAND *Dressed up in his Sunday best, a veteran of the harsh outback settlement at Birdsville struggles across the 'road' before the afternoon dust storm.*

THE SEVENTH STATE *There is always severe drought in some part of Australia. The stock animals die from starvation and thirst. Drought is such a constant companion of the outback farmer that many of them call it 'the seventh State'.*

Geoffrey Dutton described the land with no rain as 'drought country ... where the light strikes nothing but ruin as response' and time and time again observations about the drought pierce the general greyness of Australian literature with a special clarity. From Judith Wright's poem 'Drought Year':

> I heard the dingoes cry
> in the whipstick scrub on the Thirty-mile Dry.
> I saw the wagtail take his fill perching
> in the seething skull.
> I saw the eel wither where he curled
> in the last blood-drop of a spent world.

DESPERATE MEASURES *A grazier in the drought-stricken Boomi District hand-feeds his herd to keep them alive. After years without rain there is often not a blade of grass to be found.*

They say that drought runs in seven-year cycles. In 1970 on Herb and May Springer's property near Longreach in Queensland, there was not a blade of grass in sight. At that time Herb and May described their predicament. Herb said:

> This country at the present time is really finished as far as we're concerned. And a lot of other selectors on the eastern side of the Thomson River are in a similar position to myself with their stock. I would say that we'd want at least four or five years abnormal rain to bring this country back into its being. In another fortnight there won't be a sheep left on this place.

By the early seventies, graziers were walking off their properties never to return. The Springers, however, were determined to stay. Like many farmers, they owned two properties side by side. The second farm had been bought for the children but, as the drought dried up the land, that second property had to be sold. Herb went back to his old job of wool classing, working for a few farmers who still had sheep alive. The Springers prayed for rain and eventually, after seven dry years, it came. In the Australian bush, they say it never rains but it pours. For Herb and May Springer, that first

THE GRIM FACTS *Several Australian balladists have been inspired to write about the drought. But nothing can romanticise a situation so starkly grim as this one.*

rain storm is one they will never forget. May described how the drought broke and washed them out:

> We just sat and waited and hoped for the wet season until finally one night it came, and unfortunately we got nine inches overnight. It was abnormal, particularly on this drought stricken land. There was just absolutely nothing to hold the water. As a result the fences wound up like corkscrews and there was great damage done to the dams.

But in the good times the Springers had paid well. Their credit was good and their feed and land were an investment for the future.

With the support of their local stock and station agent, the banks and the Rural Reconstruction Scheme, Herb and May Springer survived their greatest crisis. After the drought broke, it took them another five years to get the property working again.

Today they own little of their former land, but they're still there—old dogs for a hard road.

Plague and Pestilence
The rabbit

In the middle of the nineteenth century, Mr Thomas Austin, a gentleman farmer of Barwon Park near Geelong, was feeling homesick. He missed his native England and he missed his favourite sport—hunting. In 1859, Mr Austin decided to import live game and later that year the first animals arrived in Victoria on the clipper ship *Lightning*. The animals Mr Austin had chosen were *Oryctolagus cuniculus*, the common European rabbit. Mr Austin had made a terrible mistake.

Domesticated pet rabbits had come to Australia with the First Fleet, but their breeding was controlled. Mr Austin's rabbits soon reproduced to the point where by 1870 they had become a popular delicacy in Melbourne society. There were now so many, they were regularly offered for sale in the Geelong *Advertiser*. The Barwon Park rabbits were

BARWON PARK *Thomas Austin's magnificent old house near Geelong in Victoria. Austin brought rabbits here to help him emulate the aristocratic life style of landholders in the old country. The Duke of Edinburgh hunted here.*

bred near the main house and became so famous that when the Duke of Edinburgh visited Australia in the 1880s, he made a special trip to Geelong to enjoy the hunt, shooting 450 rabbits in a single day. By this

time, the rabbits were breeding and spreading at an unbelievable rate, and from Barwon Park came what scientists now call the greatest animal invasion of any continent in history.

SIX O'CLOCK CLOSING *The incredible result of a few weeks of rabbits breeding in an uncontrolled environment. These rabbits gathering for a social drink were a typical scene of the 1950s. The rabbit was introduced to Australia in 1859 by Mr Thomas Austin for his favourite sport — hunting.*

RUN RABBIT *One way to keep a plague of rabbits under control is to eat them. At least that was the view of the government in 1905. These workers at the Government Meat Markets, Darling Harbour, are packing dead rabbits for export. But the rabbits who managed to stay out of a pie kept right on breeding and the plague continued for half a century.*

Ironically, while rabbits were overrunning Australia, South American countries were facing the opposite problem. Rabbits raised for meat and fur were dying from a mysterious disease called myxomatosis. Early this century, a Brazilian scientist named Dr H. de B. Aragao approached the Australian government and suggested that myxomatosis could be the answer to our problems. The government, on the advice of Australian scientists, ignored the Brazilian's solution to our ever-increasing rabbit problem. According to Professor F. J. Fenner,

author of the book *Myxomatosis:*

They poured cold water on it. They responded by saying that the rabbit was a very important animal for the carcass and fur trade. They didn't want to interfere with the trade by destroying rabbits totally. They realised that they did have to contain them but they didn't want to destroy them.

Australian scientists would soon regret their decision not to introduce myxomatosis to Australia. Within a few years rabbits were completely out of control. The pests became so

prevalent that in the west of New South Wales land which had supported fifteen million sheep in the 1890s could carry less than half that forty years later.

For half a century Australians on the land fought a futile battle against the rabbit. Trapping, shooting, poisoning and even clubbing the rabbits to death was futile. Rabbits were slaughtered by the thousands, but it made little difference.

In the 1930s a new scientist entered the myxomatosis saga. She was Dr Jean McNamara, a Melbourne paediatrician, who had been overseas studying poliomyelitis when she met a group of scientists working on myxomatosis. Dr McNamara was convinced the disease and its effect on rabbits had not been adequately tested. Myxomatosis is a particularly horrible virus which spreads only under certain conditions. A rabbit infected in the eye with ugly sores will take more than a week to die. In the meantime, the disease is transmitted to other rabbits by flies or mosquitoes. Convinced of its effectiveness, Dr (later Dame Jean) McNamara hammered away at the authorities for years. As Professor Fenner says:

> She wrote some very pointed articles in the Melbourne newspapers and insisted that myxomatosis must be given another trial. This was started in May 1950 and carried out right through the winter which, with hindsight, is when mosquitoes aren't about.

FATHER OF MYXOMATOSIS *Dr H. B. Aragao, a Brazilian scientist who isolated a natural 'pox' virus, Myxomatosis. He suggested as early as 1919 that Myxo could be used as a control in Australia.*

LADY WITH A MISSION *Dr Jean (later Dame Jean) McNamara, a Melbourne paediatrician. She campaigned for thirty years before authorities finally adopted Myxo in the war against the rabbit.*

BUNNIES BY THE MILE *The end of a rabbit 'drive' in the late 1940s. A team of men would fan out and drive the animals towards wire pens where the terrified bunnies were either clubbed to death or shot.*

But they didn't think of that at the time. The scientists had pretty well written it off as a failure. But then, just before Christmas 1950, reports came from ten miles away from Corowa, the nearest trial site, that there were rabbits with a horrible disease wandering over Corowa Common. It was obviously myxomatosis.

The myxomatosis, which had escaped from that testing site in the Murray Valley in 1950, soon changed the entire face of rural Australia. With government support a large-scale campaign was established which ensured the rapid, and deadly, spread of the myxomatosis virus throughout the Australian rabbit population. Half a century after a Brazilian doctor had first told us about myxomatosis, we finally had the rabbit plague under control.

FACING DEATH *Driven towards this chicken-wire pen by teams of professional rabbit hunters, these animals hurl themselves against the wire in a desperate attempt to avoid the death that awaits them.*

A GOOD SWAG *A professional rabbit trapper slings his haul over the saddle at the end of a busy day. The individual trapping of rabbits proved ineffectual against the millions of animals which ravaged grazing land at the height of the plague.*

THE GREEN OCTOPUS *This massive clump of prickly pear grew from a single plant. Each leaf puts down a root when it falls to the ground, and within a few years, a whole paddock is submerged beneath the green pest.*

Prickly pear

The common prickly pear, *Opuntia inermis*, an innocuous looking cactus, was first introduced to Australia as a pot plant in 1839, and grown for its decorative value at Scone in the central west of New South Wales. By 1916, the prickly pear was estimated to be increasing at the rate of a million acres a year, threatening to destroy all the pastures and arable land of Queensland and northern New South Wales. In 1920 vast areas of Eastern Australia were totally infested with the fast growing plant. It was so dense that farmers found it difficult to find their way across their own paddocks. The more prickly pear was cut back, the more it grew. Eventually the pest covered fifty million acres of Australia. How the nation came to be saved from the scourge is one of the most fascinating stories of how modern science came to the rescue.

The reason the prickly pear spread so quickly was that when the early settlers brought it to Australia, they neglected to bring its natural enemies as well. By 1920, the situation was so desperate that the newly established Prickly Pear Board sent a team of experts to America in search of insects which, if introduced to Australia, might attack and destroy the pest.

There were, however, grave dangers in introducing another pest to an already disturbed ecology. Science, playing God and tampering with the balance of nature, had found itself in trouble before. So for many years the scientists worked patiently in the Americas raising dozens of different insect species, making sure that they were free from parasites which would stop them multiplying.

PIONEERING SCIENCE *Scientists worked in this now decaying homestead in Queensland, to eradicate prickly pear. In the mid-1920s Cactoblastis eggs were supplied to farmers in tiny quills which were stabbed into the flesh of the prickly pear. Some sceptical farmers threw the quills away, and then came to regret it.*

MEMORIAL TO AN INSECT *At its height, the prickly pear menace covered 50 million acres of pasture in eastern Australia. The locals of Boonarga, a small town near Chinchilla in Queensland, were so grateful for their deliverance from the pest by the humble Cactoblastis insect, that they named their civic hall in its honour.*

Finally, in 1924, the scientists were ready to bring the insects on the long and difficult journey to Australia. Eventually, after more painstaking experiments, they narrowed down the field of candidates to one tiny creature, which now faced the extraordinary task of destroying millions of tons of encroaching vegetation.

Cactoblastis cactorum, introduced from the Argentine in 1925, proved to be as powerful as its name. Cactoblastis is a moth which lays its eggs on the prickly pear's spines. When the young caterpillars hatch, they immediately enter the pear and tunnel inside until fully grown. Then they spin cocoons and change to the chrysalis stage from which the moths emerge. The results are spectacular. After the grubs eat out the hearts of the pear, bacteria and fungus rot take over and destroy the plant completely. In the mid-1920s, cactoblastis eggs were supplied to farmers in tiny quills which were stabbed into the flesh of the prickly pear. Many farmers, sceptical of the work of the scientists, threw the quills away, and then came to regret it. Their neighbours, who'd spread the cactoblastis eggs, soon watched with amazement as their ten-year scourge was quickly

demolished. As the ground came back into view, the timber was burnt and crops planted again. Thousands of farms in Queensland and New South Wales were reborn.

In the small farming district of Boonarga near Chinchilla in Central Queensland, the locals were so grate-

ful for the way their farms had been saved that they named the modest civic hall the Boonarga Cactoblastis Memorial Hall in honour of the tiny insect. It may not be the most attractive name for a public building, but the people of Boonarga wouldn't have it any other way.

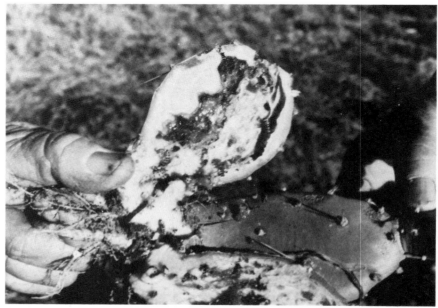

KILLER CACTOBLASTIS *Prickly pear is first disembowelled by the Cactoblastis larvae and then quickly rots. Cactoblastis brought prickly pear under control in the 1920s, and farms in Queensland and New South Wales were reborn.*

The Fly

When Chairman Mao Tse-tung came to power in China thirty years ago, one of his first edicts was that the nation must get rid of its flies. Every citizen was directed to kill at least a fly a day and, after some years, China's fly problem reportedly diminished. That sort of pest control may work when you have 800 million people to swat flies, but here in Australia we attack the problem with characteristic twentieth century biological overkill. We spend more than $20 million a year on fly sprays.

The 'Louies' we see in television commercials are actually raised in science laboratories, such as that at the Department of Entomology at the University of New South Wales. But while the scientists supply the victims for fly spray ads they don't necessarily approve of the battle strategy. Dr Eric Shipp, one of the country's leading experts on bush and house flies explains:

I don't think big companies are really aiming to try and get rid of flies and I don't think people are expecting the companies to do this. The only way to really get rid of flies is to look at their ecology and the whole background of their biology and breeding. Chemicals are not the answer to that at all. I believe someone once calculated the number of flies that would result if you started with a single pair and there was nothing to eat them, and plenty of food for them. At the end of twelve months, they would be ten to the eighteenth. That is ten million, million, million and that's not just flies, that's tons weight of flies. That's enough to cover the earth to a depth of twelve feet.

But whatever the realities of our war against the fly, a succession of anonymous blowies have left their own distinctive mark on Australian life. The characteristic wave of the hand to dislodge a persistent fly has become known as the 'great Australian salute', and there's plenty of photographic evidence that flies have been present at many of the nation's most solemn historical moments. There were flies (as well

THE PLAGUE *A Narrabri farmer surveys what is left of his oats crop after a plague of locusts has passed through.*

KNEE HIGH IN GRASSHOPPERS *Locusts, or grasshoppers, are a constant plague which decimates lush pasture land and crops once every few years. There is still no effective prevention to the invasion, one of the few remaining curses to the modern farmer.*

as Turks) at Gallipoli, and the famous flies of Canberra made the first of their many appearances on film when Prime Minister Joe Lyons introduced his Cabinet for the newsreel cameras in 1932.

And—horror of horrors—flies even turned out to plague Her Majesty Elizabeth Regina II when she toured outback areas during the royal visit of 1954. When you can't even say there are no flies on the Queen, what hope is there for the rest of us?

PEACHY *The fruit fly, scourge of every orchardist, is seen here depositing eggs onto a peach. Insects are only one of the problems facing Australian horticulture.*

347

OWZAT! *Harvey the sheepdog looks triumphant after demonstrating his prowess at Melbourne Sheep Show.*

Horses, dogs, sheep and galahs

The ceaseless battle against plague and pestilence and the elements has bred a famous stereotype ... the laconic man-on-the-land who is fazed by very little, except perhaps some bludger who misses his shout in the pub.

It would appear from Australian history that, rather than complain about his lot, the dinkum country-man has spent a good deal of his time sitting around thinking of more colourful ways to describe the adversities which beset him.

Not the least of problems facing a 'bushie' has been crook tucker. Australia has never been noted for its cuisine and yet even when faced with abysmal food somehow the bushman has managed to keep his sense of humour. What, for example, does he do when confronted with one of the world's gastronomic horrors—namely a galah? Certainly, he didn't complain but rather he invented this famous recipe as

quoted in Bill Wannan's marvellous book *Australian Folklore.*

Select three average-sized stones and place the plucked and gutted cockatoo or galah on top of them in a pot of water over a good fire. Boil hard for ten hours and then simmer for another five or six (the longer the better). Tip out the water, give the cockatoo to the dog and eat the stones.

Another version goes:

First catch your cockatoo. Pluck and gut it, and place it in the pot of hot water with two stones. Boil steadily. When the stones are soft the cockatoo is ready to serve.

Birds have always played a prominent part in the annals of the Australian bush—perhaps because they have been the only other creatures in the landscape who actually talked. Bill Wannan sources this story to one of the readers of his famous column 'Come In Spinner' which became an institution in the magazine *Australasian Post*:

ROYAL FILLY *Australia's Silver Jubilee gift to the Queen was a race horse. Here the Queen meets her new filly with the introductory honours going to the Prime Minister. It is hoped that* Australia Fair *will carry the Queen's racing colours to victory.*

I reckon the best known talking bird in Australia was Mudie's crow, a familiar figure at Alec Mudie's Federal Hotel, Bemboka (NSW), for many years.

The bird developed a habit of drinking tailings from the beer mugs, and there were times when it would stagger around. On one occasion a chalk line was drawn along the bar counter and the crow was told to walk along it.

After making several attempts the bird turned to the publican and said, 'Put me to bed, Alec, I'm as drunk as an owl.'

The Australian bird with the most famous name is the drongo, found in the north-east. Although the use of the word to describe someone as slow or 'not the full quid' comes from Drongo the racehorse of the 1920s who had a remarkably unsuccessful career. The horse was the butt of several jokes created by *the Melbourne Herald* cartoonist Sam Wells and thereafter became the national symbol of the 'no hoper'.

It is perhaps not surprising in a country so preoccupied with the problems of distance that animals, particularly horses, have featured so strongly in our folk tales. From the 'colt from Old Regret' to Carbine, our horses have been raised to an exalted position few human beings have achieved. The faster they were, the bigger the legend.

An Australian dog, on the other hand, was required to be not so fast but smart—quick on his paws, in other words. Here's a chestnut:

A kelpie dog was being discussed in a country pub in Queensland.

'That there dog of mine's a bloody marvel,' said the proud bushman. 'He does just about everything. He brings in the cows, goes out after rabbits, gets the mail from the post office, yards the sheep ... Yes, he does just about everything.'

'Well,' said the stranger, 'if he's such a flaming marvel why don't you call him in and let me buy him a beer.'

'Now, fair go,' said the bushman, 'that's one thing I won't allow. It wouldn't be right, seeing as how he's got to drive me home.'

HORSEPOWER *At the turn of the century draught horses were a more familiar sight than motor cars, these were photographed at an R.A.S. show in 1900.*

THE WINNERS' CIRCLE *To win a ribbon at the Royal Easter Show is every horsebreeder's ambition. These stallions were the champions of 1900.*

BATH TIME AT THE RIVER! *As this wood carving of the 1860s shows, the easiest way to wash a flock of sheep in those days was to throw them in the river.*

Paradoxically, though, the king of all Australian animals is one which most of the human population thinks is basically stupid. The sheep is a much maligned creature and yet Australia is so proud of her première industry that you could be forgiven for thinking that we invented wool.

The simple fact is that Australia has quite literally ridden on the sheep's back for most of its modern history. Even at the turn of the century Australia had around 100 million sheep and by the 1970s the number had nearly doubled.

CLICK GO THE SHEARS *Sheep shearing methods have come a long way since the hand clipping of the mid-nineteenth century, and wool is still one of Australia's primary products.*

THIS ISN'T A BAD SPOT *This 1905 photograph may look like a pleasant family outing, but for these settlers clearing the land was certainly no picnic.*

Sheep came to Australia with the First Fleet but the animal which really put Australia on the economic map was the Merino. We didn't create the breed but we did have a lot to do with its evolution. Its fascinating history can be traced back to MacArthur who, while he was in exile in England, bought half a dozen Spanish Merinos from the stud flock of George III.

MacArthur, who planned to develop a wool industry in NSW, was warned that if he tried to ship his Merinos to the colony they would be confiscated and he would be severely penalised. But he disregarded their warnings. He had influential friends and he obtained a special Treasury warrant to transport the animals in spite of the efforts of his old enemy, Sir Joseph Banks.

ON THE SHEEP'S BACK *When John Macarthur began breeding Merino sheep like these in the eighteenth century, he laid the foundations for Australia's greatest industry.*

351

The fears of his rivals were well founded because within two years MacArthur was back in London, flogging his fleece for a small fortune, 10 shillings a pound.

MacArthur's sheep became the backbone of an industry which determined the destiny of this country. It was a history colourful and dramatic; a story of hardship and incredible wealth — from the pound a pound days of the Korean War when American wool spinners stocks were depleted to those tragic times when sheep have been worth less than the bullets used to kill them.

The drought of the 1890s reduced Australia's sheep flock by half. It caused a major depression and at the same time it reinforced one of the earliest major industrial forces in Australia — the shearers. Between 1860 and 1890 there had already been more than 3 000 cases of strike action by shearers and the problems at the beginning of the twentieth century made them even more militant. Shearers were striking about

THE GREAT STRIKE *When drought in the 1890s caused a major depression in the sheep industry, shearers became extremely militant and there were frequent strikes. Armed militia are seen here removing strikers from the Great Strike of 1891. By the beginning of the twentieth century mechanisation had caused even more unrest.*

automation even in the early 1900s when the introduction of machine shears was considered to be a technological outrage. All in all the shearers lived in an intensely union orientated atmosphere with its own fascinating rituals. Even the cook was elected by secret ballot and

THE MARCH OF PROGRESS *This early woolshed has been converted to mechanised shearing. One die-hard in the foreground however, is still using hand shears. The adaptation to machinery did not come easily.*

according to the federal politician Clyde Cameron, a former shearing organiser whose father was a foundation member of the shearers' union, it was a decision taken with gravity and some humour.

You know the usual thing was,

'Who called the cook a bastard?' The chorus would come back, 'Who called the bastard a cook?'

We would always reckon that if the person who staggered out of the hotel almost paralytic was the cook we were going to have a

fairly good menu. The only reason I can think of is that as they became more famous and more competent they were better able to afford to get drunk, and bad cooks had to try to make up for their cooking by their sober habits.

SHORT BACK AND SIDES *Sheep at Goombargoona station, NSW. Despite competition from synthetics, wool continues to be a major world commodity.*

Today, despite intense competition from synthetics wool is still the fabric of our society. Interestingly much of the synthetic revolution has been spearheaded by the Japanese who are very much part of the Australian wool tradition. Many Japanese have been involved in the local wool scene longer than some Australian companies, and the remarkably long and complicated relationship between the two countries has survived even war and its bitter aftermath. Mr Kanematsu, founder of the famous company, was in the wool business when Ned Kelly was a boy. His company established its Australian office in the 1890s and there has been a constant interchange of business and cultures up to the present day. The only real interruption was during the Second World War when Kanematsu's Japanese staff was sent home for a few years. Discriminatory trade regulations were enforced until 1957, when it was business as usual. In the words of Hiroshi Tachibana, wool manager of Kanematsu-Gosho,

SHEARING THE GOLDEN FLEECE *The place where wool becomes wealth, the 'board' of a shearing shed in rural NSW. In a nation where there are more sheep than people, the annual clip is one of our most important statistics every year.*

We think that the Australian people are very open and very friendly and more or less optimistic. That's what we think. Typical thing is that you can say, 'She'll be all right, mate.'

Perhaps nothing represents the inexorable nature of the wool industry more than the continuing business relationship between nations through thick and thin. Eventually not even a few million lives stand

I'D WALK A MILE FOR A CAMEL *Well into the 1930s, camels were still in use hauling huge loads across the arid routes of inland Australia. The camels were descended from the beasts brought here by Afghan teams to help build the Overland Telegraph.*

WOOL FOR SALE *The scene at the sale rooms of Winchcombe Carson and Company, Sydney, 1901. The sale of wool has a colourful, and dramatic history. Our first fleeces were sold in London for a small fortune, ten shillings a pound.*

between a healthy trading situation. Wool itself is an industry which has survived tremendous ups and downs during more than two centuries of Australian life. No doubt it will suffer many more vicissitudes. It is after all a billion dollar industry based on such shaky foundations as an imported, ill-equipped animal set loose in an environment noted for its wretched excesses.

As long as there is drought and flood and fire, and a fluctuating market, working the land is always going to be a risky way to make a quid. Yet most country people wouldn't dream of changing their environment even if they could.

In the words of Dorothea Mackellar,
Core of my heart, my country!
Her pitiless blue sky,

When sick at heart, around us,
  We see the cattle die—
But then the grey clouds gather,
  And we can bless again,
The drumming of an army,
  The steady soaking rain.

Though the earth holds many
  splendours,
  Wherever I may die,
I know to what brown country,
  My homing thoughts will fly.

11

LANDMARKS IN TIME

A TWENTIETH CENTURY LANDMARK *This century has provided many Australian land-marks — in achievement, technology and architecture. But for sheer beauty, few would surpass the Sydney Opera House.*

The spirit of adventure and enterprise

There is something special about being Australian. But what is it? Maybe it's a mixture of pride and a need to prove ourselves. We seem to have a sort of 'edifice complex' whereby we build on a grand scale as if to prove there really is someone down here on the bottom of the world. Certainly this mixture of assertiveness and inferiority is reflected in our institutions and monuments.

Canberra

The story of Australia's national capital is a mixture of vision and farce, of shameless junketing and destructive bickering. But while the building of Canberra reflects government bungling on a grand scale, it also represents the realisation of a noble ideal.

Canberra is also the story of American architect Walter Burley Griffin who, like Denmark's Joern Utzon with his Sydney Opera House forty years later, was so troubled by government interference that he handed over his project to see it finished by others. Today, eighty years after Federation, Canberra still lacks the principal building for which the city was created—a permanent Parliament House. In fact, such a building, a bold design by architect Richard Thorp, is still in its planning stage, and is now due to be opened on 26 January 1988, the two-hundredth anniversary of European settlement in Australia.

In 1902, W. M. (Billy) Hughes, then the new federal member for West Sydney, led a group of parliamentarians in search of a suitable site for our national government. Choosing New South Wales, the oldest state, they journeyed from town to city, fêted and feasted by

THE PERMANENT HOME *More than fifty years after the 'temporary' Parliament House was opened, the Australian Government has chosen this bold design by Richard Thorp to be erected on the hill behind the existing building. It is hoped that the new Parliament House will be finished for the two-hundredth anniversary of European settlement in Australia, January 1988.*

ON THIS SPOT *Federal Minister for Home Affairs King O'Malley knocks in the first peg for the construction of Canberra. Until this ceremony, the only inhabitants of the gentle pastoral land in the area had been a few sheep.*

eager country folk who were hoping their district might be chosen as the lucky spot.

Through Bega, Bombala, Tumut, out to Orange and down to Albury, they stopped to tour rainforests and take a dip in cool springs. This jolly junketing at taxpayers' expense became so blatant that the Sydney magazine *Table Talk* finally thought it time to satirise their fruitless explorations with verse:

Each hill and dale, each stream and lake,
Seems all the more alluring,
When sandwiches and bottled ale,
Alleviate our touring.

Then the general public joined in the fun suggesting bizarre names for the nation's capital: Australopis, Kookaburra, Woolgold, Cooeeton.

THE GREAT CANBERRA JUNKET *Even before the Federal Parliament had decided on a site for a national capital, they had managed to turn the problem into an excuse for junketing. Climbing a fence to inspect a possible site near Albury is Sir William Lynne, Premier of New South Wales. On his left, in the light-coloured hat is Billy Hughes.*

BIRTH OF A NATION *The foundation stone is put into place on Capital Hill, Canberra, in March 1913. In the cockade hat, Governor-General Lord Denman taps the stone with his trowel, on his right, the Prime Minister Andrew Fisher. Behind, and holding a homburg, King O'Malley, who was a principal proponent of the National Capital.*

TIMES REMEMBERED *King O'Malley listens as his wife reads to him in the garden of their inner-Sydney home in 1953. Canadian born, O'Malley was a dynamic figure in the early political history of the nation.*

When, at last, a site was chosen beside the Molonglo River, months of speculation ended. It was declared 'Canberra' after its common local name. But debate still persists today on the origin of that name. Some say it means 'place of winds'. Others, that it is derived from the Aboriginal *Camberra* as the natives called Robert Campbell, owner of the original Yarralumla homestead. Or perhaps it comes from the Aboriginal word *Kanburra*, meaning a young kookaburra.

Whatever its origin, Canberra was officially named on 12 March 1913, just a few months before Walter Burley Griffin arrived to take up the position of Federal Capital Director of Design and Construction. When he won the highly coveted competition to design Australia's national capital, Griffin, thirty-six years old, was a 'modern' architect from Chicago, designing American cities for the future, cities for motor cars and electricity and aircraft. But, even before he arrived, Commonwealth public servants were criticising the design as 'too ambitious'. Griffin had planned for Canberra's development over a hundred years, but the bureaucrats refused to accept that Canberra would ever be larger than a country town. (Its population is now expected to reach half a million by the turn of the century.)

The government men often ignored Griffin's detailed instructions, even approving the construction of new buildings without his knowledge. The architect opposed the expense of putting up temporary buildings, claiming it would cost less to start work on the permanent designs.

VISIONARY ARCHITECT *Walter Burley Griffin the young American whose startling design for the new national capital of Canberra won an international competition. But by 1919 he had left the project.*

WITH ALL DUE POMP AND CIRCUMSTANCE *It was at this ceremony, in 1913, that the long awaited official name for the national capital was announced. In the cockade hat, Governor-General Lord Denman; on his left, the Prime Minister of the Commonwealth, Andrew Fisher. Lady Denman is announcing the choice of Canberra as the name for the new city, and on her left, is King O'Malley, Minister for Home Affairs. Debate persists today on the origin of the name.*

The public servants saw the affable, idealistic young American as an 'artist', the sort of person not to be trusted by 'sensible' administrators. In 1916 a Royal Commission into the National Capital criticised the bureaucrats for withholding information from Griffin, but the findings made little difference.

By 1919 Griffin's contract had ended, and he left Canberra, with at least its distinctive triangular layout already formed. But he was never to be involved again in the city's development. Griffin worked in private practice designing buildings such as Melbourne University's

Newman College and the Capitol Theatre, as well as a good part of the unusual suburbs of Castlecrag in Sydney and Eaglemont in Melbourne. Towards the end of his stay in Australia he made a living out of designing council incinerators, and those which still stand reflect his unique modern design concepts. Walter Burley Griffin, whose works in Australia ranged from our capital city to restaurants and water towers in country towns, eventually went to India on a commission to design a city. He died there from peritonitis in 1937.

Ten years before, on 9 May 1927,

Canberra had celebrated the opening of its Parliament House with the architect of the city noticeably absent from the invitation list.

It was a grand occasion. The opening of the first proper venue for our national parliament also marked the true establishment of Canberra as our national capital. As the politicians and public servants began their move up from Melbourne, what had recently been little more than a country town found itself a potentially great city. The opening ceremony was performed by the Duke of York (later George VI). Dame Nellie Melba sang the

FATHER OF A CAPITAL *Walter Burley Griffin with his wife. Griffin had to leave the Canberra he designed after arguments over how his plan was to be realised. He left the city when only its distinctive triangular lay-out was formed.*

BEAUTIFUL BURNER *The elaborate rubbish incinerator designed by Walter Burley Griffin for Willoughby Council in Sydney was one of many designed by him.*

national anthem to the enthralled spectators who had travelled by motor car, buggy and excursion train to watch the spectacle unfold among the sheep pastures.

With only two cafés in town, thoughtful organisers arranged caterers for the crowds they confidently expected to reach the grand figure of 100 000. Consequently they ordered 30 000 pies and sausage rolls, and on its opening day Canberra witnessed its first major example of over-spending. A mere 6000 people ate only 10 000 pies, and the government had to pay up for the rest. After everybody had gone home, the embarrassed officials buried 20 000 leftover Sargents pies in a mass grave on Capitol Hill behind Parliament House.

Canberra has been the butt of public service jokes ever since, but despite the funds which have been poured into the place, it is a city which now inspires most Australians with some sense of national identity. Parliament has approved a new House, but still resides in its 'temporary' building with a leaky roof, but in every other way Canberra is a crisp, clean metropolis with its sights set firmly on the future.

RIOT OF DECORATION *After leaving the Canberra project Walter Burley Griffin went into private practice. This ornate interior was the highlight of his design for the Capitol Theatre in Melbourne.*

A GOOD SHEEP PADDOCK RUINED *The local wags wasted no time in lampooning the decision to build the capital on grazing land near a sheep property called 'Canberra'. Thirty years later, Parliament House was not immune from a flock of jumbucks.*

Sydney Harbour Bridge

We're building a bridge in Sydney.
Over the harbour, too.
We'll all cross in safety
And busy trains pass through.

A wonderful thing of beauty,
Arching the skies of blue,
The best brains started it, brave men
wrought it,
Bridge Of Our Dreams Come True.

The unlikely lyrics of this old gramophone recording were sung by the popular Len Maurice, backed by Gil Dech and his Syncopators. But quaint as that song may seem now, back in 1930 it was sentimental enough to stir the souls of Sydney-siders day by day as they watched the two half arches of the Sydney Harbour Bridge inch closer together. It was truly the 'Bridge of our dreams'.

As early as 1815, convict architect Francis Greenway was designing bridges to span Sydney Harbour. The New South Wales Railways drew up plans in the 1870s and a few years later, the State Government actually negotiated to build a bridge for £850 000 but again nothing happened.

By 1900 Sydney was a thriving metropolis but virtually cut off from the north by water. The only way to move people and vehicles across Sydney Harbour was by ferry.

In 1912, Dr J. C. Bradfield, a government engineer, was commissioned to build a bridge. His early plans were delayed during the steel shortages caused by the First World War and it was 1924 before an English design for the bridge was selected and a British company contracted to build it. Against criticism of the high cost (the successful tender was for £4 217 721/11/10) the New South Wales Premier, J. T. (Jack) Lang insisted the bridge be wide enough for Sydney traffic as he foresaw it fifty years later.

The plan itself was simple. Two half arches would be built, one from Dawes Point in the city, the other from Milson's Point on the northern shore. The arches, on hinges, were cantilevered out over the water, each one held in place by giant tension cables looped through tunnels dug from subterranean granite. When the half arches were completed, the hundreds of cables were gradually slackened until the two halves closed and were riveted together.

At a time when much of the traffic was still horsedrawn, it was a stupendous engineering achievement. The span weighs 65 000 tonnes.

NORTH SHORE STEAM *Transport in the early 1900s provided a choice of carriage, tram or ferry, and here in this early photograph at Milson's Point, all three meet. Always popular, the ferry service survived the completion of the Harbour Bridge.*

THE ONE THAT GOT AWAY *As early as 1815 bridges were being designed to span Sydney Harbour. These three miniature harbour bridges were designed decades before the familiar coathanger eventually joined Sydney and the North Shore.*

EARLY DESIGN *Many Sydney Harbour bridges were drawn, including this one conceived by a Mr Parrott in the 1880s.*

SYDNEY AS IT MIGHT HAVE BEEN *In 1895, this was one 'artist's' vision of what Sydney might look like in the year 2001. Published in the* Town & Country Journal, *it had no noticeable effect on the city fathers, who continued to erect grim office blocks.*

WHAT I DID IN THE DEPRESSION *Jim Barbour, one of the few men who worked on the construction of the Sydney Harbour Bridge from start to finish. Sixteen of his fellow workers were killed on the project.*

More than a thousand men were employed building the bridge under the watchful eye of Lawrence Ennis, director of construction for the British contractors. Jim Barbour of Sydney, who worked on the bridge from 1924 to 1932, remembers Ennis well:

I was screwing a bolt with the washer on and I dropped the nut. Mr Ennis was at the back of me and he saw me drop it. 'Don't for-get to pick that up and put it on,' he said. 'That cost sixpence, that nut.'

For some men it was like any other job. The old hands became as agile as mountain goats as they strolled

TALK OF THE TOWN *As the new bridge inched its way slowly across Sydney Harbour, the crowds on the ferryboats made it their main topic of conversation. Soon most of them travelled in the trains, trams and cars, but the ferry system lived on.*

366

DOWN A BIT ON THE LEFT MATE *High above Sydney Harbour, the two halves of the arch of the Harbour Bridge edge slowly together. The workman on the left stokes the small portable furnaces used to heat rivets.*

THE KALANG SAGA *When the Sydney Harbour Bridge was opened in 1932 this craft, the car ferry Kalang was left without a job. So the Kalang, which had come out from England under her own steam, was converted to become a show boat. During the war she was stripped of her glamour and became a work horse, then it was back to the show again. In the '70s it was decided to tow the Kalang to Taiwan for scrap. But the boats towing Kalang got into difficulties. One sank and two others were wrecked.*

down the slippery steel slopes, over 90 metres above the water. But for many workers, it was bitterly tough. It was 1930 and some men, who had been forced to lie about their skills to get a job in the Depression, worked in a state of utter terror. Jim Barbour was there when the first of the sixteen who died, fell:

I remember I was standing there with one hand on the wire rope, and I had to prise my fingers off it with my other hand. I was quite safe where I was. But it was the shock—it was just seeing him go down, I knew he'd be killed.

Each time a man died, representatives were sent to his funeral and money was collected, half a day's pay from each worker, for the widow.

THE GIANT COATHANGER *The principal engineering challenge of the Sydney Harbour bridge was the construction of the arch. It was assembled progressively from each pylon, until the two sides joined in 1930, 200 feet above the water. It was another two years before the bridge was completed, at a cost of £10 million.*

Late in 1930, the two half arches had been lowered to the point where they were only inches apart. Completion of the span now depended on the weather, and twenty-four thermometers were placed along the surface to warn of even slight variations in temperature. In hot weather, the bridge might have expanded suddenly and jeopardised the complex

and delicate operation. It was a cool, cloudy August day in 1930 when the arch was successfully joined. The contractors claimed the bridge as 'a triumph for British engineering', but really it was very much an Australian achievement, and the bridge was indeed at that time one of the modern wonders of the world.

Next, huge girders were hung

from the giant arch to support the roadway that was being built like a cradle underneath. After another eighteen months the last of five and a half million rivets was driven home and the steel structure of the bridge was complete.

To show off the new marvel, imaginative public relations men ran ninety-two steam engines on to the bridge in a rather extravagant test of its strength. No one seemed too worried that if the test had failed half of the New South Wales Railways might have wound up on the bottom of the harbour. But as far as the public was concerned it did prove that our £10 million—double the original quote—had been well spent.

The opening ceremony was planned for 19 March 1932, and thousands of Sydneysiders crowded the foreshores for a long-distance glimpse of the celebrities on the bridge. The Premier, Mr Lang, made the major official speech concluding with the words:

...in a few moments I shall complete the opening ceremony by severing the ribbon stretched across the highway ...

A PUBLIC DEMONSTRATION *When the major engineering work on the new Harbour Bridge was completed, the authorities loaded the span with 92 steam locos in a public relations stunt aimed at reassuring Sydney residents that the Bridge wouldn't collapse.*

HARBOUR BRIDGE OPENED *Sydney will most probably never see a day like this again. Hundreds of thousands of people formed crowds and processions to commemorate the opening of the modern marvel.*

They were perhaps the most famous last words in our history. Just before the Premier stepped forward to perform the ceremony, a Captain Francis De Groot rode up on a horse and sliced through the ribbon with his sword, shouting:

I declare this bridge open in the name of the decent and respectable citizens of New South Wales.

In his slightly tatty uniform and mounted on a decidedly skinny horse, De Groot seemed like a latter-day Don Quixote. He was dragged to the ground by the New South Wales Police Commissioner, Bill MacKay, and carted off to the reception house.

Officials hastily restored the ribbon and the Premier was again handed the ceremonial pair of scissors. As the slashed ribbon was cut for the second time, tens of thousands of people around the harbour cheered and shouted as hundreds of ships, tugs and small craft hooted. Aircraft flew in formation across the city and over the bridge.

Captain De Groot, the villain of the day, was a member of the extreme right wing political group, the New Guard. They were violently opposed to Lang's socialistic policies aimed at combating the Depression. The following Monday, De Groot appeared in court and was fined £5 for offensive behaviour after the judge refused to declare him insane. Afterwards, he described his one moment of glory for the newsreel cameras:

A MAN AND A SWORD *Captain Francis De Groot, one of the more fanatical members of the New Guard, slashed the opening ribbon on the Sydney Harbour Bridge.*

At right: SINGULAR OCCASION *The day the Harbour Bridge was opened. For the first and last time, pedestrians were allowed on to the roadway.*

FIRST OVER THE BRIDGE *In the early 1930s, lady lifesavers were a popular part of the Sydney scene, and it was only proper that a troupe of these bronzed Amazons should lead the way during the procession which first crossed the new bridge.*

OH HAPPY DAY! *Thousands of schoolchildren make a giant tableau at the Sydney Cricket Ground on the day of the Harbour Bridge opening in 1932.*

Wearing my uniform which I wore in France, I merely joined the Governor-General's escort of 'mounteds' as they came out of Government House. I saluted the Governor most punctiliously as I passed, proceeded to the place where the ribbon was stretched, and before our Premier could get a chance to open it, slashed it through with a sword that I also wore in France.

Whatever the fun and political games of opening day, there's no doubt that the grand old pile of nuts and bolts that spans Sydney Harbour is today part of Australian folklore. It's true that workmen have been fighting the rust and repainting the bridge every day since the building started, and they even have their own special paint to ensure that the bridge never changes colour. It's true also that a man climbs the bridge each day to raise and lower the flags. Also, unfortunately, some people see

STILL IN THE RED *Despite nearly fifty years of toll collection, and the $5 million collected every year by toll-keepers, the bridge will not be paid for until 1985.*

the bridge simply as the best way to end it all. Despite nearly fifty years of toll collection, and despite the fact that the 140 000 cars cross the bridge

daily and the fact that more than $5 million is collected every year by the toll-keepers, the bridge won't be paid for until 1985.

The Holden

To most Australians, the Holden is 'Australia's own car'. It means plentiful spare parts and quick service. In the fifties, we used to say you could buy a fan belt in any milk bar. Even today television advertisements like to remind us Holden is Australian, 'We love football, mat pies, kangaroos and Holden cars . . .'

But the Holden is far from a home-grown product, and the story of how an American car became an Australian institution is one of the great marketing sagas in our history. In 1946, the first three prototype Holdens arrived on a boat from Detroit, in America. Alongside locally built prototypes they were road tested at Fishermen's Bend in Victoria and in the nearby countryside. Mr Laurence (later Sir Laurence) Hartnett, managing director of General Motors-Holden's between 1934 and 1947, recalls:

> The deal, as I saw it, was that we would be responsible for the styling, and the mechanical work would be done in Detroit. But Detroit seemed to take the whole thing under their wing. And they produced the prototype.

HORSES TO HOLDENS *James Alexander Holden founder of the famous car company.*

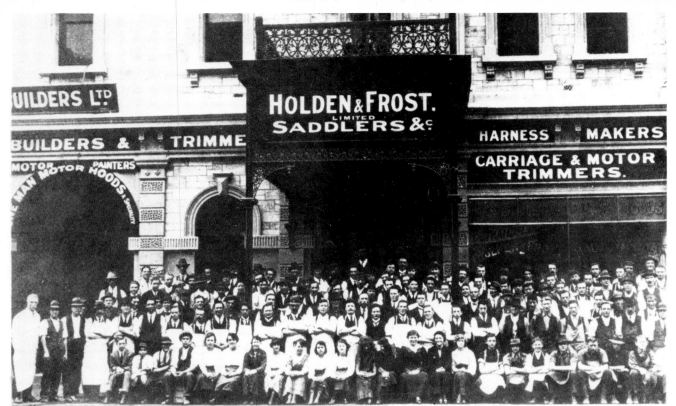

THE GANG'S ALL HERE *The massed staff of Holden and Frost, the Adelaide saddlers and coach builders who eventually became the Holden Motor Company, and gave their name to 'Australia's Own Car'.*

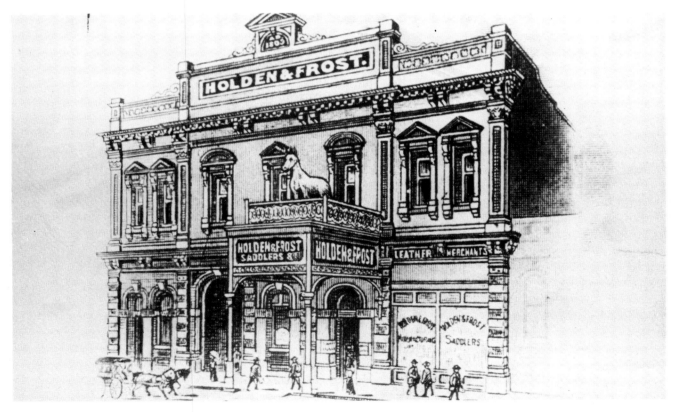

But if the first Holden was designed and built by Americans, at least the name was Australian. In the 1850s James Alexander Holden and his friend, Henry Frost, established a highly successful saddlery and coach building business in Adelaide. When the horseless carriage arrived, the Holden Company turned its hand to motor bodies.

HOLDEN AND WHO? *In the 1850s James Holden and his friend James Frost, established a successful saddlery and coach business at these premises. Later they turned to producing motor bodies.*

FATHER OF THE HOLDEN *Sir Laurence Hartnett, the father of the first Holden, stands somewhat forlornly beside his own car The Hartnett, built after he left GMH in 1948. He disagreed about what sort of car was suitable for Australia.*

FAMILIAR SHAPE *Under the skilled hands of a clay modeller in the General Motors design workshop, the familiar shape of the legendary first Holden emerges. Called the 48/215, the car was in production from 1948 to 1953.*

In the early twenties, General Motors came to Australia. It made good sense for the local and overseas companies to work together. By the end of the decade, they were making everything from flivvers to hearses.

When the Depression struck, the two companies merged and continued to produce the General Motors range of Oldsmobiles, Pontiacs, Chevrolets and a variety of other vehicles in Australia. But the business merger did not work out so well, and soon the company began to run at a loss. In 1934 a young engineer, Laurence Hartnett, was sent out from England to untangle the mess. With Hartnett at the wheel, the losses turned into profit and the company expanded its operations, building a new plant at Fishermen's Bend.

MAGIC MOMENT *The legendary Holden 'Ute' rolling off the production line in the early 1950s. The characteristic Holden grille is about to be fitted in front of the 'straight six' motor.*

Hartnett's long-cherished dream was to produce an Australian car for Australian conditions, and he was greatly encouraged by the wartime Prime Minister John Curtin, and his successor Ben Chifley. He went to America to persuade his American superiors to help fulfil the dream. But the boss of General Motors, H. P. Sloane, considered the Australian government of the day 'dangerously socialist'. Hartnett countered with the argument that it was in fact the military and not private enterprise which had built America's proudest achievement, the Panama Canal, and he got the begrudging go ahead. He was allowed to take an existing prototype, which he considered was the ideal basis for an Australian car, from a backlot in Detroit.

AUSTRALIA'S OWN CAR? *This prototype of the first Holden was in fact fresh off the boat from America. The car was designed and built in Detroit, but Australians accepted it as their own and bought thousands of them.*

THE HOLDEN THAT NEVER WAS *This is a rare photograph of the Holden we would have had if it had really been designed in Australia. Laurence Hartnett wanted a cheap car, but Detroit decided what would be 'Australia's Own Car' and the prototype came from America.*

375

But from then on the Americans dictated what type of vehicle 'Australia's own car' would be. Despite Hartnett's vision of a cheap car for the local market—a car with straight-pressed body sides and 'no fancy chrome grille'—the Americans were insistent. They were the biggest business in the world and they drove some very hard bargains with the Australians. They would be taking their share of the profit, but they would not be tying up their capital. For that, Hartnett had to take loans from the Commonwealth Government and the Bank of Adelaide.

Eventually, when it seemed inevitable to Hartnett that the 'Holden' was going to be simply a scaled down version of other General Motors cars, he gave up his struggles and resigned on the eve of the release of the first car. The honour of greeting the first one off the assembly line on 29 November 1948 went to his friend and mentor Ben Chifley.

Those original Holdens were the 48/215 (now commonly and mistakenly called the FX) and they sold

PEOPLE'S CAR *Prime Minister Ben Chifley sees a private dream come true when the first Holden comes off the production line on November 29, 1948. The Labor leader's idea was of a low-cost, 'people's car', and that is what the Holden became.*

HARDLY HOME GROWN *Despite a publicity campaign stressing the Australian origins of the Holden, the automotive industry was well aware of the car's American ancestry.*

376

STILL GOING STRONG *The latest model to bear the Holden name is the VC Commodore range featuring revised styling, added luxuries and mechanical changes over previous models.*

STYLE, LUXURY AND PERFORMANCE *The SLE Commodore has certainly been a winner for GMH, with its improved economy, additional power, stylistic interior and refined handling.*

MASS PRODUCTION *A proud and happy team of production workers from General Motors Holden pose beside the 100,000th Holden motor car manufactured at the Fishermen's Bend plant in Victoria. Later, a second assembly plant was opened at Pagewood in Sydney.*

for £733/10/-. The first car off the line, Holden Number One, stands today in the GMH plant at Fishermen's Bend. GMH built just 163 cars in that first year. By 1951 they were producing a hundred a day, and Australians bought them as fast as they reached the showrooms. The basic design hardly changed for the best part of a decade. In 1953 they made a small alteration to the grille and called it the FJ. Today the FJs are nearly thirty years old but there are still quite a few on the roads.

With the hindsight of history, perhaps the Americans had a better idea of what Australians really wanted in a motor car. By 1960 one million Holdens had been built and the second million took only another six years. Today, Toranas, Commodores and Geminis can claim engineering pedigrees stretching from Germany to Japan, but they all sport the Holden name and the familiar tag, 'Australia's own car'.

The real sequel to the story is the fate of little Larry Hartnett, the 'father of the Holden'. He still had dreams of building a cheap 'people's car'. After resigning from GMH he produced a small, French designed car called the Hartnett. But government contractors failed to supply essential parts, and while Hartnett won a massive damages case in the courts, the delays killed the project. Only 350 were ever built and one is lovingly kept under a tarpaulin in a shed on Sir Laurence's spectacular estate at Mount Eliza. The registration expired in 1950.

Qantas

Qantas is the second oldest international airline in the world (after KLM) and its bald-tyred beginnings can be traced back a long way, to a stony paddock and a galvanised iron shed in the town of Longreach in central Queensland.

These days the closest Qantas goes to Longreach is about eight kilometres straight up, but in 1920 this was the scenario. After you'd collected your tickets at the old wooden verandahed building in Duck St you made your way out to the hangar at the aerodrome. There was only one plane to choose from, an Avro 504K. It did 65 miles an hour (about 105 kilometres an hour) and it wasn't cheap. A joy flight cost three guineas and charter flights were 2/- a mile. The facilities weren't exactly luxurious but right from the start there was a healthy demand in the remote centre of Queensland. Qantas was soon ferrying mail and the odd grazier between Cloncurry to the north and Charleville to the south.

The story of the birth of Qantas is as intriguing as the name itself; the letters stand for Queensland and Northern Territory Aerial Services and it was begun by two men who, in 1919, had the task of surveying by motor car the proposed route for the £10 000 competition for the first flight between England and Australia. While Ross and Keith Smith took the glory for that flight, two other young pilots named Hudson Fysh and P. J. McGinness founded Qantas with the backing of a group of graziers. Hudson Fysh (later Sir Hudson) once recalled:

> Our first trip into Queensland nearly ended in disaster. We ran into some very rough weather, and the clouds closed right in on me and I got lost in them and I'm afraid I came out of them in the first turn of what could have been a fatal spin. However, I righted the plane and managed to land on the side of a hill near what turned out to be Redhead Coalmine. We taxied up this hillside and to a miner's cottage and the miner's wife rushed out and offered us a cup of tea.

THE VERY FIRST *Queensland grazier Alexander Kennedy, who invested in the foundation of Qantas when it was better known by its full name of The Queensland and Northern Territory Aerial Service. Kennedy's investment was partly in return for enjoying the honour of holding ticket Number 1.*

The Queensland and Northern Territory Aerial Services Limited.

No. **1**

22/11/22 _____ 192

PASSENGER TICKET.

NOT TRANSFERABLE,

PLEASE CONVEY

Mr. *A. Kennedy,* From *Longreach* to *Cloncurry,*

By Aeroplane intended to leave *Longreach* at *5-30* ᵃ·ᵐ· on *Nov 2ⁿᵈ* *1922*

First passenger from Longreach to Cloncur

FARE £ *11 / 1 / ~*

Extras *1 / 1*

TOTAL *11 / 1*

In addition to the conditions and regulations stated on the back hereof subject to which this ticket is issued by the Company and accepted by the passenger, the Company hereby expressly stipulates and provides that it will not be responsible for and shall be exempt from all liability in respect of any detention, forced landing, overcarriage, loss, damage, or injury (whether resulting in death or otherwise) whatsoever of or to the person of any passenger or of or to any luggage, property or effects belonging to or carried by, with, or for any passenger, whether such luggage, property or effects is conveyed in the same Aeroplane or other conveyance as the passenger or in any other Aeroplane or conveyance, and whether such detention, forced landing, overcarriage, loss, damage, or injury shall occur on land, in the air or elsewhere (all exemption attaching immediately such luggage etc., is received and continuing until it is delivered by the Company), and whether the same shall arise from or be occasioned by the act of God, of the King's enemies, dangers of the air, navigation, collision, fire, thefts, whether by persons directly or indirectly in the employment or service of the Company or otherwise, accidents to or by machinery or defects latent or otherwise in the Aeroplane or other conveyance, accidents, negligence, unskilful, improper or careless navigation or flying or driving, or any acts, defaults, or neglect of any pilot, passengers, Company's agents or servants of any kind whatever, or loss, delays, or any consequence arising from combinations of workmen and others, strikes and civil commotion, or from the restrictions of quarantine whatsoever imposed.

H Griffin

FOR THE QUEENSLAND AND NORTHERN TERRITORY
AERIAL SERVICES LIMITED.

NOTE This Ticket is the property of the Company, and is issued to and accepted by the passenger, subject to the conditions and regulations described on the face and back hereof, and must be given up when demanded by any of the Company's Officers.

PILOT *Hudson Fysh.*

SIGNATURE OF PASSENGER *A Kennedy*

ENGINEER *On Board*

UP, UP AND AWAY! *It was this model of an imported bi-plane, an Avro 504K, which served as the first passenger plane for Qantas. The first flights were in 1920 with Hudson Fysh as pilot. The passengers travelled in an open cockpit.*

A MATTER OF SCALE *The modest Avro 504K which served the airlines operations back in 1924 is dwarfed by the Boeing 707 which saw Qantas into the jet age, making it one of the world's great airlines.*

Soon young bush pilots were buzzing around the outback delivering people and mail. They were harum-scarum days, when you chocked the wheels with a mallee log and didn't worry too much about smoking on the tarmac, and took off and landed in a cloud of dust.

The first Qantas passengers flew open cockpit but it wasn't long before the 'propeller set' were getting a bit fussier. In 1924 Qantas bought its first cabin aeroplane and a brochure told the passengers 'Flying cap and goggles are quite unnecessary, sit at ease in your machine because your movements will not affect its balance whatsoever.' It sounded pretty good but for those who were still a bit queasy about flying there were some really comforting words. 'The fact that many invalids have used our facilities including people with weak hearts,' it said, 'demon-

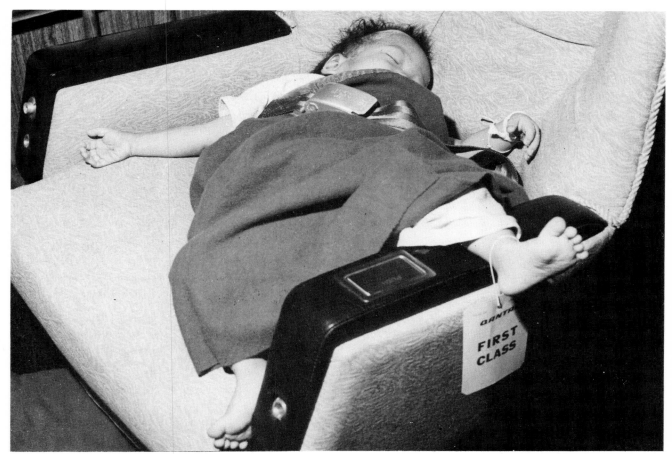

QANTAS TO THE RESCUE *Australia's own airline has taken part in mercy flights at home and abroad. When Cyclone Tracy hit Darwin mothers and children were first to board flights in a massive airlift. Orphans from war ravaged Saigon, like this baby, were also flown to Australia by Qantas. All the seriously ill children were identified by a first class label.*

strates the ease of air travel.' Not that everyone enjoyed the luxury. While the passengers travelled inside the pilot stayed out on top in the wind and the weather. Over the years Qantas would fly a host of different aircraft including the pretty little DH86s which made Singapore seem like a long way indeed. They were grounded after a series of crashes but the airline repainted older aircraft and pressed on with its ambitious plans.

And then came the golden years of the Empire Flying Boats, run in partnership with a British company. They were extremely popular; Sydney to Southampton took nine and a half days but it was luxurious travel. The fifteen passengers were provided with reclining seats, a smoking cabin and a promenade deck. In 1947 the first of the huge but graceful Lockheed Constellations arrived in Sydney for service on the now famous Kangaroo route.

BACKYARD AIR DISASTER *When this airliner crashed into a backyard at Guildford, Western Australia, eighteen people died. Air disasters are rare, and Australians claim an outstanding record of air safety.*

The next decade saw a period of rapid expansion. At the beginning of the seventies the airline which had been started in the scrub by two men barely out of their teens was half a century old and proudly taking delivery of its first Jumbo Jet.

Qantas is now the ninth biggest airline in the world and is seen in twenty-four countries on five continents. The airline has seventeen of the magnificent birds with the familiar flying kangaroo on the tail, and considering each one costs about fifty million dollars they make quite a flock and help to give Qantas an annual turnover of one hundred and fifty million dollars and earn more than a hundred million in foreign exchange.

AT LEFT: SHOW A LEG *Qantas hostesses are always up-to-the-minute in fashion. In 1973 it was the mini skirt.*

THE ONLY WAY TO TRAVEL *First class passengers on board a Qantas 747 in the upstairs Captain Cook lounge, which was part of the Captain's Club facilities for discerning travellers.*

PASS THE BOTTLE *Dr N. Blewett M.P. christens Qantas', 'City of Elizabeth' with champagne. With him are Sir Lenox Hewitt and Hostess Maureen Robertson, who appears to have brought along a spare.*

AND BELOW US WE HAVE ... *A 1971 Qantas Boeing 747B cruises in over Sydney Harbour. From a single plane in a paddock in Central Queensland in the 1920s, Australia's international airline has grown to be the ninth largest in the world.*

Victa and Hills

Mr Merv Richardson, an engineer and compulsive tinkerer, was almost sixty when he emerged from the garage of his suburban house in 1952 with the contraption that would soon revolutionise the Australian weekend. What he had produced from some billycart wheels, old piping and even a peach tin, is now almost an archaeological relic. Mr Richardson had made number one of 3 000 000 Victa lawnmowers.

At first he sold the mowers direct from the garage, but after placing a tiny advertisement in the local paper, demand outstripped supply so quickly that he knew he'd stumbled on a bonanza. Within a year Richardson was building a small factory and even the carpenter on the roof couldn't help noticing how much Victa business was booming. The carpenter, Mr Ken Blight, is now sales promotion manager for Victa Limited:

Well, you see, they needed the space so badly that by the time we got a roof and some walls up, they were moving in to start the manufacturing of the lawnmower. There were about six fellows working there then and it fascinated me so much that I just couldn't keep my interest on the factory, as a matter of fact. To be honest, I hated every minute of the factory roof; when it rained I was delighted to get down and go inside and help them building lawnmowers. They really excited me.

In fact, they seemed to excite most of the adult population of Australia. Helped along by slogans such as 'Turn Grass Into Lawn' and advertising, which even gives the big horsepower mowers some of the mystique of sports cars, Victa is now a nine acre complex.

Merv Richardson spent a frustrating and unsuccessful period of his life trying to develop a local aircraft manufacturing industry, but the mowers remained the firm foundation of the empire. Statistically, the chances are that almost every backyard in Australia has at some time had a going over from a Victa.

The other great Australian backyard success story revolves around the rotary clothes hoist. In some Australian suburbs there are more Hills Hoists than trees.

The story began when Mr and Mrs Lance Hill of Adelaide planted two orange trees in the backyard of their home to commemorate the birth of their daughter. While Lance was at the war the trees grew and grew until there was little space left to hang clothes across the yard.

So the dutiful husband built his wife a rotary clothes hoist, and soon afterwards he was travelling to town in a tram when he overheard a conversation. Lance Hill recalls the words that changed his life:

There were two ladies sitting opposite me in the tram and I couldn't help but hear their conversation and one said, 'I'm going into town to buy a rotary clothes hoist because my line's just broken

PULVERISES PASPALUM *An early newspaper advertisement for the new Victa rotary lawn mower. In 1954, the company could not secure exhibition space at the Royal Easter Show, and for some obscure reason, decided to advertise the fact.*

and all my washing is down in the mud.' And number two replied, 'Well, you can't get them. They are not available.' Number one said, 'They are available somewhere, because my neighbour's just got one.' So, with that in mind, I stewed it over and I got out of the tram next stop and caught the following tram back

home and said to Mum, 'We're going to make clotheslines.'

Just as Merv Richardson had done, they gathered up material to make half a dozen units and put a small ad in the paper. The calls started at 6.00 a.m. and continued all day and all the next day. People arrived at the Hills' house and left cash for the first hoist available. Lance Hill:

We had a long verandah on the house which had been converted into a kitchen and at the end of that was a little old cash box and people would say, 'Here's £5 or £7' or what have you. Sunday night my voice had gone and the cash box was overflowing on to the floor, and we were most ecstatic. We just didn't know that things could be like this. We'd never seen so much money.

Materials were extremely scarce but the demand was so great that Lance Hill was soon going to the most extraordinary places to get his precious tubing. A lot of material for the early hoists came from the submarine boom which had been stretched across Sydney Heads during the war. Early deliveries were made by the Hills and their relatives pushing a handcart. By the seventies Hills Industries was a multi-national company exporting to many countries, and responsible for planting 3 000 000 hoists in the backyards of this country alone.

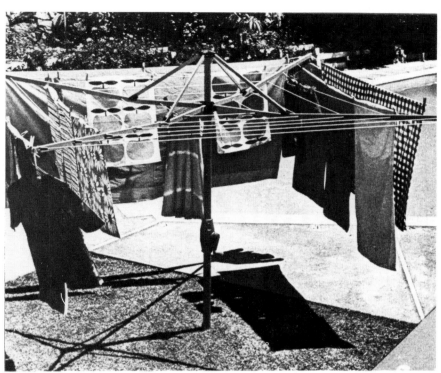

IT LOOKS LIKE A CLOTHES HOIST *It is a clothes hoist — but one with a difference. This is the Hill's Foldaline, you simply fold it up and store it away.*

ONE IN EVERY BACKYARD *Standing in front of their backyard bonanza, Mr and Mrs Hill, the couple who made the rotary clothes hoist an Australian institution. Mr Lance Hill came back from the war to find his wife's washing trailing in the mud. Handy with tools, he knocked her up a rotary hoist. By the mid-sixties Hills Industries was a multi-million dollar concern.*

The Sydney Opera House

If ever there was a symbol of modern Australia it is the Sydney Opera House. Overseas it is as familiar an image as the kangaroo, the boomerang and the Sydney Harbour Bridge. The Opera House has become an indelible part of the Australian consciousness in a comparatively short time, and no doubt this is because it came into being after twenty years of trials and tribulations. It was a difficult birth.

As early as 1948 Eugene Goossens had advocated an Opera House for Sydney and his idea was taken up by an unlikely crusader, the Labor Premier J. J. (Joe) Cahill. Opera is essentially not a sport of the working class, and although there were few votes in it for Joe Cahill he pushed ahead with zeal.

In 1956 his $10 000 international design competition attracted 216 entries from thirty-six countries. The four-man panel of judges chose a bold sketch of graceful sails by a

ELABORATE SHED *Until it was demolished to make way for the Opera House, an ornate brick structure served as Sydney's tram shed.*

THE DREAM *New South Wales Premier Joe Cahill (left) displays the imaginative drawing by Danish architect Joern Utzon that captured first prize in the competition for a design for a Sydney Opera House.*

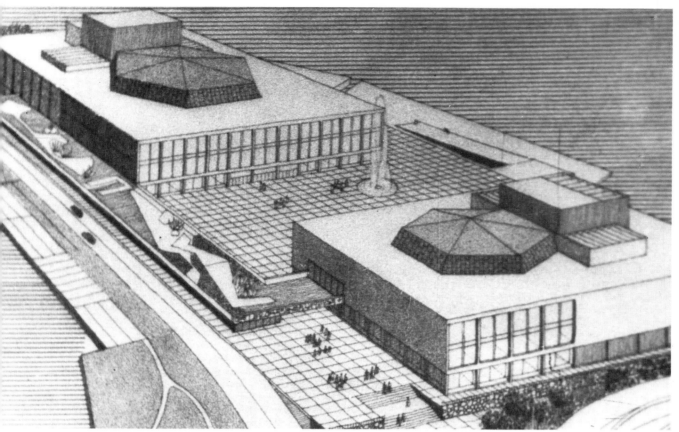

THERE BUT FOR ... *Third prize in the competition for a design for Sydney Opera House. Although this building may have been quicker and cheaper to build, it would not have provided Sydney with the spectacular tourist attraction it boasts today.*

thirty-seven-year-old Danish architect Joern Utzon. Utzon, an associate of such architectural giants as Frank Lloyd Wright and Le Corbusier, started work on the Opera House in 1957. At that time the cost was quoted at about $7.5 million.

The trouble was that nothing quite like Utzon's building had ever been built. Utzon did not really know how his magnificent sails could be constructed and soon, like Griffin before him, he ran into tremendous difficulties with the bureaucrats and politicians. As he and the contractors grappled with incredibly complex engineering, the costs began to mount. Soon we had a monumental architectural problem on the scale of the pyramids, except of course the Pharaohs did not have the benefit of a pyramid lottery. The $100 000 Opera House lottery made the extraction of money relatively painless.

The problems seemed interminable and, at times, insoluble. The battles between Utzon and the authorities were complicated still further by different demands from the eventual tenants of the building, including the ABC. Half way

through the project it was decided to change the whole nature of the building. At one stage, $3 million worth of stage machinery had to be scrapped when the ABC demanded the main hall for its symphony

concerts and this pushed opera into the smaller second hall. Joan Sutherland, La Stupenda herself, joined the fray saying, 'The concert hall is better. If only the ABC hadn't taken it for themselves.'

OPERATIC PILL BOX *Second prize in the international competition for a Sydney Opera House design went to this rather severe, upright concept which reminded many Australians of a pill box.*

THE WINNER *Joern Utzon, the Danish architect whose winning design for the Sydney Opera House was to cause so many problems.*

BEGINNINGS OF A DREAM *The first day of site preparation for the Opera House. As the bulldozers turned the 'first sod' a decade of hopes and conflicts began.*

The wars went on for more than a decade. The opposition in State Parliament found the Opera House a wonderful weapon with which to bludgeon the government. When the Liberals came to power in 1965, Utzon had to deal with a new and tough Minister for Public Works, Mr Davis Hughes. Hughes pinned most of the blame for the troubles on the hapless architect. In February 1966 he made a move to downgrade him from controlling architect to design consultant.

More than 1000 architects and artists marched through the streets of Sydney in protest. They formed the 'Utzon in charge' group, opposed by the 'Utzon go home' faction. Michaelangelo's letters describing the problems he faced building St Peter's in Rome were reprinted and distributed by the Sydney University Architects Club. A Sydney sculptor even went on a three-day hunger strike in protest over the government's treatment of Utzon. Reluctant to continue as the centre of controversy any longer, Joern Utzon left Australia in April 1966 with his wife and family, under assumed names to avoid publicity. In an interview in Denmark in 1972, Utzon said:

I left with great great regret. I fought for the perfect idea. The years I worked with my team were marvellous but very hard and we gave up only because I couldn't see the alternatives Mr Hughes wanted. I thought our work would be ruined and as it actually has proved now, it is ruined. You cannot make a piece of art and let somebody else finish it. I think if the architects who took over had been slightly more 'good colleagues', it could have been settled easily. But they were very eager to grab the case. Normally in this, if you take something over from another architect, you're not supposed to do that before the first architect is completely satisfied with his fees and everything else.

BUILDING BLOCKS *The towering shells of the Sydney Opera House roof presented staggering engineering problems for the designers, engineers and builders. Eventually they were fabricated in sections on the ground and then hoisted into place.*

AWAKENING GIANT *On the magnificent Bennelong Point site on the edge of Sydney Harbour, the unique shape of the Sydney Opera House begins to emerge from the massive concrete base.*

Utzon has never returned to Australia. The job of finishing the Opera House was passed to a conglomerate firm of Sydney architects, Hall, Steele and Littlemore. One of the architects, Peter Hall, recalled the appointment years later:

I suppose I was fairly young and reckless. I thought it was a fascinating idea. The job wasn't represented as what it turned out to be. The drawings that were left did not describe the kind of building the community thought it was getting.

I thought it would be necessary for us to complete drawings and build what Utzon had designed for the interior. But he hadn't designed very much. We did all the working drawings and made the final decisions on colour. There was a great deal more designing to do than I'd bargained for.

I think people imagined that because I came into the job, it stopped Utzon finishing it. In fact

THE REPLACEMENT *Australian architect Peter Hall, who after Joern Utzon's resignation took on the daunting task of completing the design work and supervising the final construction of the Opera House project.*

EMPTY HOUSE *The sweeping lines of the Sydney Opera House Opera Theatre as seldom seen by the audience. These seats have been filled to capacity on many glittering occasions.*

THE MIGHTY FALLEN *After his resignation from the Opera House Project, and departure from Australia, architect Joern Utzon's name is removed from the site hoarding.*

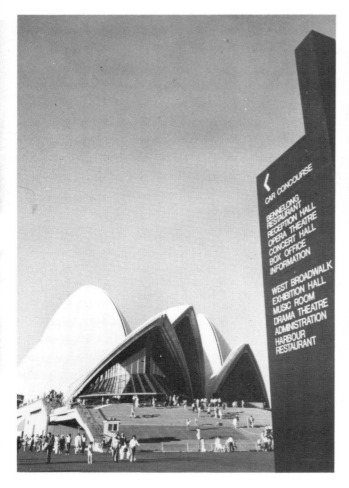

THE DREAM BECOMES REALITY *The dream of Sydney's own Opera House took a long time to unfold and was not without its difficulties. The realisation of that dream made it all worthwhile.*

At left: **TAKE YOUR PICK** *The Sydney Opera House has a great deal more to offer than just opera — in fact, it is a huge theatre complex with entertainment to suit just about everyone.*

he'd left the country. I spoke to him and I gave the Utzon faction full information as to where the negotiations were between the Minister and me. If he'd wanted to re-open negotiations at the eleventh hour, it was definitely open to him.

When the Opera House was finally completed just in time for the Queen to open it in 1973, Utzon did not attend. The cost had risen to more than $100 million, and Australians flocked to Bennelong Point in their thousands to see what their lottery money had bought. There was criticism that the outside and the inside of the building didn't match, which was to be expected since it had been created by different minds. But, on the whole, Sydneysiders love their Opera House. It has numerous flaws, but it compensates by being a most magnificent piece of sculpture. Like the pyramids it is not so much a functional object but a decorative symbol—the jewel of Sydney Harbour.

START WITHOUT ME *The Opera House was completed in 1973 just in time for the Queen to open it. Utzon, its architect, did not attend the opening.*

Now a tradition is the New Year's Eve party on the forecourt of the Opera House, with jazz, rock, disco and a brilliant fireworks display.

The building has had thousands of knockers. One Sydney wit said, 'It would have been cheaper if they built it overseas and sailed it across.' And another dubbed it 'the New South Whale'. But others, like Sir Tyrone Guthrie, have said, 'Although Australians might consider the Sydney Opera House the stock joke, the rest of the world is not giggling. It will lift Sydney out of its crimson imitation of British suburbia.'

Joern Utzon is now in his sixties, an architect of international repute. In 1978 he was awarded the Queen's Gold Medal for Architecture for his design of the Sydney Opera House. His recommendation came from the British Institute of Architects and it was said of Utzon at the award ceremony that he was 'the greatest architect of the twentieth century'.

Ultimately there's not too much more to be said about the story of

WORLD PREMIERE *Celebrated American bass Paul Robeson sings for construction workers on the Sydney Opera House site in 1960, becoming the first performer to have given a concert on the site. Robeson died before the Opera House was completed.*

THE GREAT DAY *After ten years of controversy, the long awaited opening of the Opera House in October, 1973.*

the Sydney Opera House. The public has forgotten the controversy and Australians now revel in the pride of owning one of the modern wonders of the world. The Opera House is a monument to our era and it's a far cry from the small, grey stone obelisk which we erected to celebrate the birth of our nation in Centennial Park, a few kilometres from the Opera House, eighty years ago: the monument which celebrates Federation on 1 January 1901, the first day of the twentieth century . . . *This Fabulous Century.*

A CITY CELEBRATES *Balloons, bunting, streamers and flags — Sydney was in a festive mood on the day the Queen opened the Opera House. Crowds packed the foreshores and a gaily-decked flotilla of small craft danced across the harbour.*

INDEX

Aboriginal Land Rights 69, 70
Aborigines 53, 54, 68
Acton, Prue 237
ACTU 66
Adam-Smith, Patsy 123
Adams, Phillip 98, 101, 305
Adamson, E. A. 23
Adler, Larry 103
'Adventures of Robin Hood, The' 309
Advertiser, Geelong 341
Age, The Melbourne 14, 15
Agostini, Antonio 262
    Linda 262, 263, 264
Agua Caliente Handicap 77
Alda, Frances 36
Alexander III, Czar 79
Allan, Police Commissioner Norman 60
'Alvin Purple' 306
America 176
America's Cup 59, 176, 177
Amphlett, Patricia
    See Little Pattie
Amundsen, Roald 92
Angry Penguins 46
Angus and Robertson 54
Anthony, John Douglas 332–334
Antipodeans, The 49
Anzac Cove 28
Anzac Day 29, 31
Anzacs 29
Anzacs, The 123
Argus, The 12, 125
Armstrong, Charles 80
    George 78
    Neil 66
Arnott, Arthur 20
Archibald, Bill 268
Archibald Prize 46
Ashbolt, Allan 314
'Ashes', The 40, 181, 182
Ashton, Julian 21
Aspro Company 22
Aurora, The 95
Austin, Thomas 341
Austral, Florence 78
Australia 179
Australia Calls 26
Australia, Miss 238–244
'Australian Folklore' 348
Australian Inland Mission 26
    Iron and Steel Company 36
    Rules 17, 185, 186
Australian, The 60
'Australis' 272
Avro-Avian biplane 32

Baird, James Logie 324, 325
Baker, Reg 'Snowy' 307
Banks, Sir Joseph 351
Bannister, Roger 50, 174
Barassi, Ron 185, 186
Barbour, Jim 366
Barnett, Walter 12
Barry McKenzie 306
Bartlett, Ellis Ashmead 29
Bartolomeo Colleoni 44
Barton, Edmund 15, 194, 195
Barwick, Sir Garfield 198
Battarbee, Rex 55
BHP 62
Beardsley, Aubrey 66
Beatles, The 61
Beauchamp, Lord 103
Beaurepaire, Frank 150
Bell, Ron 278
Benbow, Dr 264
Benghazi Handicap 44
Bennett, Major General H. Gordon 45
Benny, Jack 102
Bentley, Dick 108
Bialoguski, Dr Michael 214
Bien, Hoa 59
Bikini 50, 234
Bill, Immigration Restriction 16
'Bitter Springs' 311
Blacksmith, Jimmy 18
Blamey, Thomas 41
Blair, Ron 289
Bleriot 23
Blight, Ken 383
'Blue Andromeda' 273
'Bluebird' 190
'Blue Hills' 286, 321, 322
Blue Streak 61, 66

'Bodyline' bowling 182
Bogle, Dr Gilbert 59
Bonner, Neville 68
Booth, Herbert 13
Borge, Arne 151, 152
    Christine 234, 235
Bource, Henri 257
Boxer Rebellion, The 19
Bradfield, Dr J. C. 364
Bradley, Stephen Leslie 265, 268
Bradman, Sir Donald 36, 37, 74, 81–85, 182, 318
Brassiere 231
'Breaker Morant' 306
Bronhill, June 78
Brookes, Norman 22, 157, 158
Brooklands, Riley 189
Brown, Noeline 328
    Norman 36
    Warren 189
Bruce, Stanley Melbourne 33–37, 40–42, 201–206
Bryant, Gordon 71
Bulletin, The 12, 33, 61, 100
Budge, Don 57
Burdon, Alec 186
Burley Griffin, Walter 26
Burns, Tommy 166
Bury, Leslie 64
'Bush Christmas' 311
Butler, Samuel 19
Butt, Dame Clara 36, 80
Buzo, Alex 289
Byers, Herbert 18

Cabas, Louise 26
Cabban, Peter 271
Cactoblastis Cactorum 346
Caddie 306
Cahill, J. J. (Joe) 386
Cairns, Dr Jim 199
Calling Australia 140, 141
Caltex 51
Calwell, Arthur Augustus 56, 58, 61, 62, 216–218
Cameron, Clyde 353
Campbell, Donald 60, 190
    Robert 361
Canberra 358–363
Captain Blood 309
Carroll, Gerald 139
Carruthers, Jimmy 50, 57, 169
Carter, Jimmy 38
Caruso, Enrico 80
Casey, Richard 38, 42
Cavill, Arthur 150
    Dick 149
    Fred 148
    Sydney St Leonards 149
Cazaly, Roy 185
Centennial Park 15, 16
Cerutty, Percy 173, 174
Chaliapin 36
Chalmers, Rob 207
Chamberlain, Neville 40, 41, 43
Chandler, Mrs Margaret 59
Chant of Jimmy Blacksmith, The 306
Charge of the Light Brigade, The 309
Charleston, The 226, 331
Charlton, Andrew 'Boy' 151, 152
Chater, Gordon 328
Chauvel, Charles 42, 302, 303
Chiang-Kai-Shek 35
Chicago, US Cruiser 136
Chief Havoc 46
Chifley, Ben 37, 38, 47, 48, 50, 211, 375, 376
Chloe 245
Christie, Moss 152
Cinesound 39
Clark, Alan, Detective Sergeant 267
Clarke, Ron 53, 175
Clay, Cassius 169
'Club, The' 289
Cobb and Co. 34
Cockerill, George 15
Coles, Arthur 28
    Dave 28
    George 28
    Jim 28
Coming of Stork, The 289
Commonwealth Arbitration Court 51
    Bank 48
Conscription 125–128
Consider Your Verdict 327
Conzinc Rio Tinto 62
Cook, Joseph 28
Coombs, Dr H. C. 50, 287

Covent Garden 79
Crapp, Lorraine 53
Crawford, Jack 37, 40, 159
Credit Squeeze 214
Creyton, Barry 328
Cricket 180–184
Crime 259–261
Cronin, M. 186
Cross, Stan 99
Crucified Venus, The 21
CSIRO 36, 53
Cuba 19
Cuban Rebel Girls 310
Culotta, Nino 54
Current Affair, A 62
Curtin, John 37–39, 42–44, 47, 74, 127, 135, 210, 211, 375
Custance, Fred 23, 24
Cuthbert, Betty 53
Cutler, Sir Roden 132, 133, 145
Cyclone Tracy 67, 252, 277

Dad and Dave 98
Dad and Dave Come to Town 313
Daily Telegraph 58
Dame Pattie 178
Dancing 226–229
Darcy, Les 29, 75, 103, 166–169
Darley, Sir Frederick 195
Davey, Jack 107–111
Davies, George 22
Davis Cup 22, 49, 157, 159, 160
    David, J. 75
    Dwight 157
Deakin, Alfred 20
De Fries, Colin 23
De Gaulle, Charles 56
De Groot, Francis 40, 197, 370
Dennis, C. J. 99, 100, 296
Depression 33, 36, 37, 39, 40, 74
Devil's Playground, The 306
'Dinks and Onkus' 104
Disasters 269–283
Disney, Walt 19
Dobell, William 46
Don's Party 289
Drive-in theatres 224, 225
Drysdale, Russell 49
Duigan, John 24
Duke of Edinburgh 341
    Orleans 79
    York 36
Dumas, Lloyd 125
Dunlop Cup 188
    Rubber Company 188
Dunstan Keith 98, 101, 235
Durack, Fanny 150
    Mary 339
Dutton, Geoffrey 340
Dyer, Bob 74, 107, 108, 111, 112, 113
    Dolly 111–113

Edmonson, Ray 296
Edinburgh, Duke of 341
Edwards, Vic 162, 164
Egan, Ted 71
Eliza Frazer 306
Elizabethan Theatre Trust 50
Elliott, Herb 174, 175
England Made Me 314
Ennis, Lawrence 366
Erehwon Revisited 19
Erwin, Dudley 65
Evans, Lindley 80
Evatt, Herbert Vere 35, 43, 61, 212
Eve, Dick 149
Eve in Ebony
    see *Jedda*
Everage, Edna
    see Barry Humphries

Fadden A 43, 44, 106, 210
Fads 222–229
Fairweather, I 49
Falk's Photographic Studios 12
Far From the Madding Crowd 314
Fashion 230–237
Federation 15
    Celebrations 14
Feminism 232
Fenner, Professor F. J. 342–344
Ferrier, Noel 115
Film Industry 290–306
Finch, Peter 42, 313, 314

Fingleton, Jack 83
Fisher, Andrew 27, 28, 43
Fisk, Sir Ernest 316, 325
Fitzgerald's Circus 14
Flappers 232
Flies 347
Floods 335–337
Floyd, Dr 46
Flynn, Errol 39, 308–311
Football 185, 186
Forty Thousand Horsemen 42, 302, 311
Fosky, Ray 134
Foxtrot 226
Foy, Mark 177
Frank E. Evans 272
Fraser, Dawn 53, 59, 60, 154, 155
    Malcolm 34, 64, 65, 199, 332
    Ron 328
Frost, Henry 373
Fysh, Hudson 33, 378

Game, Sir Philip 40, 197, 198
Gale, Sadie 102
Gallagher, Harry 154
Gallipoli 28, 29
Garonne 41
General Motors 41
Glenn, John 59
Gocher, William 22
Golden Gate, The 33
Goolagong, Evonne 162, 163, 164, 165
    (Mrs Evonne Cawley)
Gone to the Dogs 105
Gorton, John 61, 62, 64, 65, 305
Goossens, Eugene 386
Governor, Jimmy 17–19
Granville bridge disaster 275, 276
Greenway, Francis 364
Greer, Germaine 50, 250, 251
Gregory, S. E. 19
Gretel 177, 178
Gretel II 178
Greycliffe 280, 281
Griffin, Walter Burley 361, 362
Griffiths, Harry 107
    Tom 262
Grout, Wally 58
Guillaux, Maurice 27
Gunston, Norman
    see Garry MacDonald
Guthrie, Sir Tyrone 392
Gyngell, Bruce 54, 326

Hair 66
Hall, Ken 300
    Peter 390, 391
Halls, Archibald 134
Hancock, Lang 51
Hargrave, Lawrence 23
Harmon, Bill 328
Harmony Row 104
Harris, Max 46, 100
Hart, William 24, 26
Hartnett, Sir Lawrence 41, 372, 374, 377
Hasluck, Paul 64
Hathaway, Marcia 256
Hawke, Bob 66, 70
Hawker, De Havilland 26
    Harry George 26, 27
    Siddely 26
Helpmann, Sir Robert 36
Hertz, Car 12, 13
Hewett, Dorothy 289
Hibberd, Jack 289
Hill, Lance 384, 385
Hills rotary clothes hoist 384, 385
Hinkler, Bert 31–33, 36
Hiroshima 43, 47
Hitler, Adolf 34, 35, 43, 47
Hoad, Lew 50, 57, 159–162
Hogan, Paul 99, 117, 119
Holden Car 372–377
    J. A. 373
    Motor Body Works 41
    Motor Company 48
Holland, Fritz 167
Holt, Harold 61–63, 218, 219, 305
Homicide 327
Hopetoun, Lord 15, 16, 194, 195
Hopman, Harry 159, 162
Horne, Donald 61, 202
Houdini, Harry 23, 24
Howard, Jenny 105, 106
Hula Hoops 223

Humphries, Barry 50, 54, 64, 99, 114, 116, 119, 289
Hughes, Davis 388
    Richard 137
    W. M. (Billy) 29–31, 86, 125–127, 201–206, 358

Illawarra, Lake 275
Immigration Restriction Bill 16
In Melbourne Tonight 327
In the Wake of the Bounty 39
Inland Mission, Australian 26
Intrepid 178

Jack Davey Story, The 110
Jacka, Albert 74
Jackson, Marjorie 50
Jedda 302
Jitterbug 226, 227
Johnson, Jack 166
Jones, Barry 305
    Charles Lloyd (Sir) 318
Joyce, Eileen 227

Kahanamoku, Duke 152
Kanakas 16
Kellerman, Annette 245–247
    Marcel 247
Kelly, Ned 291
Kennedy, President John 56, 59
    Graham 327
Kenny, Senior-Sergeant 126
Kerr, Sir John 197, 199, 200
Kertz, Helena 118
Kim 19
Kindergarten of the Air 46
Kings in Grass Castles 339
Kingsford Smith, Charles 36, 74, 86–91
    Charles Arthur 89
Kipling, Rudyard 15, 19
Kirkpatrick, John Simpson
    see Simpson and his donkey
Kiwi boot polish 20
Knowles, Adrian 141
Kocan, Peter 216, 217
Kokoda Front Line 142
Kookaburra, The 88
Kormoran 44
Kramer, Jack 50
Kunoth, Ngarla
    see Rosalie Monks
Kurtzman, Bill 162, 164
Kuts, Vladimir 54
Kuttabul, ferryboat 136

La Bohème 78, 80
'La Milo' 19
'La Stupenda' 50
Labor Party split 214
Lady Southern Cross, The 90, 91
Lamington, Baron 36
Landy, John 50, 53, 174, 175
Lane, Fred 17
Lang, Jack 35, 37, 40, 66, 196–198, 364, 369
Larwood, Harold 182
Last Wave, The 306
Latham, John 38
Lautrec, Toulouse 19
Laver, Rod 57, 66
Lawler, Ray 50, 115, 288
Lefebvre, Chevalier Jules 245
Leigh, Vivien 50, 286
Let George Do It 104
Lightning, The 341
Lillee, Dennis 19
Limb, Bobby 111
Lindbergh, Charles 86
Lindrum, Walter 37
Lindsay, Norman 21, 66   Rose 230
Lingiari, Vincent 69, 70
Linkletter, Art 109
Lipton, Sir Thomas 176
Little Pattie 229
London, Jack 166
Lone Hand, The 22
Longford, Raymond 26, 99, 296
Louisville 282
Lovely, Louise 26
Lucas Heights 56
Lucia di Lammermoor 79
Lumière Brothers 12
Lyell, Lottie 26
Lyne, Sir William 15, 195
Lyon, Harry 87
Lyons, Enid 38, 248–250
    Joseph 38, 42, 43, 209, 248

MacArthur, General Douglas 44, 127
    John 351, 352
McBride, Dr William 59
McCackie, Mo 99
MacDonald, Garry 118, 119
McDowall, Dr Val 324
McGinness, P. J. 33, 348
McKay, Bill 262, 264, 370
    Heather 58
Mackellar, Dorothea 332, 355
McKenzie, Barry 114
    Stuart 53
McKinley, President W. 19
McMahon, Sonia 236
    Sir William 63, 65, 71, 199, 236
Macmillan, Harold 56
McNamara, Dr Jean 342, 343
McNeil, Jim 289
McIntosh, Hugh D. 166
McIver, Wilma 162
Mack, Dolly
    see Molly Dyer
    Monica 240
Mahon, Hugh 33
Mahony, Marie 22
Maitland floods 335, 337
'Malley, Ern' 46
Malvern Star 171
Mannix, Archbishop Daniel 29, 126
Marchesi, Madame Mathilde 78
Marconi, G. 19
Martyn, Norma 230
Matthews, Marlene 53
Mawson, Douglas 92–95
Mavis Bramston Show 286, 328
Mein Kampf 35
Melba, Nellie 36, 74, 78–81, 93
    peach 36
Melbourne, HMAS 62, 66, 269–273
Melbourne Cup 12, 75, 78, 234, 235
    Opera House 12
Men's fashion 230
Menzies, Sir Robert Gordon 37, 38, 42–44, 47–49, 52, 53, 56, 58, 59–62, 64, 127, 199, 207–215
Meredith, Gwen 321, 322
Merino sheep 351
Mertz, Xavier 92, 94
Messenger, Charles 177
    Dally 'the Boot' 186
Milk bars 222
Miller, Godfrey 49
Mills, Beryl 246
    John 304
Milne Bay 45
Milo, La 19
Mini-golf 223
Minsec 63
Missingham, Hal 240
Mitchell, Ray 108
Mockridge, Russell 50, 173
Monash, Colonel John 130
Monks, Rosalie 303, 304
Montague, Pansy 19
Morant, 'Breaker' 19
Morgan, Anna 264
    J. P. 19
Morosi, Junie 199
Moses, Sir Charles 318, 319, 321
Motor sport 188–191
Movietone 39, 107
Muggeridge, Malcolm 51
Murder, Bogle-Chandler 59
    pyjama girl 37, 40 shark arm 37, 40
Murray, Jack 'Gelignite' 190
Murrumbidgee Irrigation Scheme 26
Murrumbeena Girls' Home 14
Mussolini, Benito 32, 43, 47
Mutiny on the Bounty 311
My Brilliant Career 306
My Country 332
Myer Music Bowl 56
Myxomatosis 342–344

Nagasaki 43, 47
Namatjira 54, 55
Nathan, Trent 237
Neptune's Daughter 247
Network 313, 314
Newcombe, John 66
New Guinea 30, 46, 127, 143
New South Wales Married Women Act 40
Ninnis, Belgrave 92, 93
Niven, David 309
Nixon, Richard 236

No Love for Johnnie 314
Noack, Errol 128
Nolan, Sydney 46, 49
Number 96 328

O'Grady, John 54, 305
Oil 51
O'Keefe, Johnny 56
Oldfield, Bert 182
Olivier, Laurence 50, 286, 313
Olympic Games 17, 50, 53, 54, 60, 150, 152, 154, 155
On the Beach 56
Opera House, La Scala 79
    Melbourne 12
    Sydney 50, 53, 56, 386–393
Opperman, Hubert 36, 171
O'Reilly, Bill 83
Ord River Project 59
O'Shea, Sergeant Laurence 265
Overlanders, The 311

Packer, Frank (Sir) 54, 58, 177, 179
    Kerry 183
Page, Earle 42, 203, 209, 211
Panama Canal 19
Parer, Damien 142–144
Park, Centennial 15, 16
Parliament House 34, 36, 362, 363
Parsons, Freddie 103
Partridge, Frank 74
Paterson, Banjo 19
    Dinks 104
Pavlova, Anna 36, 93
Payne, Alan 177, 179
Peach Melba 81
Peacock, Andrew 65
Perry, Joseph 13, 14
Pethybridge, Tommy 90
Petrov, Evdokia 50, 213, 214
    Vladimir 50, 212–214
Phar Lap 36, 37, 74–77, 103
Phillips, Nat 28, 102
Phone box stuffing 225
Pick-a-Box 74
Picnic at Hanging Rock 306
Pike, Jim 77
Pogo sticks 225
Pollice Verso 21
Port Kembla Steelworks 36
Poseidon 63
Powell, Mary 89
Prickly pear 34, 345, 346
Pride of Erin 226
Prince of Wales 33
Princess Theatre, Melbourne 12
Private Eye 114
Profumo scandal 59
Puccini 78
Pugh, Clifton 218
Pyjama Girl case 262–264

Qantas 33, 34, 378–382
Queen Elizabeth 50, 215, 391
    Mary 148, 159
    Victoria 16, 19, 79
Queen Elizabeth, battleship 29

Rachmaninoff 19
Radio 316–322
Rafferty, Chips 42, 311
Ramsay, Alan 65
Ratcliffe, Jill 258
Raye, Carol 328
Reade, Eric 14
Reard, Louise 50
Redex Trials 190
Reeks, Walter 176
Regalia
    see *Rodney*
Removalists, The 289
Rene, Roy (Mo) 28, 102–104, 108, 119
Rickards, Harry 12
Richard Earning His Breakfast 14
Richardson, Merv 383
    Sir Ralph 287
Rigoletto 79
Robb, Ken 293
Robbery Under Arms 294
Robertson, Captain John 270–272
    Sir John 15
Roche, Tony 66
Rocks, The 16
Rodney 282

Romance of Margaret Catchpole, The 26
Romeo and Juliet 78, 99
Roosevelt, President F. 19, 47
Roots of Heaven, The 310
Rose, Murray 53
Rosewall, Ken 50, 57, 159–162
Rugby League 186
    Union 186
Rusty Bugles 288
Ryan, Ronald 62

Sailing 176–179
Saker, Harold 260
Salvation Army 13
Sachse, Bert 36
Sceptre 177
Scott, Robert 92
Scullin, J. H. 37
Sedgman, Frank 50
Seixas, Vic 160, 161
Sentimental Bloke, The 26, 99, 296
Sestier, Maurice 12
Sharks 254–258
Sheep 350–355
Shipp, Dr Eric 347
Shrimpton, Jean 234, 235
Simpson and his donkey 28, 129, 130
Simpson, Bobby 84
    Mrs W. 41
Sixty Minutes 62
Sleeping Prince, The 286
Sloane, H. P. 375
Small, Sir Bruce 171, 172
Smiley 311
Smith, Artie 227
    Joshua 46
    Keith 31, 86, 378
    Margaret (Court) 164
    Ross 31, 86, 378
Smith's Weekly 36, 99
Snedden, Billy Mackie 64
Snowy Mountains Scheme 47, 48
Soccer 186
Soldiers of the Cross 13, 14, 290, 291
Sopwith, T. O. M. 26
Southern Aurora 66
    Cloud 40, 89
    Cross (plane) 87, 89, 90, 91
    Cross (yacht) 179
Spears, Steve 289
Springer, Herb 340
    May 340
Squatter's Daughter, The 300
St John, Edward 64, 65, 271, 272
Stevens, Duncan 271
Stewart, Colin 255
'Stiffy and Mo' 28, 102, 104
Stirling, Alfred 205
Stomp 228, 229
Stone, Wizard 31
Story of the Kelly Gang, The 290, 291
Stralia, Elsa 78
Strike Me Lucky 103
Strike, New South Wales Coal 36, 47
Stubbs, John 214
Sturrock, Jock 53, 177, 178
Summer of the Seventeenth Doll 50, 115, 287, 288, 304
Sun Also Rises, The 310
Sunday Bloody Sunday 314
Susumo, Iso 137
Sutherland, Joan 50, 387
Swimsuits 234
Sydney, (battleship) 44, 45
Sydney Morning Herald 58
Sydney Harbour Bridge 364–372
    Hobart Yacht Race 177
    Opera House 386–393

TAA 47
Tahiti 280, 281
Tait, Charles 293, 294
    John 293, 394
Tarrant, Colonel H. 19
Tasker, Rolly 53
Tasminex 63
Taylor, George 23
    Joseph Leslie 'Squizzy' 36, 259, 260, 261
    P. G. 89
Television 50, 53, 54, 324–328
Telford, Harry 75, 77
Ten-pin bowling 225
Theatre 286–289
Theosophist temple 223, 224
They're a Weird Mob 54, 305

This Day Tonight 62
Thompson, Billy 189
    Herbert 19
    Peter 50
    Steam Phaeton 19
Thorne, Basil 265
    Belinda 265
    Freda 265
    Graeme 265–268
    Kidnapping 265–268
Thorndike, Dame Sybil 102, 287
Thresher, submarine 59
Times, London 47
Tobruk 44
Torrey, Reverend Dr 226
Toweel, Vic 50, 170
Town Like Alice, A 314
Townsend, Simon 128
Trabert, Tony 160, 161
Tracy, Cyclone 66
Trudgeon, The 17
Truman, President H. 47
Tudawalli, Robert 304
Tully, Mrs Mary 91
Twenty-four Hours 62
Twist, The 228

Ulm, C. 36, 86–90
Uranium 49, 94
Ure Smith 54
U.S. Steel Corporation 19
Utzon, Joern 53, 387, 388, 390, 391

Van der Sluice, Harry
    see Roy Rene
Versailles Peace Treaty Conference 30
Verstak, Tania 243, 244
Vesteys, The 69–71
Vickery, Dr Joyce 266
Victa lawnmower 383, 384
Victoria, Queen 16, 19, 79
Voce, Bill 182
Voyager 59, 269–272
Vyner Brooke, The 138, 139

Wake in Fright 311
Wales, Prince of 33
Walkley, Bill 41, 51
Wallace, George 99, 104–106, 117
Wallis, Reverend 229
Wannan, Bill 348
WAPET 51
War Cry 14
War, First World 26–30, 43, 69, 100, 122–127
    Korean 48, 51
    Precautions Act 168
    Second World 26, 40, 43–46, 132–145
    Spanish Civil 41
    Vietnam 48, 59, 61, 62, 64–66, 74, 122, 128
Warner, Jim 87
Watson, John Christian 16
Weatherly 177, 178
We Were the Rats 46
Wells, H. G. 43
    Sam 349
West Gate Bridge collapse 274
Western Mining Corporation 63
Wheatly, 'Dasher' 74
Whickam, Alick (Prince Wickyama) 150
White, John Michael 49
Whitlam, Gough 28, 58, 59, 61, 66, 114, 199, 200
    Nicholas 214
Willessee at Seven 62
Williams, Maslyn 142–144
Williamson, David 289
Wilson, Harold 219
    President Woodrow 30
Wimbledon 16, 22, 40, 50, 57, 66, 157, 160
Woodchopping at the Metropole 14
Woodcock, Tommy 75–77
Woodfull, Bill 182
Wool 354, 355
'World Series Cricket' 183
Wright Brothers 23, 24
    Flyer 23
    Judith 340
    Lew 106, 108, 109
Wunderlich Tile Company 17

York, Duke of 36
Young and Jackson's Hotel 245
Yo-yos 225

Zampatti, Carla 237

Picture Index

Abigail 327, 328
Aboriginal stockmen 69
Ada and Elsie 320, 325
Adams, Phillip 99
Agostini, Linda 262
    Antonio 262, 263, 264
Agua Caliente Handicap '77
Airliner crash 381
Amanda Miller, supertanker 68
American paratroopers 144
American sailors 138
America's Cup 179
Amiss, Dennis 184
Amphlett, Patricia
    See Little Pattie
Anderson, Keith 88
Anti-conscription cartoon 124
Anzac Parade, Sydney 34
Anzacs
    Gallipoli landing 29
Aragao, Dr H. B. 343
Armstrong, G. 179
Arnott's parrot trademark 20
Austin, Thomas 341
Australia Fair 348
Australian Broadcasting Commission
    Commissioners 319
Australian cavalry 123
Australian Light Horse Brigade 29
Aviation
    Bert Hinkler 31, 32
    experimental kite 23
    first flight in Australia 22
    first home-grown aircraft 24

Baird, James Logie 324
Baker, Reg 'Snowy' 307
'Bandstand' 326
Barbour, Jim 366
Barton, Edmund 17, 194, 195
Battle of Rothbury 35
Beatles, The 60
Beauty contests 238, 239
Becher, Rear Admiral 270
Berrima Jail, NSW 130, 131
Blamey, (General) Sir Thomas 41, 43, 209
Blue Hills 323
Boer War
    Australian riflemen 122
Bondi Beach 137, 149
Bonner, Senator Neville 68
Bource, Henri 257, 258
Boxing
    World heavyweight title, 1908 167
    World heavyweight title, Jimmy Carruthers &
        Vic Tourel 169
Brabham, Jack 189
Bradley, Stephen 268
Bradman, Sir Donald 82, 83, 84, 85
Bramston, Mavis 328
Bridges
    Sydney Harbour 365
British 'Lions' 186
Brookes, Sir Norman 158
Brown, Noeline 329
Bruce, S. M. 35, 201, 203, 204
Bryant, Betty 302
Bunny, Rupert, 'Portrait of Nellie Melba' 78

Cactoblastis insect 346
Caddie 306
Cairns, Dr Jim 128, 199
Calwell, Arthur 52, 216, 217
Campbell, Donald 61
Camels 354
Cameraman 298
Capitol Theatre 363
Car racing
    (see Motor racing)
Carlisle, Forbes 156
Carroll, Gerald 138
Carruthers, Jimmy 57, 169, 170
Casey, Sir Richard 207
Cavill family swimming centre 149
Cazaly, Roy 185
Centennial Park, Sydney 123
    Rotunda 11
Centennial Park Cemetery, Adelaide 128
Cerruty, Percy 174
Changi Prison 141
Chappell, Greg 184
    Ian 184
Charlton, Andrew 'Boy' 151
    Michael 32

Chauvel, Charles 302, 304, 313
Chifley, J. B. 48, 210, 376
Chloe by Lefebvre 245
Chinatown, Darwin, destruction of 134
Chou-en-lai 200
Christie, Moss 152
Clarke, Ron 174
Cobb & Co. 34
Cornell, John 116
Country property 332
Court, Margaret 164
Crawford, Jack 159
Creyton, Barry 329
Cricket
    Adelaide Test, 1932–33 182
    Australian Test side, 1905 181
    Centenary Test 1977 184
    First Test, West Indies v Australia, 1960–1 183
    Ladies stand, 1919 231
    Notice, London Sporting Times 181
    Richmond Paddock 180
Cross, Stan
    cartoon 99
Crucified Venus 21
Curtin, John 43, 127, 210
Cutler, Sir Roden 133
Cutmore, 'Snowy' 261
Cyclone Tracey 67, 252, 277

Dame Edna Everage 116
Darcy, Les 166, 167, 168
Darwin, bombing of 135
    Cyclone Tracey 67, 277
    Chinatown 134
    harbour, February 1942 135
Davey, Jack 100, 106, 107, 108, 109, 110, 111, 190
De Groot, Captain Francis 370
Demonstrations 200
Denman, Lord 260, 361
    Lady 26, 27
Dennis, C. J. 101, 296
    The Sentimental Bloke, illustration 100, 297
Digger 126
Digger's farewell 133
Dobell, W. *Portrait of Joshua Smith* 46
Draught horses 349
Drive-in movies 224
Drought 237, 238, 239, 240
Duigan, John 24
Dunlop car rally, 1905 188
Dunlop Reliability Trial 19
Durack, Fanny 150
Dyer, Bob 110, 112, 113
    Dolly 110, 112

Edna Everage, Dame 54
Edwards, Vic 164, 165
Elliott, Billy 74
    Herb 174, 175

Fadden, Arthur 44, 210
Fads
    drive-in movies 224
    fast-food 222
    hula-hoop 223
    hokey-pokey dance craze 227
    jitterbugging 226, 227
    mini-golf 39, 223
    pinball machine 222
    pogo stick 223
    ten-pin bowling 224
    the twist 228
    the stomp 228, 229
Farm labourers 334
Farmer, sugar cane 333
Fashion
    see Women's Fashion
Fashion parade 234, 242
Fast-food 222
Federation
    first Federal Ministry 17
Film
    A Girl from the Bush 209
    Caddie 306
    Captain Blood 309
    Dad and Dave Come to Town 313
    early newsreel cameras 300
    Forty Thousand Horsemen 302
    French Without Tears 314
    In the Wake of the Bounty 309
    Jedda 303, 304
    Judith 315
    Melbourne Cup, oldest film in Australia 12
    Mr Chedworth Steps Out 314

Neptune's Daughter 298
Newsreel cameraman 298
Picnic at Hanging Rock 306
Rats of Tobruk 314
Soldiers of the Cross glass slide 13, 14
Story of the Kelly Gang 293, 294, 295
The Talkies 300
The Overlanders 312
They're A Weird Mob 305
Fisher, Andrew 360, 361
Finch, Peter 313, 314, 315
Fisk, Sir Ernest 316
Floods, Maitland 335, 336
Flynn, Errol 308, 309, 310
Football
    Australian Rugby League team, 'Kangaroos' 186
    engraving, Australian Rules football
        Melbourne v Carlton 1876 185
    Rugby League Grand Final 1963 187
    VFL Grand Final 1906 186
Forty Thousand Horsemen, Chauvel 302
Fruit fly 347
Funeral, of Private E. W. Noack 65

Gainford, Judy 241
Gale, Sadie (Mrs Roy Rene) 102
Game, Rosemary 197
    Sir Phillip 198
General Motors Holden
    production workers 377
German gymnasts 132
Goolagong, Evonne 164, 165
Gorton, John 64
Gould, Shane 156
Gramophone 317
Granville rail disaster 276
Greer, Germaine 250, 251
Gretel 58, 178, 179
Grey Ghost 190
Greycliffe collision 280
Griffin, Walter Burley 361, 362
    Capitol theatre 363
    Incinerator 362
Guillaux, Maurice 26, 27
Gunston, Norman
    (see Garry McDonald)
Gurindji stockmen 69
Gurney, Robyn 327
Gyngell, Bruce 55

Hall, Ken 300
    Peter 390
Hancock, Lang 51
Hasham, Joe 327
Hardy, Frank 69
Hargrave, Lawrence 23
Hart, William 25
Hartnett, Sir Laurence 374
Harvest 333
Hathaway, Marcia 256
Hawke, R. G. 70
Hawker, Harry 26
Henderson, Brian 326
Hewitt, Sir Lennox 383
Hills clothes line 385
Hill, Lance 385
Hinkler, Bert 31, 32
Hitchcock, Bob 88
Hoad, Lew 50, 160, 161, 162
Hogan, Paul 116, 117
Holt, Harold 60, 218, 219
    Zara 219
Hokey-Pokey dance craze 221
Holden car 224, 274, 375, 376, 377
Holden, James Alexander 372
Holden and Frost 373
    staff 373
Horse Racing
    Agua Caliente handicap 77
Hopetoun, Lord 15
Hopman, Harry 159
Houdini, Harry 24
Housing
    inner city 42
    1950's 'dream home' 225
Hughes, W. M. 30, 49, 125, 201, 203, 205, 206, 359
    portrait 201
    cartoon 202
Humphries, Barry 54, 115, 116
    'Bazza' McKenzie 115
    'Dame Edna Everage' 116
Hula-hoop craze 223

Jacob, Sir Ian 325

Japanese midget submarines 137
Japanese surrender 145
Jardine, Douglas 183
Jedda 303
Jitterbug 39, 226, 227
Johnson, President L. B. 66, 219
Jones, Barry 113
    Charles Lloyd 319
Joye, Col 323, 326

Kahanamoku, Duke 152
Kalang 367
'Kangaroos' 186
Kellerman, Annette 246, 247, 298
Kelly, Ned
    The Story of the Kelly Gang 293, 294, 295
Kennedy, Alexander 378
    Graham 110, 327
Kentwell, Wilbur 110
Kerr, Sir John 192
King Street Bridge 275
Kingsford Smith, Mary 90
    Sir Charles 72, 87, 88, 89, 90, 91
    portrait of 86
Knowles, Adrian 141
Kocan, Peter 216
Kokoda Trail 45
Kookaburra motif 301
Kooyong 161
Kunoth, Ngarla 303, 304
Kuttabul 136

Lady Southern Cross 90
Lane, Freddie ('Fast Freddie') 17
Landy, John 52, 174
Lane, Freddie 149
Lang, J. (Jack) 37, 40, 196, 198
Larwood, Harold 182
Lawler, Ray 115
Lehmann, Lotte 301
Leigh, Vivien 289
Lindsay, Norman 20, 21
    Norman Lindsay Museum 21
    Recruiting poster 28
Lingiari, Vincent 69
Litchfield, H. A. 89
Little Pattie 229, 323
Lockwood, Rupert 214
Locusts 347
Longford, Raymond 296
Luck, Peter 114
Lyne, Sir William 359
Lyons, Edith 38, 209, 248, 249, 250
    Joseph 38, 171, 209

MacArthur, General Douglas 41, 127
McBride, William 59
McDonald, Garry 117, 118, 119
McDowall, Dr Val 324
McEwen, John 219
McGilvray, Alan 319
McKenzie, 'Bazza'
    (see Barry Humphries)
McMahon, Sir William 63, 236
    Sonia 236
McNamara, Dr Jean 343
Mack, Dolly 110, 112
Maitland floods 335, 336
Mannix, Archbishop Daniel 124
Marx, Chico 321
'Mavis Bramston Show', cast 118
Mawson expedition
    Polar terrain 93
    Daily Mail reports 94
Mawson, Sir Douglas 92, 93, 95
May Day March Sydney 1951 212
Melba, Dame Nellie 79, 80, 81, 284
    portrait of 78
    cartoon 80
Melbourne HMAS 269, 270, 271, 272, 273
Melbourne Cup, 1965 235
Melbourne Cup Day, 1915 230
Melbourne Cup, M. Sestier's film of Melbourne
    Cup, 1910 230
Melbourne tram, 1908 185
Menzies, Pattie (Dame) 85
    Robert (Sir) 42, 49, 57, 85, 207, 208, 209, 210,
    211, 215
Meredith, Gwen 322
Mertz, Xavier 94
Mills, Beryl 240
Miss Australia Quest 240, 241, 243
'Mo'
    (see Roy Rene) 102

Mockridge, Russell 173
Monks, Rosalie 303, 304
Montague, Pansy ('La Milo') 18
Morant, Harry 'Breaker' 18
Morgan, Anna Philomena 263
Morosi, Junie 199
Morse, Helen 306
Moses, Charles 325
Motor Racing
    Australian championships 189
    Dunlop car rally, 1905 188
    Redex trial, 1954 190, 191
Murray, Jack 189
Myer Music Bowl 56

Namatjira, Albert 56
    watercolour 55
Neptune's Daughter 298
Newcombe, John 163
New Parliament House 358
Newspaper censorship 144
Newsreel footage, Damien Parer 142
Nicholas, Hilton J. 23
Nixon, President R. 236
Noack, Private E. W., funeral of 65
Noble, Patsy Ann 326
Norman Lindsay Museum 21
Number 96 328, 329

Oldfield, W. A. 182
Oldsmobile 15
Olivier, Sir Laurence 289, 321
Olympic Games, opening ceremony, Melbourne
    1956 52
O'Malley, King 359, 360, 361
On Our Selection 98
Opera House
    see Sydney Opera House
Opperman, Hubert 171, 172, 173
Outback settler 339

Packer, Sir Frank 58
Parer, Damien 142, 143
    newsreel footage New Guinea 142
    Road to Mandalay 143
Parkes, Henry 194
Parliament House 363
Parrot, Arnott's trademark 20
Paterson, A. B. ('Banjo') 18
    'Dinks' 96
Pavlova, Anna 287
Peace celebrations 145
Peach, Bill 62
Penney, William 49
Petrov Espionage Royal Commission, Document J
    214
Petrov, Evdokia 213
    Vladimir 213
Petty, Bruce, cartoon constitutional crisis 200
Phar Lap 74, 75, 76, 77
Phillipe, Robert Luis 79
Picnic at Hanging Rock 306
Picture show 290
Picture Show Man 290
Pike, Jim 76
Pinball machine 222
Pogo stick craze 223
Porritt, Barbara 52
Portrait of Joshua Smith, William Dobell 46
Prickly pear 345, 346
Prisoners of war, Syria 126
Provan, Norm 187
'Pyjama Girl'
    police poster 263
    inquest 264
Pyjama party 233

Qantas
    Boeing 707 380
    Boeing 747B 1971 383
    Captain Cook lounge 382
    City of Elizabeth 383
    passenger ticket 379
    rescue of Saigon orphan 381
    terminal, Longreach 379

Rabbit 341
    menace 342, 343, 344
Radio
    early radio 316, 318, 319
    dinner-suited announcer 321
    'simulated' cricket broadcasts 318
    sound effects 319
Rafferty, Chips 311, 312, 313, 314

Reeks, Walter 177
Remembrance Day 199
Rene, Roy 100, 103, 106
Richmond Paddock (Melbourne Cricket Ground)
    180
Roberts, Rachel 306
Robertson, Captain John 270, 271, 272
    Maureen 383
Robeson, Paul 392
Rodney ferry disaster 282, 283
Rosewall, Ken 50, 160, 162
Rothbury coal pit 36
Rotunda, Centennial Park, Sydney 11
Royal Easter Show 1900 349
Rusty Bugles 287

Saint Kilda 33
Salter, June 323
Scullin, James 37
Sentimental Bloke
    illustration 100
Sharman, Jim 59
Sharks 255, 256
    attack 257, 258
    engraving 1877 254
    netting 254
    spectators 255
    victims 256, 257, 258
Shearers 352
Sheep
    Merino 351
    shearing 350, 352, 353, 354
    washing 350
Sheepdog 348
Shrimpton, Jean 235
Skyhawk jet 273
Small, Sir Bruce 172
Smith, Joshua 46
    see 'Portrait of Joshua Smith' 46
Smith, Keith 30
    Margaret 164
Snowy Mountains Hydro-electric scheme 48
    submerged dwellings 47
'Soldiers of the Cross' 13, 14, 291, 292
Southern Cloud, remains of 88
Southern Cross 72, 88, 89, 91
Speedo bathing costume 232
Sproule, Cliff 159
Stafford, Paula 51
Stalag Luft III 139
'Stiffy' ('Stiffy and Mo') 102
Sturrock, Jock 178
Stomp 228, 229
Stone, Judy 326
Story of the Kelly Gang 293, 294, 295
Summer of the Seventeenth Doll 288, 289
Summons, Arthur 187
Surf carnival, Inaugural, Manly 148
Sydney
    artist's vision 365
    drawing by Percy Spence 195
    shoppers 1949 47
Sydney 126
Sydney Cricket Ground 'The Hill' 180
Sydney Harbour Bridge 40, 197, 366, 367, 368, 369,
    370, 371, 372
Sydney Opera House 357, 389, 390, 391, 392
    Joern Utzon's drawing 386
    opening 1973 393
    original site 386
    second prize 387
    site preparation 388
    third prize 389
Sydney-to-Hobart Yacht Race 176, 177

Tahiti collision 280
Tasman Bridge 275
Taylor, Bill 89
    George 22
    Grant 302
    Rod 323
    'Squizzy' 259, 260, 261
Television
    ABN 2, official opening 325
    'Ada and Elsie' 325
    Bandstand 326
    cathode-ray camera 326
    In Melbourne Tonight 327
    Mavis Bramston Show 328, 329
    Number 96 327, 328, 329
    transmission of early signal 324
Theosophist Temple 39, 223
Theatre Royal, Sydney, 1882 286

They're A Weird Mob 305
Thorne Kidnapping
　Basil Thorne 265
　family residence 267
　Graeme Thorne 266
　newspaper headlines 267
　police reward poster 266
Thomas, Al 113
Timbergetters 334
Tivoli showgirls 134
Traffic jam, Anzac Parade 34
Tram, Melbourne, 1908 185
Transport, North Shore 364
Travelling picture show 290
Troopships, departure of 132
Tudawalli, Robert 303
Twist, The 228

Ulm, Charles 87, 88
Underwood, Derek 184
Utzon, Joern 388

Valli, Joe 105
Verstak, Tania 243, 244
Vickers Vimy 30
Victa lawnmower 1952 384
Victorian Football League, Grand Final 1909 186
Victorian volunteers 123
Vietnam War
　anti-war protestors 66, 128
　arrival of military personnel at Richmond airbase 67
　soldiers on patrol 65

Voyager HMAS 66

Walkley, Bill 41
Wallace, George 96, 104, 105, 106
War
　anti-conscription cartoon 124
　Australian Cavalry 123
　Australian prisoners of War 140, 141
　Boer War, riflemen 122
　Changi prison 141
　conscript's grave 128
　departure of troops 132
　destruction of Chinatown, Darwin 134
　Gallipoli landing 29
　infantry, Kokoda Trail 45
　Japanese prison camp officers 140
　Japanese propaganda film *Calling Australia* 140, 141
　newspaper censorship 144
　Norman Lindsay recruiting poster 124
　The Australian Digger 126
　Victorian volunteers 123
　war brides 138
　War hero John Simpson Kirkpatrick 129
War Memorial Canberra
　Japanese midget submarines 44
Watercolour, Albert Namatjira 55
Weatherly 179
West Gate Bridge 274
　victim 275
Whickham, Alick 150
Whitlam, E. G. 70, 192, 199, 200, 229
Woodcock, Tommy 74, 75

Wollongong women's rescue and resuscitation team 151
Willessee, Mike 251
Wireless 316, 318
Women's fashion
　women's underwear 231, 232, 233, 235, 236, 242
　Speedo bathing costume 232
　beachwear 232, 240
　bikinis 234
Wool sales 355
World War One
　Australian Light Horse Brigade 29
　recruiting poster 28, 127
World War Two
　American paratroopers 144
　Damien Parer newsreel footage, New Guinea 142, 143
　Japanese midget submarines 44
　Japanese surrender 145
　16th Australian Infantry Brigade 45

Yacht racing
　America's Cup 179
　Gretel 178
　Sydney Harbour 1932 176
　Sydney-to-Hobart Yacht Race 176, 179
　Weatherly 179

Yo-Yo craze 225
Young, Rita 21

'Zeppelin' model 131

The author and publishers wish to thank the many individuals and organisations who have assisted in providing material for this book, including:
The Australian Broadcasting Commission
The Age
Angus & Robertson
Channel 7
Channel 9
Cinesound & Movietone Productions
2GB
John Fairfax & Sons
General Motors Holden
Herald & Weekly Times
Victor Joyce
The Mawson Institute
The Mitchell Library
Reg Morrison
The NSW Government Printer
The National Library
The National Film Archive of the National Library
The National War Memorial
News Ltd
Norman Lindsay copyright holder Janet Glad c/o Curtis Brown Aust Prop Ltd Sydney
D. O'Keefe
Qantas